War, Religion and Empire

What are international orders, how are they destroyed, and how can they be defended in the face of violent challenges? Advancing an innovative realist-constructivist account of international order, Andrew Phillips addresses each of these questions in *War, Religion and Empire*. Phillips argues that international orders rely equally on shared visions of the good and accepted practices of organised violence to cultivate cooperation and manage conflict between political communities. Considering medieval Christendom's collapse and the East Asian Sinosphere's destruction as primary cases, he further argues that international orders are destroyed as a result of legitimation crises punctuated by the disintegration of prevailing social imaginaries, the break-up of empires, and the rise of disruptive military innovations. He concludes by considering contemporary threats to world order, and the responses that must be taken in the coming decades if a broadly liberal international order is to survive.

ANDREW PHILLIPS is a Fellow in the Department of International Relations at the Australian National University. His research interests focus on the evolution of the global state system and the challenges that new security threats pose to the contemporary world order.

Cambridge Studies in International Relations: 117

War, Religion and Empire

Cambridge Studies in International Relations is a joint initiative of Cambridge University Press and the British International Studies Association (BISA). The series will include a wide range of material, from undergraduate textbooks and surveys to research-based monographs and collaborative volumes. The aim of the series is to publish the best new scholarship in International Studies from Europe, North America and the rest of the world.

Cambridge Studies in International Relations

Series list continues after index

War, Religion and Empire

The Transformation of International Orders

ANDREW PHILLIPS

CAMBRIDGE UNIVERSITY PRESS
Cambridge, New York, Melbourne, Madrid, Cape Town, Singapore,
São Paulo, Delhi, Dubai, Tokyo, Mexico City

Cambridge University Press
The Edinburgh Building, Cambridge CB2 8RU, UK

Published in the United States of America by Cambridge University Press, New York

www.cambridge.org
Information on this title: www.cambridge.org/9780521122092

First published 2011

Printed in the United Kingdom at the University Press, Cambridge

A catalogue record for this publication is available from the British Library

Library of Congress Cataloguing in Publication data
Phillips, Andrew, 1977–
War, religion and empire : the transformation of international orders /Andrew Phillips.
p.   cm. – (Cambridge studies in international relations; 117)
ISBN 978-0-521-12209-2 (pbk)
1). International Orders – Constitution and Transformation   (2). Latin Christendom, History
1000–1500   (3). East Asia, History 1650–1950   (4). Islam, Terrorism and World Politics,
1950–Present   (5). International Orders and Liberalism – Future
BV630.3.P47   2010
201′.7270902–dc22
2010030393

ISBN 978-0-521-19128-9 Hardback
ISBN 978-0-521-12209-2 Paperback

This book is dedicated to my Mum and Dad
and to Natalia
with love and gratitude.

Contents

List of tables

Acknowledgements

This is an ambitious book, and the debts I have incurred in writing it have been correspondingly large. My interest in great transformations in world politics dates from my undergraduate experiences at Monash University, where Chris Reus-Smit first introduced me to the discipline of international relations. Since that time, Chris has been both a fantastic mentor and a great friend, whose inspiration and encouragement have assisted me on every step of my intellectual journey. In particular, Chris's exhortation that I 'think big' gave me the courage necessary to pursue my academic passions, most likely sparing both myself and the Australian legal fraternity a lifetime of mutual frustration.

At Cornell University, where this book began life as a dissertation, I continued to be blessed by great mentors and great friends. Peter Katzenstein's reputation as a brilliant mentor is well known and even better deserved. Peter's intellectual guidance throughout every stage of this project was remarkable, as was the extraordinary kindness, sensitivity and patience he demonstrated towards me from my first days in Ithaca. I remain especially grateful to Peter for his generosity in reading the book manuscript in its entirety, and for suggesting revisions that have immeasurably improved the final product. Matthew Evangelista and Richard Bensel also provided inspiring intellectual leadership throughout my time at Cornell, constantly challenging me to make my arguments more rigorous and my prose more readable. I owe all three a personal and intellectual debt I can never adequately repay, and I only hope that I will be able to emulate their examples in my own teaching career. Special thanks are also due to Allen Carlson, Lacy Davey, Richard Ned Lebow, Daniel Nexon, Daniel Philpott, Loren Ryter and Martin Weber for their generosity in reading portions of earlier versions of this work, and for their trenchant comments and suggestions, which sharpened my arguments considerably. Helpful comments were also provided by seminar participants at both the Australian National University and the University of Queensland. I am also grateful to Shogo Suzuki and Scott Pacey for their patient and cheerful assistance in helping me to standardise Chinese words in the text to modern pinyin, and I of course accept full responsibility for any remaining transliteration errors in the final text. Manuscript revisions were largely undertaken during my time as a lecturer in the School of Political Science and International Studies at the

University of Queensland, and I thank all of my colleagues in Brisbane for providing me with a welcoming and intellectually stimulating environment in which to work. For their camaraderie, insightful criticisms and warm friendship I particularly thank Stephen Bell, Alex Bellamy, Roland Bleiker, Morgan Brigg, Melissa Curley, Sara Davies, Richard Devetak, Jean-Louis Durand, Marianne Hanson, Andy Hindmoor, Emma Hutchison, Sebastian Kaempf, David Martin Jones, Phil Orchard, Richard Shapcott, Jason Sharman and Heloise Weber. I also remain especially grateful to Gillian Whitehouse, who as head of department made me feel welcome and provided constant support and encouragement. Financial support for this project came from the Mellon Foundation, Cornell University's Peace Studies Program, and the University of Queensland's Social and Behavioural Sciences faculty, and is also gratefully acknowledged. At the Department of International Relations at the Australian National University, where this book was completed, I thank my wonderful colleagues for their sustained and consistent support during the book's final stages of development. At Cambridge University Press, I would also like to thank John Haslam for recruiting this book to be in the Cambridge Studies in International Relations Series, and also Carrie Parkinson and Tom O'Reilly, whose editorial guidance in shepherding me through the challenges of finalising the manuscript proved at all times invaluable. Jeremy Langworthy's painstaking efforts in carefully reading through and copy-editing the final manuscript were also very much appreciated.

I thank all of my friends for vicariously experiencing the rigours of writing first the dissertation and then the manuscript with both sympathy and good humour. In Ithaca, many thanks to Devashree Gupta, Barak Mendelsohn, Scott Siegel and Steve Watts, both for their insights and for their fine company. In Brisbane and Canberra, I owe special thanks to Daniel Celm, Sophie Devitt and Chris King, both for their generous hospitality and for their gastronomic resilience in surviving my rare forays into the kitchen.

My greatest individual debt is owed to my parents, Bob and Judy Phillips, who have always given me their unconditional love and support. From as far back as I can remember, dinner-table conversations were enlivened by discussions about politics, and I will always be grateful to my father for conveying to me his passionate interest in all things political. I also thank my mother for reminding me to keep some sense of perspective when my academic preoccupations threatened to become all-consuming.

Finally, thanks to Natalia Kowalczyk for her love, wisdom, courage and understanding, without which nothing I have achieved would have been possible, and also to her family for their precious friendship, which I will always treasure.

Canberra
February 2010

Introduction

International orders do not last forever. Throughout history, rulers have struggled to cultivate amity and contain enmity between different political communities. From ancient Rome down to the Sino-centric order that prevailed in East Asia as recently as the nineteenth century, the impulse for order was most often realised via the institution of empire. The rulers of the Greek city-states, their Renaissance counterparts and the feuding kings of China's Period of Warring States alternatively secured order within the framework of sovereign state systems. The papal–imperial diarchy that prevailed in Christendom from the eleventh century to the early sixteenth century provides yet a third form of international order, which was neither imperial nor sovereign but rather heteronomous in its ordering principles.

Their great differences notwithstanding, two features unite the orders mentioned above. First, in each instance, international order was secured through the mobilisation of both authoritative and coercive forms of power. Both practices of communicative action and practices of organised violence have worked in uneasy combination to cultivate co-operation between polities, while simultaneously corralling conflicts between them within manageable bounds. Secondly, each of the aforementioned orders eventually proved finite. Rome's fall, Christendom's collapse and the Sinosphere's liquidation all testify to international orders' impermanence. Equally, the sorry fate of orders past should remind us of the fragility of the present world order, and caution against the conviction that history has definitively ended with the emergence of a global system of sovereign states.

What are international orders, what accounts for their transformation, and how can they be preserved in the face of violent challenges to their integrity? These are the three questions that drive this inquiry. The problem of order has long preoccupied international relations scholars, who have acknowledged both the necessity and the frailty of ordering institutions in world politics.[1] In the

---

[1] The *locus classicus* on this subject remains H. Bull, *The Anarchical Society: A study of order in world politics* (London: Macmillan Press, 1995), but see also J. A. Hall, *International Orders* (Cambridge: Polity Press, 1996); and M. Wight, *Systems of States* (London: Leicester University Press, 1977).

1

face of challenges ranging from terrorism and failed states through to an accelerating global ecological crisis, the fragility of institutions first forged to combat the twentieth-century horrors of the total state and total war has become painfully apparent. This discrepancy between ordering institutions and emerging threats to world order has in turn prompted speculation about the state system's future.[2] In this study, I bring a new perspective to debates on international systems change by anchoring them firmly within a comparative historical account of international orders' transformation. My concerns in undertaking this study are simultaneously theoretical, historical, practical and ethical in nature.

Theoretically, the discipline's focus on the problem of order in world politics invites two questions. First, what are international orders and how are they maintained? And secondly, how are international orders destabilised, contested and eventually transformed? I address both of these questions in this study. In the last decade, several landmark constructivist studies have collectively enriched our understanding of international orders' culturally and historically variable character.[3] But while these studies have undermined the sparse and asocial conceptions of the international realm that once dominated the discipline, they nevertheless serve in this book as both foils and inspirations. For while I reaffirm constructivist claims regarding international orders' socially constructed character, I also seek to correct the excessive idealism of constructivist accounts of international orders' constitution and transformation. Practices of communicative action and shared authoritative institutions are undeniably crucial in sustaining international order. But international order is equally sustained by corresponding practices of legitimate organised violence. In placing disproportionate emphasis on the former, I contend that existing constructivist accounts have provided us with an artificially bloodless account of international orders' constitution and operation. Conversely, in according equal significance to authoritative and coercive institutions, I aim to provide a conception of international orders that more accurately captures the paradoxical essence of international politics, as a realm in which the struggle for power and the pursuit of the good remain irreducibly important and unavoidably intertwined spheres of action.

---

[2] See for example the collection of essays in K. Booth and T. Dunne (eds.), *Worlds in Collision: Terror and the future of global order* (Basingstoke: Palgrave, 2002). See also C. Kennedy-Pipe and N. Rengger, 'Apocalypse now? Continuities or disjunctions in world politics after 9/11', *International Affairs*, 82(3) (2006), 539–52.

[3] See M. Bukovansky, *Legitimacy and Power Politics: The American and French Revolutions in international political culture* (Princeton University Press, 2002); R. B. Hall, *National Collective Identity: Social constructs and international systems* (New York: Columbia University Press, 1999); D. Philpott, *Revolutions in Sovereignty: How ideas shaped modern international relations* (Princeton University Press, 2001); and C. Reus-Smit, *The Moral Purpose of the State: Culture, social identity, and institutional rationality in international relations* (Princeton University Press, 1999).

Whereas my analysis of international orders' constitution serves as simultaneously a confirmation and corrective to established constructivist studies on international order, my points of reference on the question of orders' transformation are more eclectic. For while constructivists have convincingly demonstrated the centrality of ideational factors in driving great transformations in international politics, these insights have recently been complemented by the works of scholars who have alternatively stressed the materialist and institutional dimensions of international political change. In addition to the constructivists cited above, my thinking on great transformations in world politics has been heavily influenced by these more recent contributions, most particularly by the arguments of Daniel Deudney and Daniel Nexon.[4] Given these eclectic influences, my task in conceptualising the dynamics of international orders' transformation has been one of synthesis and integration rather than either the outright ratification or refutation of existing frameworks. Accordingly, my explanation for international orders' transformation accords equal primacy to the ideational, institutional and material drivers of international systems change, offering an account that remains sensitive to the particularities of each case, while nevertheless identifying a common causal constellation underpinning otherwise disparate episodes of historical change.[5]

My theoretical and historical preoccupations with regard to the question of order transformation inevitably overlap, and are explored empirically through a comparative investigation of the transitions to sovereign international orders in Reformation Europe and nineteenth-century East Asia. Conventional accounts of European and Asian transitions to sovereignty have emphasised the dissimilarities distinguishing these cases, with the dynamics of the state system's genesis regarded as being fundamentally different from those underwriting its subsequent export to the non-European world. In the following pages, I tell a different story, illuminating the startlingly similar dynamics that underpinned these transitions. In both Europe and East Asia, a combination of military innovation and religiously tinged ideological polarisation destroyed the material and normative bases of existing international orders. Equally, the transition to a sovereign international order in both Europe and Asia was also completed only after imperial alternatives were decisively foreclosed. That such parallels manifested themselves in environments as culturally and historically distinct as those of early modern Europe and nineteenth-century East Asia suggests a common logic of international systems change that demands explication. In

---

[4] See D. Deudney, *Bounding Power: Republican security theory from the polis to the global village* (Princeton University Press, 2007); and D. Nexon, *The Struggle for Power in Early Modern Europe: Religious conflict, dynastic empires and international change* (Princeton University Press, 2009).

[5] This eclecticism is consistent with that recently advocated by Georg Sorensen in G. Sorensen, 'The case for combining material forces and ideas in the study of IR', *European Journal of International Relations*, 14(1) (2008), 5–32.

retracing the processes through which the modern state system was forged in Europe and then exported to East Asia, I seek to illuminate broader continuities in European and Asian political development that have hitherto remained largely unacknowledged and unexplored in the discipline of international relations. More broadly, my goal is to advance a general account of the dynamics of international change that both improves our understanding of the modern state system's genesis and expansion, while also enabling us to better comprehend its contemporary challenges and long-term prospects.

This study's concerns are predominantly conceptual and historical, but I have undertaken this inquiry with contemporary concerns firmly in mind. At the practical level, this study is driven by the necessity of better comprehending a global security environment that has been radically reshaped by processes ranging from the growth of transnational terrorism and religious fundamentalism, through to widespread post-colonial state failure and the accelerating spread of weapons of mass destruction to both state and non-state actors. In the wake of 9/11, many commentators have invoked these challenges to justify their advocacy of fundamental revisions in the practice of sovereignty, most notably including the adoption of a more permissive regime governing the use of force than that presently authorised under the UN Charter.[6] Conversely, the international community's rapid post-9/11 counter-mobilisation against Al Qaeda suggests that the state system may be capable of responding to these challenges without fundamentally compromising its liberal principles.[7] Whether or not world leaders will successfully adapt to the new security environment depends critically on their ability to comprehend the origins, nature and magnitude of emerging threats. In situating contemporary developments within a historical frame, I hope to delineate with greater precision the vectors of change with which the international community will need to contend if the present order is to be preserved.

Finally, this project is framed by an ethical concern for the state system's future. For all of its manifold imperfections, the international order forged after 1945 institutionalised a host of moral advances worthy of preservation. The global generalisation of the sovereignty regime; the institutionalisation of norms of non-aggression and non-intervention; the articulation of human rights covenants curbing the arbitrary exercise of state power – each of these

---

[6] From a neoconservative perspective, see for example D. Frum and R. Perle, *An End to Evil: How to win the war on terror* (New York: Random House, 2003); and more generally C. Krauthammer, 'The unipolar moment revisited', *The National Interest*, 70 (2002/03), 5–17. From a liberal perspective, see for example L. Feinstein and A.-M. Slaughter, 'A duty to prevent', *Foreign Affairs*, 83(1) (2004), 136–50; and A. Buchanan and R. O. Keohane, 'The preventive use of force: A cosmopolitan institutional proposal', *Ethics and International Affairs*, 18(1) (2004), 1–22.

[7] On this point, see generally B. Mendelsohn, *Combating Jihadism: American hegemony and interstate cooperation in the war on terrorism* (The University of Chicago Press, 2009).

is justly celebrated as having contributed to international stability in the post-war era. But in the face of endemic state failure, an unprecedented spread of destructive capabilities to anti-systemic actors, and resurgent religious funda-mentalist hostility to the present order, the long-term durability of these principles is far from assured. In emphasising the impermanence of past orders and the fragility of the present one, I hope to lend added urgency to the search for solutions to contemporary threats that reconcile the timeless desire for order with the historically contingent task of preserving the liberal principles upon which the present world order has been built.

The argument

Conceptual building blocks and methodology

Already, I have introduced concepts into this discussion that demand defini-tion. The most important of these is the concept of *international orders*. International orders are defined here as the constellation of constitutional norms and fundamental institutions through which co-operation is cultivated and conflict contained between different political communities. This concep-tion of international order, while consistent with that advanced by many constructivists, nevertheless differs from them in two ways.[8] First, while my focus lies with the order-producing norms and institutions that define interna-tional orders, I also acknowledge that international orders depend on the existence of an order-enabling material context. This acknowledgement informs my argument that transformations of international order are propelled by a combination of ideational and material forces, rather than being driven by the force of revolutionary ideas alone.

Secondly, I argue that international orders are inherently dualistic in their constitution, incorporating both positive and negative (or alternatively, Aristotelian and Augustinian) dimensions into their animating purposes. On the one hand, international orders seek to advance a normatively thick and culturally and historically contingent vision of the good. The moral values that inform these visions inevitably reflect the perspectives of the dominant actors within international orders. However, in stable orders these values generally secure wide assent among the order's constituent polities. Simultaneously, however, international orders are also dedicated to the more basic objective of containing violent conflict between different polities within manageable bounds. Of necessity, these positive and negative dimensions of international order inform one another, an observation that is reflected in international orders' fundamental institutions. International orders are sustained through a

---

[8] See for example Hall, *National Collective Identity*; Philpott, *Revolutions in Sovereignty*; and Reus-Smit, *The Moral Purpose of the State*.

combination of authoritative institutions, which attract agents' compliance through their concordance with shared standards of legitimacy, and coercive institutions, which compel agents' compliance through the application of authorised practices of organised violence. In giving equal primacy to author-itative and coercive institutions in sustaining international orders, I hope to 'bring violence back in' to accounts of international change, without abandon-ing constructivists' emphasis on the centrality of shared legitimacy concepts in conditioning international orders' purposes and fundamental institutions.

International orders can be distinguished from one another along the follow-ing axes: (a) principle of differentiation – the organising principle that governs relations of authority between different political communities; (b) purposive orientation – the particular vision of the good that an international order seeks to advance; (c) institutional form – the precise combination of authoritative and coercive institutions upon which an international order relies to promote co-operation and contain enmity between its constituent communities; and (d) distribution of capabilities – the distribution of material capabilities (par-ticularly capabilities for organised violence) among the different actors inhab-iting a given order. These axes of comparison inform my conceptualisation of different types of *international systems change*. At the lowest level of magnitude, international orders may be buffeted by instances of *positional change*, whereby the relative distribution of power and prestige between different political units is altered, but in which an international order's fundamental institutions, constitutional values and principle of unit differentiation all remain unchanged.[9] France's relative decline vis-à-vis Britain following the Seven Years War, which marked a dramatic shift in the global balance of power without witnessing any substantial changes to the constitutional values or fundamental institutions of the international *ancien regime*, stands as a clear example of positional change. Conversely, *institutional change* entails signifi-cant revisions to an international order's fundamental institutions, and would therefore encompass developments such as the establishment (in both 1918 and 1945) of permanent universal conferences of states as mechanisms of interna-tional order maintenance.

Purposive changes in an international order's constitution in turn involve both a transformation of its underlying moral purposes and a comprehensive revision

---

[9] My conception of positional change is roughly comparable to Robert Gilpin's conception of systemic change, which he defines as entailing 'changes in the international distribution of power, the hierarchy of prestige, and the rights and rules embodied in the system'; see R. Gilpin, *War and Change in World Politics* (Cambridge University Press, 1981), p. 42. However, whereas Gilpin conflates changes in the international distribution of power and prestige with alterations in the rights and rules of the international system, thus assuming that changes in the distribution of power unproblematically translate into changes in rights and rules, I see the relationship between the two as being contingent rather than necessary, hence my distinction between positional and institutional change.

of its fundamental institutions.[10] Historically, purposive change is embodied most distinctly in the protracted transition from an Absolutist state system grounded in monarchical sovereignty, towards a state system predicated on popular sovereignty.[11] Finally, international orders may experience *configurative changes*, whereby an order's principle of unit differentiation changes along with its constitutional values and fundamental institutions. The transition from the heteronomous order of Latin Christendom to a Westphalian sovereign state system stands as the classic instance of configurative change in modern European history.[12] Unless otherwise stated, when I refer to the *transformation of international orders*, this term refers to instances of configurative change only.

Despite their profound differences, I argue that both Christendom and the Sinosphere were transformed as a result of structurally similar configurative crises. These crises were driven by a combination of institutional decay, the collapse of prevailing social imaginaries and the accompanying emergence of anti-systemic ideologies, and increases in violence interdependence both within and between political communities. Given the importance of these concepts to my argument, a brief definition of each follows. *Institutional decay* refers to a decline in both the capacity and the legitimacy of an international order's fundamental institutions. While the exact causes of institutional decay historically vary, the manifestations of decay are similar across each of my cases. These symptoms of decay include rising ideological dissent, increasing popular dissatisfaction with existing governance structures, and a decrease in rulers' ability to manage violent conflicts within existing institutional forms. Institutional decay is protracted in character, and provides the permissive context for the operation of the macro-processes that then actively propel international orders towards transformation.

International orders collapse as a result of concatenating ideational and material transformations operative at a systemic level, which simultaneously rob fundamental institutions of both their legitimacy and their practical effectiveness in managing violent conflict between political communities. Turning first to the ideational aspect of my argument, I contend that international orders are purposive rather than merely practical associations, and are undergirded by a coherent set of 'thick' constitutional values. These values articulate a shared vision of the good that binds otherwise feuding polities together, while also providing the normative glue that imbues fundamental authoritative and coercive institutions with the legitimacy necessary for them to maintain a modicum

---

[10] Both the distinction between purposive and configurative forms of systems change and the terminology distinguishing the two types are drawn from Reus-Smit, *The Moral Purpose of the State*, pp. 164–5.

[11] On this transition, see generally *ibid.*, Ch. 6.

[12] On the dynamics underwriting this episode of configurative change, see generally J. G. Ruggie, 'Territoriality and beyond: Problematizing modernity in international relations', *International Organization*, 47(1) (1993), 139–74.

of order. Transformations of international order are catalysed in part through a breakdown of the consensus values that sustain these fundamental institutions. This breakdown manifests itself in several ways. At the level of consciously articulated beliefs, it entails the emergence of anti-systemic ideologies that explicitly contest either part or all of the normative complex underpinning the existing international order. At a more holistic if also a more tacit level, this process of normative breakdown also entails the collapse of the prevailing social imaginaries that make communicative action – and thus the articulation of shared visions of the good and their accompanying fundamental institutions – possible in the first instance.[13] The significance of social imaginaries in providing the conditions of possibility necessary for international orders to emerge will be explored in subsequent chapters. For now, it is necessary to briefly canvass the more direct role that ideological schisms play in tearing international orders apart.

The term *ideological schism* refers to the emergence of an anti-systemic ideology that explicitly repudiates the existing order's animating purposes and constitutional norms. Anti-systemic ideologies subvert international order in two ways. First, they destroy the normative consensus necessary to sustain the operation of fundamental institutions, effectively paralysing collective capacities to manage and contain violent conflict. Secondly, they polarise polities both internally and internationally between defenders and opponents of the existing order. In Latin Christendom, an ideological schism was precipitated by the outbreak of the Reformation, and culminated in the Wars of Religion, which in turn catalysed the establishment of a sovereign international order. In East Asia, by contrast, the Sinosphere's normative coherence was compromised first by the intrusion of Western 'standards of civilisation', before then being challenged internally with the eruption of first millenarian and then revolutionary nationalist rebellions against the Chinese Confucian social order.

The lethal interplay of institutional decay with crises of social imaginaries and ideological schisms was compounded in each of my cases by technologically driven increases in the scale and scope of violent international conflict. Following Daniel Deudney, I refer to this phenomenon as an increase in *violence interdependence*.[14] Increases in violence interdependence arise from broader technological improvements that increase the scope for both peaceful and violent kinds of interaction between polities. Nevertheless, central to the concept of violence interdependence is the development of qualitatively more

---

[13] The concept of social imaginaries invoked here derives from the works of Charles Taylor, as expounded for example in C. Taylor, 'Modern social imaginaries', *Public Culture*, 14(1) (2002), 91–124.

[14] This concept of violence interdependence is taken from Deudney, *Bounding Power*, p. 18. The materialist dimension of my account of transformations of international order draws much of its inspiration from Deudney's work in this area.

destructive forms of warfare than existed previously. In Christendom, increasing violence interdependence was already corroding the old order's material foundations prior to the Reformation. Nevertheless, it was ultimately Christendom's religious polarisation combined with the advent of Europe's first 'military revolution' that condemned Christendom to destruction.[15] Similarly, in East Asia, international order had historically rested upon China's uncontested hegemony as Eurasia's most successful 'gunpowder empire'.[16] The industrialisation of warfare beginning in the mid nineteenth century finally permitted the Western powers to force China open to foreign commercial and cultural influences. This forced opening and the destabilisation that it wrought in turn catalysed a cluster of internal rebellions that gravely weakened the Qing Empire, thereby enabling East Asia's subsequent incorporation into a Western-dominated state system.

Having laid out my core concepts, a brief note on my methodological and theoretical orientation is necessary before I proceed to my analysis. Throughout this inquiry, I abjure exclusive commitments to any single theoretical paradigm in international relations. Instead, I favour an analytically eclectic approach to the study of complex social phenomena, one that has become increasingly popular within the discipline in the past decade.[17] This commitment to analytical eclecticism flows in part from my conviction that the processes through which international orders are constituted, maintained and destroyed are too complex to be adequately captured through singular adherence to any one theoretical framework. The rise of insurgent belief systems and forms of collective identity, processes of institutional decay and breakdown, and material increases in agents' destructive capabilities each plays vitally important roles in the making and unmaking of international orders. Moreover, these processes concatenate in intricate and varied ways at different stages of international orders' evolution, precluding attempts at analysis that afford causal primacy to any single factor.

Considerations of causal complexity thus warrant an analytically eclectic stance for pragmatic reasons. However, my attachment to analytical eclecticism stems equally from its compatibility with my hybrid realist–constructivist theoretical orientation. This book's central argument, derived from a problem-

---

[15] On the nature and consequences of Europe's early modern military revolution, see generally G. Parker, *The Military Revolution: Military innovation and the rise of the West 1500–1800* (Cambridge University Press, 1996).

[16] The concept of 'gunpowder empires' is drawn from W. H. McNeill, *The Age of Gunpowder Empires 1450–1800* (Washington DC: American Historical Association, 1989).

[17] On analytical eclecticism as an approach to the study of international relations, see for example generally J. J. Suh, P. J. Katzenstein and A. Carlson, *Rethinking Security in East Asia: Identity, power, and efficiency* (Stanford University Press, 2004); and R. Sil and P. Katzenstein, *Beyond Paradigms: Analytic eclecticism in the study of world politics* (London and New York: Palgrave Macmillan, 2010).

driven engagement with the question of international orders' transformation in both Western Europe and East Asia, is that international orders depend on both authoritative and coercive fundamental institutions for their constitution and operation. These fundamental institutions remain anchored in shared visions of the good and an order-enabling material context for the duration of their existence, and international orders are transformed when the permissive ideational and material conditions that underpin their fundamental institutions cease to obtain. The conceptual framework underpinning my inquiry thus defies easy categorisation within the discipline's dominant theoretical paradigms, both because of its dualistic emphasis on political orders' authoritative and coercive aspects, and also because of its equal incorporation of the ideal, institutional and material drivers of international systems change. Nevertheless, as I will shortly argue, the constitutional dualism at the heart of my framework is not without precedent, finding diverse antecedents in ancient Western and Eastern political philosophy and the classical realist canon, as well as much more recently in an emerging literature on 'realist constructivism'.[18] This book is thus unapologetically eclectic in its mode of analysis, its theoretical orientation and its intellectual pedigree, reflecting the irreducibly complex and contradictory social realities I have sought to capture in the following pages.

Plan of the book

This study seeks to account for international orders' constitution, transformation and preservation. Accordingly, the book is organised in three parts to engage respectively the study's conceptual, historical and contemporary concerns. In Part I, I critique existing treatments of international order before advancing my own alternative. Central to my approach is a desire to transcend the established polarity between realist and constructivist accounts of international order. These approaches have respectively privileged either the conflictual or the co-operative dimensions of international politics, and have further emphasised respectively the causal force of either material or ideational factors in accounting for international orders' constitution and transformation. Opposing these approaches, I demonstrate that international orders have historically been designed for the two purposes of cultivating co-operation and managing enmity between different political communities. These purposes have been realised through a complementary reliance on both authoritative and

---

[18] Examples of realist constructivist scholarship include J. S. Barkin, 'Realist constructivism', *International Studies Review*, 5(3) (2003), 325–42; and H. R. Nau, *At Home Abroad: Identity and power in American foreign policy* (Ithaca: Cornell University Press, 2002). For an outstanding argument concerning the centrality of values and identities in informing realist conceptions of politics and the implications of same for international orders, see also generally R. N. Lebow, *A Cultural Theory of International Relations* (Cambridge University Press, 2008).

coercive fundamental institutions. These fundamental institutions have relied in turn for their operation on the existence of enabling ideological and material conditions. That these conditions have historically proved transient cuts to the essence of my account of international orders' transformation, which is outlined in Part I before being empirically illustrated in Part II.

In Chapters 3 to 9, I illustrate my argument through reference to the transformation of two historical orders, specifically Latin Christendom and the Sinosphere. Chapters 3 to 5 detail Christendom's constitution, decay and collapse, before then recounting the generative trauma of the European Wars of Religion that ultimately yielded the Westphalian international order. I attribute Christendom's collapse to the combined impact of the Reformation and the early modern military revolution. In a world in which religion was conceived as referring to an embodied community of believers rather than to an abstract body of beliefs, Protestantism's rapid spread undercut Europe's most basic governing principles and rites of social integration. With the coming of the Reformation, the authority of canon law as mechanism of order maintenance was irrevocably destroyed, prompting Charles V's quixotic effort to reconstitute Christendom along imperial lines. Once the Habsburg bid for empire had in turn been defeated, European rulers sought to re-establish order in their own kingdoms through the forcible imposition of confessional conformity, conflating religious dissent with political treachery and thereby condemning Europe to a century of violence. The correspondence of this crisis with the military revolution radically raised the destructiveness of the ensuing wars, which were then further aggravated by the absence of any systemic ordering institutions to prevent localised conflicts from metastasising throughout the international system. Ultimately, it was only in the wake of a series of cultural and intellectual innovations forged in the maelstrom of the Wars of Religion that a new international order based on sovereign principles crystallised, a process that was begun but was by no means completed by 1648.

Whereas Chapters 3 to 5 recount a transformation of international order that is already familiar to international relations scholars, Chapters 6 to 9 concentrate on the comparatively under-studied but no less significant epochal shift from a suzerain to a sovereign international order in East Asia. Chapter 6 outlines the constitutional features of the old East Asian order of the Sinosphere, before then detailing its creeping decay in the decades immediately preceding large-scale Western encroachment. Chapters 7 and 8 then consider this system's crisis and collapse in the face of the combined pressures of Chinese dynastic decay, millenarian rebellion, and increasing foreign predation catalysed by the rise of industrial warfare from the late nineteenth century. Finally, Chapter 9 charts East Asia's traumatic transition towards a consolidated sovereign international order in the forty years following the Qing dynasty's collapse in 1912. As with Western Europe in the decades leading up to Westphalia, so too in East Asia the interval between two international orders was punctuated by a combination of ideological polarisation, imperial aggression and a transformation in the material means and social purposes of warfare. The contours of this chaotic interregnum, and its resolution in the form of the sovereign international order that emerged after 1945, are considered in the chapter's concluding section.

Whereas Part II analyses international orders' transformation, Part III focuses on questions of order preservation as they pertain to the contemporary world order. Since 2001, the global state system has been destabilised by the intertwined threats of Islamist radicalism and transnational terrorism. These threats have in turn prompted US-led interventions in Afghanistan and Iraq that have been characterised as imperial by both advocates and critics alike, calling into question the robustness of a global state system predicated on norms of sovereign equality and non-intervention.[19] I argue that when seen from a historical vantage point, the threats to world order posed by both jihadist terrorism and its American imperial counterpoint appear more transient and less profound than many have assumed. This observation aside, the 'war on terror' has nevertheless obscured deeper frailties in the present order that must be addressed if it is to endure. The revival of authoritarian Great Powers and accelerating competition for the Middle East's scarce energy resources; the burgeoning 'nuclear renaissance' in the Persian Gulf and its accompanying spur to nuclear weapons proliferation; the wrenching political and economic dislocation anticipated to flow from climate change, particularly in the failing states of the Afro-Asian 'Islamic crescent' – these structural forces are together likely to both complicate and amplify the threats already posed by terrorism and the confrontation between Western liberalism and radical Islam. Consequently, this study concludes by situating these challenges within their larger macro-historical context, before then speculatively considering the ordering imperatives they are likely to engender in the coming century.

---

[19] For positive assessments of America's post-9/11 imperial turn, see for example N. Ferguson, *Colossus: The rise and fall of the American empire* (London: Penguin Books, 2005); and S. Mallaby, 'The reluctant imperialist: Terrorism, failed states, and the case for American Empire', *Foreign Affairs*, 81(2) (2002), 2–7. For more critical accounts, see for example M. Mann, 'The first failed empire of the 21st century', *Review of International Studies*, 30(4) (2004), 631–53; J.N. Rosenau, 'Illusions of power and empire', *History and Theory*, 44(4) (2005), 73–87; and G. Steinmetz, 'Return to empire: The new U.S. imperialism in comparative historical perspective', *Sociological Theory*, 23(4) (2005), 339–67.

PART I

Conceptual framework

1 | *What are international orders?*

You must understand, therefore, that there are two ways of fighting: by law or by force. The first way is natural to men, and the second to beasts. But as the first way often proves inadequate one must needs have recourse to the second. So a prince must understand how to make a nice use of the beast and the man. The ancient writers taught princes about this by an allegory, when they described how Achilles and many other princes of the ancient world were sent to be brought up by Chiron, the centaur, so that he might train them this way. All the allegory means, in making the teacher half beast and half man, is that a prince must know how to act according to the nature of both, and that he cannot survive otherwise ...

Niccolo Machiavelli, *The Prince*.[1]

Order under the centaur's shadow

In taking the centaur to personify the dualistic character of political power, Machiavelli captured an essential truth about the nature of order, one that obtains equally in the domestic and international spheres. Both the power of moral suasion and the force of material sanctions sustain political order. This elementary observation is worth emphasising, precisely because it is so often overlooked in the study of international relations. Far from constituting mere decorative artifice, the rules, norms, principles and moral conventions that infuse political orders provide the essential media through which co-operation is realised and conflict mitigated between social agents. Equally, recourse to organised violence frequently fortifies and perpetuates political orders rather than undermining them. Political orders crystallise at the intersection of ethical and coercive modes of action. For the duration of their existence, they are sustained by these modes of action. And it is precisely when the tentative reconciliation between these factors fails that political orders are destroyed.

The next two chapters outline this book's conceptual framework. I begin by exploring the nature of political order, explaining both why it is necessary and

---

[1] N. Machiavelli, *The Prince*, trans. G. Bull (London: Penguin Books, 1999), p. 56.

how it is produced. I then narrow the discussion to consider the specific problems of realising order internationally, before then advancing my own conception of international order. In Chapter 2, I then critically evaluate existing explanations for the transformation of international orders, before then articulating my own account of how and why international orders are transformed.

The nature of political order

Security, community and the need for political order

Throughout history, humans have constructed communities that have transcended the small circles of sympathy delimited by the bonds of family and friendship.[2] I argue that this impulse towards community has been profoundly motivated by a quest for both physical and ontological security. As embodied beings, we remain forever hostage to certain basic physical needs. We need food, drink and shelter to survive, but we can undertake the productive activities necessary to secure them only once we have mitigated the immediate threats to our physical survival posed by potential predators. The quest for physical security consequently finds expression in the development of fundamental institutions – ranging from culturally prescribed practices of private vengeance through to the establishment of violence-monopolising Weberian states – that aim to mitigate the threat of violent predation, while also providing the stability required for agents to enjoy at least the minimal standard of material welfare necessary for their survival.[3]

In contrast to the quest for physical security, the search for ontological security flows from the fact that we are meaning-seeking creatures as well as corporeal beings.[4] Our aspirations extend beyond bodily needs, encompassing also a yearning for the mental maps necessary to orient us in our relationships within both the social world and the larger universe. Ontological security consequently concerns itself with nothing less than the requirements of individual and collective self-understanding, and entails the creation of shared systems of meaning that articulate and institutionalise a community's most basic moral, social and frequently even spiritual values and ideals.[5] Shared

---

[2] Berger and Luckmann refer to this trans-historical imperative towards community as the 'constitutional sociality' of man. See P. L. Berger and T. Luckmann, *The Social Construction of Reality* (Middlesex: Penguin Books, 1966), p. 119.

[3] Within the Western political tradition, the classic statement on the centrality of physical security as a rationale for the establishment of political institutions remains T. Hobbes, *Leviathan* (London: Penguin Books, 1985).

[4] On humans as 'meaning-seeking creatures', see K. Armstrong, *A Short History of Myth* (Edinburgh: Canongate, 2006), p. 2.

[5] On the role of 'symbolic universes' in providing both a framework of meaning for individuals and a broader legitimating structure for established institutional orders, see generally Berger and Luckmann, *The Social Construction of Reality*, pp. 110–22.

visions of the good; collective identities that transcend the limits of intimate familiars; common narratives that situate us in relation to our collective past and future; even ritual practices that enact the distinctiveness of imagined communities of tribe, faith and nation – these phenomena practically manifest the imperative towards ontological security, and provide the affective cement necessary to constitute political communities.

While the search for physical and ontological security draws us together to form communities beyond the limits of intimate familiars, several powerful constraints nevertheless limit the possibility of sociability among strangers. First, communities must contend with the reality of continuous struggles between their members for power, prestige and wealth. Both the inescapable condition of scarcity and the inherently positional nature of some desired social goods guarantee conflict in even the most well-ordered societies. Secondly, attempts to enlarge the boundaries of solidarity among strangers are often endangered by agents' more parochial allegiances and their accompanying tendencies towards discriminatory sociabil-ity. Finally, the very attempt to provide ontological security through the gener-ation of a shared conception of the good is an inherently fraught enterprise, inviting as it does principled conflicts over the nature of the good that cut to the very essence of what it means to be a member of a particular community.

Security, both physical and ontological, can only be found in community. But the security that community promises is always endangered by the centrifugal forces outlined above. Political orders thus arise out of the need to reconcile the quest for security through community with the equally irresistible human pro-pensity for conflict. They fulfil this task through the provision of fundamental authoritative and coercive institutions, which acquire social legitimacy through their perceived concordance with a shared vision of the good. For this reason, the construction of political order is simultaneously both a regulative project and an interpretive enterprise, entailing the tasks of both institutional design and the articulation of the common identities and shared conceptions of the good that imbue fundamental institutions with moral and political legitimacy.

How political order is achieved: The two faces of political order

Having identified political orders' chief purposes, it is now necessary to sketch the processes by which these orders are generated and sustained. Within the Western canon, two traditions have proved particularly influential in shaping conceptualisations of political order. The first of these, referred to here as the Aristotelian tradition, envisages the polis as constituting the highest form of collective association, and conceives of it as being held together by a shared commitment to the pursuit of a supreme good. For Aristotle, humanity is by nature a political animal (a *zoon politikon*).[6] Having been uniquely endowed

---

[6] Aristotle, *The Politics*, trans. T. A. Sinclair (Baltimore: Penguin Books, 1962), p. 28.

with the capacity for reasoned speech, humans possess the ability to engage in public deliberation, enabling them to articulate common standards of justice and a shared conception of the good.[7] The Aristotelian tradition thus foregrounds the communicative dimension of political action, and conceptualises the state as being above all a distinctly moral association.

Conversely, the Augustinian tradition conceives of the polis as forming a repressive, remedial order intended only to preserve a modicum of peace in the temporal world. For Augustine, the City of Man was merely a temporal and transient order founded on coercion and domination, which contrasted with the spontaneous order of love and fellowship embodied in the ethereal City of God.[8] Those following the Augustinian political tradition have thus typically downplayed the communicative and deliberative aspects of political action in favour of its coercive aspects.[9] Rather than conceptualising political order as a sphere for the articulation and institutionalisation of shared moral visions, the Augustinian tradition emphasises political institutions' prosaic and instrumental character. Through this lens, political institutions contribute to order not by making humans more just and virtuous, but rather by securing their conformity with laws through the deployment of mechanisms of coercion and punishment.[10]

At first glance, the Aristotelian and Augustinian traditions seem to offer conceptions of politics that preclude the possibility of fruitful synthesis. Aristotle's emphasis on polities as co-operative moral associations, together with his emphasis on the critical significance of public deliberation for the constitution and functioning of political orders, initially suggests a highly idealist – and idealistic – conception of politics. Similarly, Augustine's conception of the polis as being primarily an apparatus of coercion, founded on force and rendered necessary because of Fallen Man's inherently conflictual nature, ostensibly confronts the reader as being unequivocally realist in character. Positioning these two thinkers in this way fortifies a long-established idealist–realist faultline – with Plato and Confucius on the one side and Hobbes and the Chinese Legalists on the other – that pervades both Western and Eastern political thought, and finds its echoes in international relations in the contemporary constructivist–realist divide. Critically, however, a closer consideration of these thinkers reveals a more nuanced understanding of order, one

---

[7] *Ibid.*

[8] Augustine, *City of God* (London: Penguin Books, 1984), pp. 593–7. See also H. Deane, *The Political and Social Ideas of Saint Augustine* (New York: Columbia University Press, 1963), p. 117.

[9] On the influence on Augustine of twentieth-century realism, see for example M. Loriaux, 'The realists and Saint Augustine: Skepticism, psychology, and moral action in international relations thought', *International Studies Quarterly*, 36(4) (1992), 401–20.

[10] Deane, *The Political and Social Ideas of Saint Augustine*, p. 141.

that offers a means of transcending the constructivist–realist divide, and which furthermore fundamentally informs my conception of international order.

While their respective emphases differed, both Aristotle and Augustine acknowledged the role played by the imperatives of physical and ontological security in bringing communities into being. Thus, Aristotle openly acknowledged the polis's protective function alongside its higher role in enabling communities to collectively realise the supreme good.[11] Similarly, for Augustine, the search for ontological security was the starting point of his political theology. While Augustine reduced the polis to a mechanism of physical protection, he nevertheless saw its legitimacy deriving from its role in providing the temporal order necessary for humans to pursue the ultimate end of spiritual salvation.[12] Under both Aristotle and Augustine, the search for security and meaning, order and justice were thus explicitly incorporated into their understandings of the nature and purposes of collective association. Equally, while their analytical emphases differed vastly, both of these thinkers also recognised both the communicative and coercive dimensions of political life.

Nomos and *kratos* – expressed respectively in inter-subjectively shared systems of moral meaning and structures of organised coercion – form the twin foundations of political communities. This acknowledgement of the constitutional dualism inherent in political order has all too frequently been overlooked by both constructivists and modern realists, who have alternatively privileged either the communicative or the coercive dimensions of political life in their characterisations of international politics. In contrast, I seek to transcend this idealist–realist faultline by embracing the constitutional dualism characteristic of both ancient political thought and the classical realist tradition. Specifically, I argue that political orders are inherently Janus-faced in their constitution, possessing both Aristotelian and Augustinian aspects. Political orders seek both to advance a concrete conception of the good, and to secure the physical safety of their members. Furthermore, they do so by relying on both authoritative and coercive forms of power. Moral suasion and material sanctions, the respective arts of man and beast embodied in Machiavelli's centaur, are equally essential for the maintenance of political order. Authoritative and coercive forms of power are sometimes portrayed as residing at different ends of a continuum of forms of social power.[13] Thus, whereas authoritative power is seen to attract subjects' voluntary compliance with rules or commands deemed

---

[11] Aristotle, *The Politics*, p. 107.

[12] On the claim that the Earthly City's legitimacy is directly concordant with its degree of legitimacy to the imperatives of the City of God, see for example Augustine, *City of God*, p. 600.

[13] See for example C. Reus-Smit, *American Power and World Order* (Cambridge: Polity Press, 2004), p. 58.

by them to be morally legitimate and therefore compulsorily binding, coercive power is conceived as extracting subjects' otherwise unwilling compliance through the use or threatened use of force.[14] While this distinction is not without value, I maintain both that authoritative and coercive power typically work in conjunction with one another to produce order, and that the marshalling of both forms of power is necessary for societies to realise their elementary goals.

Political order involves first the imposition of ethical and institutional restraints on agents' freedom of action. While these restraints are necessary to cultivate co-operation between actors and limit enmity between them, their imposed character makes it vital that they be recognised as legitimate if they are to command compliance. Authoritative power relies upon the issuing of rules and commands, the obligatory force of which increases the more closely they are identified with agents' subjectivities, their essential purposes and their most deeply held ethical convictions. Where agents inhabit what Habermas calls a common 'life-world' – that is, where they share a 'storehouse of unquestioned cultural givens' that form the backdrop for practices of communicative action – authoritative power acquires a particularly strong purchase over agents' actions.[15] This is because the close identification between a ruler's commands and a community's shared moral values creates the obligation to obey a routine social expectation on the part of the dominated. This expectation in turn increases agents' compliance with authority and thereby reduces the need for costly recourse to coercive power to maintain political authority.[16] Where a close fit exists between a society's constitutional values and the rules and commands of governing agencies, the legitimacy accorded to these agencies grows, the scope for the exercise of authoritative power expands, and the stability of the prevailing order increases accordingly.

The ability of authoritative power to attract actors' voluntary compliance makes it indispensable, but authoritative power alone is insufficient to maintain political order. This is because even in the most well-integrated orders, the basic asymmetries of power and opportunity between rulers and ruled will inspire resistance in some quarters. This resistance may assume the form of a direct attack on the order by actors that deem it illegitimate, and who seek to overturn it in favour of a purportedly more just alternative.[17] Alternatively, it may manifest itself in a more indirect and unprincipled way, with actors ignoring or defying rules, norms and laws for the sake of advancing their own interests at

---

[14] *Ibid.*

[15] J. Habermas, *Moral Consciousness and Communicative Action* (Cambridge, MA: MIT Press, 1990), p. 135.

[16] On this point, see D. C. North, *Structure and Change in Economic History* (New York: Norton, 1981), p. 47.

[17] On the threats of this nature posed to political orders by 'extremists and doctrinaire theorists', see Aristotle, *The Politics*, pp. 214–15.

the expense of others. What unites both instances of resistance is the imperviousness of the actors involved to the normative force upon which authoritative power relies. It is precisely because some will always be beyond the reach of authoritative power that coercive power becomes necessary.

Coercive power, entailing the use or threatened use of material sanctions to compel actors' compliance, where authoritative power has failed to elicit it voluntarily, fulfils a variety of functions germane to the maintenance of order. Coercive power can punish transgressors and deter future violations of the existing order by providing actors with strong negative inducements to comply with existing arrangements.[18] It can also be deployed to enforce established norms, rules, laws and commands and thereby preserve the existing order in the face of principled and unprincipled efforts to undermine it.[19] Coercive power can also be deployed in a restorative sense to reverse or mitigate injuries sustained by the victims of transgressors, in so doing upholding communally shared conceptions of justice that the prevailing order purports to embody. Finally, coercive power can also serve a pedagogical purpose, reaffirming in the punishment of transgressors the key constitutional values of society, while simultaneously providing renewed opportunities to reflect, reiterate and communicate these values and identities back to the community.

In stable orders, authoritative and coercive power form complementary and mutually indispensable modes of action. Exclusive reliance on authoritative power is unsustainable in the long term, for the failure to punish violators of norms, rules, laws and commands inhibits a political order's capacity to provide elementary social goods, inviting negative assessments of its performance that corrode its legitimacy over time. Equally, excessive reliance on coercion is suggestive of an order's lack of legitimacy and its ineffectiveness in attracting voluntary compliance. Only by maintaining strong reserves of both authoritative and coercive power, deploying the former where possible and the latter where unavoidable, can a political order be successful in providing the social goods of physical and ontological security that are its *raison d'être*.

The constitution of international orders

A prefatory note on order and pluralism

Just as within the state every government, though it needs power as the basis of its authority, also needs the moral basis of the consent of the governed, so an international order cannot be based on power alone, for the simple reason that mankind will in the long run always revolt against

---

[18] On this point, see for example Bull's discussion of war as a fundamental institution contributing to the maintenance of order in modern international society. See Bull, *The Anarchical Society*, pp. 180–3.

[19] *Ibid.*, p. 182.

naked power … The fatal dualism of politics will always keep considerations of morality entangled with considerations of power …

E. H. Carr, *The Twenty Years' Crisis.*[20]

Just as order relies within political communities on both authoritative and
coercive power, so too does this 'fatal dualism' obtain between political communities. Admittedly, the existence of multiple centres of power and solidarity
within international systems complicates the task of maintaining order. This is
so for two reasons. First, the diffusion of coercive power between political
communities immediately introduces the problem of the security dilemma
into social life, suffusing inter-polity relations with mistrust and thus corroding
prospects for co-operation.[21] Secondly, the existence of multiple political communities would initially appear to inhibit convergence towards a consensus on
the 'thick' constitutional values necessary to support the development of robust
authoritative institutions. In reality, however, the magnitude of these challenges
should not be overstated. Turning first to the question of coercive power, its
broad diffusion within international systems presents a less insurmountable
challenge to the generation of order than might first be supposed. Hedley Bull's
paradoxical characterisation of the institution of war in international societies,
which has historically threatened order while also working to sustain it, illustrates the fact that organised violence plays a vital role in the generation of order
between political communities as well as within them.[22] Similarly, neo-realists
have long emphasised the importance of concepts such as the balance of power
and conventional and nuclear deterrence in underpinning international order,
although they have sometimes cast these concepts in excessively materialist
terms.[23] What a closer consideration of practices of organised violence across
different international orders reveals is that coercive power works to sustain
rather than subvert order when it operates within the parameters of a shared
justificatory framework. When corralled within a framework prescribing the
circumstances when violence is justified, the agents that may legitimately
employ it, the purposes to which it may be directed and the ways in which it
may be deployed, organised violence fulfils similar ordering purposes internationally as it does within political communities. The punishment of transgressors, the enforcement of laws, the rectification of injuries and the
enactment of shared conceptions of justice each provides warrants for the

---

[20] E. H. Carr, *The Twenty Years' Crisis, 1919–1939: An introduction to the study of international relations* (New York: Harper and Row, 1946), pp. 235–6.
[21] On this point, see generally K. N. Waltz, *Man, the State, and War: A theoretical analysis* (New York: Columbia University Press, 1959), Ch. 6.
[22] Bull, *The Anarchical Society*, Ch. 8.
[23] See, for example, K. N. Waltz, *Theory of International Politics* (New York: Random House, 1979), Ch. 6; and more generally J. J. Mearsheimer, *The Tragedy of Great Power Politics* (New York: W. W. Norton and Company, 2001).

legitimate use of violence internationally. To make such an observation is not to underestimate the often intense security anxieties actors confront internationally, nor is it to deny international orders' fragility in the face of illegitimate applications of violence by powerful actors. But just as the state's recourse to violence domestically may be productive of order rather than subversive of it, so too does this situation frequently obtain internationally.

That violence may be legitimately employed to promote international order begs larger questions concerning the identity of those who are authorised to confer the judgement of legitimacy, as well as the criteria by which such assessments are to be made. More broadly, it raises questions concerning the scope for the exercise of authoritative power within systems populated by a plurality of different power centres. Authoritative power operates through the medium of practices of communicative action. These communicative practices in turn require as a condition of possibility the existence of a shared life-world that binds agents together and that provides the backdrop of common cultural assumptions enabling effective communication to take place. In international systems, this then raises two questions. First, to what extent do an international order's constituent polities inhabit a common life-world? And secondly, what scope exists internationally for effective communicative action and the marshalling of authoritative power in the service of order?

The cases I consider below demonstrate that the existence of a common life-world has been an antecedent condition for the generation of international order across a range of contexts, and that the use of authoritative power has been vital in producing order in each of these cases. Latin Christendom, the Sinosphere and the contemporary global state system were or are all purposive rather than merely practical associations. As with all orders, authoritative power in each case acquired its persuasive force precisely because of agents' prior subscription to a world-view incorporating a common collective identity, shared purposes and an agreed moral framework. Certainly, in each instance, systemic norms and collective identities co-existed alongside more particularistic identities and values operative within polities. Nevertheless, in each case subscription to a common set of constitutional values was critical to the development of the fundamental institutions necessary to realise order between different polities. Even more critically, in each case it was the partial or total breakdown of consensus over these values – and thus the withering of agents' capacities to deploy authoritative power in the service of common goals – that presaged the decay (and in two cases, the eventual transformation) of international orders.

How, then, is order generated internationally? More specifically, what are international orders? International orders are understood here as systemic structures that cohere within culturally and historically specific social imaginaries, and that are composed of an *order-producing* normative complex and its accompanying fundamental institutions. Both an international order's normative complex and its fundamental institutions rest in turn on a permissive *order-enabling* material foundation. An international order's normative complex confers upon actors a shared collective identity, as well as providing ethical prescriptions to regulate actors' behaviour and a justificatory rationale to stabilise and sustain relations of organised domination. The constitutional values expressed in this complex are practically realised through its fundamental institutions. These institutions comprise recognised loci of authoritative and decision-making power, a legal or ritualistic framework through which relations of co-operation are fostered and conflicts mitigated, and authorised practices of violence through which order is enforced, transgressors punished and the order's values reaffirmed. Finally, the order-enabling foundation sets concrete material constraints on the scope and character of agents' interactions. While not determining an international order's character, the material foundation indirectly shapes it by providing the permissive context within which orders are forged.

International orders are composed first of a web of shared meanings that make the exercise of authoritative power possible between polities, and which I refer to throughout this inquiry as an international order's normative complex. Normative complexes provide actors with the 'maps of meaning' necessary to navigate social life, conferring upon them a shared collective identity, as well as a common ethical system and a framework for recognising and legitimising political authority. They articulate the foundational suppositions of a given order, and are as such crucial in enabling the collective practices – in the form of authoritative institutions such as ritual and law and coercive institutions such as feud and war – through which order is practically realised. The exact constitution of normative complexes will be outlined momentarily. For now, it is necessary to emphasise that these normative complexes themselves crystallise within historically and culturally specific social imaginaries, understood as the deep background of tacit assumptions, images and symbols that make possible the prescriptive propositions that constitute normative complexes.[24] Social imaginaries encompass our most basic and mostly unarticulated assumptions about social reality, extending even to those that condition our experience of categories as allegedly basic as time, space, language and embodiment.[25] The contrast between 'messianic' time and linear, historical time; the distinct conceptions of space implied in the medieval *mappe mundi* versus the profane Mercator map; the different forms of sociality mediated respectively via 'sacred' versus vernacular scripts; even the diverse forms of embodiment represented by

---

[24] For a fuller exposition on the significance of social imaginaries in constituting social orders, see generally Taylor, 'Modern social imaginaries'; C. Taylor, *Modern Social Imaginaries* (Durham NC: Duke University Press, 2004); and C. Taylor, *A Secular Age*, (Cambridge, MA: Belknap Press of Harvard University Press, 2007).

[25] Taylor, *A Secular Age*, pp. 171–5.

the 'porous' bodies of late medieval Europe versus the 'buffered' selves of the modern age – each of these comparisons advert to the deep constitutive influence of social imaginaries, as diffuse but pervasive phenomena that structure the mental horizons within which international orders come into being.[26] While my discussion below focuses on the articulated corpus of beliefs that sustains international orders, it is critical to recognise that these beliefs in turn rest on a more diffuse and an unarticulated social imaginary, which provides a primary condition of possibility for orders' constitution and operation.

Normative complexes can be disaggregated into a composite of overlapping norms that perform identity-constitutive, ethical-prescriptive and power-legitimating functions.[27] Identity-constitutive norms integrate an order's communities by conferring upon them a shared identity, and providing consensus on the ultimate purposes of collective association. They answer such basic questions as 'who am I?' and 'what do I want?', offering agents what Taylor has referred to as the 'inescapable frameworks' operative in all societies that link concepts of the self with concepts of the good.[28] Identity-constitutive norms provide societies with a sense of the ultimate *sources* of morality, be they the revealed Word of God, the divine mandate of the Son of Heaven, or cosmopolitan ethical principles discernible from the exercise of human reason. They also help agents to locate themselves within the world, allowing them to orient themselves in relation to the higher purposes of collective association.

While identity-constitutive norms integrate orders by providing consensus on the ultimate *sources* of moral obligation, ethical-prescriptive norms seek to regulate agents' behaviour by articulating the *nature* and *content* of these obligations. Whereas identity-constitutive norms give actors a sense of what the good is, ethical-prescriptive norms give them a sense of how to go about being good, establishing shared standards of rightfulness against which the legitimacy of actors' actions may be judged. The existence of such a shared moral vocabulary is critical if order is to endure, for authoritative power can only operate in an environment in which actors share a common sense of what is right and wrong. Politics by its nature involves intense and often violent

---

[26] For an instructive contrast between the distinctive social imaginaries informing modern conceptions of the nation and those that underpinned earlier religious and dynastic forms of imagined community, see B. Anderson, *Imagined Communities: Reflections on the origins and spread of nationalism* (London: Verso, 1991), Ch. 2. On the distinction between the pre-Reformation 'porous' self and the post-Reformation 'buffered' self, and on the different social imaginaries these different forms of embodiment reflected, see Taylor, *A Secular Age*, pp. 37–41.

[27] My conception of the component elements of international orders' normative complexes derives strong inspiration from Christian Reus-Smit's interstitial conception of political rationality as articulated in C. Reus-Smit, 'The politics of international law' in C. Reus-Smit (ed.), *The Politics of International Law* (Cambridge University Press, 2004), pp. 25–30.

[28] C. Taylor, *Sources of the Self: The making of modern identity* (Cambridge, MA: Harvard University Press, 1989), p. 3.

struggles over the ethical evaluation of actors' motives and actions, but the existence of such interpretive contests in no way suggests the marginality of ethical-prescriptive norms to the generation of order. On the contrary, such contests testify to the practical political importance actors perceive in being seen to be 'good', thereby indirectly affirming the power of ethical-prescriptive norms in conditioning actors' political judgements and thus corralling conflict within shared moral parameters.

Politics necessarily entails relations of organised domination, hence the existence of power-legitimating norms that stabilise the relations of domination upon which international orders depend. In a sense, power-legitimating norms constitute a subset of ethical-prescriptive norms, inasmuch as their function is to convince agents that political obedience is both necessary and consistent with the demands of morality. Simultaneously, however, they also fortify established structures of domination by situating them as necessary expressions of politically salient collective identities, whose continued operation is essential if the community's shared purposes are to be realised. Power-legitimating norms therefore harmonise the imperatives of morality and identity with the realities of power, legitimising and securing the relations of domination that are characteristic of all political orders.

The overlapping identity-constitutive, ethical-prescriptive and power-legitimating norms sketched above constitute the ideological cement that holds international orders together, providing consensus on questions such as 'who are we', 'what do we want', 'how should we act' and 'how should we organise ourselves politically to get what we want'.[29] Normative complexes pacify relations between polities by unifying them around a common moral ontology and shared purposes, creating the shared life-world within which communicative action becomes possible. They regulate agents' behaviour through the codification of binding standards of rightfulness, and they legitimise and stabilise the relations of domination within and between polities that are necessary for the realisation of order. Additionally, normative complexes also profoundly inform institutional design, shaping the fundamental institutions within which authoritative and coercive power are marshalled to the task of producing order.

The fundamental institutions of international orders are composed of the following: (i) authoritative institutions that wield supreme authority within a given issue area and/or territory; (ii) a legal or ritual framework that codifies agents' rights and obligations and provides the medium through which relations of amity are fostered and relations of enmity contained; and (iii) authorised practices of legitimate violence through which order is enforced, violators are punished, and injuries are remedied. It is through this framework that the

---

[29] C. Reus-Smit, 'Politics and international legal obligation', *European Journal of International Relations*, 9(4) (2003), 607–8.

imperatives encoded in orders' normative complexes are practically realised. Inevitably, in all international orders, attempts to institutionalise visions of the good fall well short of stated ideals. But such imperfections do not detract from the necessary role these institutions play in mitigating conflict and promoting order.

The diversity of the normative complexes informing different orders is reflected in the distinctiveness of their accompanying fundamental institutions. In Christendom, power was organised along heteronomous lines, with actors ensnared in webs of cross-cutting, territorially non-exclusive and frequently mutually contradictory obligations.[30] Social power crystallised overwhelmingly at the local level in medieval Europe, with the system's coherence deriving from the operation of a loose diarchy composed of the Church and the empire, serving as Christendom's respective pinnacles of sacred and temporal power.[31] This framework contrasted starkly with the hierarchical order of the Sinosphere, in which the Chinese emperor laid claim to supreme spiritual and temporal power throughout the empire proper, as well as over a penumbra of adjacent tributary states.[32] The Sinosphere differs in turn from the modern sovereign state system, in which political authority is concentrated primarily in territorially exclusive and formally equal sovereign states, but also secondarily in multilateral institutions that derive their legitimacy from their perceived concordance with the collective will of their member states.[33]

The papal–imperial diarchy, the Sino-centric tributary state system and the global sovereign state system each epitomises different ways of organising authoritative power internationally. In each of these orders one finds not only different configurations of authoritative power, but also historically specific legal or ritual frameworks through which this power is deployed. These legal or ritual frameworks are accompanied also by authorised practices of violence through which coercive power is brought to bear in the service of order. The joint operation of these authoritative and coercive institutions in producing order can be demonstrated through a brief comparison of this dualism as it manifested itself in Christendom and the Sinosphere.

---

[30] On heteronomy as the organising principle of medieval Christendom, see J. G. Ruggie, *Constructing the World Polity: Essays on international institutionalization* (London: Routledge, 1998), pp. 146–7.

[31] M. Mann. *The Sources of Social Power*, 2 vols. (Cambridge University Press, 1986), I, p. 394.

[32] J. K. Fairbank, 'A preliminary framework' in J. K. Fairbank (ed.), *The Chinese World Order: Traditional China's foreign relations* (Cambridge, MA: Harvard University Press, 1968), pp. 6–8.

[33] On this point, see generally J. Meyer, 'The world polity and the authority of the nation-state' in A. Bergesen (ed.), *Studies of the Modern World-System* (New York: Academic Press, 1980), pp. 109–37; and also Reus-Smit, *The Moral Purpose of the State*, Ch. 6.

In Christendom, a combination of canon law and feudal law codified the matrix of social relations through which conflicts were mediated. As the supreme interpreter of canon law, the papacy was empowered to authoritatively adjudicate temporal as well as spiritual disputes, with its ability to threaten excommunication to recalcitrant parties ensuring a notably high rate of compliance with papal courts' rulings.[34] This system of papal mediation and adjudication functioned side by side with a system of violent self-help, in which an armed aristocracy routinely resorted to violence as a means of seeking legal redress within the parameters of a shared corpus of feudal law.[35] Rather than operating as alternative and antithetical systems of dispute resolution, papal adjudication and feudal self-help complemented one another in an environment in which spiritual and legal power was highly concentrated, but capacities for organised violence remained widely dispersed.[36]

A similar complementarity in the exercise of authoritative and coercive power was observable in the Sinosphere. In the Sinosphere, authoritative power was deployed principally through the ritual affirmation of asymmetric bonds of benevolence and obedience linking the emperor to his domestic and foreign vassals. *Li*, understood as proper adherence to divinely sanctioned forms and ceremonies, was seen as vital to the transmission of ethical principles and the maintenance of moral, social and cosmic order within the Sinosphere.[37] In China's relations with its tributaries, *li* manifested itself most regularly in vassals' highly ritualised tribute missions to the imperial court, and also in the less frequent but arguably more important investiture missions undertaken on the emperor's behalf to confirm the authority of newly appointed kings in vassal states.[38] Conversely, where the proper enactment of ritual was insufficient to secure order, the imperial court resorted to *fa*, understood as the rectification of error through the punitive use of force against those unwilling to submit to the requirements of *li*.[39] Internationally, *fa* was intermittently manifest in imperial interventions to punish outlaws (such as the *wako* pirates active between the

---

[34] R. Lesaffer, 'Peace treaties from Lodi to Westphalia' in R. Lesaffer (ed.), *Peace Treaties and International Law in European History* (Cambridge University Press, 2004), pp. 24–6.

[35] On the fundamentally litigious character of aristocratic legal feud, see generally P. J. Geary, 'Living with conflicts in stateless France: A typology of conflict management mechanisms, 1050–1200' in P. J. Geary (ed.), *Living with the Dead in the Middle Ages* (Ithaca: Cornell University Press, 1994), pp. 125–60.

[36] Lesaffer, 'Peace treaties from Lodi to Westphalia', p. 11.

[37] F. T.-S. Chen, 'The Confucian view of world order' in M. W. Janis and C. Evans (eds.), *Religion and International Law* (Leiden: Martinus Nijhoff Publishers, 2004), p. 33.

[38] K.-H. Kim, *The Last Phase of the East Asian World Order: Korea, Japan, and the Chinese Empire, 1860–1882* (Berkeley: University of California Press, 1980), pp. 7–9.

[39] A. Bozeman, *The Future of Law in a Multicultural World* (Princeton University Press, 1971), pp. 152–3.

fourteenth and seventeenth centuries), and to defend tributary states from external attack by 'barbarians'.[40]

The normative complexes and fundamental institutions of international orders provide them with the ideological unity and institutional capacity needed to produce order between political communities. But these norms and institutions are themselves embedded within an order-enabling material context. The three most salient features of this context are: (i) the aggregate social capacities for organised production and destruction extant within a given order; (ii) the configuration of mobilisational networks – organised around principles of kinship, patronage, contract or bureaucratic command – through which collective action may be channelled; and (iii) the volume and density of interactions (the systemic interdependence) operative between the order's communities.[41] These features collectively help determine both the social resources available to the would-be architects of order and the magnitude of governance problems that they must confront.

Both the capacities to generate and appropriate liquid wealth and the capacities to organise and project armed force are central to the generation of political order. Across the cases examined in this book, variations in capacities for production and destruction left profound imprints on international orders' constitutions. Thus, for example, we can only fully understand Christendom's constitution with a prior recognition of medieval Europe's poverty, its technological backwardness, and the radical dispersion of capacities for violence among the aristocratic nobility. For it was only in such an environment, where economic and military power remained largely localised and the economy centred predominantly around subsistence agriculture, that the crazy-quilt of overlapping authority claims characteristic of a heteronomous system could effectively function as a viable governance structure.[42] Conversely, the continuing viability of the hierarchical order of the Sinosphere over several centuries cannot be comprehended without an appreciation of the qualitatively higher levels of wealth and war-making capacity that the Ming and Qing dynasties were able to access vis-à-vis their medieval European counterparts.[43] Equally, contemporary leaders' ambitions to eradicate war and poverty from the world are only imaginable because of the unprecedented levels of liquid wealth and popular pacification that have been delivered by the advent of a global market economy and the universalisation of the nation-state.

---

[40] D. Kang, 'Hierarchy in Asian international relations: 1300–1900', *Asian Security*, 1(1) (2005), 59.

[41] My emphasis on systemic interdependence as a vitally important determinant of international order is drawn from B. Buzan, C. Jones and R. Little, *The Logic of Anarchy: Neorealism to structural realism* (New York: Columbia University Press, 1993), pp. 66–80.

[42] P. Hirst, *War and Power in the 21st Century: The state, military conflict, and the international system* (Cambridge: Polity Press, 2001), pp. 129–30.

[43] Kang, 'Hierarchy in Asian international relations', pp. 57–9.

The raw levels of wealth and war-making capacity that rulers are able to tap clearly condition international orders' constitution, as do the mobilisational capacities available within a given social milieu. Social networks governed by principles of kinship, patronage, contract or bureaucratic command provide the media through which collective identities crystallise and material resources are mobilised and channelled into concerted action. Thus in Christendom, aristocratic kinship and patronage networks formed the vital media through which power was projected by both the emperor and the rulers of emerging dynastic kingdoms.[44] Meanwhile, from the eleventh century onwards, the papacy crafted a system-encompassing Church governed firmly on principles of legal–bureaucratic command.[45] Conversely, within the Sinosphere, a conspicuously modern bureaucratic apparatus and centralised patronage networks formed the twin bulwarks of imperial power within the empire, while rigorously administered commercial networks linked the Middle Kingdom to its tributary states.[46] Finally, in the contemporary state system, order is crafted from the operation of bureaucratically organised nation-states and multilateral organisations, with each depending on the wealth generated by formally depoliticised and world-straddling commercial networks for the perpetuation of order.[47]

Aggregate capacities for production and destruction and mobilisational networks form the raw materials out of which ordering institutions are constructed. The level of systemic interdependence evident within international systems in turn influences the magnitude of the problems these institutions must manage. All other things being equal, the potential for inter-polity conflict increases as the volume and density of interactions rises between polities. This observation holds true particularly when considering the *violence interdependence* of international systems.[48] Violence interdependence refers here to the scope for violent confrontation between an order's constituent polities, as determined through the interplay of unchanging geography and changing technologies of communication, transportation and production.[49]

The level of violence interdependence decisively shapes the magnitude of governance challenges that international orders' custodians must face. By

---

[44] Mann, *The Sources of Social Power*, I, p. 385.

[45] *Ibid.* On the Gregorian revolution and its import for the evolutionary trajectory of Christendom more generally, see H. Berman, *Law and Revolution: The formation of the Western legal tradition* (Cambridge, MA: Harvard University Press, 1983).

[46] Fairbank, 'A preliminary framework', pp. 7–8.

[47] On the relationship between the authoritative power of the nation-state and the wealth-generating capacities of transnational corporations, see generally S. Krasner, 'Power politics, institutions, and transnational relations' in T. Risse-Kappen (ed.), *Bringing Transnational Relations Back In* (Cambridge University Press, 1995), pp. 257–79.

[48] D. H. Deudney, 'Regrounding realism: Anarchy, security, and changing material contexts', *Security Studies*, 10(1) (2000), 27.

[49] *Ibid.*

Table 1.1 *International orders at a glance*

Latin Christendom	The Sinosphere	The Global State System
Medieval Social Imaginary	Confucian Social Imaginary	Modern Social Imaginary
Normative Complex	**Normative Complex**	**Normative Complex**
• Salvation through Church as *raison d'être* of collective association • Christian ethics as articulated by the Church • Augustinian political theology and social ideology of tri-functionality	• Achievement of temporal state of harmony (*ping*) in concordance with cosmic order • Confucian ethics • Sacerdotal conception of emperor and Confucian norms of asymmetric benevolence and obedience	• Popular eudemonism, human emancipation, and augmentation of collective and individual capacities for self-determination • Cosmopolitan ethical framework institutionalised within global human rights regime • National self-determination and international regime of sovereign equality
Fundamental Institutions	**Fundamental Institutions**	**Fundamental Institutions**
• Heteronomous system of overlapping jurisdictions loosely governed by papal–imperial diarchy • Canon law and feudal law • Aristocratic feud as a legitimate means of legal redress ('peace in the feud')	• Suzerain state system governed by the Chinese emperor as Son of Heaven • Ritual enactment of shared identities (*li*) through investiture missions and tribute trade • Imperial resort to judicial sanctions and violence (*fa*) to rectify error and restore cosmic order	• Sovereign state system collectively governed by permanent universal concert of formally equal states • Global legal framework based on multilateralism and contractual international law, supplemented by issue-specific regimes claiming technocratic authority (e.g. World Trade Organization) • State monopolies on violence supplemented by collective maintenance of order

Table 1.1 (*cont.*)

Latin Christendom	**The Sinosphere**	**The Global State System**
Medieval Social Imaginary	Confucian Social Imaginary	Modern Social Imaginary
		through use of force authorised by UN Security Council
Material Context	**Material Context**	**Material Context**
• Feudal mode of production and aristocratic oligopoly over organised violence • Aristocratic kinship and patronage networks predominate alongside bureaucratic Church hierarchy • Low concentration and low accumulation of coercive means (low violence interdependence)	• Proto-capitalist mode of production organised within the framework of gunpowder empire • Dominance of imperial bureaucracy and centralised imperial patronage networks • High concentration and low accumulation of coercive means (moderate violence interdependence)	• Global market capitalist system ordered within framework of states possessing industrial (and in some cases nuclear) capacities for violence • Dominance of state and inter-governmental bureaucracies and formally depoliticised global commercial networks • High concentration and high accumulation of coercive means (high violence interdependence)

contemporary standards, social relations in Christendom were suffused with violence, given the aristocracy's oligopolistic control over violence and the universal acceptance of feud as a means of legal redress. However, Christendom's poverty, its technological backwardness and the poor quality of its transportation infrastructure all conspired to keep violence interdependence relatively low. By contrast, the Sinosphere's greater wealth and technological sophistication ensured significantly higher violence interdependence, although the ordering challenges that this presented were mitigated by the Chinese state's very high accumulation and concentration of coercive power.[50]

---

[50] Kang, 'Hierarchy in Asian international relations', pp. 61–2.

Within the contemporary state system, the unprecedentedly high concentration of Clausewitzian war-making capabilities that America presently enjoys invites loose parallels with the Sinosphere's imperial peace. However, the countervailing diffusion of destructive capacities to non-state actors as a result of globalisation has raised systemic violence interdependence beyond all prior experience, presenting challenges of an intensity not witnessed in my historical cases.

A tabular representation of Christendom, the Sinosphere and the global state system is presented in Table 1.1. The presentation is necessarily a schematic simplification of a far more complex reality, and is intended as a reference point for the reader rather than as a comprehensive portrait of any of these orders. What Table 1.1 cannot show is that international orders are rent by internal tensions and inconsistencies, and that they are capable only of mitigating and containing inter-polity conflict rather than eliminating it. International orders are susceptible to crises of legitimacy and are vulnerable to breakdown if they fail to contain sentiments of enmity between their constituent communities. It is entirely possible for there to be an international system without an international society, in which antagonisms play out without the civilising bridle of shared values and institutions to moderate hatred and mitigate human suffering. International orders are contingent constellations of norms and institutions that operate effectively only within a permissive ideational and material milieu. International orders are fragile. International orders are flawed. And international orders are finite.

Accounting for the transformation of international orders

Existing accounts for the transformation of international orders

How are international orders transformed? A range of suggestive but incomplete answers may be drawn from the literature on international systems change. Cyclical theories of order emphasise international orders' dependence on the fate of great power sponsors, with their transformation being driven by shifts in the balance of power away from conservative status quo powers and towards more dynamic revisionist powers. Linear-process theories, conversely, see international orders as the systemic residue of largely endogenous processes of state formation. Seen through this lens, the nation-state's contemporary ubiquity is a testament to a centuries-long process of Darwinian institutional selection, with the global state system representing nothing more than the most efficient available means of organising political authority on a global scale. A third set of perspectives conceptualises international systems change in terms of punctuated equilibria, affording causal primacy either to far-reaching transformations in the mode of production or destruction, or to the irruption of subversive new forms of collective identity in explaining orders' transformation. Each of these accounts provides valuable insights, but none by itself is adequate as an explanation for international orders' transformation.

International orders and the rise and fall of Great Powers

The notion that international orders are hostages to the fortunes of their Great Power sponsors superficially has much to commend it. Intuitively, it makes sense that orders would reflect the interests of the powerful, and that they would tend towards disintegration as their sponsors' relative power ebbed.[1] The idea that international orders rise and fall in tandem with successive hegemons is also attractive in its simplicity and potential generalisability across a broad range of cases. Paul Schroeder's account of the post-Vienna Congress of

---

[1] For a sophisticated rendition of this argument, see T. L. Knutsen, *The Rise and Fall of World Orders* (Manchester University Press, 1999).

Europe, a collective security system that was guaranteed by the dual hegemony of the United Kingdom and Imperial Russia as Europe's respective sea and land-power giants and that crumbled as these powers' interests diverged, accords well with this approach.[2] 'Rise and fall' theories also seem to find confirmation in the fate of the League of Nations, which failed through a combination of Allied neglect and the active assaults of ascending totalitarian empires.[3] The credibility of 'rise and fall' theories is further fortified by their status as realists' favoured default explanation for the collapse of international orders.[4] The very familiarity of such theories demands that they be critically engaged before alternative accounts are considered.

Cyclical power-transition explanations for international orders' transformation can be faulted first on conceptual grounds. Power-transition theories are of limited value when trying to comprehend the transformation of international orders as they are conceived in this study. For an international order such as Christendom or the Sinosphere did not merely reflect the interests of dominant actors such as the Church or the reigning imperial dynasty. Rather, these orders constituted the taken-for-granted normative and institutional matrix within which these actors crystallised. As such, the causal pathway assumed by cyclical theories must be reversed – far from *reflecting* the interests of dominant actors, international orders worked to *constitute* these actors and their interests instead.

Secondly, and relatedly, to claim that revisionist states intentionally over-throw international orders in Herculean acts of statesmanship designed to remake the world in their own image is to misunderstand international orders' character as systemic social constructs. International orders constitute the shared mental and institutional framework within which social interaction takes place between polities, with their collapse punctuating the terminal crisis of an entire world outlook. They collapse only after a protracted period of decay, with their continued viability during this time being threatened by indifference and neglect rather than hostility or overt subversion. Moreover, when international orders finally do expire, their ideological coherence is often shattered not by Goliath but by David, not by revisionist Great Powers but by

---

[2] P. Schroeder, 'Did the Vienna settlement rest on a balance of power?', *The American Historical Review*, 97(3) (1992), 683–706. It must be acknowledged, however, that Schroeder's broader account of the Vienna settlement accords great significance to the development of norms and processes of peaceful conflict mediation and resolution between the five Great Powers, and that his larger account of the era thus cannot be easily reduced to a realist position.

[3] See for example P. M. Kennedy, *The Rise and Fall of the Great Powers: Economic change and military conflict from 1500 to 2000* (London: Fontana Press, 1987), Ch. 6.

[4] See generally Carr, *The Twenty Years' Crisis*; Gilpin, *War and Change in World Politics*; Kennedy, *Rise and Fall of the Great Powers*; and J. Kugler and A. F. K. Organski, 'The power transition: A retrospective and prospective evaluation' in M. I. Midlarski (ed.), *Handbook of War Studies* (Ann Arbor: The University of Michigan Press, 1996), pp. 171–94.

inchoate insurgent groups – such as the Protestant confessional networks of the Reformation – operating at the interstices of the existing order.

Positional power conflicts played out *within* decaying orders are undeniably important in both accelerating that decay and exacerbating the chaos that follows an order's collapse. The relative power of different actors is also of critical importance in shaping reconstituted orders that emerge from the ruins of their predecessors – the order that succeeded Christendom, for example, would have looked very different had the Habsburgs defeated France and Sweden in the Thirty Years War. But the fact remains that international orders only collapse following decades of decay, a process that is in turn driven by developments that are generally not the product of deliberate human action. Moreover, when international orders collapse, they do not simply sweep away the accumulated privileges of declining powers. Rather, they dissolve the most basic institutions of international societies, as well as representing the comprehensive failure of the world-views that sustained them. Christendom's dissolution and the Sinosphere's disintegration respectively represented not just the humbling of the Church and the Qing dynasty, but the discrediting of entire cosmologies as well. Ruptures of this magnitude simply cannot be explained by the power-transition approaches favoured by realist international relations scholars.

State formation, linear process theories and the collapse of international orders

Power-transition theories perceive international orders as top-down constructs, imposed by Great Powers in their fleeting moments of dominance to perpetuate their interests at a systemic level. Conversely, an alternative 'bottom-up' perspective might imagine international orders as practical associations, collectively negotiated by rulers in parallel with domestic state-building projects to secure the realisation of essential social goods at systemic as well as unit levels. In place of recurrent cycles of Great Power turnover and the accompanying dramas of order collapse and reconstitution, a bottom-up perspective rather conceives of historical change in terms of a linear development from less to more efficient forms of domestic and international political organisation. Seen through this optic, less efficient forms of international order do not collapse so much as fade away, with rulers collectively and incrementally sloughing off inefficient practices of international governance in the same manner that less efficient polity forms were eventually sidelined in favour of the sovereign state.[5]

---

[5] On the elimination of city-states and city leagues in favour of the more efficient polity form of the sovereign state, see generally H. Spruyt, *The Sovereign State and its Competitors* (Princeton University Press, 1994). For a sophisticated approach to the question of international systems change that emphasises the predominance of accretive rather than revolutionary transformations over time, as well as tracing the secular tendency towards more

There are undoubted insights to be found in approaches of this kind. Both Christendom and the Sinosphere showed advanced signs of decay in the decades preceding their demise, with both systems increasingly failing to maintain order within environments convulsed by large-scale economic and geopolitical change. In acknowledging that international orders do not merely embody the interests of the powerful, but rather work to safeguard the common interests of their members, it becomes possible to mount plausible arguments linking environmental changes (e.g. technologically driven increases in violence interdependence) to a decline in the perceived effectiveness of international orders in securing their members' common interests. The resulting legitimacy deficit may then be cited as the catalyst for institutional innovations that subsequently evolved to restore a modicum of order within international societies.

The world's developmental trajectory since 1500 offers continuities that seem to support efficiency-driven linear-process models. When considered over the broad arc of history, both Christendom and the Sinosphere present as decidedly inefficient international orders, swept away with the rise and spread of the modern sovereign state. Seen through this prism, processes of contracting and coercion in late medieval Europe forged a new form of polity in the sovereign state, which eventually proved more efficient in mobilising capital and violence and more effective in commanding popular legitimacy than any of its contemporary rivals.[6] Through processes of Darwinian selection, the sovereign state saw off its competitors, forcing, through its ascendancy, a reorganisation of political authority within Europe from a heteronomous to a sovereign state system.[7] From Westphalia onwards, the principles governing relations between rulers were then refined and perfected, enabling sovereigns to consolidate their power domestically while containing international conflict within manageable bounds. The efficiency with which the European state system was then able to reconcile international pluralism with a continuing expansion of Europe's productive and destructive capabilities laid the foundation for European international society's triumphant global expansion. In so doing, it necessarily doomed irredeemably pre-modern non-European orders like the Sinosphere to destruction.[8]

---

complex modes of international governance, see generally K. J. Holsti, *Taming the Sovereigns: Institutional change in international politics* (Cambridge University Press, 2004).

[6] On this process, see generally C. Tilly, *Coercion, Capital, and European States,* AD *990–1992* (Cambridge, MA: Blackwell, 1992).

[7] *Ibid.*

[8] The notion that Europe's pluralistic and intensely competitive geopolitical environment fashioned a range of institutional and military innovations that laid the basis for Europe's subsequent geopolitical expansion is well rehearsed in the literature on so-called Western exceptionalism; see generally Kennedy, *Rise and Fall of the Great* Powers, Ch. 1, pp. 20–38; W. H. McNeill, *The Rise of the West: A history of the human community* (The University of Chicago Press, 1963); D. C. North and R. P. Thomas, *The Rise of the Western World: A new economic history* (Cambridge University Press, 1973); and Parker, *The Military Revolution*. I have however yet to read a treatment of the 'rise of the West' that gives sustained analysis

While superficially plausible, linear-process accounts are unsustainable upon closer analysis. At the most fundamental level, one can contest the artificially thin conception of international order that sustains this line of argument. The realisation of common interests such as the security of life and property is of undeniable importance in driving the construction of international orders and the perception that a given order is failing to achieve these functions is certainly conducive to the onset of a legitimation crisis. But across the cases I consider, the more prosaic functions of international orders were joined with more historically and culturally contingent goals such as the pursuit of salvation through the Church, the maintenance of a Confucian cosmic and social order, or the promotion of popular eudemonism and human emancipation. Assessments of institutional efficiency, far from operating through the application of timeless and universal standards of rationality, were rather suffused with the substantive value orientations of agents operating within these historically and culturally specific environments. To take but one example, Christendom's dependence on feud as an acceptable method of aristocratic legal redress seems by current standards to be not only morally perverse, but also highly inefficient as a means of enhancing the security of agents' lives and property. Within the cultural context of Christendom, however, a system-wide ideology of tri-functionality that celebrated the armed vocation of the nobility provided ample justification for the feud as a normal and morally acceptable mechanism for resolving disputes.[9] Endemic non-state violence did not by itself inspire late medieval rulers to consciously aspire for a more efficient international order. Rather, it was only after Christendom's cultural unity had been decisively shattered, and then only in the wake of Europe's devastating Wars of Religion, that Europe's rulers were forced by necessity to reconstitute an international order on the basis of sovereign principles.

The loss of legitimacy is indeed critical to the collapse of international orders, and the hardships endured *after* an order has disintegrated provide a crucial catalyst for the construction of a new order. But hard-headed assessments that a given order is inefficient at realising common interests, and that it must be reformed if those interests are to be achieved, are conspicuously absent in the cases I consider. The empirical record suggests not an organic process of linear evolution towards more efficient forms of order, but rather the periodic collapse of old orders, followed by a bloody and prolonged interregnum out of which a qualitatively different order eventually emerges. For this reason, claims that international orders are a systemic residue of processes of state formation must be discounted.

---

to the role of sovereignty as an ordering institution in providing the political stability in Europe necessary to facilitate the colonial powers' subsequent global expansion.

[9] See again generally Geary, 'Living with conflicts in stateless France'.

Punctuated equilibria models of international systems change I: The collapse of international orders as the product of changes in modes of production or destruction

In contrast to either cyclical power-transition theories or linear-process theories, punctuated equilibria models more accurately capture the historical dynamics of order transformation. Given international orders' holistic character and the protracted nature of the crises leading to their transformation, attempts to hitch the fate of these orders to tectonic transformations in underlying modes of production or destruction have definite appeal.

In recent years, Marxist international relations scholars have convincingly demonstrated international orders' embeddedness within broader structures of production, cognition and destruction.[10] The value of Marxist approaches is illustrated clearly in Benno Teschke's analysis of the constitutive role played by transformations in social property relations in reconfiguring both units of political authority and the geopolitical orders within which they are embedded.[11] That the medieval, Absolutist and modern international systems in Europe displayed distinctive geopolitical logics is hard to contest. Teschke convincingly shows that these different geopolitical logics were at least partially explicable through reference to changing logics of accumulation and concomitant shifts in dominant forms of social property relations.[12]

What Marxist approaches indicate is that international orders' transformation are at least partially derivative of systemic shifts in their material foundations. This insight is reinforced through a consideration of theories that focus on transformations in the mode of destruction as an engine of change. Both the Revolution in Military Affairs and the contemporary prominence of non-traditional security threats have spawned a growing literature on the changing nature of warfare as a socio-cultural institution.[13] Thus, for example, Andrew Latham discerns distinctive feudal, modern and emerging post-modern forms of warfare, with organised violence being pursued for radically different

---

[10] See for example J. Rosenberg, *The Empire of Civil Society: A critique of the realist theory of international relations* (London: Verso, 1994); and B. Teschke, *The Myth of 1648: Class, geopolitics, and the making of modern international relations* (London: Verso, 2003).

[11] Teschke, *Myth of 1648*.

[12] *Ibid.* See also B. Teschke, 'Geopolitical relations in the European Middle Ages: History and theory', *International Organization*, 52(2) (1998), 325–58.

[13] The literature on this topic is voluminous. See for example J. Arquilla and D. Ronfeldt (eds.), *Networks and Netwars: The future of crime, terror, and militancy* (Santa Monica: RAND, 2001); R. Bunker, 'Epochal change: War over social and political organization', *Parameters*, 27(2) (1997), 15–25; L. Freedman, *The Transformation of Strategic Affairs*, Adelphi Paper 379 (New York: International Institute for Strategic Studies, 2006); T. X. Hammes, 'War evolves into the fourth generation', *Contemporary Security Policy*, 26(2) (2005), 189–221; and Hirst, *War and Power in the 21st Century*.

purposes and being undertaken by historically distinctive collectivities in each of these epochs.[14] Permutations of this theme can be found also in the works of Kaldor, Cerny and van Creveld.[15] While none of these scholars can be accused of subscribing to mono-causal narratives, they nevertheless share a common focus in identifying the transformative significance of changes in the mode of destruction for the legitimation of political authority and the organisational configuration of domestic and international orders.

Macro-structural accounts have much to offer in aiding our understanding of international orders' transformation, but they are nevertheless by themselves inadequate. The most obvious weakness of these accounts lies in their relative neglect of ideational factors in accounting for systemic change. While war-centric narratives are more willing to trace correlations between dominant modes of destruction, political organisation and collective identification, the independent causal significance of transformations in collective identity in effecting transformations of order is generally neglected. This observation obtains even more strongly for Marxist accounts. While Gramscian analyses of the contemporary international system accord at least some independent significance to ideology, culture and other 'superstructural' characteristics of the present world order, historically oriented accounts of the evolution of international systems more typically neglect the independent significance of ideational factors as drivers of change.[16] Thus, for example, in Teschke's analysis of the emergence of Absolutist and modern geopolitical orders, minimal mention is made of either the Reformation or the French Revolution as independent catalysts for systemic change, despite the pivotal significance of both in transforming European international society.

The materialist bias of macro-structural accounts is problematic, given that in my historical cases a critical catalyst for the destruction of international orders was the emergence of subversive ideologies that fatally undermined the old order's normative complex. Certainly, shifts in the material foundations of both Christendom and the Sinosphere weakened the effectiveness and legitimacy of these orders. But it was the shattering of ideological unity and the ensuing breakdown of existing ordering mechanisms that triggered the shift from a chronic to an acute legitimation crisis in both cases. Neither the Reformation nor the Taiping rebellion can be easily reduced to epiphenomenal expressions of changes in underlying modes of production or destruction.

---

[14] A. Latham, 'A Braudelian perspective on the revolution in military affairs', *European Journal of International Relations*, 8(2) (2002), 231–66.

[15] P. G. Cerny, 'The new security dilemma: Divisibility, defection, and disorder in the global era', *Review of International Studies*, 26(4) (2000), 623–46; M. Kaldor, *New and Old Wars: Organized violence in a global era* (Stanford University Press, 2001); and M. van Creveld, *The Transformation of War* (New York: Free Press, 1991).

[16] On Gramscian approaches to the problem of world order, see for example R. Cox, 'Social forces, states, and world orders: Beyond international relations theory', *Millennium: Journal of International Studies*, 10(2) (1981), 126–55.

Unfortunately, this observation merely illuminates an additional weakness of macro-structural accounts, namely their tendency towards structural determinism and their relative neglect of agency. Macro-social accounts leave limited room for considering the active role played by agents in shaping international orders' normative composition. In so doing, they neglect the processes through which coercive and authoritative power are tentatively reconciled to produce international orders, thus eliding also the dynamics through which these tentative reconciliations are then subsequently torn apart. Macro-structural accounts risk assuming a highly deterministic character, with successive international orders mechanistically reflecting the functional requirements of the larger social totalities of which they are a part. Seen through such an optic, the distinctive and pressing human dilemmas that are provisionally resolved through the construction of international orders – such as the reconciliation of force with legitimacy or the balancing of rulers' autonomy with requirements of systemic stability – are in danger of being overlooked.

Finally, the Eurocentrism typical of macro-structural accounts further weakens them, with the periodisations from which their categories are constructed most often drawing on the particular experience of Western Europe. In basing supposedly universal claims on the European experience, macro-social accounts can divine universal correspondences where contingent constellations in fact exist. This danger is illustrated for example in the emphasis placed by 'mode of destruction' accounts on the importance of Europe's military revolution as the catalyst for the emergence of both the modern state and the modern state system. The military revolution's importance in triggering the rise of a sovereign state system in Europe is undeniable. But the fact that a roughly synchronous military revolution merely strengthened the suzerain order of the Sinosphere suggests that the causal linkages drawn between changing modes of destruction and changing international orders are contingent rather than universal.[17] Consequently, attempts to reduce the transformation of orders to mere symptoms of deeper transformations in modes of production or destruction must be regarded with scepticism.

Punctuated equilibria models of international systems change II:
The collapse of international orders as the product of
transformations in collective identity

The notion that transformations in collective identity are pivotal in catalysing international systems change has been persuasively advanced in a range of studies. The empirical emphases and causal narratives advanced by authors

[17] On this point, see for example N. di Cosimo, 'Did guns matter? Firearms and the Qing formation' in L. A. Struve (ed.), *The Qing Formation in World Historical Time* (Cambridge, MA: Harvard University Press, 2004), pp. 121–66.

such as Daniel Philpott, Rodney Bruce Hall and Mlada Bukovansky naturally vary. Philpott emphasises the role played by heretical identities and ideas as mechanisms of contradiction producing 'crises of pluralism' that then catalyse the development of new international constitutions.[18] Conversely, Hall posits a causal pathway whereby transformations in co-constituted individual and collective identities produce a social dissonance between agents' interpretive frameworks and existing social orders.[19] This dissonance ultimately resolves itself in the formulation of new legitimating principles of global and domestic social order, yielding transformations in institutional forms of collective action and with them transformations in international order.[20] This perspective contrasts again with Bukovansky, who emphasises the pivotal significance of contradictions in hegemonic international political cultures in establishing the normative and strategic terrain within which legitimacy contests between the *ancien regime* and proponents of counter-hegemonic legitimacy principles are played out.[21]

These differences in argument notwithstanding, the contributions of these scholars have definitively established the importance of ideational changes in explaining international orders' transformation. This ideational emphasis accords well with the conception of international orders advanced below, and the importance I ascribe to crises of social imaginaries and ideological shocks in precipitating international orders' collapse relies heavily on insights drawn from the constructivist tradition. Where my position differs from existing constructivist accounts lies in the more systematic links between material and ideational transformations that I stress in explaining international orders' transformation. While constructivists have been careful not to argue for the complete sufficiency of ideational transformations in explaining systems change, their efforts to demonstrate the necessity of ideational changes in accounting for this process have often led to a relative neglect of material forces as catalysts of systems change. In this respect, constructivists are guilty of an idealist bias comparable to the materialism of the macro-structural accounts considered above.

That international orders founder with the irruption of subversive collective identities and the ensuing breakdown of their ideological unity is central to my argument. But ideological shocks occur only following protracted processes of institutional decay, in which changes in the material environment render established governing frameworks increasingly less effective in maintaining order. Changes in collective identities are critical to international orders' transformation, but ideational changes are of only secondary importance in bringing international orders to the edge of the precipice in the first instance. Material

---

[18] Philpott, *Revolutions in Sovereignty*, p. 4.
[19] Hall, *National Collective Identity*, p. 47.
[20] *Ibid.*   [21] Bukovansky, *Legitimacy and Power Politics*, pp. 10–11.

changes – and most especially increases in violence interdependence – are instrumental in corroding the effectiveness of the ordering institutions of international societies long before their collapse. For it is only once these ordering institutions have been degraded that heretical movements can strip away the residual normative consensus underpinning international orders to such devastating effect.

Constructivists are correct to emphasise the importance of transformations in collective identity in explaining international orders' breakdown. For without a basic consensus on the sources and content of morality and the character of legitimate political domination, agents lack a shared life-world, and effective communicative action – and thus the deployment of authoritative power internationally in the service of order – becomes impossible. But authoritative power by itself is insufficient to maintain order. Coercive power, in the form of authorised practices of organised violence, is equally necessary if order is to endure. And changes in the material context within which coercive power is deployed can exert profoundly destabilising consequences, rendering old methods of order enforcement ineffectual while empowering actors with new and unprecedented levels of destructive power. Heresies in isolation can be suppressed, while ordering institutions can adapt to expansions in coercive capacities if given sufficient time to do so. However, it is when heresy and military innovation explosively intersect that international orders fail.

Explaining the transformation of international orders

The transformation of international orders: Fundamental assumptions

I have argued that international orders, like all other political orders, arise out of communities' universal aspirations to achieve some measure of ontological and physical security. These orders are fashioned within particular cultural and material milieus, with their constitutional structures being profoundly conditioned by prevailing social imaginaries and geopolitical contexts. Order is produced through the combined influence of communicative and coercive forms of social power, and is manifest in shared authoritative and coercive institutions, including ritual and law on the one hand, and feud and war on the other. These propositions form the conceptual bedrock of this study, and are presented in Table 2.1.

International orders rely on fundamental authoritative and coercive institutions to provide their members with a modicum of physical and ontological security, and these institutions are in turn predicated on the existence of a shared social imaginary and a supportive geopolitical context. Consequently, I argue that international orders are transformed when they experience systemic legitimacy crises occasioned by a combination of institutional decay, disruptive military innovations, and ideological shocks that terminally destabilise existing social

Table 2.1 *How international order is constituted*

Imperatives (what we want)	Ontological security	Physical security
Contexts (the environment in which we seek to advance these imperatives)	Ideal – social imaginaries	Material – geopolitical environment
Modes of social power (how we seek to advance these imperatives)	Communicative action	Organised violence
Institutional structures (the structures we build to satisfy these imperatives)	Authoritative institutions (e.g. ritual and law)	Coercive institutions (e.g. feud and war)

imaginaries and thus shatter the normative consensus upon which international orders depend. As I will shortly demonstrate, the role and significance of ideational and material factors in driving these crises vary in the different stages of an order's decay, crisis, collapse and eventual reconstruction. Before I do so, however, I must first briefly outline my understanding of legitimacy and specify the meaning and significance of 'legitimacy crises' within this inquiry.

Regardless of its necessity, political order remains difficult to secure and is always provisional in nature. This is so because the character of political order as a form of organised domination inevitably raises the problem of justification. Hans Morgenthau observes of man that '[He] is born a slave, but everywhere he wants to be the master ... Out of this discord between man's desire and his actual condition arises the moral issue of power, that is, the problem of justifying and limiting the power which man has over man.'[22] While Morgenthau and other classical realists acknowledged domination as an inevitable aspect of political life, they also recognised that this domination is continuously subject to moral evaluation, and that it must at least partially meet its members' ethical demands if it is to survive for any length of time.[23] It is

---

[22] H. Morgenthau, *Scientific Man vs. Power Politics* (The University of Chicago Press, 1946), pp. 168–9.

[23] Certainly, it is possible for a political order to endure in the absence of legitimacy if its custodians choose instead to rely on coercion and repression as their primary mode of governance. However, political orders of this nature are likely to be rigid and brittle rather than truly strong, and are susceptible to rapid collapse in the face of exogenous shocks such as defeat in war or financial collapse. The pervasive propaganda characteristic of modern totalitarian governments is evidence enough of the importance that even the most brutal and terroristic rulers place on cultivating the appearance of popular legitimacy.

precisely because agents are continuously evaluating the legitimacy of political orders that they are so fragile, for evaluations of legitimacy are necessarily subjective and can be revised at any time.

Judgements about political orders' legitimacy turn on questions of purpose, process and performance.[24] Questions of purpose centre on the extent to which an order's declared purposes accord with agents' most deeply held moral convictions. Questions of process relate to the degree to which agents believe that an order's purposes are properly reflected in the design and operation of its fundamental institutions. Finally, questions of performance concern agents' judgements about the effectiveness of these institutions in fulfilling the purposes to which they have been dedicated. Inevitably, in any order, different agents' judgements about questions of purpose, process and performance – and thus their assessments of an order's legitimacy – will vary considerably. Consequently, the durability of a given order is partially determined by its capacity to elicit positive evaluations of its legitimacy that will translate into continued support for its perpetuation. Equally, its durability will also be determined by its capacity to manage sentiments of estrangement arising from negative assessments of its legitimacy.

Political orders depend for their survival both on the cultivation of legitimacy and on the maintenance of institutional capacities to suppress subversion, accommodate dissent and mobilise loyalty and support. Given the centrality that I accord legitimacy in the maintenance of order, it follows that a key point of vulnerability for these orders lies in their susceptibility to legitimacy crises. I use the term legitimacy crises here to denote episodes in which political orders become debilitated as their members deem the existing order to be illegitimate and withdraw their support for its perpetuation. Legitimacy crises may present in either chronic or acute forms.[25] Chronic legitimacy crises are characterised by the insidious leakage of support away from an existing order, and are punctuated by agents' increasing unwillingness to comply with the rules, norms, laws and commands of established authorities. The increasing unwillingness of agents to accord legitimacy to established authorities progressively corrodes rulers' capacities to govern. This corrosion of institutional capacity in turn feeds back into negative assessments of the order's performance, further diminishing its perceived legitimacy and institutional capacity.[26]

---

[24] This typology is my own, but has been inspired by and builds upon Fritz Scharpf's discussion of the distinction between input-oriented and output-oriented (or in my terms, purposive and process-oriented versus performance-oriented) accounts of legitimacy. See F. Scharpf, 'Economic integration, democracy, and the welfare state', *Journal of European Public Policy*, 4(1) (1997), 19.

[25] C. Reus-Smit, 'International crises of legitimacy', *International Politics*, 44(2/3) (2007), 168.

[26] On the reciprocal relationship between polities' institutional capacities and their level of popular legitimacy, and the possibility of negative feedback between the two contributing to a downward spiral of institutional effectiveness and performance, see F. Fukuyama,

While chronic legitimacy crises are protracted and insidious, acute legitimacy crises entail a more precipitate decline in an order's institutional capacities, as well as involving a more direct challenge to its legitimacy. Whereas in chronic legitimacy crises, the political order's deterioration is marked by a steady swelling of the ranks of the disaffected and an incremental erosion of support for existing institutional arrangements, in acute crises one observes instead a polarised confrontation between radically alienated challengers and mobilised supporters of the status quo. Moreover, while a nominal commitment to a shared world-view may persist among the members of an order mired in chronic crisis, acute crises are characterised by a violent confrontation between proponents of mutually antagonistic world-views. Analytically, it remains useful to distinguish between chronic and acute legitimacy crises, for chronic crises need not presage the collapse of a political order – prolonged stagnation or renovation and renewal both present as alternative possibilities to collapse.[27] In the cases considered below, however, chronic and acute legitimacy crises constituted successive phases of a single overarching crisis encompassing the decay of an order and its subsequent dissolution.

Decay, crisis, collapse and reconstruction: The constituent phases of international orders' transformation

International orders are progressively transformed through the unfolding of systemic crises that may be divided up into successive phases of decay, crisis, collapse and reconstruction. An international order's transformation begins with a protracted period of deterioration marked by institutional decay, increasing ideological dissent and cultural innovation, and growing violence interdependence occasioned by a combination of commercial expansion and technological change. The specific causes and dynamics of institutional decay vary across my cases, but manifest themselves in each instance in a growing contrast between the claims legitimising an order and its growing inability to fulfil those claims. As the prevailing order proves less capable of providing physical and ontological security, the legitimacy accorded to its fundamental institutions wanes, further weakening their effectiveness and thus locking the system into a vicious spiral of diminishing institutional effectiveness and legitimacy.

The weakening of established institutions generally accelerates processes of cultural innovation, as agents seek to apprehend the ultimate causes of institutional decline and begin grasping – with lesser and greater degrees of self-consciousness – for alternatives to the status quo. In its early stages, this search for alternatives typically occurs within the broad parameters of the existing order, with agents drawing upon existing cultural repertoires and reviving neglected or half-forgotten

---

State-Building: Governance and world order in the 21st century (Ithaca: Cornell University Press, 2004), p. 68.

[27] On the possibilities of taking remedial action to resolve international crises of legitimacy, see Reus-Smit, 'International crises of legitimacy', pp. 169–73.

traditions in order to make sense of the accumulating disorder around them. Thus, in fifteenth-century Europe, for example, we witness intensified efforts to draw upon Roman law and ancient pagan political thought to legitimise Western Europe's emerging Renaissance monarchies.[28] Simultaneously, the increasingly worldly character of the Church precipitates a growth in unorthodox expressions of popular piety.[29] The significance of these cultural mutations lies less in the direct challenge they pose to the existing order, and more in the fact that they signal the increasingly mutable character of the social imaginary underlying that order. For a time, the old order may prove capable of suppressing or appropriating the new innovations, but they are generally too diffuse and too pervasive to be entirely contained. Moreover, the incremental shifts in social imaginaries that they reflect provide a crucial condition of possibility for the subsequent outbreak of more overtly destabilising ideological shocks to the old order.

In addition to institutional decay and creeping mutations in social imaginaries, international orders are also undermined by material changes, most particularly increases in violence interdependence. Increases in violence interdependence accumulate in the decades prior to an order's collapse and steadily undercut its institutional capacity to manage armed conflict. The fundamental institutions of international societies emerge out of historically finite material contexts, and the efficacy of these institutions is dependent upon a perpetuation of these initial conditions. Paradoxically, however, the very increases in wealth accumulation and technological development that the maintenance of order enables eventually yield material innovations that undercut its continued stability. Specifically, the development and diffusion of new means of destruction heighten agents' security anxieties, while the observed ineffectiveness of existing fundamental institutions corrodes their legitimacy and thereby diminishes their ability to maintain order. Increases in violence interdependence accelerate processes of geopolitical consolidation, paradoxically *integrating* international *systems* within tighter webs of coercive interaction while simultaneously exposing the inadequacy of existing institutions and thus paving the way for the eventual *disintegration* of international *societies*.

Institutional decay, incremental shifts in social imaginaries, and increases in violence interdependence together propel international orders into the chronic phase of a legitimacy crisis. Nevertheless, it is only with the coming of a systemic ideological shock that an order shifts from a chronic to an acute crisis phase. Ideological shocks subvert international orders by breaching the

---

[28] On the fifteenth-century growth of a discourse on the political as a sphere of human conduct potentially separable from considerations of religion, see S. S. Wolin, *Politics and Vision: Continuity and innovation in Western political thought* (Princeton University Press, 2004), p. 177.

[29] D. MacCulloch, *Reformation: Europe's house divided, 1490–1700* (London: Penguin Books, 2004), pp. 35–8.

integrity of the normative complexes that help constitute these orders. Recall that international orders are partly composed of normative complexes consisting of identity-constitutive, ethical-prescriptive and power-legitimating norms. These norms integrate actors around shared identities and purposes, regulate behaviour through the articulation of standards of rightful conduct, and justify and stabilise the relations of organised domination upon which international order rests. Ideological shocks destabilise orders by destroying the consensus embodied in these normative complexes. In place of shared identities and common purposes, ideological shocks polarise international societies between radically alienated opponents of the old order and mobilised supporters of the status quo. Where ethical-prescriptive norms previously restrained violence between adversaries within manageable bounds, ideological polarisation robs these norms of their constraining power. Opponents that might previously have been fought so that they could be brought to terms become ontological enemies falling outside the circle of moral obligation, who must be annihilated if order is to be restored. Finally, ideological shocks subvert power-legitimating norms, with defenders of the old order confronting actors who repudiate the principled bases of organised domination in international societies.

In challenging the normative bases of international order, ideological shocks rob actors of the shared life-world needed to make communicative action possible and authoritative institutions practically effective. At base, the effectiveness of authoritative institutions depends upon the maintenance of consensus on the constitutional values that inform these institutions. This is because, without this consensus, the capacity of authoritative institutions to attract agents' voluntary compliance with existing rules, norms, commands and laws is fatally diminished. In destabilising the normative bases of international orders, ideological shocks paralyse authoritative institutions, thus fatally compromising agents' ability to contain conflict within manageable bounds.

Systemic legitimacy crises eventually culminate both in the collapse of an international order's fundamental institutions, and in the dissolution of the social imaginaries that sustained it. In practice, it is nevertheless usually difficult to pinpoint the precise moment at which an international order dies. This is partially because conservative forces may momentarily rally to the old order's defence, perhaps even fashioning expedients that temporarily preserve it in a modified form. Thus, following the First Opium War and the ensuing Taiping cataclysm, the Qing dynasty succeeded for a time in managing the threats of foreign predation and millenarian rebellion by establishing a modus vivendi between the Manchu court, the Confucian Han scholar gentry, and the 'barbarian intruders'.[30] Old orthodoxies also die hard, and both the symbolic

---

[30] The achievements and limits of the Qing dynasty's post-Taiping recovery are discussed in detail in M. C. Wright, *The Last Stand of Chinese Conservatism: The T'ung-Chih restoration, 1862–1874* (Stanford University Press, 1957).

vocabularies and codified beliefs that helped constitute the old order are frequently reasserted with even greater vigour as they come under challenge. In an insight that is as applicable to *fin de siècle* China as it is to Reformation Europe, Michael Walzer has observed that 'the official political theory during periods when symbolic forms are being questioned and replaced is likely to consist entirely of dogmatic reiterations and amazing elaborations of the old images and analogues'.[31] In both Christendom and the Sinosphere, the respective shocks of the Reformation and the Western encroachment catalysed an insistent reassertion of orthodoxy at the very moment that it was being undone. These reassertions of orthodoxy can appear in retrospect to be self-serving, futile and even somewhat tragic in their Sisyphean defence of a doomed order. But to dismiss them as merely the death throes of reaction is to understate the nature and magnitude of the crises of meaning they express, and to misapprehend also the profound sentiments of existential disorientation and despair that accompany international orders' collapse.

With the final collapse of an international order, the cosmic certainties that had previously underpinned it fall away, giving way to a heightened appreciation of the radically contingent character of the social world. At the same time, the collapse of old imaginaries and ordering institutions deprives agents of the ability either to arrive at convergent understandings regarding the legitimate purpose and nature of political association, or to contain the inevitable conflicts arising from the resulting clashes between divergent visions of the good. The emergence of these principled disagreements – which typically interweave with and exacerbate more straightforward contests for power and prestige – then plunges international systems into a protracted state of chaotic disorder until such time as a new international order can emerge.

Barry Buzan's concept of 'immature anarchy', which describes a condition in which polities violently pursue their interests in the absence of any normative constraints and without heed to even their adversaries' most basic interest of survival, powerfully captures the broad texture of international politics following the collapse of international orders.[32] But it is to Carl Schmitt that we must turn if we are to fully grasp the intensity of the antagonisms that beset international systems in the interval between the death of the old order and the birth of the new. In his *Theory of the Partisan*, Schmitt identified three different forms of enmity in political life.[33] The first of these, which he dubbed conventional

---

[31] M. Walzer, 'On the role of symbolism in political thought', *Political Science Quarterly*, 82 (2) (1967), 198.

[32] On the notion of immature anarchy as a state of unregulated mortal conflict between different polities, and its distinction from a state of mature anarchy, in which the benefits of political fragmentation are enjoyed without the accompanying instability, see B. Buzan, *People, States and Fear* (London: Harvester Wheatsheaf, 1983), pp. 96–101.

[33] C. Schmitt, *The Theory of the Partisan: A commentary/remark on the concept of the political* (Detroit: Michigan State University Press, 2004).

enmity, typified the rule-bound character of European conflicts following the Congress of Vienna, in which combatants were clearly distinguished from non-combatants, wars were conducted within a common framework of norms of *jus ad bellum* and *jus in bello* and states regarded their opponents as conventional enemies to be brought to terms rather than existential enemies to be annihilated.[34] Schmitt contrasted this conventional enmity with the real enmity characteristic of unconventional conflicts between partisan irregulars and foreign occupiers, in which both sides fought one another without mercy and without reference to shared ethical and legal constraints.[35] This form of enmity – unrestricted in its intensity but territorially limited in its scope and objectives – contrasted again with the absolute enmity of the nomadic revolutionary, who wages unrestricted warfare as part of a global struggle to overthrow the existing political order.[36]

While the ethos of conventional enmity generally characterises armed conflict within functioning international orders, the spirit of both real and absolute enmity typically suffuses conflicts following an international order's collapse. Across the cases I consider, the breakdown of old orders was either accompanied or swiftly succeeded by attempts to reconstitute a new universal order under the banner of empire. The resulting clashes between expanding empires and local nodes of resistance solidified particularistic identities at the expense of imperial visions in each instance, thereby facilitating the eventual transition to a sovereign international order. Significantly, these struggles between empire and its enemies were overlaid by systemic conflicts over the very nature and purposes of collective association, in which the spirit of absolute enmity was conspicuously present. What distinguishes war in the interregnum between two international orders is thus the tendency for adversaries to regard their opponents as existential enemies worthy only of annihilation. The hardening of mutually antagonistic collective identities that accompanies the outbreak of sentiments of absolute enmity epitomises the breakdown of order that marks the aftermath of international orders' collapse. Paradoxically, however, the emergence of these new forms of social identity under conditions of absolute enmity also stimulates the rise of new social imaginaries, thereby laying the cognitive and affective foundations for the new international order to come.

The reconstitution of a new international order from the ashes of the old presupposes the emergence of a social imaginary capable of sustaining the new norms and institutions needed to maintain order within a radically changed ideal and material environment. This process of re-imagining order is both painful and protracted, and is made even more so by its coalescence within a context of endemic warfare fuelled by disruptive military innovations and the breakout of sentiments of absolute enmity both between and within existing political communities. As will be explained in greater detail below, war plays an

---

[34] *Ibid.*, p. 6.   [35] *Ibid.*, p. 14.   [36] *Ibid.*, p. 39.

ambivalent role in my narrative, serving both as a symptom of the old order's demise and as a herald of the new order's emergence. The trauma of war sharpens and solidifies new collective estrangements and solidarities, reconstituting the affective bases of political communities and thus profoundly shaping the contours of the succeeding international order. At the same time, the very chaos that war engenders and expresses catalyses a renewed frenzy of cultural innovation and institutional adaptation, as agents desperately seek respite from the heightened physical and ontological insecurity they experience following the old order's collapse.

International orders thus re-emerge out of a complex set of recursive processes linking transformations in social imaginaries with the emergence of new forms of violence and collective identity. As agents' mental horizons metamorphose, and as the experience of war dissolves old identities while consolidating new ones, alternative ways of re-conceiving political community become first imaginable and then later self-evident. Thus, within post-Reformation Europe, a conception of religion as referring to an embodied community of believers gives way to a conception of religion as referring to a private body of beliefs, establishing the ontological foundations for the later re-emergence of a stable multi-confessional sovereign European order.[37] Accompanying this shift, a social imaginary conceiving of order under the metaphor of 'harmonious integration' steadily crumbles in favour of one focused instead on 'anarchy of movement', providing a new problem of order on which to fixate, and with it a new implied solution in the form of the Absolutist sovereign state.[38] Similarly, in post-Qing China, an identification of China as being synonymous with civilisation itself eventually yields to a new conception of China as an imagined national community, the defence of a hierarchical Confucian order likewise giving way to the overriding imperative of securing China's sovereign independence within a formerly anarchic system of states.[39]

With the emergence of new social imaginaries and their accompanying social identities, the common life-world necessary for communicative action to take place both between and within political communities becomes possible once again, thereby facilitating the growth of shared authoritative institutions and with it the stabilisation of international order. Natural international law in Absolutist Europe and contractual international law in post-World War II East Asia provided critical mechanisms for order preservation, but their efficacy in turn rested on shared understandings about the purpose and nature of political

---

[37] On the Reformation's role in helping to precipitate this ontological shift, see H. Berman, 'Religious foundations of law in the West: An historical perspective', *Journal of Law and Religion*, 1(1) (1983), 15.

[38] Walzer, 'On the role of symbolism in political thought', p. 199.

[39] J. R. Levenson, *Confucian China and Its Modern Fate*, 3 vols., I: *The Problem of Intellectual Continuity* (London: Routledge and Kegan Paul, 1958), p. 104.

community born of prior transformations in social imaginaries, and predicated as well on new collective identities forged in the foundries of systemic crisis and war. At the same time, within both Absolutist Europe and post-war East Asia, new international orders took shape only with the harnessing of new forms of violence to the task of order preservation. Both the European military revolution and the coming of industrial warfare to East Asia radically accelerated the collapse of old orders. But these phenomena were implicated also in the reconstitution of orders through the transformations in collective identity and new practices or organised coercion that they eventually spawned. Limited war in Absolutist Europe and the practices of 'people's war' (in both its conventional and guerrilla forms) in post-war East Asia provided the primary institutions through which conflict was expressed within reconstituted international orders. Disruptive military innovations made their emergence possible, but it was only once they were incorporated within new understandings of political authority and community that they could acquire their order-stabilising character. This tentative reconciliation between the authoritative and coercive dimensions of political life was and is always fragile and provisional, and the reconstitution of new international orders is typically protracted and uneven. Nevertheless, it is only once new fundamental institutions have emerged, legitimised through the framework of a common social imaginary and an accompanying vision of the good, that the transition from one international order to another can be said to be complete.

Looking back and looking forward: Faith, war and empire in international orders' destruction and reconstitution

The preceding pages provide a schematic outline of the argument that follows. A more detailed exposition must await articulation in my case studies. In the meantime, however, a few words are necessary to explain the significance of religion, war and empire as three themes that dominate the ensuing narrative, and that are each vitally implicated in international orders' destruction and reconstitution.

Render unto Caesar? Religion, the transcendent/immanent divide and crises of international order

From the Axial Age onwards, spiritual life in sedentary agro-literate societies has been conditioned by a heightened awareness of the sacred and the mundane as distinct realms, as well as by a recognition of the existence of a fundamental tension between these worlds.[40] This tension has expressed itself in international

---

[40] S. N. Eisenstadt, 'The Axial Age: The emergence of transcendental visions and the rise of clerics', *European Journal of Sociology*, XXIII (1982), 296.

orders' constitutional structures, which rest on ontological assumptions regarding the appropriate relationship between the spiritual and social worlds. Latin Christendom's Augustinian political theology, the Sinosphere's Mandate of Heaven, even the contemporary state system's avowedly secular foundations – each of these embodies clear ontological claims regarding the proper relationship between the transcendent and immanent domains.[41]

The significance of this observation lies in the fact that it is precisely because international orders rest on such constructs that they remain susceptible to religiously inspired challenges to their legitimacy. The perceived lack of harmony between the cosmic and the mundane provides agents with a rationale for rebellion that is indefeasible in character and potentially apocalyptic in its implications.[42] Additionally, agents' capacities to reflexively appreciate inconsistencies between their religious and political obligations have historically increased with time, being aided by developments such as the growth of literacy and the emergence of public spheres operating beyond the exclusive control of clerical and bureaucratic elites.[43] Such developments have empowered agents to critically consider existing orders without the mediation of an orthodox priestly or bureaucratic class, thereby increasing these orders' vulnerability to fundamental challenges to their integrity.

The normative complexes that help constitute international orders thus remain continuously susceptible to challengers seeking to overturn the established terms of the relationship between the transcendent and the immanent realms. An acknowledgement of this vulnerability is essential for understanding the deep background of the legitimacy crises considered in this book. It is also crucial if we are to comprehend the exact nature and magnitude of these crises. For the challenges that have historically destabilised international orders were so disruptive precisely because they contested the existing order all the way down to its ontological foundations. Consequently, I use the term 'ideological shock' advisedly to denote this phenomenon, and with the caveat that we would be understating the magnitude of transformative crises if we were to understand them exclusively as intellectually grounded contests over the legitimate terms of political authority. For the crises that engulfed Christendom and the Sinosphere

---

[41] On the political significance of secularism as a foundation of the contemporary global order, see generally E. S. Hurd, *The Politics of Secularism in International Relations* (Princeton University Press, 2008); and S. M. Thomas, 'Taking religious and cultural pluralism seriously: The global resurgence of religion and the transformation of international society', *Millennium: Journal of International Studies*, 29(3) (2000), 815–41.

[42] On this point, see generally M. Juergensmeyer, 'The logic of religious violence' in R. Howard and R. Sawyer (eds.), *Terrorism and Counter-Terrorism: Understanding the new security environment, readings and interpretations* (Guildford, CT: McGraw Hill/Dushkin, 2002), pp. 149–52.

[43] Eisenstadt, 'The Axial Age', 297. See also Taylor, *A Secular Age*, p. 68.

were not merely crises of political authority confined to lettered elites. Nor was their expression confined to the irruption of new and subversive principled propositions concerning the terms of legitimate rule. On the contrary, they entailed far-reaching cultural mutations that touched virtually all members of affected societies, and that forever altered the social imaginaries within which institutions of governance – both political and religious – were anchored.

War as both a symptom of order destroyed and a herald of order renewed

Transformations of international order encompass not only crises of ontological security, but also crises of physical security. In foregrounding the importance of increasing violence interdependence in transforming international orders, I seek to correct the relative neglect of material changes that has characterised most constructivist accounts of international systems change. This observation notwithstanding, my emphasis on violence interdependence does not imply a deeper commitment to understanding war through a predominantly materialist lens. On the contrary, war as a social institution is constituted as much by emerging forms of subjectivity as it is by evolving technological capabilities. Thus, the new forms of organised violence that manifested themselves in my cases instantiated and consolidated emergent forms of collective identity that were deeply subversive of the old order. Equally, however, these new forms of collective identity often became profoundly implicated in the constitution of the orders that emerged in the wake of systemic crises. In instantiating and consolidating nascent forms of collective identity, the new forms of violence that emerged in each of my cases played a productive as well as a destructive role, helping to inscribe in blood and iron the contours of the orders that succeeded transformative crises.

Both the destructive and reconstitutive roles of war can be illustrated through a consideration of the impact of industrial warfare in driving the suzerain-to-sovereign transition in East Asia. From the First Opium War onwards, the industrialisation of warfare enabled first Western and then Japanese imperialists to challenge and then overturn a regional order that had historically rested on China's unchallengeable military might.[44] Following the Sinosphere's collapse, however, industrial warfare also played a productive role in laying the foundations for a sovereign regional order. It did so principally through its role in stimulating the growth and popular diffusion of radical Chinese nationalism.[45] The spread of Chinese nationalism beyond educated elites in the 1920s

---

[44] This point is developed in greater detail in Chs. 6–8 below.

[45] On this point, see generally H. J. van de Ven, *War and Nationalism in China: 1925–1945* (New York: RoutledgeCurzon, 2003); and A. Waldron, *From War to Nationalism: China's turning point, 1924–1925* (Cambridge University Press, 1995).

facilitated the re-establishment of centralised political authority in China, helping to ensure the eventual consolidation of an East Asian sovereign state system. Critically, this revolution in popular subjectivities was forged in the crucible of the cluster of wars that followed the Qing dynasty's demise. The emergence of 'people's war' was both a symptom of the disorder that followed the Sinosphere's collapse and a violent backlash against Tokyo's attempts to reconstitute a suzerain order under the Japanese imperial sceptre.[46] More than this, however, it also instantiated and consolidated Chinese nationalism as a coherent popular identity, thereby enabling mainland China's reunification and the ensuing consolidation of a regional sovereign state system following Japan's defeat.

Across both of my cases, new forms of collective identity and new forms of violence co-evolved in a complex and recursive manner to refashion the social imaginaries that eventually underpinned succeeding international orders. The Wars of Religion and the conflicts following the Sinosphere's collapse each witnessed the evolution of highly disruptive military innovations. These innovations were important not merely as short-term accelerants of disorder, but also as expressions of nascent forms of collective identity that were later implicated in the norms and institutions of reconstituted international orders. Significantly, across my cases, the new modes of organised violence that emerged following the collapse of international orders assumed hegemonic and insurgent forms. These in turn reflected the polarisation between the imperial advocates of renewed universalisms and their parochial nemeses, whose success in subverting imperial designs laid the foundations for the sovereign state system's genesis and worldwide extension. Thus, it is lastly to this theme of empire and its nemeses that I now turn.

Empire and its nemeses: Imperial visions and parochial rebels in times of transition

The significance of empire for this study thus derives from the recurrent propensity for transformative crises to provide the powerful with both the motive and the opportunity to seek order via imperial consolidation. Empire-builders have historically exploited the expanded destructive means available during epochal transitions to pursue such ambitions. Additionally, the ideological ferment attending international orders' collapse has also compelled empire-builders to either fashion new orthodoxies or extensively revise existing ones in order to bind their constituent territories together and more effectively mobilise support for the imperial cause. Thus, the Habsburgs' identification with the Counter-Reformation and Japan's promotion of anti-Western

---

[46] See generally C. Johnson, *Peasant Nationalism and Communist Power: The emergence of revolutionary China, 1937–1945* (Stanford University Press, 1962).

Pan-Asianism both sought to provide the ideological glue necessary to hold their imperial conglomerations together.

In both cases, would-be empire-builders nevertheless failed to construct viable alternatives to the orders they sought to replace. For the ideological schisms that destroyed old orders and the new forms of violence that emerged following their demise together generated new social identities that gravely undermined imperial projects. Thus in Reformation Europe, confessional polarisation and the military mobilisation of trans-polity networks of co-religionists combined to thwart successive Habsburg bids for hegemony.[47] Similarly, in East Asia, the growth of radical Chinese nationalism and its accompanying forms of 'people's war' fatally jeopardised Tokyo's bid for regional dominion.[48] Confessional identity in Reformation Europe and national identity in East Asia worked to thwart imperial designs in both cases. Against a backdrop of ideological polarisation and increasing violence interdependence, it was partially the very struggle against empire that brought into being the new social identities and forms of organised violence that would help constitute the sovereign international orders that succeeded these transformative crises.

The destabilisation of orthodoxies prescribing the proper relationship between the transcendent and the immanent realms; the co-evolution of new forms of social identity and new forms of organised violence out of transformative crises; the bloody battle between imperialists and their enemies in the struggle to reconstitute international order – these three themes of faith, war and empire form the common backdrop for the historical transformations that follow. The sheer complexity of these transformations can only be conveyed through the narrative that follows. The secularisation of international orders, the rationalisation and bureaucratisation of organised violence and the delegitimation of empires together form the grand Weberian subtext underpinning this inquiry, and I will conclude this investigation by considering the significance of these developments as they relate to the global state system's contemporary travails and long-term prospects. For now, it is towards an examination of the first historical intimations of these developments, in Latin Christendom's decay and dissolution, that I turn.

---

[47] See generally H. G. Koenigsberger, 'The organization of revolutionary parties in France and the Netherlands during the sixteenth century', *The Journal of Modern History*, 27(4) (1955), 335–51. On the complementary role played by a religiously tinged 'Mosaic' proto-nationalism in defeating Habsburg imperialism, see for example P. S. Gorski, 'The Mosaic moment: An early modernist critique of modernist theories of nationalism', *The American Journal of Sociology*, 105(5) (2000), 1428–68.

[48] P. Calvocoressi, G. Wint and J. Pritchard, *Total War: The causes and courses of the Second World War*, 2 vols., II: *The Greater East Asia and Pacific Conflict* (London: Penguin Books, 1989), p. 84; Johnson, *Peasant Nationalism and Communist Power*.

PART II

The historical transformation of international orders

3 | The origins, constitution and decay of Latin Christendom

Religio vincula societatis [Religion is the bond which holds society together]

In 1577, six years after Philip II's victory over the Turks at the Battle of Lepanto, Pope Gregory XIII called Europe's final crusade in an attempt to press home Christendom's recent triumph over its Islamic nemesis.[1] From the eleventh century, the institution of the Crusade had embodied Latin Christendom's spiritual unity, as well as demonstrating the Church's power to mobilise the European nobility in the service of Holy War. While Jerusalem had long since been lost, the crusading spirit was far from dead as Europe entered the modern age. The Turkish conquest of Constantinople in 1453 had signalled the emergence of a powerful new threat to Christendom on her eastern doorstep, while the completion of the Spanish *Reconquista* in 1492 marked a parallel resurgence of Christendom in the western Mediterranean. By the latter half of the sixteenth century, the continuing proximity of the Turkish threat, combined with the religious fervour of the Counter-Reformation and the waxing of Spanish power all suggested scope for a renewed Holy War against the Ottomans.

That the pope ultimately failed to rally Christendom for a new crusade is illustrative of the final collapse of Christian unity and of Latin Christendom's disintegration as a viable international order by the late sixteenth century. Far from pressing home his advantage against the Ottomans after Lepanto, Philip instead made peace with the sultan in 1578 so as to pursue the more urgent task of crushing Calvinist rebels in the Spanish Netherlands. Similarly, France proved equally reluctant to answer the call of crusade while the monarchy's very survival was being threatened by sectarian rebellion. If faith remained the primary focus of collective identity in sixteenth-century Europe, it was a faith

---

[1] On Gregory's repeated failures after Lepanto to rally Christendom to a renewed war against the Ottoman Empire, see R. F. Kerr (ed.), *The History of the Popes from the Close of the Middle Ages*, 40 vols., XIX: *Gregory XIII (1572–1585)* (London: Routledge and Kegan Paul Ltd, 1952), pp. 354–7, 369–75.

that had become bitterly divided along confessional lines, with the duty to eradicate heresy taking absolute priority over obligations to wage Holy War against infidels. In Gregory's call to arms, one finds the last dying echo of Europe's medieval unity, and with the failure of his crusade, a final confirmation of Christendom's collapse.

In this chapter, I begin my inquiry into the transformation of international orders by reviewing Latin Christendom's genesis and consolidation in the High Middle Ages, before then examining the fundamental institutions that helped constitute it as an international order. Having sketched Christendom's contours, I then proceed to an analysis of the processes of decay that were apparent within this order from the late fourteenth century. Whereas Chapter 3 focuses on Christendom's constitution, operation and decay, Christendom's collapse and Europe's subsequent descent into immature anarchy form the respective subjects of Chapters 4 and 5. If by 1500 Christendom was in an advanced state of decay, it was far from inevitable then that it would be succeeded by a sovereign international order. That Europe failed to replicate the dominant Eurasian pattern of imperial consolidation demands explanation, thus it is to a consideration of Europe's prolonged crisis that I turn in Chapter 4. As anticipated in earlier chapters, my argument privileges military revolutions and cultural *qua* ideological shocks – in this case the Reformation – as the primary catalysts for Christendom's collapse. Briefly stated, the introduction of gunpowder and the subsequent military revolution dramatically increased Christendom's level of violence interdependence, undermining the effectiveness of existing fundamental institutions at a time when the Reformation was shattering Christendom's religious *cum* ideological unity. The combined impact of increased violence interdependence and ideological polarisation precipitated in turn a chain of conflicts that destroyed the last vestiges of medieval heteronomy while also arresting the consolidation of an imperial order organised under the Habsburg sceptre. It was only after Christendom had become irretrievably broken and the Habsburg imperial alternative had been foreclosed that the emergence of a sovereign international order became possible.

Chapter 4 details both the structural drivers of Christendom's disintegration, while also exploring the role played by the Habsburgs' multiple enemies in thwarting Christendom's reconstitution along imperial lines. In Chapter 5, the French Wars of Religion and the Thirty Years War are examined, both as conflicts that are representative of the chaos that followed Christendom's collapse, and also for their formative role in generating the normative and institutional innovations that eventually facilitated the construction of a sovereign international order. My analysis concludes with a reinterpretation of Westphalia's significance as a definitive settlement that restored to Europe the stability required for the subsequent decades-long reconstruction of a new international order along broadly Absolutist sovereign-territorial lines.

The origins, consolidation and ordering mechanisms of Latin Christendom

Origins

The story of Latin Christendom's origins is one of failure, specifically the failure of Rome's heirs to reconstitute a viable governance system to succeed the Western Roman Empire. Following the fall of Rome, Western Europe descended into a prolonged period of political anarchy, economic contraction and cultural regression from which it would not recover until the eleventh century. Certainly, attempts to construct supra-local governance structures during the early medieval period were not entirely without success. The Carolingian emperors' attempts to revive the imperial dignity kept the idea – if not the actuality – of empire alive in Western Europe, while the Church meanwhile extended the skein of a common Christian high culture to Europe's northern and eastern peripheries.[2] Nevertheless, if the precursors to the papal-imperial diarchy of the High Middle Ages can be dimly discerned during this period, neither of these institutions was then sufficiently robust as to sustain a viable order in the centuries following Rome's demise. Without the protection of an overarching imperial order, the trading networks that had flourished under Roman suzerainty withered, accelerating de-urbanisation and attenuating Western Europe's cultural and commercial contacts with other civilisational centres.[3] This process of fragmentation accelerated in the tenth century with the collapse of royal and comital authority, and the cascading downwards of military and political power to the level of the castellany, or in some instances even down to the individual knight.[4] Across Western and Central Europe, an overwhelmingly illiterate peasantry eked out a subsistence existence within the parameters of localised, non-monetised economies, while control over organised violence remained radically dispersed among a predatory nobility.[5] With the Carolingian Empire dissolved and the papacy yet to decisively assert its authority over the Church, all forms of social power crystallised at the local level. As Europe approached the millennium, centrifugal forces seemed inexorably in the ascendancy.

---

[2] On Carolingian concepts of empire, see generally R. Folz, *The Concept of Empire in Western Europe: From the fifth to the fourteenth century* (London: Edward Arnold, 1969), Ch. 1. On the spread of Christianity throughout Europe's northern and eastern peripheries, see N. Davies, *Europe: A history* (London: Pimlico, 1997), pp. 275–90.

[3] On the de-urbanisation of society in the western half of the Roman Empire during the late antique and early medieval periods, see generally W. Liebeschuetz, 'The end of the ancient city' in J. Rich (ed.), *The City in Late Antiquity* (London: Routledge, 1992), pp. 1–49.

[4] On the collapse of public authority and the accompanying process of 'encastellation' across the lands of the former Carolingian Empire, see J.-P. Poly and E. Bournazel, *The Feudal Transformation, 900–1200* (New York: Holmes and Meier, 1991), pp. 25–6.

[5] Mann, *The Sources of Social Power*, I, p. 394.

The consolidation of Latin Christendom

Europe's fragmented social landscape in 1000 CE initially presents as an unlikely seedbed for the formation of any stable order. However, from the eleventh century onwards a cluster of processes conspired to generate a distinctive international order undergirded by the unifying religious and cultural identity of Latin Christendom. The years 1000–1250 CE witnessed a trebling of Europe's population, a demographic upswing made possible by a commercial revival that had begun in the late eleventh century.[6] The breakdown of centralised political power following the Carolingian Empire's demise facilitated both the growth of merchant towns in North-west Europe, as well as the establishment in the countryside of a system of banal lordship predicated on the intensified extraction of surplus from a newly enserfed peasantry.[7] Academic opinion remains divided as to the relative priority that should be placed on the revival of long-distance trade versus the feudal intensification of agricultural surplus extraction as engines of the economic revival.[8] However, there is consensus that the interaction of these processes provided European elites with access to a growing pool of labour and taxable wealth over time.[9]

This increase in the availability of material resources coincided with a process of elite consolidation and differentiation among Europe's lay and clerical elites. Under pressure to preserve their patrimonies in an environment of growing population pressures, Europe's nobility abandoned a system of partible inheritance in favour of one predicated on principles of patrilineal primogeniture.[10] Previous conceptions of family as one of loose clans of collateral kindreds gave way in the eleventh century to a more exclusive conception of family as patrilineal dynasty.[11] The nobility's growing adoption of heraldic emblems and toponymic surnames meanwhile reflected a growing aristocratic self-consciousness and sense of corporate distinctiveness from both

---

[6] R. I. Moore, 'The birth of Europe as a Eurasian phenomenon' in V. Lieberman (ed.), *Beyond Binary Histories: Re-imagining Eurasia to c.1830* (Ann Arbor: The University of Michigan Press, 2002), p. 140.

[7] Poly and Bournazel, *The Feudal Transformation*, pp. 38–9.

[8] The disagreements among economic historians of medieval Europe are reflected in the approaches of social scientists concerned with international systems change in the medieval and early periods. Thus, whereas Hendrik Spruyt affords greater significance to the revival of long-distance trade in accounting for the economic revival, Benno Teschke conversely emphasises that the economic revival was driven principally by developments endogenous to a feudal economy based upon intensified aristocratic exploitation of an enserfed peasantry. On this controversy and its relevance for their approaches to international systems change, see Spruyt, *The Sovereign State and its Competitors*, pp. 61–3; and Teschke, *The Myth of 1648*, pp. 95–6.

[9] On this point, see Spruyt, *The Sovereign State and its Competitors*, pp. 62–4.

[10] Moore, 'Birth of Europe', p. 145.

[11] G. Duby, *The Chivalrous Society* (London: Edward Arnold, 1977), pp. 147–8.

the peasantry and the priesthood.[12] Similarly, the priesthood's corporate identity dramatically increased following the contemporaneous establishment of papal dominance over the Church. Previously, Western Europe's pervasive disorder had necessitated clerics' involvement in local political intrigues, both to protect the interests of the Church and also to advance their own worldly interests. The resulting enmeshment of the priesthood within aristocratic webs of kinship and patronage had weakened the Church's moral authority, while also threatening its absorption within a social milieu dominated by the Frankish warrior caste.[13] In asserting the supremacy of canon law within the Church hierarchy and prohibiting both the sale of Church offices and the marriage of priests, Pope Gregory VII and his successors extricated the priesthood from entanglement within the family politics of the local aristocracy.[14] In so doing, the Church prevented the usurpation of its assets by priests connected by marriage to local dynasties, while also forging a new cadre of celibate officials whose identity was now tethered exclusively to advancing the Church's salvation mission.[15]

As Europe grew in wealth and population and its elites became more consolidated as distinct estates, the availability of the 'social technologies' required to administer large collective associations also increased.[16] The growth in trade and the operation of the Church hierarchy respectively required the co-ordination of market transactions and the conveyance of bureaucratic commands over long distances.[17] Both processes necessitated the creation of a greatly expanded class of literate administrators, trained from the twelfth century onwards at the newly established universities emerging in urban centres such as Oxford, Paris and Bologna.[18] In addition to generating a class of literate professionals, the growth of universities also permitted the systematisation of knowledge in the fields of law, theology and philosophy.[19] This in turn enabled growing elite-level cultural integration across Christendom, exemplified in the diffusion of the crucifix as the pre-eminent symbol of Christianity from the late eleventh century.[20] Just as importantly, the systematisation of knowledge also provided elites with a shared conceptual vocabulary through which to articulate binding

---

[12] R. Bartlett, *The Making of Europe: Conquest, colonization, and cultural change, 950–1350* (Princeton University Press, 1993), pp. 49–51.

[13] On the relationship between the weakness of temporal authority in Dark Ages Europe and the eventual defensive reaction it inspired in the growth of pontifical authority and power within the Church, see M. Gauchet, *The Disenchantment of the World: A political history of religion* (Princeton University Press, 1997), p. 152.

[14] Berman, *Law and Revolution*, p. 108.   [15] *Ibid.*

[16] The term 'social technologies' is taken from S. J. Kaufman, 'The fragmentation and consolidation of international systems', *International Organization*, 51(2) (1997), 183–4.

[17] On the dramatic growth in the pool of trained clerics capable of executing these functions over the course of the twelfth and thirteenth centuries, see J. Strayer, *On the Medieval Origins of the Modern State* (Princeton University Press, 1970), pp. 24–5.

[18] Davies, *Europe*, p. 361.   [19] Moore, 'Birth of Europe', p. 149.   [20] *Ibid.*

authority claims to critical audiences. Admittedly, conflicts such as the Investiture Contest demonstrated the inability of Church and emperor to peacefully resolve disputes over the scope of their respective authority claims. But the very ability of these parties to engage in such a polemic was indicative of Christendom's growing cultural cohesiveness during this time.

Demographic and commercial expansion, elite consolidation and differentiation, and increases in the social technologies of administrative capacity and cultural integration each fed into a highly tentative process of political centralisation, which was initially most precociously apparent in England, France and the Spanish kingdoms, before then diffusing more gradually elsewhere.[21] If it is premature to speak of the emergence of the state by the fourteenth century, one can nevertheless argue for a much greater degree of systemic integration than had previously existed. From 1000 CE onwards, Latin Christendom had witnessed a sustained increase in its territorial reach, material wealth, institutional sophistication, ideological and cultural integration, and political centralisation. As with all orders, Christendom would prove ultimately ephemeral, beginning a long process of decay from the mid-fourteenth century onwards. But before this process may be considered, a more thorough investigation of Christendom's constitutional structure is in order.

The constitution and ordering mechanisms of Christendom

As with all international orders, Christendom was held together first and foremost by a normative complex composed of overlapping identity-constitutive, ethical-prescriptive and power-legitimating norms. At the identity-constitutive level, Christendom was united in its commitment to spiritual salvation as the *raison d'être* of collective association.[22] Medieval Europe was first and foremost a community of faith, with religion being understood not as referring to a privately held body of abstract doctrine and beliefs, but rather as referring to an embodied community of believers.[23] The medieval *mappe mundi*, which depicted the world as the Body of Christ, with Christ's head next to paradise, his arms gathering the temporal world, and Jerusalem – navel of the world – at the centre, metaphorically captured the conflation of the temporal with the spiritual that was emblematic of the beliefs undergirding Christendom's unity.[24] At a more concrete level, throughout Christendom, the ritual of the Mass routinely confirmed the centrality of

---

[21] Strayer, *On the Medieval Origins of the Modern State*, p. 35.

[22] See generally M. Bloch. *Feudal Society*, 2 vols., I: *The Growth of Ties of Dependence* (The University of Chicago Press, 1961), pp. 81–7.

[23] Thomas, 'Taking religious and cultural pluralism seriously', p. 820.

[24] J. B. Harley and D. Woodward (eds.), *Cartography in Prehistoric, Ancient, and Medieval Europe and the Mediterranean* (The University of Chicago Press, 1987), p. 310.

faith to medieval European identity, as well as reinforcing the perception that membership of the community was synonymous with membership of the Church. The Church's cosmology and moral ontology were systematically communicated to the populace through the Mass's re-enactment of Christ's expiatory sacrifice as penance for man's sins, a sacrifice that made possible reconciliation between God and man and thus opened up the possibility of salvation.[25] Even more critically, the Mass formed a vital social integrative function, with the individual's participation in Communion (common union) symbolising not only wholeness of Christ and his Church, but also the social solidarity of those united in their faith in Christ.[26]

The Church provided medieval Europeans with not only a shared collective identity and understanding of the ultimate purposes of collective association, but also a common ethical framework. While there is no question but that the Church legitimised the medieval world's pervasive inequalities, the egalitarian and pacifist dimensions of the Christian message also found comprehensive expression in the Church's teachings. The notion that all humans are made in God's image and are capable of salvation extended the bonds of moral obligation beyond the limits of family and friends, while the claim that acts of violence and injustice directly contradict God's will exercised similarly powerful pacifying effects. The normative force of these prescriptions was evident in the Church's frequently successful efforts to mobilise religious sanctions to restrain the worst excesses of seigneurial violence.[27] Moreover, even where the Church saw the need to reconcile Christian ethics with the realities of princely violence, it nevertheless exercised a powerful restraining influence through its development of a coherent and richly articulated doctrine of just war.

Christian ethics provided the basis of the normative restraints on violence that held Christendom together. The universality and the efficacy of these normative restraints were admittedly circumscribed by several factors. Externally, the ethos of Holy War posited a stark moral dichotomy between Christians and others, rehearsing on Christendom's bloody borders an ethic of religiously sanctioned annihilatory violence that would later punctuate the Wars of Religion. Internally, the reach of Christian ethics was limited by the accommodations struck between Europe's lay and clerical elites, which found

---

[25] On this point, see J. Bossy, 'The Mass as a social institution 1200–1700', *Past and Present*, 100 (1983), 34.

[26] *Ibid.*

[27] The Peace of God movement in medieval France and Spain constituted an early example of the Church's ability to jointly utilise its unique moral authority alongside peasant mobilisation to forge new normative constraints on predatory aristocratic behaviour. See generally T. N. Bisson, 'The organized peace in Southern France and Catalonia, ca.1140–ca.1233', *American Historical Review*, 82(2) (1977), 290–311. See also T. Head and R. A. Landes, *The Peace of God: Social violence and religious response in France around the year 1000* (Ithaca: Cornell University Press, 1992).

expression in the power-legitimating structures of a social ideology of tri-functionality and an Augustinian political theology. Turning first to tri-functionality, this concept legitimated and sacralised the notion of society as a divinely conceived organic totality, with feudal society's pervasive inequality being justified on the basis of its concordance with God's vision of a rigidly stratified world divided between clerics, warriors and peasants.[28] The concept of tri-functionality legitimised and perpetuated inequality by assigning to priest, knight and peasant the respective vocations of worship, combat in defence of the Church and cultivation of the land in support of priests and nobles.[29] The popular passivity and social immobility this concept engendered was further reinforced by the Church's Augustinian justification for temporal authority. Juxtaposing the City of God with the City of Man, Augustine had conceived of the latter as a remedial order imposed on man as punishment for original sin.[30] While Augustine conceded the necessity of temporal authority, given Fallen Man's inability to peacefully co-exist without its restraining influence, this endorsement clearly subordinated the imperfect order of man to the perfect order of God, a celestial order given earthly institutional expression in the Church.[31] In embracing Augustine's justification of temporal authority, the Church provided vital theological support for princely power.[32] However, at the same time, the terms of this endorsement clearly affirmed the Church's supreme moral authority, thereby confirming the undiminished centrality of the Church's salvation mission within the medieval imaginary.[33]

Christendom's constitutional norms found their practical expression in its fundamental institutions, at the apex of which stood the papal–imperial diarchy. The papal–imperial diarchy constituted the highest expression of the often fractious accommodation between clerical and lay elites upon which order in Christendom relied. Church doctrine proclaimed that both Church and empire were divinely ordained institutions fulfilling distinct but complementary functions. The former was responsible for assuring humanity's submission to Christ and securing the salvation of souls, while the latter was charged with securing the temporal order necessary for the Church to realise its divine mission.[34] The Church thus accorded the emperor a special significance as the *primus inter pares* among temporal rulers; although, as the emperor's function was derivative of the Church's salvation mission, the Church still regarded the emperor as being subordinate to the pope.[35] This interpretation was inevitably challenged by imperial propagandists, who sought,

[28] On the centrality of the ideological construct of tri-functionality in dominant conceptions of social order in the Middle Ages, see generally G. Duby, *The Three Orders: Feudal society imagined* (The University of Chicago Press, 1978).
[29] *Ibid.*, p. 5.
[30] On this point, see Deane, *The Political and Social Ideas of Saint Augustine*, p. 117.
[31] *Ibid.*   [32] *Ibid.*, p. 152.   [33] *Ibid.*
[34] On this point, see Folz, *The Concept of Empire*, pp. 81–9 *passim*.   [35] *Ibid.*, p. 89.

with very limited success, to invoke ancient Roman precedents to sustain a more capacious conception of the imperial office.[36]

The tensions between papacy and empire eventually exercised a profoundly corrosive effect on the capacity of each to sustain order. However, for the duration of its existence, the diarchy provided a loose ordering framework for Christendom that embodied the synthesis of authoritative and coercive power that is constitutive of political order. Moreover, while the centrality of Church and empire as ordering institutions should not be understated, one must also acknowledge the limited character of their authority claims. While both pontiff and emperor claimed throughout Christendom the right of *auctoritas* (the power to judge the legitimacy of lower office-holders and the legality of their actions), neither consistently sought to translate this claim into one of *potestas*, understood as the right and ability to enforce compliance with one's commands.[37] Instead, the systemic and at times quite notional authority claims of pope and emperor helped integrate an order in which reserves of material wealth remained low, capacities for organised violence remained radically dispersed and social power crystallised at an overwhelmingly local level.

Throughout Christendom, social power resided predominantly both in the Church and within the nobility's kinship and patronage networks.[38] Unsurprisingly, the authoritative and coercive institutions through which order was maintained bore strongly the imprint of these different power networks. The most important of Christendom's authoritative institutions was the system of canon law administered by the papal courts. Down to the sixteenth century, confirmation by religious oath served as the main constitutive act in the process of ratifying treaties between disputants, with signed paper documents (where they existed at all) serving merely as accessory guarantees for such agreements.[39] Christendom's religious unity and the Church's supremacy in adjudicating spiritual matters provided a framework for mediating conflicts and safeguarding treaty commitments, thereby assuring the credibility of such commitments and maintaining a modicum of social order.[40] As the breaching of a religious oath was perceived as a sin in violation of canon law, breaches of oaths necessarily fell under the jurisdiction of papal courts.[41] By confirming the

---

[36] *Ibid.*, pp. 109–10.
[37] On the distinction between *auctoritas* and *potestas* as Roman legal concepts and the implications of this distinction for the shape of the international order of Latin Christendom, see the helpful discussion in A. Osiander, 'Before sovereignty: Society and politics in *Ancien Regime* Europe', *Review of International Studies*, 27(5) (2001), 123–5.
[38] Mann, *Sources of Social Power*, p. 385.
[39] Lesaffer, 'Peace treaties from Lodi to Westphalia', p. 24.
[40] On this point, see generally W. Ullman, 'The medieval papal court as an international tribunal' in W. Ullman (ed.), *The Papacy and Political Ideas in the Middle Ages* (London: Variorum Reprints, 1976), pp. 365–71.
[41] Lesaffer, 'Peace treaties from Lodi to Westphalia', pp. 24–6.

terms of a treaty through a religious oath, contracting parties agreed to submit to the papal courts' jurisdiction, thereby exposing themselves to a range of spiritual penalties should they be found to be in breach of their commitments.[42] Given the very real political consequences that could flow from an adverse ruling – the sanction of excommunication absolved vassals from allegiance to an excommunicated lord, thereby exposing the latter to the threat of dispossession, deposition or even death – the threat of papal sanctions could restrain even those with little concern for their own spiritual welfare.[43]

Canon law and the system of papal jurisdiction worked alongside a richly elaborated system of feudal law to maintain order within Christendom. Over the course of centuries of aristocratic intermarriage, Europe's polities had become enmeshed in extraordinarily complex webs of criss-crossing genealogical ties. Given the centrality of marriage and inheritance as mechanisms of property transference in medieval Europe, a common corpus of feudal law was necessary to mediate the disputes that inevitably arose within such a tightly integrated environment.[44] Critically, while feudal law provided a common medium within which aristocrats could articulate their competing claims, neither the existence of feudal nor canon law could prevent Christendom from being riven by endemic aristocratic feuding. That feuding remained commonplace in spite of the existence of both canon and feudal law would initially appear to speak to the irrelevance of authoritative institutions in contributing to order within Christendom. Nevertheless, such an impression would be misplaced given the role played by the feud itself as an ordering institution. In contrast to the modern opposition between private violence and public law, noble violence was inseparable from litigation in an environment in which no centralised agency existed to promulgate and enforce a uniform legal code.[45] Feuding did not occur within a legal vacuum, but was rather informed by feudal laws pertaining to matters such as the rights and duties of vassals and the rules for the proper dispensation of landed property. As medievalist Philip Geary notes, nobles' purpose in engaging in feuds was rarely to achieve the extermination of the opponent, but was rather to seek legal redress, with the end goal being the renegotiation of a continuing social bond with the opposing party on more favourable terms.[46] Contrary to the situation obtaining in a nation-state enjoying a coercive monopoly, aristocratic violence was not antithetical to existing legal structures. Rather, the feud formed an integral part of the legal structures themselves, at least among the nobility.[47]

The final contributor to order within Christendom flowed directly from its material context. Simply stated, Christendom's poverty and technological

---

[42] *Ibid.*, p. 26.   [43] *Ibid.*

[44] On the development of feudal law as a pan-European legal institution, see generally Berman, *Law and Revolution*, Ch. 9.

[45] Geary, 'Living with conflicts in stateless France', p. 145.   [46] *Ibid.*   [47] *Ibid.*

backwardness placed strict upper limits on the scale and destructiveness of violent conflicts. For much of the Middle Ages, the subsistence nature of the European economy foreclosed the possibility of diverting large numbers of men from agricultural pursuits for participation in military campaigns.[48] Moreover, even if economic constraints had permitted the temporary mobilisation of large infantry hosts, the bureaucratic and logistical capacities necessary to train, arm, equip and deploy large-scale armies had withered with the fall of Rome.[49] The dilapidated state of European roads further slowed the pace of armed confrontations and limited their operational range, while the dispersed character of military power curtailed the ambitions of lords and vassals alike.[50] Given the dominance of shock cavalry in medieval warfare and the largely non-monetised nature of the economy, rulers had long been compelled to provide grants of land in exchange for promises of military services from the nobility.[51] The result was the formation of political systems in which rulers were not qualitatively much stronger than their most powerful subjects, and were consequently painfully dependent upon the fickle loyalties of their vassals when contemplating war. Admittedly, from the mid-fifteenth century, Christendom's violence interdependence began to rise markedly, signalling an imminent transcendence of the technological and physical limits on conflict that had previously prevailed.[52] Nevertheless, for much of the life of Latin Christendom, physical limitations on the scale and scope of conflicts did much to reinforce the efficacy of ordering institutions and the pacifying effects of ideological unity already described.

Like all orders, Latin Christendom was far from perfect. Religious unity provided the normative cement necessary to hold Christendom together, but the Christian imperative of non-violence co-existed uneasily with other constructs that conceded a necessary role to aristocratic violence in defending the Church and maintaining temporal order. Similarly, Christendom's ordering institutions were both inadequate and indispensable in mitigating violent conflict. Treaties guaranteed by religious oath and enforced by the papal courts could be partially effective in securing peace, but this peace was always likely to be provisional while such treaties were perceived as being neither binding upon a prince's successors, nor even necessarily binding upon the vassals nominally under his control.[53] Equally, the institution of feud may have been inseparable from processes of aristocratic litigation, but the mere fact that recourse to

---

[48] Mann, *The Sources of Social Power*, I, p. 393.

[49] R. Bean, 'War and the birth of the nation state', *The Journal of Economic History*, 33(1) (1973), 217–18.

[50] Hirst, *War and Power in the 21st Century*, p. 19.

[51] Mann, *The Sources of Social Power*, I, p. 393.

[52] These processes are discussed in some detail in W. H. McNeill, *The Pursuit of Power: Technology, armed force, and society since* AD *1000* (The University of Chicago Press, 1982), Ch. 3.

[53] Lesaffer, 'Peace treaties from Lodi to Westphalia', pp. 15–21.

Table 3.1 *The international order of Latin Christendom, 1000–1350*

Normative complex	Governing institutional framework	Order-enabling material context
Identity-constitutive norms Salvation through the Church as *raison d'être* of collective association	**Ordering framework** Heteronomous system of overlapping jurisdictions loosely governed by papal–imperial diarchy	**Aggregate capacities for production and destruction** Feudal mode of production and aristocratic oligopoly over organised violence
Ethical-prescriptive norms Christian ethics as articulated by the Church	**Authoritative institutions** Canon law and feudal law	**Mobilisational networks** Aristocratic kinship and patronage networks predominate alongside bureaucratic Church hierarchy
Power-legitimating norms Augustinian political theology and social ideology of tri-functionality	**Coercive institutions** Aristocratic feud as a legitimate means of legal redress ('peace in the feud')	**Violence interdependence** Low concentration and low accumulation of coercive means (low violence interdependence)

violent self-help was recognised as an ordering mechanism is demonstrative of the fragile character of order within Christendom. Finally, as we will shortly see, Christendom's very success in generating a modicum of order ironically permitted the acceleration of processes that would ultimately corrode the material limitations on conflict that were operative in the medieval period.[54]

The decay of Latin Christendom, 1350–1500

The crisis of the papal–imperial diarchy and the onset of institutional decay

Any consideration of Christendom's decay must begin by surveying the decline of the papal–imperial diarchy. While ostensibly complementary as the temporal and spiritual legatees of Roman universalism, empire and papacy remained locked in conflict throughout the Middle Ages in a struggle encompassing

[54] This point is made with some eloquence in K. W. Deutsch, 'Medieval unity and the economic conditions for an international civilization', *The Canadian Journal of Economics and Political Science*, 10(1) (1944), 30.

ideological, infrastructural and eventually even geopolitical dimensions. Ideologically, the Church claimed both temporal and spiritual supremacy within Christendom.[55] Moreover, while the Church conceded the empire's legitimacy, it tied this legitimacy exclusively to the emperor's position as the Church's anointed defender on earth.[56] This perspective contrasted sharply with the views propounded by imperial propagandists, who stressed the empire's Roman and Frankish origins, and claimed that the emperor derived his authority directly from God rather than through delegation from the Church.[57] At the level of infrastructural conflict, the Church sought to assure its independence by confirming the pope's exclusive right to control the appointment of bishops within imperial territories. This inevitably aroused resistance from the emperor, for whom control over the appointment of bishops was crucial as a source of elite patronage.[58] Finally, from the mid-twelfth to the mid-thirteenth centuries, the conflict between papacy and empire assumed a geopolitical dimension, as the Church tried to stave off a bid by the Hohenstaufen emperors to unite the German, Burgundian and Italian kingdoms under the imperial sceptre. As the emperor's success would have jeopardised the Papal States' autonomy and thus potentially undermined the Church's liberty, successive popes conspired successfully with the Hohenstaufens' enemies to prevent the empire's consolidation.[59]

With the death of Frederick II in 1250 and the subsequent neutralisation of Frederick's heirs, the papacy succeeded in preventing a central polity from coalescing around the great trading city-belt stretching from northern Italy to the Baltic Sea.[60] Consequently, successive emperors were unable to effectively

---

[55] For a comprehensive summation of the theory of papal monarchy, see J. A. Watt, *The Theory of Papal Monarchy in the Thirteenth Century* (New York: Fordham University Press, 1965).

[56] The political import of the papacy's subscription to a doctrine of spiritual supremacy over the empire was that it conferred upon the pope a right to call for the deposition of an emperor deemed to have been delinquent in fulfilling his obligations to the Church. Such a doctrine clearly compromised the autonomous power of the emperor, and was as such fiercely opposed by imperial propagandists from the Investiture Contest onwards, who attempted to argue that the emperor derived his power directly from God rather than via the institution of the papacy. See Folz, *The Concept of Empire*, pp. 110–12.

[57] *Ibid.*   [58] Berman, *Law and Revolution*, p. 97.

[59] On papal fears concerning the potential threat to the Papal States posed by Hohenstaufen imperialism, see J. A. Watt, 'The papacy' in D. Abulafia (ed.), *The New Cambridge Medieval History*, V: *c.1198–1300* (Cambridge University Press, 1999), p. 130.

[60] For a detailed description of the great urban dorsal spine of Central Europe and its influence on the sequencing of state formation on the Continent, see P. Flora, S. Kuhnle and D. Urwin (eds.), *State Formation, Nation-Building, and Mass Politics in Europe: The theory of Stein Rokkan, based on his collected works* (Oxford University Press, 1999), p. 179. On the role played by the defeat of the Hohenstaufens in facilitating the consolidation of princely territorial jurisdiction within Germany and in opening up political space for the emergence of city-states and city-leagues in Europe, see Spruyt, *The Sovereign State and its Competitors*, pp. 114–16.

tap the massive surpluses locked up in capital containers such as the Italian city-states, thereby denying them the resources necessary to politically unify Latin Christendom's cultural and economic heartland.[61] Instead, with the road to capital-intensive empire-building blocked, processes of state formation subsequently advanced most rapidly in areas outside of Europe's core zone of taxable wealth.[62] Coming at a time when vast swathes of Eurasia were being unified under the Mongol yoke, the defeat of Hohenstaufen imperialism further compounded Western Europe's entrenched pluralism, once again distinguishing Christendom's development from the Eurasian imperial norm.

In the aftermath of the empire's defeat, the papacy enjoyed a fleeting period of supremacy that can retrospectively be seen as an Indian summer for Christendom as a coherent international order. In comparison with the contemporary global state system's ordering institutions, the authority of the papal court within Christendom seems particularly impressive. The papal court contrasted starkly with the modern International Court of Justice inasmuch as its jurisdiction was compulsory; it explained, interpreted and developed the law through the issuing of papal decretals; and it could reasonably anticipate – by dint of its spiritual authority over all believers – the reliable enforcement of its decisions.[63] At the height of its power, the Church routinely struck down the laws of lesser powers, ordered the revision or annulment of treaties, and even deprived kings and emperors of their powers through deposition or excommunication.[64] From its mid-thirteenth-century apogee, the papacy nevertheless began a process of decline that accelerated rapidly in the fourteenth century. Having defeated the Hohenstaufens with the help of Christendom's petty princelings, the pontifical imperialism inaugurated by Innocent III and sustained by his successors sparked resistance in its turn from temporal rulers anxious to guard their privileges against an overreaching Church. Additionally, the Church's heavy reliance on Western European kings to balance the emperor established a relationship of increasing dependence that would reach its zenith during the Avignon papacies.[65] As the

---

[61] Interestingly, D. J. A. Matthews also hypothesises that the preservation of a coherent empire in Western Europe may have provided Latin Christendom with a more effective framework through which to defend Eastern Europe from the confrontation with the Mongols beginning in 1241; given the profound influence exercised by the Mongol incursions on Eastern Europe's (and particularly Russia's) subsequent development, one cannot help but speculate on the possible trajectory of East–West relations that might have emerged had the empire been able to assist in the manner raised by Matthews. See D. J. A. Matthews, 'Reflections on the medieval Roman Empire', *History – Journal of the Historical Association*, 77(251) (1992), 389.

[62] On this great paradox of European development, whereby strong states emerged most rapidly at the periphery of the old empire, see Flora, Kuhnle and Urwin, *State Formation, Nation-Building, and Mass Politics in Europe*, p. 145.

[63] Ullman, 'The medieval papal court as an international tribunal', p. 356.

[64] *Ibid.*, pp. 362–4.

[65] G. Leff, 'Heresy and the decline of the medieval church', *Past and Present*, 20 (1961), 38.

fourteenth century progressed, and the papacy experienced first the Babylonian Captivity and then the Great Schism, the efficacy of papal jurisdiction over Christendom consequently waned. Notwithstanding their public lamentations over the polarisation of Christian loyalties between two (and later three) popes, Europe's temporal rulers exploited the Church's weakness to further encroach on its prerogatives within their own territories.[66] The subsequent post-Schism division within the Church between defenders of papal supremacy and conciliarists (those insisting upon the pope's ultimate accountability to a general council of the Church) provided further scope for monarchical aggrandisement at the Church's expense.[67] While successive popes successfully quashed conciliarists' calls for reform, temporal rulers' continued cultivation of the conciliarist faction left the Church internally divided, further diminishing its capacity to fulfil its ordering functions within Christendom.[68]

The growth of dissent and the weakening of Christian unity

By 1500 both papacy and empire were immeasurably weakened. This process was reinforced by a discernible loosening in the grip of Church orthodoxy over the medieval imagination. The challenges to Christendom's normative unity were both indirect and direct in nature. Indirectly, the recovery of classical knowledge posed a potentially grave threat to the Church's power. Initially, the Church's near-monopoly on literacy enabled it to marshal classical legacies to the cause of promoting universal papal monarchy.[69] Over time, however, it was Europe's ruling families who more effectively appropriated the classical heritage to justify their increasing centralisation of power. The Church's Augustinian understanding of political authority explicitly subordinated the temporal to the sacred. In this formulation, kings derived their power from the top down – that is, their power was the product of divine sanction, and the pope as Christ's vicar on earth could thus effectively adjudicate the legitimacy of its exercise.[70] By contrast, Aristotelian conceptions of the polis as an autonomous community – one brought into being by man's natural propensity towards sociability – suggested an alternative, 'bottom up' justification for political authority not tied to the Church's salvation mission.[71] In providing an alternative, secular conceptualisation of political authority, the recovered classical heritage

---

[66] *Ibid.*, pp. 38–9.   [67] Wight, *Systems of States*, pp. 131–4.

[68] *Ibid.*, p. 134. Wight goes as far as to argue that Christendom was in effect headless by the mid-fifteenth century, and that there existed at this time sovereign states but not a sovereign state system. While I agree that Christendom was in an advanced state of decay by the mid-fifteenth century, I believe Wight overstates the case in this regard, for reasons that should become evident in the remainder of this chapter and the next two chapters.

[69] See generally Watt, *The Theory of Papal Monarchy*, pp. 97–105.

[70] Ullman, 'The medieval papal court as an international tribunal', p. 367.   [71] *Ibid.*, p. 366.

provided Europe's rulers with legitimating principles that reduced their ideological dependence on the Church, potentially undermining Christendom's
ordering structure.

As it transpired, however, the recovery of Europe's classical heritage did not
immediately destroy Christendom's foundations, even though it contributed
mightily to the atmosphere of intellectual tumult that prefigured its destruction.
Aristotelian conceptions of political community had first resurfaced in the
Latin West as far back as the thirteenth century, at which time the Church
had demonstrated a robust capacity for assimilating the classical inheritance
and adapting it to its own purposes. This assimilative capacity had been most
evident in the writings of Aquinas, whose argument that humans could attain
knowledge of God through the exercise of reason skilfully reconciled Greek
rationalism with Judeo-Christian revelation. Aquinas's endorsement of
Aristotelian conceptions of humans as political animals by nature had admittedly lent a dignity to temporal power superior to that formerly provided by
Augustinian conceptions of political authority.[72] At the same time, however,
this reclamation of Aristotle had not weakened the Church's pre-eminence, for
Thomistic conceptions of the law provided a far more elaborate and coherent
set of normative constraints on the exercise of temporal power than had
previously existed. If Aquinas's recovery of Aristotle had lent temporal power
a greater dignity than it had previously possessed, his conception of kingdoms
as embedded within a wider community of believers had also conversely
reinforced Christendom's heteronomous tendencies, as had his understanding
of temporal rulers as being enmeshed within webs of divine, natural and human
law that prohibited the unfettered exercise of worldly power.[73]

At the height of its powers in the mid-thirteenth century, the Church had
thus proven eminently capable of harnessing revived pagan ideas and subordi-
nating them to its own vision of the good. By 1500, however, the challenge
of assimilating the classical inheritance had become considerably more
difficult. Following Constantinople's fall, the westward flood of Greek texts
across the Mediterranean fuelled an insatiable hunger for ancient wisdom
among Europe's intellectuals, while the invention of the printing press helped
to disseminate the resulting interpretations of recovered texts far more swiftly
than would previously have been possible.[74] From the ensuing ferment arose
two potentially disruptive tendencies for the Church. The first of these was the
growth of civic humanism, which blossomed first in the Italian city-states

---

[72] Wolin, *Politics and Vision*, p. 122. See also E. L. Fortin, 'St Thomas Aquinas' in L. Strauss
and J. Cropsey (eds.), *History of Political Philosophy* (The University of Chicago Press,
1987), pp. 253–5.

[73] Fortin, 'St Thomas Aquinas', p. 258; and Wolin, *Politics and Vision*, p. 126. See also
J. B. Elshtain, *Sovereignty: God, state, self* (New York: Basic Books, 2008), pp. 16–20.

[74] MacCulloch, *Reformation*, p. 78.

before then diffusing more broadly throughout transalpine Europe. Finding its most iconoclastic expression in Machiavelli's writings, civic humanism proffered an alternative moral foundation for political community that preferred ancient *virtu* and republican liberty to Christian charity and the Church's salvation mission.[75] That civic humanists such as Machiavelli were able to even formulate secular theories of politics at this time is indicative of the fact that a sovereign European international society was certainly imaginable by 1500. Conversely, however, the visceral hostility with which Machiavelli's works were initially received also attests to the continuing centrality of sacral forms of collective identity in Europe, and also to the mutually entwined character of religious and political power structures in Christendom as it stood on the cusp of dissolution.[76] More generally, if ancient conceptions of political authority proved ever more accessible to both republican civil humanists and royalist propagandists in the fifteenth and early sixteenth centuries, in practice this did not prompt the former to abandon religious legitimations of princely power. Rather, at least with respect to Christendom's ascending Renaissance monarchs, the classical revival more often merely increased the self-consciousness and sophistication with which they were able to advance their authority claims, providing them with the intellectual resources necessary to renegotiate rather than directly sever their ties to the Church.[77]

While the more iconoclastic civic humanists challenged the Church's vision of the good openly but generally unsuccessfully, a second and more insidious consequence of the classical revival was the fillip it gave to humanists seeking to more accurately access religious truth through the analysis of newly discovered ancient texts. Where previously the Church's power had rested strongly on its unchallenged authority to interpret and communicate the truths expressed in the Latin Vulgate Bible, the recovery of ancient Greek texts dating from the time of Jesus increasingly exposed the Vulgate's manifold mistranslations and inconsistencies.[78] In their quest for religious truth, humanist scholars thus inadvertently began to destabilise the intellectual and epistemological foundations of the Church's power. This was expressed not only in their emphasis on the independent authority of recovered texts, but also in both

---

[75] On Machiavelli's attack on Christianity for its alleged subversion of civic life and corruption of the public ethos necessary to sustain republican liberty, see Q. Skinner, *The Foundations of Modern Political Thought*, 2 vols., I: *The Renaissance* (Cambridge University Press, 1978), p. 167.

[76] On the hostility with which Machiavelli's works were received (at least publicly), see MacCulloch, *Reformation*, p. 44.

[77] The concordats signed between the Church and the French and Spanish kings in the period immediately preceding the Reformation – agreements that kept these realms within Christendom while dramatically increasing the religious authority of both monarchs within their kingdoms – are emblematic of this process of renegotiation.

[78] MacCulloch, *Reformation*, p. 81.

the premium they placed on historical authenticity over centuries-old tradition and on the increasingly introspective and textually oriented form of devotion many humanists favoured. As MacCulloch notes, the activities of these pious humanists set an ominous precedent, even where as in most instances they had no intention of challenging the Church's authority: '*Ad fontes*, back to the sources, was the battle-cry of the humanists, and the Protestants would take it from them.'[79] Initially at least, the threat posed to the Church by the humanists' activities was not immediately evident. But when it was finally conjoined with the upsurge of popular religious fervour that overtook Europe in the fifteenth and early sixteenth centuries, this humanist emphasis on textual authority would have devastating consequences for Christendom's constitution.

In emphasising nature over divinity, human reason rather than human sinfulness, and the polis over the Church as a focal point of human association, the classical revival generally presented as a slow-acting, indirect and somewhat ambiguous threat to Christendom's normative unity. A much more direct threat came in the growth of popular heretical movements in late medieval and early modern Europe. The forces driving the growth of heresy were manifold, but foremost among them was disillusionment with the Church owing to its perceived worldliness, corruption and neglect of its pastoral duties. The combination of monarchical centralisation, intensified geopolitical competition and the increasing financial demands of late medieval warfare had driven a creeping usurpation of the Church's prerogatives and material assets in many parts of Western Europe.[80] In response, the Church resorted to a range of expedients – from the sale of offices to the increased sale of indulgences – that momentarily relieved its financial situation while simultaneously eroding its moral authority.[81]

While the pressures that compelled it to adopt such self-subverting expedients were beyond its immediate control, the Church's ability to manage challenges to its moral and spiritual authority was further weakened by its increasingly inflexible response to heterodox religious movements. Whereas earlier waves of lay religious fervour had been successfully canalised into monastic and mendicant orders under the Church's control, the Church proved unwilling from the thirteenth century onwards to countenance further accommodations with lay pietist movements.[82] The establishment of the papal inquisition at the height of the Church's power in the 1230s thus marked a decisive shift from co-optation to coercion as the Church's preferred method of dealing

[79] *Ibid.*
[80] This was particularly evident in the case of the Hundred Years War, where the financial exigencies of sustaining the conflict saw a sustained monarchical usurpation of Church powers and material assets on both sides of the English Channel. On this point, see Leff, 'Heresy and the decline of the medieval church', p. 38.
[81] *Ibid.*   [82] *Ibid.*, p. 41.

with religious dissent.[83] Subsequently, the Church identified popular impulses for spiritual renewal with heresy, even when practitioners sought merely to enjoy a more immediate experience of the divine by emulating the austere lifestyle of Christ's early followers.[84] The wisdom of such a strategy may always have been questionable, but as the Church's capacities to maintain its ideological hegemony waned in the fourteenth and fifteenth centuries, it served only to radicalise religious dissenters and further heighten the likelihood of a systemic ideological challenge to the Church's authority.

The collision between the Church's ideological rigidity and an upsurge in popular piety in the late medieval period exposed the Church to the risk of direct challenges to its legitimacy. This threat manifested itself most acutely in the Lollard and Hussite heresies that blossomed during the Great Schism. Given the localised character of these heresies and their limited scope for cross-regional transmission prior to the invention of the printing press, the immediate systemic consequences of these heresies were limited. Nevertheless, they merit attention, and not merely for their significance as forerunners of the Reformation. Unlike earlier movements that had emerged when the papacy was in the ascendancy, fifteenth-century heresy blossomed in an environment of institutional weakness on the part of the Church. Throughout its evolution, a common faith had provided the ideological cement holding Christendom together. But as the fifteenth century advanced, the Church's decay called forth movements that signalled the potential transience of this unity.

The wrath of Khan: Guns, money and material transformations in the decay of Latin Christendom

The institutional decay and incipient religious fragmentation of the late medieval period substantially weakened Christendom. This deterioration was exacerbated by changes in Christendom's material foundations. Ironically, the very stability that Christendom's ordering institutions provided hastened material processes that would ultimately be implicated in its destruction. While initially restricted to long-distance trading circuits centred around urban enclaves and occasional trade fairs, the market economy increasingly permeated the Western European social fabric as the Middle Ages progressed. Medieval improvements in metallurgical techniques increased the yields of Central Europe's silver mines, raising the amount of specie money in circulation and thus further driving the commercialisation of the economy.[85] This increase in the supply of specie

---

[83] On the broader institutional and social dynamics driving the Church towards an increasingly rigid and inflexible stance over time, see generally R. I. Moore, *The Formation of a Persecuting Society: Power and deviance in Western Europe, 950–1250* (Oxford: Blackwell, 1987).

[84] Leff, 'Heresy and the decline of the medieval church', pp. 40–1.

[85] McNeill, *The Pursuit of Power*, p. 71.

money paralleled the further growth in long-distance trade in the thirteenth–mid-fourteenth centuries occasioned by the emergence of a Eurasia-wide *Pax Mongolica*.[86] Both of these processes in turn stimulated the development of deeper credit markets, dramatically expanding the pool of liquid wealth available for borrowing, taxation or confiscation.[87]

In addition to stimulating Christendom's economic development, the commercial expansion facilitated by Eurasia's brief integration under Mongol arms also enabled the transmission from China to Europe of a series of disruptive military innovations. From the mid-ninth century to the late thirteenth century, the Chinese developed a number of important military inventions, including gunpowder, metal-barrelled guns and cannons.[88] The transcontinental trading circuits that Mongol imperialism made possible enabled the transfer of these inventions to Christendom, where they interacted with ongoing improvements in European war-fighting techniques to dramatically alter Christendom's material foundations. Anticipating the early modern military revolution, some scholars have argued for the existence of a comparable late medieval military revolution, with increased recourse to projectile weapons and infantry pikemen heralding the decline of feudal shock cavalry even prior to the introduction of gunpowder into European warfare.[89] It is not necessary to fully embrace the analogy between late medieval innovations and subsequent military revolutions to accept that European warfare was becoming progressively more decisive and destructive as the Middle Ages waned. In addition to these endogenous changes in European warfare, the introduction of gunpowder artillery dramatically – if only temporarily – shifted the advantage in warfare to the offence, enabling monarchs to rapidly reduce the fortresses of rebellious subjects.[90] Simultaneously, the growth of credit markets enabled rulers to transcend the restraints of feudal warfare by recruiting mercenary armies, either with money drawn directly from loans or by drawing upon cash payments provided by vassals in exchange for the commutation of their military obligations.[91] Unsurprisingly, the commercialisation of military violence manifested itself most precociously and prominently in the wealthy city-states of northern Italy

---

[86] On the pivotal importance of the *Pax Mongolica* in facilitating a Eurasia-wide surge in long-distance trade, see J. L. Abu-Lughod, *Before European Hegemony: The world system AD 1250–1350* (Oxford University Press, 1989), Ch. 5.

[87] McNeill, *The Pursuit of Power*, p. 72.

[88] J. M. Hobson, *The Eastern Origins of Western Civilization* (Cambridge University Press, 2004), pp. 58–60.

[89] For a general argument for the existence of a medieval Revolution in Military Affairs, see for example C. Williams, '"As if a new sun had risen": England's fourteenth century RMA' in M. Knox and M. Williamson (eds.), *The Dynamics of Military Revolution, 1300–2050* (Cambridge University Press, 2001), pp. 15–34.

[90] Bean, 'War and the birth of the nation state', pp. 207–8. See also McNeill, *The Age of Gunpowder Empires 1450–1800*, p. 6.

[91] McNeill, *The Pursuit of Power*, pp. 72–3.

before spreading unevenly throughout Christendom.[92] Its uneven geographical diffusion notwithstanding, the systemic consequences of this process of commercial integration and military innovation were both undeniable and inimical to Christendom's survival.

Commercialisation and military-technological change were both derivatives of the stability afforded in Western and Central Europe by the order of Latin Christendom, and across Eurasia by the fleeting supremacy of the Mongol imperium. These processes together contributed to Christendom's dissolution through the increase in violence interdependence they begat. What little order existed in medieval Europe was owed to both religious unity and Christendom's fundamental institutions, but it also stemmed from a material context that limited the destructive scale and destabilising consequences of aristocratic violence. Medieval Europe's poverty and its technological backwardness constituted irreducibly material parametric constraints on violence that were essential to the preservation of order. Consequently, as Christendom's material foundations shifted, as warfare became more decisive and more destructive, ordering mechanisms designed to function in a more benign material environment began to diminish in effectiveness. Simultaneously, the same conflict-producing elements that had earlier fuelled endemic feuding – an aristocratic culture of existential bellicosity, a wide dispersal of coercive resources throughout the social fabric, a noble preoccupation with territorial aggrandisement – continued to operate in a more combustible geopolitical context. Neither Mammon nor the cannonball brought down Christendom. But the two working in combination did tighten and enlarge the web of coercive interactions the order was trying to contain. Alongside advanced institutional decay and growing ideological dissent, this increase in violence interdependence constituted the final degenerative macroprocess eating away at Christendom's foundations.

Christendom's decline and statements of possibility in 1500

Superficially, the foregoing portrait suggests a picture not of Christendom's decay so much as of its incipient disintegration by 1500. As it is, however, several considerations militate against this interpretation, necessitating a more detailed exploration of the forces responsible for Christendom's destruction. The first of these relates to the basic distinction that must be drawn between decay and collapse. That Christendom's institutions, normative unity and material foundations were all being corroded prior to its disintegration is undeniable. But to extrapolate from decay to collapse is perilous precisely because it risks obscuring the continuing vitality of system-integrating forces that remained strong down to the Reformation. Certainly, the fifteenth century witnessed a growth in popular heresies, but these movements did not fundamentally detract from

---

[92] *Ibid.*

Christendom's remarkable religious unity. The contemporary maxim *religio vincula societatis* – 'religion is the bond of society' – captured the universally held assumption that religious unity was central to the maintenance of temporal order, and also integral to the very identity of early modern Europeans.[93] The centrality of sacral forms of collective identity within Christendom remained undiminished in 1500, and would if anything soon radically intensify with the shock of the Reformation and the contemporaneous growth of Turkish power on Christendom's south-eastern flank.

Though greatly diminished in importance from the thirteenth century, the institutions of canon law and the papal courts also continued to function as essential adjudicatory structures within Christendom. Confirmation of treaties by religious oath remained the constitutive act in the process of treaty ratification down to the 1540s, and parties continued to agree to submit to ecclesiastical jurisdiction in the event of an accused breach of treaty terms.[94] More generally, the Church continued to exercise ecclesiastical jurisdiction throughout Christendom, preserving a pervasive legal influence throughout Western and Central Europe.[95] However imperfectly it fulfilled its pastoral functions, the Church also continued to assume responsibility for the masses' moral education at the village level, providing the only effective supra-local governing presence within most communities.[96] Finally, while monarchs steadily chipped away at the Church's assets and prerogatives, the sacerdotal conceptions of kingship they relied upon to legitimate their power remained intimately tied to the Church's political theology.

In addition to its religious unity, Christendom remained integrated by the existence of an exceptionally dense web of trans-polity aristocratic genealogical ties, along with an accompanying corpus of feudal laws for regulating dynastic succession and property disputes. The growing violence interdependence of late medieval Christendom had increased the destructiveness of war without changing either its ultimate objects or the legal structures through which it was mediated. The existence of trans-polity aristocratic webs, the institution of proprietary dynasticism and the persistence of dynastic strategies of territorial accumulation such as marriage, transfer and inheritance guaranteed a condition of perpetual conflict within the European nobility.[97] But this

[93] H. Schilling, 'Confessional Europe' in T. A. Brady Jr, H. A. Oberman and J. D. Tracy (eds.), *Handbook of European History 1400–1600 Late Middle Ages, Renaissance, and Reformation*, II: *Visions, Programs, and Outcomes* (Leiden: E. J. Brill, 1995), p. 642.

[94] Lesaffer, 'Peace treaties from Lodi to Westphalia', p. 24.

[95] W. Ullman, *Law and Politics in the Middle Ages* (Cambridge University Press, 1976), p. 45.

[96] Schilling, 'Confessional Europe', p. 642.

[97] On the persistence of proprietary dynasticism in Europe down to the late eighteenth century, see generally H. H. Rowen, *The King's State: Proprietary dynasticism in early modern France* (New Brunswick: Rutgers University Press, 1980). On the continuing salience of supposedly archaic dynastic patrimonial interests for the conduct of international relations throughout the early modern period, see J. Black, *Kings, Nobles*

very same interconnectedness also worked alongside the aristocracy's sense of a shared corporate identity to bind Christendom together.

While demonstrating signs of advanced decay, Latin Christendom was far from dead by the sixteenth century. Quintessentially 'medieval' features of this order continued to form part of Christendom's fundamental structure, belying narratives that project Christendom's demise as far back as the fifteenth century.[98] In addition to the significance of these medieval survivals, the archaic nature of the Renaissance monarchies must also be stressed. When judged relative to the frailty of feudal kingdoms, the centralising initiatives of the Renaissance monarchs appear impressive. But when evaluated against the Absolute monarchies that eventually succeeded them, the power of the Renaissance monarchies appears positively anaemic. While France had pioneered the development of standing armies, becoming the first kingdom to deploy such a force from 1445, authority and control over organised violence remained the aristocracy's collective prerogative as Europe approached the Reformation.[99] Sovereigns exercised neither a monopoly on violence, nor even a monopoly on representing their territories or entering into peace treaties with other princes.[100] To the extent that the 'new monarchies' represented an improvement over existing political forms, they did so inasmuch as the Renaissance kings were able to centralise patronage more effectively than had their predecessors. Conversely, the construction of robust sovereign states governed by a rational-legal bureaucracy was still far off in the sixteenth century.

Western Europe's centralising new monarchies certainly constituted a powerful subversive influence within Christendom, and they both profited from and contributed to the further corrosion of both papacy and empire. But to conceive of late medieval and early modern state formation as the locomotive driving the shift from medieval heteronomy to modern sovereign anarchy is empirically unsustainable.[101] While the latter half of the fifteenth century had seen a surge in state formation along Western Europe's Atlantic fringe, these processes of state formation were if anything abating rather than accelerating by 1500.[102] Furthermore, the new monarchies in the sixteenth century constituted merely one of a number of institutional forms – alongside city-states and city-leagues – extant at this time, and their unqualified triumph as Europe's modal political form was at this point far from guaranteed.[103] Each

---

and *Commoners: States and societies in early modern Europe, a revisionist history* (London: I. B. Tauris, 2004), pp. 68–9.

[98] For a variant of just such an argument, see for example Wight, *Systems of States*, Ch. 5.

[99] D. Kaiser, *Politics and War: European conflict from Philip II to Hitler* (Cambridge, MA: Harvard University Press, 2000), p. 23.

[100] Lesaffer, 'Peace treaties from Lodi to Westphalia', pp. 15–16.

[101] Philpott, *Revolutions in Sovereignty*, pp. 138–41. [102] *Ibid.*

[103] On this point, see generally Spruyt, *The Sovereign State and its Competitors*, Chs. 4–7.

of these forms also continued to dwell in an environment constituted by a combination of feudal and canon law, a factor that further retarded the evolution towards the dominance of the sovereign state and the crystallisation of a European state system.

The final observation of Christendom in 1500 that needs to be made concerns the trajectory not taken. Specifically, the possibility of Christendom evolving from medieval heteronomy to modern empire must be mentioned, if only to underscore Christendom's radical fluidity and indeterminacy at Reformation's eve. Throughout Eurasia, the sixteenth century witnessed a wave of imperial consolidation under the banner of newly ascendant 'gunpowder empires'.[104] In the Muslim world, the Ottomans, the Mughals and the Safavids each exploited the power of gunpowder to subdue local potentates and construct sizeable empires across Eurasia's Islamic crescent.[105] Similarly, the century also witnessed the further consolidation of imperial forms in both Muscovy and Ming China.[106] In Western Europe, contrarily, the papacy's early defeat of the Hohenstaufens had consolidated a heteronomous order that had persisted down to the modern era. But in the sixteenth century, the vagaries of dynastic diplomacy, the shock of the Reformation, and the looming Turkish threat raised the tantalising prospect of a Christendom united under the Habsburg imperial standard. That such a possibility was even conceivable is suggestive of Christendom's extreme fluidity in a period in which the old international order had seriously decayed, but in which the lineaments of a new order were not yet clearly in prospect.

History teaches us that Western Europe would eventually transition from the heteronomous world of Latin Christendom to an Absolutist sovereign international order. But for such a transition to occur, medieval survivals would need to be dissolved, alternative imperial possibilities foreclosed and at least rudimentary ordering mechanisms for the emerging sovereign order constructed. Christendom's decay provided the permissive context out of which this evolutionary sequence emerged. But the road to a sovereign international order was far from straight. Before a new international order can emerge, its predecessor must first have collapsed, a process that necessarily entails enormous violence followed by a period of prolonged, chaotic disorder as power-holders scramble to construct new ordering institutions to fit radically changed material and ideal conditions. As Chapter 4 illustrates, Christendom would prove to be no exception to this rule.

[104] W. H. McNeill, *The Global Condition: Conquerors, catastrophes, and community* (Princeton University Press, 1992), p. 116.

[105] *Ibid.* See also more generally C. A. Bayly, *Imperial Meridian: The British Empire and the world, 1780–1830* (London: Longman, 1989), Ch. 1.

[106] McNeill, *The Global Condition*, p. 116.

4 | The collapse of Latin Christendom

> Let no-one think that the world can be ruled without blood; the sword of the ruler must be red and bloody; for the world will and must be evil, and the sword is God's rod and vengeance upon it ...
>
> Martin Luther[1]

By 1500 CE, Western and Central Europe remained integrated within the decaying but still discernible order of Latin Christendom. By the mid-seventeenth century, this order had been swept away, its place taken by an embryonic sovereign international order. The following two chapters chronicle the story of this transformation. In this chapter, I limit my analysis to the period beginning with the Reformation's onset in 1517 and concluding with the Peace of Augsburg in 1555. My purposes here are twofold. First, I aim to demonstrate *how* the systemic shock of the Reformation, working in conjunction with processes of geopolitical consolidation and institutional decay already evident from the late medieval period, worked to fatally undermine Christendom as an international order. Secondly, I seek to explain *why* Christendom's rulers were unable to collaborate either to save Christendom from destruction or to contrive a viable alternative once it became clear that the old order was beyond redemption.

Whereas Chapter 4 focuses on the immediate *causes* of Christendom's collapse, Chapters 5 and 6 explore the *consequences* of its collapse for Europe's subsequent evolution. I argue that Europe in the century following Christendom's demise reverted to a condition of immature anarchy marked by poisonous sectarian division, pervasive civil and international war and the partial or total breakdown of centralised structures of political authority. Far from laying the foundations of a sovereign international order, the combined forces of confessionalisation and military revolution initially exerted profoundly centrifugal effects upon early modern Europe, inspiring a series of maladaptive responses from rulers that compounded rather than alleviated systemic disorder. Ultimately, the return to order was made possible only by

---

[1] *Works of Martin Luther*, ed. Charles M. Jacobs, 6 vols. (Philadelphia: Muhlenberg Press, 1915–32), IV, p. 23, cited in Wolin, *Politics and Vision*, p. 142.

a series of cultural and intellectual innovations forged during this bloody interregnum. Of these innovations, the articulation of notions of divine right Absolutism, the formulation of *politique* solutions to the problem of religious pluralism, and the generalisation of norms of mutual recognition and non-intervention proved most critical in establishing the normative complex of a new order. It was only with the maturation of these constructs that Europe's rulers were able to reconcile themselves to the transformed ideal and material context yielded by religious schism and military revolution, thus permitting an end to the disorder that prevailed in the century after Christendom but before sovereignty.

The crisis opens

Christendom's changing strategic landscape

From the mid-fifteenth century onwards, a cluster of forces dramatically destabilised Christendom. The most basic of these forces, specifically the increase in violence interdependence, has already been mentioned. Recapitulating briefly, the introduction of modern artillery into European warfare signalled a transient but nevertheless critical shift towards offence dominance on the battlefield.[2] Cannon batteries could now rapidly reduce previously impregnable fortifications, a trend that generally favoured crown over nobility and thus accelerated the centralisation of political power.[3] Similarly, the growth of mercenary companies, disembedded from their original social context and often indifferent to the political intrigues being played out within their host societies, provided the nuclei of embryonic standing armies that could be used for both domestic pacification and territorial aggrandisement.[4] Finally, the growth of international credit increased monarchs' capacity to field ever larger armies, driving up the costs of war and thereby catalysing the further consolidation of power within a shrinking number of expanding political units.[5]

In 1453, the strategic stalemate of the Hundred Years War between England and France was finally broken, with French cannon destroying the castles of the English king's French vassals and bringing the war to a successful climax for the Valois monarchy.[6] Similarly, in the east, cannon operated and maintained by Christian mercenaries enabled the Ottoman Sultan Mehmet II to conquer

---

[2] On this point, see generally G. H. Quester, *Offense and Defense in the International System* (New Brunswick, NJ: Transaction Books, 1988), p. 49.

[3] Bean, 'War and the birth of the nation state', pp. 207–8.

[4] On this point, see generally V. G. Kiernan, 'Foreign mercenaries and absolute monarchy' in T. Aston (ed.), *Crisis in Europe, 1560–1660* (London: Routledge and Kegan Paul, 1965), pp. 117–40. See also Quester, *Offense and Defense in the International System*, pp. 48–9.

[5] Bean, 'War and the birth of the nation state', p. 208.

[6] McNeill, *The Age of Gunpowder Empires*, p. 6.

Constantinople in the same year.[7] The year 1477 witnessed the defeat of Charles the Bold of Burgundy and the partitioning of his patrimony between the Valois and Habsburg monarchies, further hastening the emergence of a bitter rivalry between the two dynasties.[8] Most spectacularly of all, in the fifty years between 1477 and 1527, the successful conclusion of a series of highly speculative marital alliances propelled the Habsburg monarchy to near hegemony in Western and Central Europe. At its furthest extent, the Habsburg conglomeration would encompass approximately 40 per cent of Western and Central Europe's population, incorporating all of its great financial centres as well as both the silver mines of Central Europe and the vast silver and gold reserves of the New World.[9] The very size of the Habsburg patrimony ensured a significant increase in Europe's strategic interconnectedness, even if its far-flung nature would eventually inhibit its permanent institutionalisation.

Christendom's geopolitical consolidation occurred against a backdrop of institutional decay already detailed in Chapter 3. By 1500, the papacy had recovered from both the Great Schism and the conciliarists' bid to strengthen the powers of Church councils at the expense of papal authority. Far from reviving the Church, however, the papacy's suppression of conciliarism merely estranged it from many Christians whose spiritual and pastoral needs the Church was increasingly failing to meet. By the early sixteenth century, monarchs were already undermining the Church's traditional exemption from royal taxation, while the papacy was neglecting the reform of the Church in favour of the pursuit of its power-political interests in Italy.[10] Similarly, while the meteoric growth of Habsburg power revived medieval fears and hopes of universal monarchy, the institutional power of the imperial office remained limited. Certainly, the emperor's *auctoritas* continued to be widely recognised into the sixteenth century within the territorial confines of the empire. But the emperor's *potestas* remained almost entirely notional.[11]

Latin Christendom thus entered the sixteenth century in an exceptionally fragile state. In an environment in which gunpowder, credit and mercenarism had made warfare more costly, more violent and (temporarily, at least) offence-dominant, the institution of the feud no longer supported order but instead subverted it, providing rulers with a familiar rationale for their bellicosity in

---

[7] *Ibid.*   [8] *Ibid.*, pp. 7–10.

[9] W. Blockmans, *Emperor Charles V 1500–1558* (London: Arnold, 2002), p. 36. In addition to Antwerp, Seville and Augsburg, Charles's Italian wars with France would yield Milan (1525), Genoa (1528) and Florence (1530) to the Habsburg patrimony.

[10] On the progressive erosion of the Church's exemptions from royal taxation and the eventual large-scale secularisation of Church property even in countries that remained confessionally aligned to Rome, see J. Gelabert, 'The fiscal burden' in R. Bonney (ed.), *Economic Systems and State Finance* (Oxford: Clarendon Press, 1995), pp. 547–8.

[11] On the distinction between *auctoritas* and *potestas*, see again Osiander, 'Before sovereignty', pp. 122–3.

an environment in which feuds *qua* wars had become qualitatively more destructive than before. Equally, the interminable struggle for primacy between Church and empire had left both institutions weakened, diminishing the capacities of either emperor or pope to mobilise authoritative power in the service of order. Simultaneously, the rise of the 'new monarchies' on Christendom's Atlantic fringe, the Habsburg ascendancy, and the growth of Ottoman power called forth powerful new entities that further unsettled Christendom's ordering framework. To the extent that a modicum of order prevailed in Western and Central Europe at all in 1500, it derived from the continuing integrity of Christendom's normative complex, a complex firmly anchored in Christendom's religious unity. Even after the material context out of which it had arisen had changed, even as its ordering institutions successively succumbed to processes of decay abetted and accelerated by these material changes, Christendom's normative unity endured. It was only once this unity was shattered that Christendom collapsed.

The Reformation and the onset of Latin Christendom's collapse

At first glance, Martin Luther presents as an unlikely agent of revolution. An Augustinian monk and professor of theology, Luther was steeped in the intellectual tradition of the Church, and his ninety-five theses critiquing clerical abuses were initially intended to catalyse reform within the Church rather than precipitating irreparable schism.[12] This qualification aside, Lutheran theology nevertheless posed a holistic challenge to Christendom's normative complex, particularly as Luther's ideas matured in the face of persecution. An enormous literature has been written on the import of Luther's ideas for Europe's subsequent evolution, but for present purposes it is sufficient to note the interweaving theological, political and ontological aspects of the Lutheran challenge.

Central to Luther's critique of the Church was his doctrine of *sola fide*, or justification by faith alone. Whereas the Church stressed the importance of good works, prayer and fasting as means of securing salvation, Luther conversely argued that salvation was possible only by abandoning oneself to God's mercy and to the messages of the Gospel.[13] Having accepted the notion of God's omnipotence, Luther argued that it was blasphemous for humans to assume that they could through their own actions compel justification in the eyes of God.[14] Stressing Augustine's conception of man's essential sinfulness and his estrangement from the divine, Luther claimed that it was only through the gift

---

[12] G. R. Elton, *Reformation Europe, 1517–1559* (London: Blackwell, 1999), pp. 1–2.

[13] M. Luther, 'The freedom of a Christian' (1520) in J. M. Porter (ed.), *Luther: Selected political writings* (Philadelphia: Fortress Press, 1974), p. 28.

[14] *Ibid.* See also Elton, *Reformation Europe*, pp. 1–2.

of faith that man could again be reconciled with God and achieve salvation. Faith, rather than works, was the key to salvation, and faith in turn could best be cultivated by devoted study of Christ's message and His sacrifice as recorded in Scripture.[15] Lutheran theology thus constituted a full-frontal assault not merely upon clerical abuses, but also upon the whole moral economy of penances and indulgences underpinning Church theology.

As a corollary of his conception of justification by faith alone, Luther also rejected the intercessionary relationship between God and man that the Church had reserved for itself, arguing instead for the existence of an invisible priest-hood of all believers linked directly to God by their faith in Him.[16] In attacking the idea that salvation was possible only through the Church, and with it the justification for the existence of a separate priestly caste to mediate between God and man, Luther assaulted the most basic power-legitimating norms underpinning Christendom. Lutheranism attacked the legitimacy of the only effective supra-local governance structure common to Christendom, while also simultaneously contesting Church teachings elevating ordained officers of the Church above the laity.[17] Luther's public burning of the canon law books in 1520 represented in the most symbolic way his denial of the Church's ecclesi-astical jurisdiction.[18] In denying the authority of canon law, Luther rejected a pivotal component of Christendom's legal infrastructure, one that not merely governed matters pertaining to religious observance, but that also mediated vertical relations between subjects and rulers and horizontal relations between rulers.

Luther's theological iconoclasm found a final expression in his invocation of the principle of *sola Scriptura*, referring to the self-sufficiency of Scripture alone as the expression of divine truth. For Luther, papal claims to exercise a monopoly on the interpretation of Scripture were nothing more than an 'out-rageous fancied fable', a usurpation he condemned as unjustified by Scripture and therefore inherently illegitimate.[19] In keeping with the egalitarian notion of a priesthood of all believers and the rejection of the Church as a necessary intermediary between humanity and the divine, Luther proclaimed that access to the divine truth was directly attainable for the common believer through the study of God's Word. Far from clarifying the Gospel's meaning, the teachings of the Church served only to obscure and pervert the meaning of God's message to the faithful.[20] Only by stripping away the accumulated excesses of Church teaching and focusing exclusively on God's Word could believers truly

---

[15] Elton, *Reformation Europe*, pp. 1–2.
[16] Luther, 'The freedom of a Christian' (1520), p. 32.   [17] *Ibid.*
[18] On this point, see Berman, 'Religious foundations of law in the West', p. 14.
[19] M. Luther, 'To the Christian nobility of the German nation concerning the reform of the Christian estate' (1520) in Porter (ed.), *Luther: Selected political writings*, p. 45.
[20] Wolin, *Politics and Vision*, p. 135.

apprehend the Gospel, and thus open themselves up to the gift of God's grace.[21] In rejecting the papacy's claim to be the final interpreter of Scripture, Luther disturbed the very basis of the Church's authority within Christendom, thus portending a wider systemic crisis of legitimacy within the territories in which its writ had formerly prevailed.[22]

Given the interlocking character of religious and political power in early modern Europe, Luther's teachings held weighty implications for the organisation of political authority in Christendom. Church doctrine from Boniface VIII onwards centred on the organic unity of Christendom and emphasised the inseparability of the civil and ecclesiastical realms. The doctrine of the Two Swords held that the Church was supreme in both the ecclesiastical and the civil spheres, but that responsibility for the exercise of civil jurisdiction had been provisionally delegated by the Church to earthly rulers.[23] Opposing this vision of the civil and ecclesiastical as representing distinct but interlocking realms, Luther articulated instead a doctrine of the Two Kingdoms. In view of Luther's conception of the Church as a purely spiritual community, an invisible body of believers united in their faith in Christ rather than through their submission to a corporeal 'worldly' institution, a clearer distinction could be drawn between the celestial and the terrestrial than had existed previously.[24] In reconceptualising the Church as an invisible body of believers and divesting Rome of lawmaking powers, Lutheranism invited an identification of the institution of law as an institutionalised expression of the will of the ruler.[25] Equally, in denying the writ of canon law, Lutheranism struck at Christendom's legal canopy, further weakening its already fragile constitution.

Finally, the Reformation inaugurated by Luther contradicted the most basic ontological assumptions about the nature of spiritual and social life held by all Christians, precipitating a crisis in Christendom's social imaginary that eventually percolated to the level of the individual parish. Specifically, Lutheranism and its offshoots opposed a traditional conception of religion as magical, ritual and communal with a reconceptualisation of religion cast in an ethical, intellectual and individualistic mould.[26] In Church doctrine, the ritual of the Eucharist was held as the central constitutive experience of the Christian faith. The Mass re-created and reaffirmed Christ's sacrifice on behalf of man, a sacrifice deemed cosmically necessary to repay the debt man incurred to God with his initial disobedience at the Fall.[27] With Christ's sacrifice, a restitution for man's disobedience was secured, making possible a reconciliation between

---

[21] *Ibid.*   [22] *Ibid.*, p. 139.   [23] Watt, *The Theory of Papal Monarchy*, p. 66.

[24] Berman, 'Religious foundations of law in the West', p. 15.   [25] *Ibid.*, p. 19.

[26] P. S. Gorski, 'Historicizing the secularization debate: Church, state and society in late medieval and early modern Europe, *ca*.1300 to 1700', *American Sociological Review*, 65(1) (2000), 148.

[27] J. Bossy, *Christianity in the West, 1400–1700* (Oxford University Press, 1985), p. 4.

man and God.[28] The ritual of the Mass reaffirmed the bond between God and man made possible by Christ's sacrifice. In addition, it also performed a vital social and sacramental function. In entering into communion with other believers through participation in the Eucharist, Christians affirmed both their membership within the universal Church, and also the integrity and unity of the body social, encompassing both the living and the dead.[29]

The Eucharist – as the Church's central institution – was magical, in that it called for divine intervention in the social world through the priestly performance of a sacred rite; was ritual, in that it centred around the formulaic performance of an established set of propitiatory acts; and was communal, inasmuch as it centred around the collective remembrance and recreation of a sacrifice that secured salvation for both the living and the dead.[30] Official doctrine thus contrasted starkly with Luther's focus on justification by faith alone, his denial of the miracle of transubstantiation and with it of the need for priestly intercession in the performance of the Eucharist, and his emphasis on individual prayer and the study of Scripture as the preferred means of drawing closer to God. In challenging the accepted interpretation of the Mass, Lutheran theology compromised its indispensable function as both a mechanism of social integration and a collective means of affirming the unity of the body social. In an era in which religion was popularly understood as referring not to a privately held body of beliefs but rather to a corporeally embodied community of believers, Protestant theology polarised Christendom around mutually exclusive and antagonistic confessional identities. The Reformation thus shattered the symbolic wholeness of the community of the faithful, effecting a rupture that would ramify throughout Christendom.

In the longer term, the Reformation would produce fundamental changes in the conception and experience of religion throughout the West. In both Protestant and post-Tridentine Catholic societies, the Reformation and Counter-Reformation would together propel a shift away from embodied collective experience and towards the reflexive internalisation and acceptance of a codified body of beliefs as the primary mode of religious encounter.[31] Similarly, Protestantism's rejection of an immanent conception of the sacred in favour of one of radical transcendence would eventually prevail throughout Europe.[32] Both the conception of religion as referring primarily to reflexively apprehended beliefs and the evacuation of the sacred from the social sphere that now characterise the Western world trace their origins to the crisis of social imaginaries inaugurated by the Reformation. Critically, however, this

---

[28] *Ibid.*   [29] Bossy, 'The Mass as a social institution', p. 37.

[30] This point is drawn directly from Gorski, 'Historicizing the secularization debate', pp. 148–9.

[31] P. A. Mellor and C. Shilling, *Re-Forming the Body: Religion, community, and modernity* (London: Sage, 1997), p. 106.

[32] *Ibid.*

secularisation of international order would develop over centuries, and was preceded by the civilisation-rending trauma of Christendom's collapse and the Wars of Religion. For in the immediate aftermath of its emergence, Protestantism presented to those who remained loyal to the Church as an existential threat to the unity of the body social. Similarly, even for converts to the new faith, Protestantism in its rapidly multiplying forms threatened old certainties regarding the nature of the relationships both between humanity and God, and also between rulers and ruled. In stressing humanity's Fallen nature and the necessity of a coercive temporal order to restrain mortal depravity, Luther followed Augustine. But in departing from Augustine in his embrace of a transcendent rather than immanent conception of the sacred, Luther unmoored the temporal order from its earlier embeddedness within the cosmos, thereby accentuating its fragile, precarious and disturbingly unstable nature.[33] The new reflexivity in religious belief heralded by the doctrine of *sola fide* and the Protestant stress on individual conscience brought with it also a heightened reflexivity concerning existing political arrangements, as well as an accompanying awareness of their contingent and therefore mutable nature.[34] In their varying ways, the magisterial Reformations, the Peasants' War and the Anabaptists' short-lived New Jerusalem in Münster all expressed this new uncertainty, as different actors appropriated and reinterpreted Luther's teachings in accordance with their own religious, political and social imperatives. In place of a unified Christendom bound by a common faith and cohering within a stable social imaginary, the Reformation thus brought division, uncertainty and pervasive ontological insecurity in its train. The immediate institutional consequences of this division and uncertainty for Christendom will now be considered.

The institutional consequences of the Reformation

The Reformation carried with it profound institutional implications that gravely imperilled Christendom's survival. At the systemic level, the effects of the Reformation were entirely disintegrative, with the doctrine of the Two Kingdoms striking like a sledgehammer against the brittle framework of canon law that had previously served as Christendom's mechanism for adjudicating international disputes. The order-maintaining capacity of canon law depended on a recognition of its validity and of the Church's unquestioned authority to interpret and apply it to individual cases. In providing actors with a principled justification for rejecting the Church's authority, Lutheranism fatally undercut the legitimacy and efficacy of canon law as a mechanism of conflict management.

---

[33] Wolin, *Politics and Vision*, p. 141.   [34] Mellor and Shilling, *Re-Forming the Body*, p. 107.

At the same time as it weakened one of Christendom's few remaining authoritative institutions, the Reformation also overlaid an already conflict-prone environment with intense confessional rivalries. Certainly, the Reformation did not destabilise an otherwise peaceful international system. Processes of geopolitical consolidation had already led to a marked increase in the scale and intensity of conflict within Christendom.[35] However, in polarising Europe's polities along confessional lines, the Reformation destabilised bonds of collective identity that had previously exercised a modest pacifying effect on relations between Christendom's rulers. Admittedly, the heightened dynastic competition for power and prestige that had punctuated Christendom's dying decades invites scepticism as to the restraining influence of religious unity upon rulers' conduct prior to the Reformation. But this scepticism is qualified once the radicalising effects of confessional strife upon dynastic policies in the decades after the Reformation are considered. Christendom's moral break-down, evidenced in the interjection of an ethos of Holy War into Europe's internecine conflicts, did not fully manifest itself until after the Habsburg bid to reconstitute Christendom along imperial lines had been thwarted. However, this breakdown was prefigured and made possible by the prior splintering of Christendom into competing confessions, a process that was inaugurated by the coming of the Reformation.

In contrast to its entirely destructive effects on Christendom itself, the Reformation's impact on Christendom's constituent polities was decidedly more ambiguous. On the one hand, Luther's doctrine of the Two Kingdoms provided a powerful legitimation for rulers' monopolisation of law-making powers, thus strengthening moves towards political centralisation in polities that adopted Lutheranism. Paradoxically, the clear-cut conceptual distinction between the civil and religious spheres articulated by Luther practically lent itself to the institutional de-differentiation of Church and State.[36] For with the Church's ecclesiastical jurisdiction abolished, the prince assumed responsibility for exercising legislative, administrative and judicial powers as they pertained to the temporal affairs of the Church within his territory.[37] Similarly, the abolition of canon law entailed the secularisation of laws pertaining to a vast range of matters – marriage and divorce, wills, property, common and religious crimes (e.g. heresy and blasphemy) – that had previously been subject to ecclesiastical jurisdiction.[38]

More generally, even within polities that remained loyal to Rome, the Reformation precipitated a range of processes that superficially favoured the strengthening of monarchical authority. While Europe's rulers had long sought

---

[35] On the Valois–Habsburg rivalry over Italy, see generally M. S. Anderson, *The Origins of the Modern European State System, 1494–1618* (London: Longman, 1998), Ch. 4.

[36] Gorski, 'Historicizing the secularization debate', pp. 150–3.

[37] Berman, 'Religious foundations of law in the West', p. 18. [38] *Ibid.*

to identify their power with the maintenance of a divinely ordained social order, the religious schism provided them with further scope for religious legitimation by enabling them to present themselves as defenders of the 'true' faith, the indispensable earthly guardians of Christianity against the forces of heresy. The historian Heinz Schilling's observation of the Reformation period that 'the state became more sacral before it became more secular' alludes to the tightening of the alliance between spiritual and sacred authorities that could be observed throughout Europe as the century progressed.[39] Processes of confessionalisation, whereby religious and lay authorities collaborated in the intensified supervision, social disciplining and spiritual indoctrination of subjects, held out the prospect of strengthening the affective and institutional bonds between rulers and ruled, thereby dramatically augmenting rulers' infrastructural power over their subjects.[40] These processes of confessionalisation were initially slow to develop in the years immediately following Luther's revelation and were decidedly uneven in their geographic diffusion, but their genesis is inevitably linked to the systemic shock introduced by the Lutheran heresy.

Offsetting these centripetal effects, the Reformation also threatened Europe's polyglot composite monarchies with the centrifugal pressures of confessional conflict. Christendom's composite monarchies were defined above all else by their heterogeneity, being composed of a congeries of dispersed territories each with its distinctive laws, language and customs, and each relating to its nominal dynastic suzerain on the basis of its own distinctive terms of incorporation.[41] Given this heterogeneity, subscription to a common faith provided composite monarchies with one of their few mechanisms of integration. Consequently, the crystallisation of implacably opposed confessional identities in different portions of rulers' patrimonies posed a grave threat to the continued integrity of their empires. Protracted religious conflict threatened to generate socially inclusive and territorially exclusive collective identities within each of the constituent territories of dynastic empires, favouring local power-holders over dynastic monarchs. With the outbreak of confessional controversy, monarchs faced the real risk of local power-holders in each of their territories adopting different and opposed confessional identities, making the prospect of achieving an empire-wide reconciliation between religious parties virtually impossible.[42]

[39] Schilling, 'Confessional Europe', p. 644.
[40] On this point, see for example Black, *Kings, Nobles and Commoners*, pp. 39–47. On the nexus between confessionalisation, social disciplining and early modern state formation, see also generally P. S. Gorski, *The Disciplinary Revolution: Calvinism and the rise of the state in early modern Europe* (The University of Chicago Press, 2003), pp. 159–61.
[41] J. H. Elliott, 'A Europe of composite monarchies', *Past and Present*, 137 (1992), 51.
[42] For an outstanding exposition of the subversive impact of categorical confessional identities upon the strategies of imperial rule favoured in early modern European dynastic agglomerations, see again generally Nexon, *The Struggle for Power in Early Modern Europe*, Ch. 4.

In an era in which religious unity was held as being a prerequisite for the maintenance of political and social stability, the Reformation posed the danger of dissolving the most basic constitutive bonds holding society together. Lutheran theology challenged Christendom's most crucial power-legitimating norms, contested the validity of established boundaries between the sacred and mundane, and deranged the operation of the Mass as Christendom's central ritual of worship and social integration. Additionally, the Reformation also denuded canon law of the universal legitimacy necessary for it to function as a mechanism of conflict mediation and adjudication, while overlaying existing conflicts within and between Europe's composite monarchies with poisonous sectarian rivalry. As the Lutheran 'heresy' and its rapidly multiplying offshoots spread throughout the empire and beyond, the last of the struts supporting Latin Christendom were gravely compromised. With its normative unity unravelling, its ordering institutions decaying, and its material foundations already substantially transformed through processes of geopolitical consolidation, the international order of Latin Christendom stood on the cusp of a terminal crisis.

The collapse of Latin Christendom and the failure of the imperial alternative, 1517–55

After the Fall: The residual tug of Church and empire after Wittenberg

The transition from the medieval *Republica Christiana* to a sovereign international order in Europe was of such historical significance that it is easy to retrospectively assume its inevitability. However, a closer consideration of the tortured manner of this transformation reveals that an alternative developmental trajectory, from heteronomy to imperium, was still faintly possible in the Reformation's early decades. Admittedly, the rupture of Europe's spiritual unity precipitated by the Reformation ultimately proved irreparable. But at least down to the 1540s, the conviction persisted among many that a permanent reconciliation between Protestants and the Church was both desirable and possible. For while Protestantism repudiated power-legitimating norms sustaining the Church as the essential mediator between humanity and God, Protestants continued to affirm both Christianity's ethical prescriptions, and Christendom's identity-constitutive norms prescribing preparation for salvation as the overriding purpose of collective association. Similarly, the subversive political implications of Protestantism in the short term should not be overstated. Certainly, the Reformation inflamed popular radical and millenarian impulses throughout Christendom, as evidenced by convulsions such as the Peasants' War and the Anabaptists' seizure of Munster. But these episodes served only to fortify Lutheranism's already profound political conservatism.[43] Their ripening religious differences notwithstanding, the majority of educated Catholics and Protestants remained committed to the defence of magisterial authority, and with it to the preservation also of Christendom's rigidly inegalitarian social order.

Despite the vituperative character of the theological debate that followed Luther's ninety-five theses, educated Europeans thus continued to subscribe to a wide range of common principles relating to the character of the spiritual and social world. In Habermasian terms, the common 'life-world' of shared values and cultural givens necessary to sustain authoritative institutions had yet to completely disintegrate. Nor for that matter was the Church's failure to conciliate religious dissenters necessarily foreordained. On the contrary, the Church had historically demonstrated an admirable capacity to canalise sentiments of popular piety into institutions (e.g. the monastic and mendicant orders) that supported rather than undermined its spiritual authority.[44] Moreover, once the Peace of Augsburg had confirmed Europe's permanent religious division, the Church proved eminently capable of reviving popular religious enthusiasm among Catholics, while also collaborating successfully with temporal authorities to roll back Protestantism across large swathes of Europe in the seventeenth century.[45] That the post-Tridentine Church was capable of substantially rolling back Protestantism in the late sixteenth and seventeenth centuries, at a time when confessional identities had become firmly entrenched in the popular consciousness, is at least suggestive of Christendom's *potential* capacity to have contained Protestantism at an earlier time, when nascent sectarian divisions had yet to mature into permanent estrangements.

In addition to the residual hold of Christian universalism and the Church's latent adaptive genius, the vagaries of European dynastic diplomacy produced a third centripetal force in post-Reformation Christendom in the form of the vast Habsburg conglomeration of Charles V. At its peak, the Habsburg patrimony constituted the largest single political entity in Europe to have existed since the fall of the Western Roman Empire, encompassing the Low Countries, modern-day Spain, northern and southern Italy, the Habsburgs' hereditary stem-lands in Austria and Switzerland, a swathe of territories in what is now Eastern France

---

[43] This political conservatism found its most notorious expression in Luther's response to the Peasants' War, as articulated in M. Luther, 'Against the robbing and murdering hordes of peasants' in Porter (ed.), *Luther: Selected political writings*, pp. 85–9.

[44] On this point, see Leff, 'Heresy and the decline of the medieval church', p. 50.

[45] The magnitude of the Counter-Reformation's long-term success is reflected in the fact that whereas in 1590, approximately half the European land-mass was under the control of Protestant governments and/or culture, by 1690 this figure was only around a fifth, with the greatest Protestant reverses being recorded in Central and South-eastern Europe in the wake of early Habsburg victories in the first half of the Thirty Years War; see MacCulloch, *Reformation*, pp. 669–70.

and substantial holdings in Germany as well.[46] For a time, the Habsburgs nominally held sway over 40 per cent of Europe's population, while also accounting in the Low Countries, northern Italy and southern Germany for all of Europe's major financial centres and the lion's share of its major trading entrepôts.[47] Beyond Europe, the dynasty had also acquired substantial possessions in the New World that would eventually yield massive infusions of bullion into the imperial coffers. Militarily, the Habsburgs possessed a precociously modern infantry-dominated army composed in the main of highly disciplined pikeman and harquebusiers; this army would ultimately constitute the renowned Spanish *tercios*, arguably the most formidable fighting force of the sixteenth century.[48]

To the Habsburgs' formidable material power was joined also the considerable prestige associated with possession of the imperial title. Despite the weakness of imperial institutions, the emperor's *auctoritas* was widely recognised within the empire and, even beyond the empire itself, Europe's rulers grudgingly acknowledged the emperor's status as *primus inter pares*.[49] The very size of the Habsburg patrimony and the inevitable comparisons it drew with ancient Rome also triggered revived interest in imperial visions for organising Christendom. These visions of revived imperial unity would in turn come to fundamentally inform the policies of Charles V, who as emperor approached the task of defending Christendom against heretic and infidel alike with implacable determination. Personally devout, Charles divined the hand of God in the Habsburg dynasty's good fortune. The suddenness with which the Habsburgs had won their empire – in Europe through marriage, election and inheritance; in the New World through discovery and conquest – suggested to Charles and his courtiers that their ascendancy was providentially ordained.[50] That the dynasty's rise occurred contemporaneously with the breakdown of Christian unity and the waxing of Turkish power suggested a divine purpose in the Habsburgs' blessings: namely, to restore the unity of the Church and lead Christendom on a victorious crusade against the infidel.[51]

Blinded by the handicap of hindsight, we presume too easily that the crisis of European order produced by the Reformation yielded a sovereign international order as its necessary consequence. Given the magnitude of the Reformation crisis and the long-term impetus it gave to the consolidation of territorially exclusive categorical identities, this presumption is understandable. But the final consequence of Christendom's collapse should not be allowed to obscure the countervailing forces that first slowed its disintegration and then left open the fleeting possibility of its reconstitution in an imperial form. Throughout early modern Eurasia, the political and religious crises of the sixteenth and

---

[46] Blockmans, *Emperor Charles V*, p. 36.   [47] *Ibid.*
[48] Elton, *Reformation Europe*, p. 23.   [49] *Ibid.*, p. 98.
[50] On this point, see *ibid.*, pp. 17–18.   [51] *Ibid.*, p. 19.

seventeenth centuries witnessed the expansion and strengthening of empires; thus it is precisely the failure of Christendom to reconstitute itself along imperial lines that marks it as distinctive from a world historical perspective. The Occidental *Sonderweg* must be explained, and a fundamental part of this explanation lies in an understanding of the dynamics underlying the defeat of the Habsburg imperial project. It is to this task that I now turn.

The vulnerability of empire: Structural impediments to the Habsburg bid for universal monarchy

The failure of the Habsburg bid for universal monarchy was not inevitable. However, it was nevertheless strongly conditioned by structural impediments to imperial consolidation emanating both from the constitution of the Habsburg patrimony itself, and from the broader systemic context out of which it had originated. Turning first to the frailties of the Habsburg estate, we must begin by acknowledging that at no time in its existence did Charles's patrimony possess a common currency, a common treasury, or a common governing bureaucracy.[52] The constituent territories of the imperium were each acquired through marriage, election or inheritance on their own distinct terms, with local power-holders retaining extensive fiscal, legal and social prerogatives and privileges.[53] Such privileges, often rooted in custom and institutionalised in representative bodies originating from the medieval period, severely restricted Charles's access to the latent wealth of his vast patrimony. Imperial attempts to encroach on these prerogatives typically met with hostility and organised resistance, up to and including violent rebellion.[54] The existence of a thicket of jealously guarded privileges proved no more pronounced than in the shatter-belt of the approximately 1,000 distinct cities, ecclesiastical territories and princely states comprising the empire itself. In the German-speaking portion of the Habsburg imperium, burghers and princes had long conspired to limit the authority of the imperial office, both to safeguard their own autonomy and also to consolidate power within their own possessions. Consequently, the empire lacked a centralised system of government, depriving Charles of the institutional framework needed to effectively mobilise his resources in pursuit of imperial ends.[55]

---

[52] *Ibid.* The promulgation of a uniform legal code for the empire stands out as Charles's only substantive achievement towards developing a common institutional framework for governing his possessions.

[53] H. G. Koenigsberger, 'The empire of Charles V in Europe' in G. R. Elton (ed.), *The New Cambridge Modern History*, II: *The Reformation 1520–1559* (Cambridge University Press, 1990), pp. 350–1.

[54] On this point, see S. Subrahmanyam, 'A tale of three empires: Mughals, Ottomans, and Habsburgs in a comparative context', *Common Knowledge*, 12(1) (2006), 75.

[55] Koenigsberger, 'The empire of Charles V', p. 348.

In the absence of common institutions around which collective loyalties could develop, the Habsburg imperium remained irredeemably diverse, with the crown providing the only point of commonality shared by all of Charles's subjects. As a result of this disunity, Charles constantly struggled to solicit the political and financial support required to defend the monarchy against its enemies. The lack of mutual identification between Charles's subjects ensured that when emergencies broke out in discrete territories within his imperium, the resources needed to confront these threats were provided belatedly and grudgingly – if at all – by subjects not immediately affected by the crisis.[56] By themselves, medieval constitutionalism and regional parochialism posed impediments to empire-building that were hardly unique to the Habsburgs. However, these challenges were further magnified by the singular vastness of the Habsburg imperium, and the formidable command-and-control challenges thereby presented for a polity in which major decision-making power remained concentrated in the Imperial Chancellery, and more specifically in the emperor himself.[57] The fragile bonds of fealty linking Charles to local elites required regular renewal through imperial visitations, forcing the emperor to adopt a perpetually itinerant lifestyle at a time when the communications and transportation infrastructure then available remained rudimentary.[58] The extent of the Habsburg domains and their geographic centrality also brought them into contact with a multitude of prospective enemies that feared the Habsburgs' power, and could be tempted into co-ordinating their actions to jointly weaken Habsburg hegemony.

For all of its strengths, the Habsburg imperium was thus a sort of geopolitical Frankenstein, composed of a hodgepodge of different territorial appendages and sewn together with the fragile threads of marriage, election and inheritance. Consequently, it was arguably too big, too diverse and too incoherent from the outset to serve as the basis for a reunified Christendom. However, to these constitutional weaknesses of the Habsburg imperium must be added also the obstacles to imperial consolidation evident at a systemic level. The most basic of these was the quickening cultural and political integration of Europe's kingdoms evident from the mid-fifteenth century onwards, and the inevitable brake this imposed on the universal authority claims of pope and emperor alike. Across fifteenth-century Europe, the technology and expertise necessary to deploy fortress-destroying artillery pieces had rapidly diffused, enabling the consolidation of rival dynastic empires that could not be easily subordinated to Habsburg imperial designs.[59] Equally, by the 1520s, the development of virtually impregnable *trace italienne*-style artillery fortresses had returned European warfare to its former state of being costly, protracted, indecisive

---

[56] Blockmans, *Emperor Charles V*, pp. 28–30.
[57] Koenigsberger, 'The empire of Charles V', p. 350.   [58] *Ibid.*
[59] McNeill, *The Age of Gunpowder Empires*, p. 6.

and typically defence-dominant, thereby favouring the survival of these very same dynastic empires in the face of the Habsburg ascendancy.[60] The fitful consolidation of dynastic authority under the Tudors in England, the Valois kings in France, the Vasas in Sweden and even the Jagiellons of the Polish-Lithuanian Commonwealth consequently hemmed in Habsburg power, even as the criss-crossing genealogical ties between these competing dynasties provided the Habsburgs with opportunities for expansion. Similarly, the invention of the printing press, the flowering of Renaissance humanism and the coming of the Reformation together hastened the standardisation of distinct national vernaculars, creating further cultural barriers to imperial consolidation. It would be grossly anachronistic to equate the resulting sense of group distinctiveness catalysed by the rise of the 'new' monarchies and the strengthening of national vernaculars with modern nationalism.[61] But it would be equally misleading to ignore the increasingly distinct solidarities then developing in Christendom's constituent *regna*, and the impediments these solidarities presented to those seeking to preserve the *Respublica Christiana*.

The perennial rivalry between papacy and empire provided a further systemic constraint on Habsburg power, and one that would eventually prove fatal to Charles's mission of correcting the religious 'errors' in Germany and thereby preserving Christian unity. This is because any effort to secure an enduring reconciliation in the empire between the Church and the dissenters required the imprimatur of the papacy if it was to succeed. But for both institutional and geopolitical reasons, the papacy had grounds for resisting conciliation. At the institutional level, an officially sanctioned dialogue with the reformers risked further empowering conciliarists within the Church at the expense of papal authority. Papal intransigence on the question of reform conversely seemed to offer the papacy the best means of preserving its supremacy within the Church.[62] Moreover, as religious controversies within Germany became ever more entwined with the political struggle between the emperor and his princely vassals, a continuation of the crisis also offered the papacy a further mechanism of leverage over the Habsburgs. Specifically, to the extent that papal foot-dragging prolonged religious and political disputes within Germany, such controversies offered the papacy an additional means by which to restrain Habsburg ambitions south of the Alps.[63] This was a particularly important consideration for Rome given the pope's status as the ruler of the Papal States,

---

[60] *Ibid.*, p. 10.   [61] MacCulloch, *Reformation*, p. 44.

[62] On the papacy's inveterate hostility towards Charles V's perceived attempts to usurp the papacy as the ultimate arbiter of Christendom's religious troubles, see Koenigsberger, 'The empire of Charles V', p. 346.

[63] *Ibid.* On the papacy's fundamental disagreements with Charles V over the relative priorities that should be accorded to reform of the Church versus doctrinal clarification of the Church's teachings, disagreements which reinforced the failures of co-operation between the two rulers, see Elton, *Reformation Europe*, pp. 135–6.

and his resulting interest in preserving the Papal States' freedom within the context of the ongoing Valois–Habsburg struggle in Italy.

The vast and amorphous character of the Habsburg estate, the persistence of medieval constitutionalism within the empire, the jealousies of Europe's emerging dynastic kingdoms and the calculated intransigence of the papacy all conspired against the possibility of preserving Christian unity under the banner of Charles V. These factors do not exhaust the forces that deflected Christendom from Eurasia's dominant imperial pathway in the sixteenth century. But their combined interaction did decisively condition the dynamics of imperial failure in the early years of the Reformation, thereby guaranteeing Christendom's extinction and heralding a new epoch of European disorder.

The dynamics of imperial destruction and the end of Christendom

Structural conditions strongly militated against the preservation of Christian unity following the dawn of the Reformation. However, the dynamics underpinning Charles V's failure to maintain Christian unity can be properly understood only through recognition also of the conjunction of a series of interlocking struggles that arose out of these conditions, and that together conspired against Christendom's preservation. Charles's rivalry with his Valois and Ottoman nemeses, his problems disciplining disobedient and heretical vassals within the empire, and the long-running contest between papacy and empire for authority within Christendom all commingled disastrously following the outbreak of the Lutheran heresy to ensure Christendom's permanent division. While a longing for religious reconciliation and the spectral legacy of Roman unity exerted a powerful influence on the calculations of both Charles and his rivals, these forces would prove insufficient to prevent Christendom's collapse.

The dream of recapturing the lost unity of the Roman Empire resonated strongly throughout the world of Charles V, and it was the force of this vision as much as Charles's commitment to preserving Christian unity that drove his imperial aspirations. Ironically, however, the very legacy of Roman unity that Charles sought to recapture also fuelled the ambitions of his enemies throughout the Mediterranean, and their combined opposition to Habsburg power contributed mightily to both the failure of empire and the consolidation of Christendom's religious fragmentation. In the west, Charles was forced to contend with the Most Christian King of France, the Valois and Habsburg monarchies being locked in a contest for dominance in Italy that preceded the Reformation by two decades, and would endure down to the Treaty of Cateau-Cambrésis in 1559. As Europe's largest single kingdom, Valois France stood after the Habsburg conglomerate as the only conceivable contender for hegemony in Western Europe.[64] Finding herself encircled by Habsburg

---

[64] Blockmans, *Emperor Charles V 1500–1558*, p. 37.

territories and simultaneously desirous of expansion into Italy at the Habsburgs' expense, France under Francis I consistently pursued an anti-Habsburg policy for a combination of defensive and offensive reasons, but always with the Valois monarchy's dynastic self-interest at the fore.[65] At one level, the contest between Charles and Francis I remained deeply personal, being suffused with classically feudal considerations of honour and glory in the defence of dynastic rights. At another level, however, the struggle also represented the most violent iteration yet of a centuries-old competition among Charlemagne's descendants to claim the imperial inheritance as Christendom's pre-eminent ruler.

Beyond the bounds of Christendom itself, the dream of reviving Roman unity also fired the imagination of Suleiman I, whose armies would come within an ace of capturing Vienna in 1529, and who would thereafter pose a potent menace on Charles's south-eastern flank. Inevitably, multiple drivers propelled Ottoman expansion in the sixteenth century, not the least of these being hunger for territorial aggrandisement and a desire also to establish control over the Mediterranean's lucrative trading routes.[66] In addition to these material motives, however, the Ottoman imperial impulse bore striking resemblances to its Habsburg counterpart, deriving from a common nostalgia for the Roman Empire, and a concomitant urge to recapture its lost unity through universal conquest. So definitively was the Mediterranean's cultural unity sundered by the spread of Islam that it is easy to overlook the deep imprint of the Roman legacy for Muslims as well as Christians in the early modern world. However, as the historian Andrew Wheatcroft explains, Ottoman rulers consistently asserted their right as Rome's legitimate inheritors, and regarded the Habsburg Holy Roman Emperors by contrast as usurpers of a title that rightly belonged to the sultan alone: 'The Habsburgs believed that their duty lay in restoring "Rome" eastwards, for one of their proudly borne titles was King of Jerusalem; the Ottomans believed that it was their destiny to reclaim the Roman empire westwards, from Constantinople.'[67]

This titanic clash of contending powers and imperial visions in the Mediterranean preoccupied Charles for much of his reign, and the combined effort of fighting his Valois and Ottoman opponents there inevitably divided and dispersed his energies at precisely the time when religious divisions were becoming ever more entrenched within the empire itself. Particularly galling for the Habsburgs at this moment was the collaboration, admittedly uneven and improvised, that transpired between the Valois monarchy and the Ottoman

---

[65] *Ibid.*

[66] The significance of Ottoman mercantile motives for expanding into the Mediterranean during the sixteenth century is accorded particular emphasis in D. L. Jensen, 'The Ottoman Turks in sixteenth century French diplomacy', *Sixteenth Century Journal*, 16(4) (1985), 451–70.

[67] A. Wheatcroft, *The Enemy at the Gate: Habsburgs, Ottomans, and the battle for Europe* (New York: Basic Books, 2009), p. 6.

Empire against Charles from 1525 onwards. While it would be anachronistic to claim that the Valois kings consciously constructed an alliance system to advance an anti-Habsburg strategy of containment, the ad hoc agreements they engineered did have the effect of fatally dispersing and diluting the Habsburgs' material strength at critical times. France's co-operation with Turkey appears to have originally been conceived as forming the south-eastern lynchpin of a broader strategy designed to divert Habsburg attention and resources eastwards, in so doing enabling Francis to retake Milan and thereby strengthen his position in Italy.[68] Ultimately, French designs in Italy were never realised, and direct Franco-Ottoman co-operation was more fitful and less consequential than either party might have hoped. This observation aside, the very threat of possible co-ordinated Franco-Turkish action compelled the Habsburgs to divide their resources across multiple theatres, thereby preventing them from bringing their strength decisively to bear against any of their enemies.[69]

Aside from the direct and compelling threat that Ottoman power posed to the Habsburg monarchy, then, the larger struggle for Mediterranean dominance constituted a constant drain on imperial resources. The resource demands imposed by these external pressures in turn exacerbated the intramural struggle for power between the emperor and his vassals that was concurrently raging in transalpine Europe, thereby further weakening the imperial position. Both the Electors and the empire's lesser princelings had long resisted recurrent imperial efforts to convert the emperor's *auctoritas* into *potestas*. This recalcitrance was further stimulated by the growth of Charles's external difficulties, together with the roughly contemporaneous onset of the Reformation. In the face of escalating Valois and Ottoman pressures, both Protestant and Catholic vassals extracted significant religious and political concessions from Charles as the price for their co-operation in financing Charles's ever more expensive military campaigns. Thus, in 1526 and in the wake of the Turks' triumph in Hungary at the Battle of Mohács, Charles was forced to guarantee the security of the Lutheran faith within the empire in exchange for aid against the Ottomans.[70] Similarly, the Catholic German princes, distrustful of the papacy and keen for the moment to avoid the prospect of religious civil war within Germany, were equally insistent in demanding a conciliar solution to the empire's religious tensions as the price for their assistance against the Turk.[71]

---

[68] Jensen, 'The Ottoman Turks', p. 453.

[69] *Ibid.*, p. 459. Jensen makes the observation that the threat of Franco-Ottoman co-operation was more powerful in its consequences than the limited co-operation that did take place, and that the constraining effects of this threat for Habsburg policy in fact diminished over time as the practical limits of Franco-Ottoman co-operation became apparent.

[70] On this point, see generally S. A. Fischer-Galati, *Ottoman Imperialism and German Protestantism, 1521–1555* (New York: Octagon Books, 1972), p. 36.

[71] *Ibid.*, p. 44.

Valois and Ottoman pressures thus distracted the emperor from comprehensively dealing with the religious question in Germany, while simultaneously forcing him to grant significant concessions to the princes that further diminished imperial authority within the empire. Later, as confessional divisions within the empire deepened, they would provide the French king with an additional means by which to destabilise the emperor through his sponsorship of the Schmalkaldic League's armed struggle against Habsburg power. Even prior to this point, however, the religious problem within the empire had become hopelessly entangled with Charles's relations with other powers, including most notably the papacy itself. From Luther's *Address to the Christian Nobility of the German Nation* (1520) onwards, Protestants had repudiated papal pre-eminence within the Church, as well as any papal claims to authority within the empire itself. Luther's revelation provided a firm theological foundation for contesting papal authority, but significantly it also tapped into a contempt for the presumed opulence and decadence of the Holy See that was widely shared among the more economically backward lands north of the Alps.[72] Critically, moreover, resentment at the perceived excesses of the papal monarchy was not confined to Protestants, but extended even to those princes that remained nominally loyal to the Roman Church. The broad antipapal sentiment among the empire's princes catalysed consistent pressures for Charles to conciliate Germany's dissidents by summoning a General Council of the Church.[73] This in turn summoned the revived spectre of conciliarism in the eyes of the papacy, further poisoning its already fraught relations with the Habsburgs and thereby contributing to the policy of papal intransigence that helped entrench sectarian divisions as a permanent feature of the empire's social landscape.

The struggle between vassals and emperor for princely liberty within the empire both paralleled and intersected with the long-standing struggle within the Church between conciliarists and the proponents of papal monarchy in the Reformation's first decades. Without papal assistance, Charles had no hope of conciliating the empire's religious factions. Such a failure threatened to derail his efforts to consolidate his power both within his patrimony and throughout Christendom more generally. Conversely, however, the papacy's continued interest in suppressing conciliarism and limiting Habsburg power in Italy counselled steadfast intransigence in the face of Habsburg entreaties.[74] The papacy's hostility to conciliarism and its fear of Habsburg successes in Italy left

---

[72] MacCulloch, *Reformation*, pp. 128–9. See also E. Cameron, *The European Reformation* (Oxford: Clarendon Press, 1991), p. 104.

[73] On the disagreements between many of the empire's Catholics and the papacy, disagreements that momentarily left open the prospect of negotiated confessional reconciliation within the empire in the 1520s, see MacCulloch, *Reformation*, p. 173.

[74] Koenigsberger, 'The empire of Charles V', p. 346.

it doubly disinclined to assist Charles in securing an early resolution to the empire's religious problems. Moreover, this combination of institutional and geopolitical motivations lent itself not merely to papal foot-dragging on the question of calling a Church council, but also to intermittent but active efforts to subvert the imperial cause.

Papal hostility to Habsburg power expressed itself in a number of ways. Initially, the papacy's conviction that the Habsburg ascendancy threatened the security of the Papal States led it to support Francis's ambitions in Italy as a means of offsetting Charles.[75] Following the failure of successive anti-Habsburg coalitions in the 1520s and the 1527 sack of Rome by Habsburg forces, the papacy generally forsook armed opposition to the Habsburgs.[76] Nevertheless, in keeping with long-standing papal suspicions of imperial ambitions, the papacy failed to support Charles's efforts to restore Christendom's lost unity. Under the pontificate of Clement VII, the papacy proved intransigent in its resistance to imperial calls for a General Council to reform the Church.[77] Moreover, even following Clement's death and the belated realisation that the convocation of a General Council was unavoidable, the papacy continued to place its interests ahead of the cause of religious reconciliation, delaying the council and then stymieing its progress until the gap between Catholics and Protestants had become unbridgeable.[78] The papacy's withdrawal of its offer of troops to support the emperor in his struggle against the Schmalkaldic League, an action taken when the League possessed more troops and the outcome of the war was far from certain, constituted a final example of the depth of distrust between pope and emperor, a distrust that further doomed Christendom's prospects for survival.

The epic struggle between Charles and his enemies for dominance in the Mediterranean; the contest for supremacy between emperor and vassals within the empire; the parallel clash between pope and conciliarists within the Church, itself projected against the backdrop of centuries-long frictions between Church and emperor – the complex interweaving of these disputes served first to divide and disperse Habsburg energies, and then to distract and delay a sustained engagement with the religious question within the empire until such time as the sectarian breach had become irreparable. Without doubt, Charles's accomplishments during his reign were considerable, but have been obscured by his larger inability to preserve either the integrity of his vast inheritance or the spiritual unity of Christendom. The failure of the first Ottoman siege of Vienna in 1529, the crushing of Valois aspirations in Italy, and the military

[75] On this point, see Elton, *Reformation Europe*, pp. 50–3.
[76] *Ibid.*, pp. 190–4.
[77] D. Cantimori, 'Italy and the papacy' in Elton (ed.), *The New Cambridge Modern History*, II: *The Reformation, 1520–1559* (Cambridge University Press, 1990), p. 290.
[78] Elton, *Reformation Europe*, p. 113.

defeat of the Schmalkaldic League in 1547 all stand out as historically significant achievements of the Habsburg crown during these decades. Conversely, however, these triumphs must be counter-balanced by the Habsburgs' failure to translate this last military victory into a religious and political settlement within the empire that was consistent with imperial interests. The short-lived character of the 1548 *Interim*, which aroused opposition as much for its perceived encroachments on princely power as for its attempted reimposition of religious orthodoxy, was in its transience emblematic of the limits of imperial power at this time. Shortly following the proclamation of the *Interim*, the French King Henri II successfully sponsored a rebellion against Charles led by the Elector Maurice of Saxony. The rebellion, which was motivated more by political than religious considerations, enabled Henri to seize Cambrai, Metz, Toulon and Verdun from Habsburg hands.[79] More significantly, however, the 'Princes' War' of 1552 underscored yet again the limits of imperial power and the impossibility of bringing the emperor's rebellious vassals permanently to heel through force alone. Equally, northern Germany's almost universal defiance of the *Interim* and the continued spread of different Protestantisms signified also that the opportunity to reconcile the empire's religious dissenters with the Church had long since passed.[80] It was thus in this spirit of resigned recognition that Charles acknowledged the permanency of the empire's religious division, paving the way for the conclusion of the Augsburg Peace and, with it, the passing of the international order of Latin Christendom into oblivion.

Liberties, empires and the collapse of Latin Christendom

On 25 September 1555 the Peace of Augsburg was proclaimed within the empire, signifying an endorsement by emperor and states alike of the principle *cuius regio, eius religio*, and with it an acceptance of the empire's immutable religious division between Catholics and Lutherans. In the same year, Charles abdicated from his positions of responsibility, dividing his massive inheritance between his brother Ferdinand and his son Philip. In so doing, he confirmed the separation of the Spanish and Austrian Habsburg lines, and with it, the end to his dreams of European imperium.[81] The attempt to reconstitute Christendom along imperial lines had failed for a variety of reasons, not the least of these being the force of established and emerging demands for liberty against

---

[79] The predominance of political over religious goals in motivating Maurice of Saxony and the other Protestant rebels in 1552 is emphasised in E. Bizer, R. R. Betts and F. C. Spooner, 'The Reformation in difficulties' in Elton (ed.), *The New Cambridge Modern History*, II: *The Reformation, 1520–1559*, p. 185.

[80] Cameron, *The European Reformation*, p. 347.

[81] Koenigsberger, 'The empire of Charles V', p. 375.

Christendom's twin pinnacles of empire and papacy. The Papal States' demands for security from Habsburg dominion, princely aspirations to preserve liberties in the face of imperial and papal fiat, and Protestant demands for religious freedom in defiance of the dictates of emperor and pope alike all conspired against processes of imperial consolidation. The liberty of the Church, the liberty of princes and the liberty of Protestants together imposed significant curbs on Habsburg ambitions in the Reformation's first decades. These obstacles were ironically reinforced by the continuing appeal of universal monarchy as a model of political community throughout the lands of the former Roman Empire, and the resulting surfeit of pretenders to the imperial title that this produced. The enduring lustre of Rome inspired dreams of revived unity for pope, emperor and sultan alike, but the clash of these competing universalisms perversely served only to further entrench particularism and fragmentation as the dominant features of Europe's political landscape.

The preceding observations hint at a highly Whiggish reading of the Reformation and the defeat of Charles V, in which Protestant dissenters successfully opposed the overweening power of both pope and emperor, thereby paving the way for the subsequent spread of religious and political liberty throughout the West. It is most certainly not my intention to endorse such a reading of the Reformation, for the reality was significantly darker and more convoluted than this. With the important exception of emerging Protestant ideas stressing the significance and inviolability of the individual believer's unmediated relationship with God, the language and political concepts of the age remained decidedly archaic. Church arguments favouring the autonomy and pre-eminence of the papal monarchy harked back to medieval precedents.[82] Similarly, advocates of princely liberty most often looked backwards to established custom and feudal privilege rather than forwards to the identifiably modern conceptions of liberty that would emerge with the social contract theorists of the seventeenth century. More ominously still, while the Reformation and the failure of Habsburg imperialism had fatally undermined Christendom's dominant institutions, the universalistic visions of order that Church and empire had respectively embodied remained predominant. A host of forces, ranging from the gunpowder revolution through to the Reformation itself, had progressively corroded the normative and institutional foundations of Christendom's unity. But by the Peace of Augsburg, the conceptual innovations necessary to grasp this new reality had yet to be imagined, while the fundamental institutions necessary to secure order in this new environment had likewise yet to be constructed.

Consequently, while the Peace of Augsburg represents the tombstone of Latin Christendom, it in no way signifies the birth certificate of a modern European state system. Instead, its historical significance lies in the fact that it

---

[82] Elton, *Reformation Europe*, p. 190.

marked the decisive collapse of Western and Central European religious unity, and with it the redundancy of the legal framework of canon law that had previously mediated Europe's conflicts. With the final collapse of Europe's religious unity and the withering of its ordering institutions, West-Central Europe was soon to be propelled into a brutal state of immature anarchy, its composite monarchies unshackled from the constraints of a heteronomous order but yet to be corralled by the ordering mechanisms of a fully articulated sovereign international order. Within this new chaos, the same processes of growing violence interdependence and confessional polarisation that had destroyed Christendom would soon accelerate rather than abate, plunging Europe into another century of division and bloodshed.

5 | *Anarchy without society: Europe after Christendom and before sovereignty*

And ye shall overthrow their altars, and break their pillars and burn their groves with fire; and ye shall hew down the graven images of their gods, and destroy the names of them out of that place ...

Deuteronomy 12:3

With the conclusion of the Peace of Augsburg and the signing of the Peace of Cateau-Cambrésis four years later between the Valois and Habsburg crowns, the possibility of a return to order in Western and Central Europe momentarily presented itself. In officially recognising the empire's permanent religious division, the Peace of Augsburg constituted an explicit acknowledgement that Christendom's spiritual unity was lost beyond recall. Equally, while the terms of Cateau-Cambrésis naturally favoured the Habsburg victors, the Habsburg patrimony's division between the dynasty's Spanish and Austrian lines removed the possibility of reconstituting international order in Western Europe in an imperial form. With the struggle between Europe's two mightiest crowns momentarily in abeyance, and with both dynasties united alongside a revived post-Tridentine Church in their determination to eradicate heresy, the prospects for stability seemed promising.

As it transpired, the period between Cateau-Cambrésis and the Peace of Westphalia would prove one of exceptional violence, with the prior breakdown of Christendom's spiritual unity and its fundamental institutions paving the way for a protracted descent into immature anarchy. While the Augsburg Peace established an uneasy truce between Germany's warring confessions, elsewhere the hardening of confessional allegiances triggered a wave of religiously inspired revolts.[1] Rulers throughout Europe struggled to balance the competing imperatives of enforcing religious conformity and maintaining civil peace, with this task made more difficult by the ease with which rebels could solicit support from neighbouring rulers and internationally dispersed networks of co-religionists. The Habsburgs' political and religious ambitions and the fears these ambitions evoked meanwhile sustained a resumption of dynastic warfare

---

[1] J. H. Elliott, 'Revolution and continuity in early modern Europe', *Past and Present*, 42 (1969), 37.

made more destructive by the continuing unfolding of Europe's first military revolution. The culmination of these tendencies in the Thirty Years War – Europe's most bloody conflict prior to World War I – symbolised in the starkest possible manner the institutional and moral breakdown that afflicted Europe in the century after Christendom, but before the advent of a sovereign international order.

This chapter offers an explanatory account of the breakdown of order that followed Christendom's collapse, before then considering the cultural and intellectual innovations that emerged from the Wars of Religion, and that eventually facilitated the re-establishment of international order in Europe after 1648. I begin by outlining the structural features of the European international system after 1560 that lent themselves towards protracted disorder, before then reviewing the dislocative forces of confessionalisation and military revolution that fuelled Europe's systemic instability during this period. The remainder of Chapter 5 then focuses on an analytic narrative of the French Wars of Religion and the Thirty Years War. My purpose in exploring these conflicts is twofold. First, these conflicts exemplified in the starkest possible manner the dynamics of disorder that characterised European politics during this period, offering an ideal lens through which to consider the problem of order as it confronted European elites in the interval between Augsburg and the Westphalian settlement. Secondly, these conflicts are singularly important for their generative role in catalysing revolutionary transformations in political thought and practice that eventually culminated in the halting consolidation of a sovereign international order in Europe after 1648. My analysis of Western Europe's transition to a sovereign international order concludes with a review of Westphalia's significance as an embodiment of the compromises that finally reconciled Europe's rulers to the transformations bequeathed by the forces of Reformation and military revolution, thereby permitting a return to order after Europe's century of chaos.

The centre cannot hold: Europe in the immediate aftermath of Christendom's collapse

The insecurity of composite monarchies in a world without rules

Any comprehension of Europe's chaotic interregnum must begin with the recognition that Europe's polities at the time dwelled within an international system but *not* within an international society.[2] Admittedly, the Valois–Habsburg wars had spurred the extension of a system of resident ambassadorial diplomacy north of the Alps, establishing the rudimentary forms upon which a sovereign

---

[2] On the vital distinction between an international system and an international society, see Bull, *The Anarchical Society*, pp. 13–16.

international order could potentially be built.[3] The sixteenth century had also seen monarchs' continuing arrogation of power to themselves, with rulers appropriating Roman legal concepts of the imperial office to support their claims towards jurisdictional supremacy within their own realms.[4] These innovations notwithstanding, neither the modern concept of sovereignty nor its accompanying principles of mutual recognition or non-intervention had been properly articulated by mid-century.[5] Regardless of their superficial resemblances to sovereign states, Europe's composite monarchies did not abide by the most basic norms of co-existence characteristic of sovereign state systems, instead engaging in practices of mutual intervention and reciprocal destabilisation as a matter of course. While mid-sixteenth-century Europe was thus endowed with some of the institutional *forms* of a sovereign international order – in the form of aggressively centralising 'state-like' entities and an expanding network of resident ambassadors – these forms lacked the necessary normative content (e.g. norms of mutual recognition and non-intervention) needed for a sovereign order to emerge.

The absence of agreed principles of co-existence aggravated the chronic insecurity Europe's rulers already experienced due to composite monarchies' inherent vulnerability to subversion. One of the most acute sources of this vulnerability stemmed from composite monarchies' extensive enmeshment within transnational aristocratic kinship webs. This lattice of kinship ties produced conflict dynamics that find no analogue among the enclosed sovereign states beloved of mainstream international relations theory. On the one hand, composite monarchies' lateral interconnectedness enabled rulers to engage in processes of rapid territorial accumulation through marriage and inheritance, as demonstrated by the Habsburgs' swift rise to near hegemony in the sixteenth century. Conversely, however, cross-polity kinship ties also provided the powerful with in-built influence vectors for destabilising neighbouring rivals, as well as providing powerful conduits for the rapid transmission of political shocks and subversive ideological influences.

In addition to the vulnerabilities flowing from their lateral interconnectedness, composite monarchies also remained hostage to pervasive factional

---

[3] On this process, see generally G. Mattingly, *Renaissance Diplomacy* (Baltimore: Penguin Books, 1964). See also Anderson, *The Origins of the Modern European State System*, pp. 52–5.

[4] G. R. Elton, 'Constitutional development and political thought in Western Europe' in Elton (ed.), *The New Cambridge Modern History*, II: *The Reformation*, p. 482.

[5] Anderson notes that even the spread of a system-wide network of resident ambassadors during this period was a far from smooth and uninterrupted process, with transnational religious antagonisms seriously disrupting the development of a modern diplomatic system for a generation after 1560. He also notes that the spread of a system-wide network of ambassadors, while beginning in transalpine Europe in the early sixteenth century, was by no means complete in the early seventeenth century. See Anderson, *The Origins of the Modern European State System*, p. 54.

rivalries among the nobility. Throughout sixteenth-century Europe, patronage networks linked wealthier and more powerful patrons to weaker clients in asymmetrical relations of benevolence and obedience.[6] These networks formed the primary loci of collective identification and mobilisation for Europe's warrior aristocrats, and were only partially subject to monarchical influence.[7] Additionally, despite rulers' growing mobilisational and extractive capacities, the armies they deployed were most often assembled and commanded by notoriously independent nobles fighting chiefly to maximise their own power and prestige.[8] Consequently, any order that monarchs were able to contrive was dependent upon their ability to ensnare the various factions within their own patronage networks and balance with and against competing factions as the need arose.[9] Rather than governing above faction, monarchs governed through faction, relying on imperial strategies of divide and rule to maintain power within their respective domains.[10] When these strategies failed, which was all too often under regency governments or under the rule of an inexperienced, frail or dying king, the risk of factional infighting and the disintegration of monarchical authority loomed large.[11]

Security challenges bedevil all political communities, but the threats Europe's monarchs faced in the century after Augsburg were particularly severe. Both the absence of agreed principles of co-existence and the structural vulnerabilities of Europe's dominant political units combined to produce a uniquely predatory environment following Christendom's collapse. In order to defend and enlarge their patrimonies, dynastic rulers were compelled as much by their own vulnerabilities as by a lust for territorial aggrandisement to engage in processes of reciprocal destabilisation against one another, with the result being the mutual enfeebling of Europe's composite monarchies. Consequently, while Europe was neither heteronomous nor imperial in its organisation at mid-century, neither had it stabilised as a sovereign international order. In light of the preceding considerations alone, it may have taken an indefinite time for a new international order to emerge. However, with the further sharpening of Europe's religious divide and the progressive unfurling of the military revolution, the task of constructing a new international order became infinitely more challenging.

---

[6] On the nature of patronage as a social institution, see generally E. Gellner, 'Patrons and clients' in E. Gellner and J. Waterbury (eds.), *Patrons and Clients in Mediterranean Societies* (London: Gerald Duckworth and Co. Ltd, 1977), pp. 1–6.

[7] Kaiser, *Politics and War*, p. 8.

[8] *Ibid.*, p. 21. Kaiser goes as far as to argue that the aristocratic armies of the early modern period resembled nothing so much as 'joint-stock companies' over which the monarch exercised little direct command and control capacity.

[9] J. H. Elliott. *Europe Divided 1559–1598*, 2nd edn (Oxford: Blackwell Publishers Ltd, 2000), p. 46.

[10] *Ibid.*   [11] *Ibid.*, p. 45.

Systemic dislocative pressures I: Confessionalisation

Far from abating in the years after Augsburg, Christendom's normative break-down radically intensified in the century's second half. The religious uniformity that had once characterised Christendom had already disintegrated in the 1520s, but confessional divisions became progressively more intractable and institutionalised over time. Following its initial resistance to reform, the Church at last embraced the need for action through a raft of doctrinal and institutional changes agreed at the Council of Trent. These reforms clarified the Church's theology, distinguishing it from both Protestant heresies and from a plethora of popular religious practices the Church deemed inconsistent with its teachings.[12] Armed with this new orthodoxy and strengthened by both internal institutional reforms and the formation of new religious orders, the post-Tridentine Church constituted a far more formidable vehicle through which to 're-Christianise' Europe than had previously existed.[13]

Processes of doctrinal refinement and institutional renovation were not con-fined to the Roman Church, but were manifest among the Protestants as well. Following the victory of confessional pluralism in the empire and magisterial 'top down' reformations in Scandinavia, Lutheranism tended towards political quiescence, even as it remained steadfast in its estrangement from the Church. Conversely, Calvinism emerged from the 1550s onwards as a dynamic, well-organised and implacable enemy of Catholicism. To established Protestant propositions disputing Rome's theology and authority, Calvin added the notion of predestination, arguing that only a very few souls were predestined for salvation, and that mortals had no way of knowing in advance whether they were among the saved or the reprobate.[14] Irrespective of whether or not they were to be saved, Calvin further insisted that all mortals were compelled to obey God's laws through subjection to rigorous physical and spiritual discipline.[15] At an organisational level, Reformed Churches were to be ruled and discipline enforced through local consistories jointly governed by Geneva-trained clerics and elders drawn from the congregation.[16] These consistories in turn would be linked to Geneva via an ascending hierarchy encompassing regional colloquys of pastors, provincial synods and national synods.[17] The rigidity and intensity of Calvinist doctrine, the self-discipline demanded of its adherents, the cellular organisation of Reformed Churches and Geneva's unremitting hos-tility towards Catholicism together rendered Calvinism a formidable adversary to the Church and its allied rulers.

---

[12] *Ibid.*, pp. 100–1.
[13] See generally MacCulloch, *Reformation*, pp. 322–30.
[14] J. Calvin, *Calvin: Theological treatises* (London: SCM Press Ltd, 1956), pp. 179–80.
[15] *Ibid.*, pp. 30–1.   [16] Elliott, *Europe Divided*, p. 76.   [17] *Ibid.*

Alongside processes of doctrinal clarification and institutional reform, the post-Augsburg era also saw the emergence of the confessions as distinct cultural configurations distinguished by their adherents' adoption of mutually antagonistic liturgical styles and forms of devotion. Writing about Lyon on the eve of the French Wars of Religion, Natalie Zemon Davis goes so far as to describe the Catholic and Reformed faiths as representing two different 'languages' embodying divergent experiential understandings of urban space, time and community.[18] In their unstinting hostility to idolatry, Lyon's Calvinists repudiated the town's sacred geography of established sites of veneration, embracing instead a desacralised orientation towards urban space that diverged radically from that of the town's Catholic inhabitants.[19] Calvinists similarly rejected the 'complex, bunched and irregular' ceremonial time of the Catholics centred around different parishes' idiosyncratic cycles of feasting, fasting and festivals, favouring rather a self-consciously more uniform and 'disciplined' form of liturgical time.[20] Finally, while the Pauline metaphor of the body figured prominently in both Catholic and Calvinist conceptions of community, profound differences demarcated the respective visions of associational life that these metaphors were invoked to symbolise. Thus, Catholics remained committed to the thoroughly somatic conception of community exemplified in the shared sacral 'eating experience' of Communion, and were equally animated by a desire to purge the body social of the spiritual pollutant of heresy.[21] Conversely, Calvinists advanced a more atomised conception of associational life, envisioning the Reformed Church as a 'nervous system' communicating with and disciplining the otherwise disparate families of believers yoked under an all-city consistory.[22]

Davis's account of sectarian polarisation in Lyon is far from unrepresentative of the cultural upheaval that characterised Western Europe's religious break-up. Its significance for this inquiry lies in its illustration of the fact that Europe's multiplying religious differences were not simply reducible to doctrinal disagreements among lettered elites. Rather, the maturation of confessional divisions both signified and extended a crisis of social imaginaries first precipitated by the Lutheran revelation. Confessional polarisation brought profound ontological insecurity in its train. Former neighbours suddenly found themselves inhabiting different cultural worlds, with the common rites and rituals that had formerly bonded them to one another having been robbed of their centripetal force following the breakdown of religious unity. For Catholics, the Protestants' rejection of the Church was tantamount to a rejection of God Himself, and the community's spiritual and temporal welfare were both imperilled while

---

[18] N. Z. Davis, 'The sacred and the body social in sixteenth century Lyon', *Past and Present*, 90 (1981), 42.

[19] *Ibid.*, p. 58.   [20] *Ibid.*, pp. 60–2.   [21] *Ibid.*, pp. 63–4.   [22] *Ibid.*, pp. 65–6.

Protestants remained unreconciled.[23] Protestants meanwhile held Rome's perceived idolatry in equally low regard, and considered the destruction of 'idolatrous' practices and beliefs a divinely enjoined imperative.[24] It would be these convictions – and their corollary identification of fidelity to God with the punishment of prideful wrongdoers – that would prove so subversive to the maintenance of civil order in the post-Augsburg era.

The ontological insecurity described above fed into and profoundly exacerbated the political conflicts of the century's second half. A fundamental reason for this correspondence lay in the tighter nexus between religious and temporal authority that emerged during the confessional age. Throughout post-Augsburg Europe, confessionalisation was extensively implicated with processes of state formation, as temporal and religious authorities collaborated intensively in the religious instruction, moral disciplining and surveillance of rulers' subjects.[25] The extent of the relationship between confessionalisation and state formation varied in different countries, being admittedly more pronounced in the lands of the empire than elsewhere.[26] Nevertheless, the broad trend throughout Europe was towards the greater sacralisation of political authority, with the result being an increased tendency to identify religious heresy with political treachery, as well as a parallel propensity for rebels to justify their defiance of established authority in religious terms. Religion continued to be conceived in relation to an embodied community of believers rather than referring to a privately held body of beliefs or doctrines. Consequently, in the eyes of rulers, religious dissent was perceived as an intolerable threat to both temporal peace and spiritual salvation.[27] Similarly, where previously rebellious subjects had been content to invoke the authority of custom in justifying their defiance of rulers, the period after 1560 witnessed the formulation of radically novel theories of resistance that justified rebellion and even the deposition of established rulers as a divinely mandated imperative.[28]

---

[23] *Ibid.*, p. 64.   [24] *Ibid.*, pp. 58–9.

[25] Schilling, 'Confessional Europe', p. 643.

[26] See for example the useful discussions in J. Deventer, '"Confessionalisation": A useful theoretical concept for the study of religion, politics, and society in early modern East-Central Europe?', *European Review of History*, 11(3) (2004), 403–25; and also T. A. Brady Jr, 'Confessionalization: The career of a concept' in J. M. Headley, H. J. Hillerbrand and A. Papalas (eds.), *Confessionalization in Europe, 1555–1700* (Aldershot: Ashgate, 2004), pp. 1–20.

[27] On the conception of religion as referring to an embodied community of believers, see for example M. Holt, *The French Wars of Religion, 1562–1629*, 2nd edn (Cambridge: Cambridge University Press, 2005), p. 2. See also N. Z. Davis, 'The rites of violence: Religious violence in sixteenth century France', *Past and Present*, 59 (1973), 57–65.

[28] See for example the characterisation of Calvinism and the Calvinist movement as being fundamentally revolutionary in character in R. M. Kingdon, 'International Calvinism and the Thirty Years War' in K. Bussman and H. Schilling (eds.), *1648: War and peace in Europe* (Münster/Osnabrück: Westfälisches Landesmuseum, 1998), pp. 229–35.

Confessional conflict thus polarised Europe around competing sectarian blocs, situating even localised conflicts within a broader narrative of spiritual struggle that resonated throughout the Continent. Confessional division threatened the unity of kingdoms, the health of the body social, and the strength of humanity's relationship to God. It disturbed temporal peace and imperilled both individual and collective spiritual salvation. Confessionalisation and the increased sacralisation of temporal authority that it brought with it ensured a corresponding sacralisation of political conflict, as well as a parallel shift in the ethos of violence from one of conventional to absolute enmity. Prior to the Reformation, Europeans had largely reserved the language and practices of total moral exclusion for infidels living beyond Christendom's borders and, less consistently, for Jews living within Christendom. Europe's Wars of Religion by contrast were distinguished by the interjection of the Holy War tradition into relations across the sectarian divide, with the heretic momentarily eclipsing the infidel as the dominant religious 'Other' and primary object of collective hatred.[29] Political and social conflicts between rulers and ruled and dynastic rivalry continued to simmer during this period as they had before Christendom's demise. But now the overlay of sectarian hostility encouraged actors to conceive of these conflicts in absolute terms, imbuing them with a larger significance as the earthly expressions of a more profound cosmic struggle between the forces of God and Satan. Residual bonds of Christian fellowship had previously imposed some moderating influence on Christendom's internecine conflicts. But with confessional schism came the logic of absolute enmity, as sectarian rivals came increasingly to be regarded as ontological enemies worthy only of annihilation. This annihilatory piety would be neither universal in its operation nor permanent in its persistence. But in the interval between Christendom's collapse and the reconstitution of order after Westphalia, the fires of confessional hatred would burn intensely, inflaming dynastic rivalries and inhibiting rulers' efforts to consolidate control over the era's composite monarchies. To this already volatile mix of religious polarisation and civil disorder, the military revolution would add revolutionary transformations in both the practice and purpose of warfare, the main lineaments of which are sketched below.

Systemic dislocative pressures II: The European military revolution

While confessionalisation introduced deep antagonisms into the fabric of early modern international politics, the resulting conflicts were made dramatically more destructive through the roughly coterminous unfurling of Europe's first military revolution. The military revolution, which progressively matured over

---

[29] On this point, see the excellent discussion in N. Housley, *Religious Warfare in Europe, 1400–1536* (Oxford University Press, 2002), pp. 194–205.

the century from 1550 onwards, is understood here to refer to the following interrelated phenomena. Technologically, the military revolution was punctuated by the ascendancy of artillery fortresses, massed musket-wielding infantry, and broadside-firing battleships as the chief instruments of violence within the European international system.[30] Organisationally, it manifested itself in a dramatic growth in the size of armies, as well as a pronounced shift in their character. With the military revolution, the ramshackle hosts of an earlier era gave way to permanent standing armies composed of systematically drilled and disciplined soldiers trained and led by a professional officer class.[31] The unprecedented costs involved in establishing and maintaining such forces in turn forced shifts in rulers' strategies of resource mobilisation, giving rise to the consolidation of permanent taxation and the development of sovereign debt as key features of government.[32] The pressures of intensified resource mobilisation in turn generated radical revisions in the governance structures mediating relations between rulers and ruled, eventually producing dramatic and lasting increases in governments' extractive and administrative powers over subject societies.[33] Finally, at its end point, the military revolution contributed to the development of new legitimating frameworks for governments, with the enhanced powers of government finding domestic justification through reference to Absolutist notions of monarchical sovereignty, and international legitimacy though reference to the imperatives of *raison d'état*.[34]

In the long term, the military facilitated both the centralisation of political power in composite monarchies and the eventual birth of a sovereign international order. But in the short to medium term it exerted immensely disruptive and decidedly ambiguous effects for Europe's rulers. At the systemic level, the immediate effect of increases in the cost, scale and destructiveness of warfare was to intensify actors' sense of vulnerability to attack, thereby elevating security anxieties and further raising the likelihood of war. Within polities, the mobilisational strains induced by the increased costs of war strained relations between rulers and ruled in an atmosphere already suffused with religious tensions.[35] Additionally, given the weak infrastructural power of early modern governments, the costs of warfare invariably exceeded rulers'

---

[30] G. Parker, *Europe in Crisis 1598–1648*, 2nd edn (Oxford: Blackwell Publishers Ltd, 2001), p. 48.

[31] Parker, *The Military Revolution*, p. 43. [32] *Ibid.*, pp. 63–4.

[33] Mann, *The Sources of Social Power*, I, p. 453.

[34] On this point, see Hirst, *War and Power in the 21st Century*, p. 58. See also R. Koselleck, *Critique and Crisis: Enlightenment and the pathogenesis of modern society* (Oxford: Berg, 1988), pp. 18–24.

[35] See for example D. Nexon, 'Religion, European identity, and political contention in historical perspective' in T. Byrnes and P. Katzenstein (eds.), *Religion in an Expanding Europe* (Cambridge University Press, 2006), pp. 269–70.

abilities to pay, forcing them to adopt short-term expedients that further magnified the socially dislocative effects of war.[36] Thus, for example, in the Thirty Years War, rulers' tendency to field far larger armies than they could possibly support forced commanders to engage in the systematic plunder of occupied populations, thereby massively increasing the devastation wrought by the conflict.[37]

Finally, and contrary to established wisdom, the military revolution did not immediately favour rulers decisively over rebels. As we will shortly see, the intractability of France's Wars of Religion stemmed in part from the entrenched position of the Huguenot rebels, who were installed in a network of formidable rebel artillery fortresses concentrated in the country's south and west.[38] Similarly, it was the Dutch rebels that first introduced systematic drilling and the inculcation of a battle culture of forbearance into the training of infantrymen, innovations that enabled them to perfect infantry musketry volleys far earlier than their more powerful Spanish opponents.[39] Once it was consummated in the post-Westphalian period, the military revolution favoured states over subjects. But during Europe's century of chaos, its effects were more uneven, tending to diffuse unprecedented destructive capabilities to rulers and rebels alike. From Augsburg to Westphalia, the increased material costs and destructiveness of war produced by the military revolution would be borne by the peasantry, who would be alternately taxed and pillaged by rulers, rebels and opportunistic military entrepreneurs alike. But the political costs of the military revolution would be no less real for Europe's most powerful dynasties. By the Peace of Westphalia, the intersection of confessionalisation with military revolution would condemn the Valois dynasty to extinction, and reduce both the Spanish and Austrian branches of the Habsburg dynasty to a shadow of their former power. While it would eventually help to lay the foundations of European Absolutism, the military revolution in its first flowering helped fuel a crisis of order that gravely imperilled the very survival of Western Europe's greatest powers, underscoring once again the extreme fluidity and violence that was characteristic of the age.

Europe's century of chaos: A reprise and a preview

The foregoing survey of the forces that defined Europe's century of chaos has been necessarily extensive. I have argued that Europe after Christendom's

---

[36] See for example Kaiser, *Politics and War*, p. 15; and also F. Tallett, *War and Society in Early Modern Europe, 1495–1715* (London: Routledge, 1992), pp. 200–1.

[37] D. A. Parrott, 'Strategy and tactics in the Thirty Years' War: The "military revolution", *Militärgeschichtliche Mitteilungen*, 38(2) (1985), 9.

[38] On this point, see Black, *Kings, Nobles and Commoners*, pp. 48–9.

[39] On this point, see McNeill, *The Pursuit of Power*, pp. 128–36.

demise possessed an international system but not an international society. While Europe possessed many of the institutional precursors of what would later emerge as a modern state system, it lacked either the minimal ordering institutions or the principles of co-existence necessary for a stable international order to emerge. Europe's composite monarchies remained embedded within transnational genealogical webs and beholden to the vagaries of dynastic diplomacy. Additionally, rulers' powers within their patrimonies were limited by the influence of patronage networks only imperfectly subject to monarchical control. Within this unsettled environment, confessionalisation and the military revolution added poisonous religious division and the diffusion of capacities for destruction on an unprecedented scale. It was in the context of this fusion of fanaticism and firepower that Europe's century of chaos unfolded. The literature on this period is voluminous and a comprehensive analysis of the era cannot be undertaken here. Instead, the French Wars of Religion and the Thirty Years War will be briefly considered, both to illustrate the dynamics of disorder that characterised the period, and also to illuminate the intellectual and cultural innovations that these conflicts called forth, and that laid the foundations of the Westphalian international order.

Into the dark valley: Europe's century of chaos, 1559–1648

The French Wars of Religion, 1562–98: The main lines of the conflict

On 28 June 1559 King Henri II of France was mortally wounded in a celebratory joust to mark the conclusion of the Peace of Cateau-Cambrésis. His death twelve days later, and the effective transfer of power to his widow Catherine de Medici and a shifting constellation of aristocratic factions, paved the way for France's descent into decades of civil war and religious violence. Between 1562 and 1598, France was wracked by no less than eight civil wars fuelled by a mixture of factional rivalry, religious fanaticism and international dynastic competition. Given the complex interplay of political and religious motives driving the protagonists, attempts to characterise the French Wars of Religion as being driven exclusively by matters of faith or faction are of limited value. Rather, the nature of these wars as expressions of Europe's broader crisis demands an appreciation of the multiple and entwined motives that made these conflicts so intense and so intractable.

That noble factional rivalries were so central to France's religious wars is unsurprising given the centrality of aristocratic patronage networks as loci of loyalty and vehicles for collective action during the sixteenth century. At one level, the wars constituted a tripolar struggle between the houses of Guise, Bourbon and Montmorency for influence over Catherine de Medici and her sons, the rightful heirs to the throne. Each of these houses maintained extensive patronage networks and independently disposed of great power in the regions they respectively dominated.[40] The monarchy's modest infrastructural power made it heavily reliant on the assistance of the great families in projecting its writ throughout the kingdom. Equally, however, the prosperity and prestige of the great noble houses was dependent upon their proximity to royal power, given the king's status as *primus inter pares* and his position as the central dispenser of patronage.[41] During the prolonged period of royal weakness following Henri II's death, the three houses were thus locked in a bitter zero-sum competition for influence over Catherine and her sons. Equally, for the Valois heirs, the age was marked by repeated and forlorn attempts to reassert the crown's pre-eminence over the factions as a condition for restoring lasting peace to the kingdom.

The situation in France after 1559 would have been volatile even without religious controversy. But the spread of Calvinism throughout France – and particularly among the higher nobility, 40 per cent of whom were at one point converts to the Huguenot cause – explosively intensified factional divisions.[42] Under the Bourbons' leadership, the Huguenots demanded the right to worship freely and in accordance with Calvinist doctrine, arguing that their religious non-conformity was in no way inconsistent with their duties of obedience to the crown. After the St Bartholomew's Day Massacre and the extermination of much of the Huguenot leadership, a reconciliation with the crown no longer seemed imaginable, and Huguenot propagandists henceforth forged a theory of resistance to monarchical authority comprising an amalgam of customary, constitutionalist and religious justifications.[43] Opposing the Bourbons, the Guise household, incidentally enjoying a near-monopoly on appointments within the Gallican Church, led the struggle to enforce conformity and relentlessly pressured the king to fulfil his coronation oath of extirpating heresy from the kingdom.[44] From 1584, as it became obvious that Henri III would die without heir and that the crown would likely pass to the Huguenot Henri of Bourbon, ultra-Catholic Monarchomachs under Guise leadership themselves embraced the cause of resistance for the larger goal of keeping the kingdom free of heresy.

That sectarian hatreds overlapped with factional cleavages provides some insight into the nature of France's religious wars, but it should not be

---

[40] Elliott, *Europe Divided*, p. 44.

[41] Interestingly, the king's powers as a dispenser of patronage had significantly increased with the large-scale sale of offices to finance the Italian campaigns, a practice that would nevertheless in the long term undercut the development of a functioning legal-bureaucratic apparatus of rule in France once Absolutism consolidated itself from 1660 onwards. On the Italian campaigns as a catalyst for the large-scale sale of offices, see Q. Skinner, *The Foundations of Modern Political Thought*, 2 vols., II: *The Age of the Reformation* (Cambridge University Press, 1978), p. 262.

[42] R. J. Knecht, *The French Wars of Religion, 1559–1598* (London: Longman, 1989), p. 14.

[43] On Calvinist resistance theory, see generally Skinner, *Foundations of Modern Political Thought*, II, pp. 225–39.

[44] On the Guise household's near-monopoly on appointments to the Gallican Church, see Kaiser, *Politics and War*, p. 50.

inferred that religious questions were of purely instrumental importance to the protagonists. On the contrary, the de-differentiation of Church and State characteristic of the age made questions of religious conformity of supreme importance not only to France's aristocratic warlords, but to the broader populace as well. For the Catholic majority, for whom faith constituted the essential glue holding society together, Huguenot non-conformity represented a spiritual pollutant that threatened the unity of the body social and thus demanded eradication.[45] Equally, sectarian hostility violently expressed itself in localities where Huguenots managed to secure the ascendancy, their public advocacy of religious toleration notwithstanding. The religious passions that animated France's civil wars were intense, heartfelt and rooted in popular assumptions about the relationship between the sacred and the social worlds, and found their expression not merely in aristocratic factional warfare but also in repeated waves of confessional cleansing aimed at restoring religious uniformity through the annihilation of heretical beliefs and heretical believers.

International dynastic competition constituted the third driver of France's civil wars. The Valois monarchy's drawn-out eclipse naturally benefited Habsburg Spain, and Philip II's sponsorship of both the Guise faction and the militant Catholic League was motivated as much by a desire to perpetuate French weakness as it was to eradicate the Huguenot heresy.[46] Similarly, the limited support Elizabethan England afforded the Huguenots from 1585 was the product of equally mixed motives. With the French crown prostrate and the danger looming of a Spanish-influenced and League-dominated puppet regime establishing itself in northern France, support for the Huguenots was dictated as much by dynastic concerns to stave off Spanish hegemony as it was by sympathy for England's co-religionists.[47] Valois France's collapse radically altered the strategic environment confronting Europe's rulers, opening up a power vacuum in the heart of Western Europe and amplifying Spain's power relative to other polities in so doing. In the absence of principles of non-intervention, dynastic ambitions and anxieties thus combined with sympathy for co-religionists to draw external powers into a series of interventions that further prolonged France's agonies and exacerbated the ensuing carnage.

The French Wars of Religion as an expression of systemic disorder

The multiple motives that drove the French Wars of Religion illuminate the broader complexities underpinning Europe's century of chaos. Confessional polarisation did not banish considerations of factional advantage or dynastic

---

[45] Davis, 'The rites of violence', p. 57.
[46] Anderson, *The Origins of the Modern European State System*, p. 169.
[47] Elliott, *Europe Divided*, pp. 208–10. See also S. Doran, *England and Europe in the Sixteenth Century* (London: Macmillan Press Ltd, 1999), pp. 95–101.

aggrandisement from actors' strategic calculations. But sectarian divisions did inject a level of venom into these conflicts that made attempts at reconciliation exceptionally difficult to effect. For the duration of the French wars, the Valois household sought unsuccessfully to manage these passions through oscillating strategies of coercion and conciliation. The failure of both of these strategies not only illustrates the weakness of central authority in France at the time, but also provides an insight into the nature of the larger environment within which Europe's wars of religion played out.

Throughout France's wars, the Huguenots pressed the king to grant them freedom to worship in Calvinist enclaves in exchange for their obedience, with these liberties to be underwritten by the maintenance of armed Huguenot strongholds within these safe havens. Catholics by contrast identified any concession to the Huguenots as an invitation to disunity and a betrayal of the king's sacred obligation to eradicate heresy. Given the irreconcilability of these positions, Catherine initially sought to transcend sectarian positions by cultivating a bi-confessional basis of support based on the nobility's common bonds of traditional fealty to the monarch. However, from 1572 onwards, the Valois court lurched towards a strategy of repression that culminated in the St Bartholomew's Day Massacre. The massacre in Paris and accompanying pogroms throughout the country eliminated much of the Huguenot leadership and permanently arrested Calvinism's spread throughout the higher nobility.[48] Nevertheless, in spite of the crown's short-term tactical successes, the strategic goal of restoring peace to the realm remained unmet, with the newly radicalised Huguenots fighting on to extort enduring concessions from the crown in the 1598 Edict of Nantes.

The Huguenots' durability in the face of repression is explicable by reference to three factors that speak more broadly to both the weakness of composite monarchies and the absence of international order in sixteenth-century Europe. First, Huguenot resilience was facilitated both by the trans-polity character of the Huguenots' support base, and by the mobilisational structures they were able to construct by synthesising the strengths of aristocratic patronage networks with those of a bureaucratically organised and internationally oriented system of Church government. From the outset, the Huguenots enjoyed ideological and organisational ties to confessional allies beyond France. Ideologically, the Huguenots drew their inspiration from Calvin's Godly Commonwealth in Geneva. A Protestant French exile, Calvin's life-long mission was the evangelisation of his homeland, and in the precociously developed printing industries of Geneva and Berne he found an ideal vehicle through which to direct a steady stream of theology and propaganda to prospective converts in France.[49]

[48] Elliott, *Europe Divided*, p. 149.

[49] R. M. Kingdon, *Geneva and the Coming of the Wars of Religion in France, 1555–1563* (Geneva: Droz, 1956), p. 93.

Throughout France's Wars of Religion, Geneva served as the Calvinist movement's spiritual and intellectual epicentre, an academy for training and despatching Calvinist missionaries having been established there as early as 1559.[50]

It was from Geneva-trained missionaries that the Huguenots derived much of their ecclesiastical and intellectual leadership. As part of a conscious strategy of proselytisation, the Genevan Academy had also successfully targeted for conversion members of the French high nobility, in the understanding that, upon converting, a noble would usually bring with him his networks of clients and dependants.[51] In so doing, the Huguenots were able to construct a highly effective apparatus of rebellion, synthesising the ideological power of an internationally trained cadre of clerics with the military power of converted noble families. This dualistic character of the Huguenot leadership found its expression also in the hybrid organisational form of French Calvinist networks. The elaborate web of kinship ties and patron-client relationships within which Huguenot nobles were enmeshed provided a powerful source of political and military power that they routinely tapped throughout the Wars of Religion.[52] Overlaying this informal structure lay a system of Church government that organised France's scattered Calvinists under a governance structure comprising a national synod, provincial synods, regional colloquys of pastors and local churches with accompanying consistories.[53] This hybrid structure – built on pre-existing kinship and patronage ties and fortified by an internationally sponsored Church bureaucracy – provided the Huguenots with truly formidable organisational capacities that sustained them throughout France's religious wars.

As well as the organisational advantages mentioned above, the Huguenot cause was aided by the absence of norms of non-intervention, and also by France's pervasive permeation by aristocratic ties linking it to other polities. Both of these factors ensured extensive foreign involvement in France's religious wars, including the provision of sympathy and support for the Huguenot cause. Thus, for example, from the 1570s, the Huguenots enjoyed a symbiotic relationship with Dutch Calvinist rebels revolting against Philip II in the Spanish Netherlands, with familial connections between the Huguenot leader Coligny and the Dutch rebel leader William of Orange working to further fortify pre-existing religious sympathies between the two rebel movements.[54] Equally, both Huguenot and Dutch rebels also received intermittent assistance from

---

[50] *Ibid.* See also Knecht, *The French Wars of Religion*, p. 7.

[51] Knecht, *The French Wars of Religion*, p. 14.

[52] On this point, see Koenigsberger, 'The organization of revolutionary parties in France and the Netherlands', p. 337.

[53] R. M. Kingdon, 'The political resistance of the Calvinists in France and the Low Countries', *Church History*, 27(3) (1958), 222.

[54] Elliott, *Europe Divided*, p. 199.

Elizabethan England and the Palatinate.[55] This international assistance – in the form of soldiers, subsidies, sanctuary for exiles and occasionally even direct military support – further fortified Huguenot resolve in the face of royal power.

Finally, the Huguenots also benefited from the opening stages of the military revolution, which in France initially favoured rebels over rulers. Despite the advances in political centralisation realised by Europe's renaissance monarchies, the aristocracy continued to exercise a collective monopoly on the use of violence in the sixteenth century, and great noble houses such as the Bourbons could summon significant coercive power through mobilising their extensive networks of clients.[56] Moreover, by the onset of the French wars, the nobility were additionally able to recruit and field larger armies than before by exploiting the burgeoning market for mercenary armies then extant throughout Europe. Consequently, France's feuding private armies were no longer limited in size or destructive capacity by the resources inhering in aristocratic kinship and patronage networks. Instead, resources indigenous to France could now be augmented by resources derived from an international mercenary market, thereby prolonging the conflict and magnifying its destructive consequences.

Not only did the ongoing commercialisation of military violence indiscriminately aid rebels as well as rulers, but the Huguenots additionally benefited from the sixteenth-century revolution in fortress design that had yielded the virtually impregnable *trace italienne* artillery fortress. Throughout the 'Huguenot crescent' of south-western France, Calvinism endured after the St Bartholomew's Day Massacre in no small part due to the formidable defensive advantages conferred by the rebels' possession of a string of fortified towns and artillery fortresses.[57] This archipelago of fortified positions provided the Huguenots with critical territorial footholds, which in the most famous instance (La Rochelle) could be supplied by sea with the help of an international network of seaborne co-religionists.[58] Consequently, in spite of a string of indecisive battlefield victories, neither the monarchy nor the Guise faction could overcome the Huguenots' entrenched positions, making outright military victory and the forcible imposition of confessional conformity impossible.

For the foregoing reasons, repression failed to resolve France's domestic turmoil. Conversely, however, for similar reasons a strategy of conciliation with the Huguenots also proved difficult to implement. For the duration of the conflict, the Catholic majority opposed any concession to the Huguenots as a concession to heresy and a sin against God. In Catholic propaganda, Huguenots were depicted as 'unclean' spiritual pollutants, to be cleansed from the body social through sacredly mandated purgative violence. Thus,

---

[55] G. Murdock, *Beyond Calvin: The intellectual, political, and cultural world of Europe's Reformed Churches* (London: Palgrave Macmillan, 2004), pp. 48–51.

[56] Elliott, *Europe Divided*, p. 46.   [57] Black, *Kings, Nobles and Commoners*, pp. 48–9.

[58] *Ibid.*, p. 49.

a Leaguer propagandist enjoined his co-religionists to the indiscriminate slaughter of Huguenots, arguing that French unity could be restored only by 'cutting off this rotten member whose stench has infected, infects, and will infect, if it is not completely separated from the others'.[59] With the unity of the body social imperilled by heresy, Christianity's preoccupation with the struggle between the forces of God and Satan was now recruited to the task of legitimising violence against confessional enemies. Previously, violence within Christendom had been corralled, however imperfectly, by the constraints of just-war doctrine and by the broader religious injunctions against violence articulated by the Church. But in the heat of confessional rivalry, these ethical constraints dissolved, to be substituted by an ethos of Holy War that mandated the use of unlimited violence against demonised and dehumanised confessional Others.[60]

The intractability of sectarian hostilities emboldened the Guise and their clients to implacably oppose all royal attempts to negotiate a *politique* compromise to the conflict. In 1576, and again from 1584 onwards, Catholic opposition to both Calvinism and sectarian conciliation was channelled primarily through the Catholic League. Like the Huguenots, ultra-Catholics enjoyed a surfeit of international connections that strengthened their will and capacity to fight continuously to advance their religious and political interests. Throughout its existence, the League drew its spiritual inspiration from Rome and remained heavily dependent upon the Spanish Habsburgs for financial and military support.[61] The conclusion in December 1584 of the Treaty of Joinville between the League and Philip II, in which both parties resolved to assist one another in preserving the Catholic character of the French monarchy and in extirpating heresy from both France and the Spanish Netherlands, provides a particularly stark illustration of both the power of France's internationally allied religious factions and the inability of the French crown to effectively discipline same. With Henri III's death in 1589 and the imminent succession of the Protestant Henri de Bourbon as his nearest legal heir, the alliance between French ultra-Catholics and foreign entities became only more pronounced, and manifested itself in sustained military interventions by Catholic powers to scotch Henri's disputed succession.[62] The

---

[59] D. M. Leonardo, '"Cut off this rotten member": The rhetoric of sin, heresy and disease in the ideology of the French Catholic League', *Catholic Historical Review*, 88(2) (2002), 252–3.

[60] On this point, see for example Housley, *Religious Warfare in Europe*, p. 198.

[61] Koenigsberger, 'The organization of revolutionary parties', p. 346.

[62] In addition to providing the League with massive financial subsidies, Spain directly supported it by landing forces in Brittany, invading Languedoc and launching no less than four offensives from the Spanish Netherlands against Huguenot forces stationed in northern France. Similarly, and again with the help of Spanish subsidies, the Duke of Savoy occupied parts of Provence, while the papacy sent an army of 10,000 soldiers to fight alongside the League in 1591–2. G. Parker, 'The Dutch revolt and the polarization of international politics' in G. Parker and L. M. Smith (eds.), *The General Crisis of the Seventeenth Century* (London: Routledge and Kegan Paul, 1978), pp. 63–4.

facility with which local ultra-Catholics were so able to tap the resources of the international Counter-Reformation in prosecuting their conflicts against both Huguenots and crown provides further insight into the obstacles impeding a *politique* solution to France's conflicts.

Given the notorious independence of France's well-armed and internationally allied aristocratic factions, and given also the chaotic environment of confessional schism and dynastic intrigue within which France's civil wars unfolded, it is unsurprising that the challenge of re-establishing monarchical power proved insurmountable for over three decades following Henri II's demise. To the perennial challenges of governing through rather than above aristocratic faction, the Reformation and the military revolution added the centrifugal influences of unbridgeable confessional division and the diffusion of enhanced destructive capabilities to rulers and rebels alike. Added to this, the absence of norms of non-intervention and the presence of ties of blood and belief linking factional warlords to foreign allies ensured the rapid escalation, internationalisation and prolongation of France's conflicts. With Christendom vanquished and the prospect of a Habsburg imperium also foreclosed, any successor order in Western Europe was always likely to take the form of a sovereign state system. Nevertheless, for this transition to occur, robust sovereign states would need to be built, a task that required the prior imagining of sovereignty as a social construct. The anarchic conditions confronting France's monarchs in the late sixteenth century hardly provided a propitious context for state-building. But they did provide an ideal context for the development of the conceptual foundations upon which the Absolutist state would subsequently be assembled.

Anticipating Absolutism: The birth of sovereignty and the end of the French Wars of Religion

With Henri of Bourbon's conversion to Catholicism in 1594 and his subsequent granting of limited toleration to Huguenots with the 1598 Edict of Nantes, France's seemingly interminable agonies were brought to a close. While France did not remain free from internal religious violence in the seventeenth century, the monarchy's new-found strength proved sufficient to prevent a return to the anarchy that had punctuated the Valois dynasty's dying decades. Indeed, so comprehensively did France recover from the religious wars that within a century a concert of powers would only narrowly defeat Louis XIV's bid for European hegemony. At the heart of this transformation lay a revolution in the conceptualisation of religious and political power, one that would undergird the formation of a new order first within France and then subsequently throughout Europe as a whole.

The ideological revolution was of course Jean Bodin's formulation of a recognisably modern theory of state sovereignty. While royal propagandists had long drawn from principles of Roman law to assert that the king acts as emperor within his own realm, it was in Bodin's writings that modern notions of sovereignty first received systematic expression. Bodin's notion that there can be no order without an orderer, and that that orderer must be absolute in their authority, was in hindsight an understandable response to the turmoil of the French wars. Nevertheless, the timeliness of Bodin's theory should detract from neither its novelty nor its enduring significance. In the context of this inquiry, the implications of Bodin's theory for prevailing conceptions of law, violence, religion and the relationships of each to monarchical authority deserve particular attention. Turning first to law, Bodin's conception of sovereignty was distinguishable by its emphasis on the centrality of legislative power as the constitutive act that defines the sovereign.[63] Whereas previous conceptions of monarchical power had placed great emphasis on the crown's adjudicatory function, Bodin instead invested law-making as the sovereign's defining prerogative.[64] Thus, the sovereign was said to replicate in his law-making powers God's creative role in ordering the universe out of chaos by the exercise of divine command.[65]

Bodin's conception of law as sovereign command was critical as an attack on theories of mixed government that both Huguenots and Leaguers had exploited in justifying rebellion against the crown. In investing sole legislative power in the sovereign, Bodin's theory wrong-footed the justifications previously advanced by feuding aristocrats in subverting the monarchy and plunging France into civil strife. While the sovereign was obliged to act within the confines of custom, divine natural law and the fundamental customs of the kingdom, the unprecedented arrogation of law-making powers to the crown necessarily carried weighty implications also for the control of violence within and beyond the kingdom. Bodinian sovereignty did not directly call for the monarch's monopolisation of the means of violence, but the sovereign's ordering function implied a harnessing of aristocratic violence towards the realisation of the sovereign's will. Given the crucial centripetal role Bodin assigned to the sovereign power, neither feudal 'self-help' nor confessional 'Holy War' justifications for aristocratic violence could be admitted where such prerogatives clashed with the objective of maintaining political and social

---

[63] See for example J. Bodin, *The Six Books of the Commonwealth* (Oxford: Basil Blackwell, 1956), p. 35, where Bodin characterises law as a social institution as follows: 'Law is nothing else than the command of the sovereign in the exercise of his personal power.'

[64] *Ibid.* See also J. H. Burns, 'The idea of Absolutism' in J. Miller (ed.), *Absolutism in Seventeenth Century Europe* (London: Macmillan, 1990), p. 27.

[65] On this point, see N. O. Keohane, *Philosophy and the State in France: The Renaissance to the Enlightenment* (Princeton University Press, 1980), pp. 70–1.

order.[66] In this regard, Bodinian sovereignty provided a crucial ideological justification for rulers' rationalisation and centralisation of violence once Europe's religious wars ended.

Finally, Bodin's theory of sovereignty opened the way for a *politique* reformulation of the relationship between religion and political authority. Bodinian sovereignty admittedly drew heavily upon existing sacerdotal conceptions of kingship.[67] But in identifying the maintenance of social order as the sovereign's *raison d'être*, Bodinian sovereignty permitted a reassessment of the formerly axiomatic identification of religious dissent with political treason. Certainly, the *politique* thinkers who followed Bodin and who rationalised the crown's accommodation of the Huguenots in no way embraced religious toleration as a positive ideal, preferring to regard it instead as a regrettable (and hopefully temporary) expedient necessitated by the categorical imperative of securing the civil peace.[68] But in locating sovereignty in the will of the monarch, and in identifying submission to the sovereign's will as the subject's primary moral obligation, Bodin at least admitted the possibility of the existence of the loyal and obedient heretical subject. In so doing, Bodin's theory of sovereignty anticipated the re-conceptualisation of religion – from an embodied community of believers to a privately held body of beliefs – that would ultimately enable the genesis of a sovereign state system and with it a resolution to Europe's century of crisis.

None of the foregoing is intended to imply that Bodin's theory was by itself sufficient to bring an end to France's Wars of Religion. Still less do I maintain that Absolutist theory unproblematically begat corresponding practices and institutions.[69] Nevertheless, Michael Walzer's observation, that the state 'must be personified before it can be seen, symbolized before it can be loved, imagined before it can be conceived', remains apposite.[70] With the formulation in France of a modern theory of sovereignty – a development that arose as a direct response to the turmoil of the French religious wars – the first lineaments of a sovereign international order begin to be discernible. Tragically, it would require a catastrophe of even greater magnitude before the construct of

---

[66] On the significance of both customary and confessional justifications for rebellion against monarchical authority for the French Huguenots, see Skinner, *Foundations of Modern Political Thought*, II, pp. 325–6.

[67] Bodin, *The Six Books of the Commonwealth*, pp. 40–2. See also Keohane, *Philosophy and the State in France*, pp. 70–1.

[68] On this point, see for example W. F. Church, *Richelieu and Reason of State* (Princeton University Press, 1972), p. 53.

[69] The dissonance between the theory of Absolutism and its actual practice has been masterfully laid bare in N. Henshall, *The Myth of Absolutism: Change and continuity in early modern European monarchy* (London: Longman, 1992). See also generally Black, *Kings, Nobles and Commoners*.

[70] Walzer, 'On the role of symbolism in political thought', p. 194.

sovereignty could be further elaborated and redeployed as an ordering arrangement at a systemic level.

The Thirty Years War and the crisis of European political order

The main contours of the conflict

Much like the French Wars of Religion, the causes of the Thirty Years War have been the subject of considerable debate. Traditional interpretations of the conflict stressed its German and religious character. The war was thus portrayed as essentially a contest between an aspiring Absolutist Counter-Reformation monarch and a coalition of princes fighting to preserve and if possible extend their religious and political liberties, with opportunistic outsiders weighing in on either side to advance their own agendas.[71] More recent analyses have conversely emphasised the conflict's European character and accorded greater primacy to dynastic over religious motives in animating the protagonists.[72] The literature on the 'general crisis' of the seventeenth century provides yet a third lens for comprehending the conflict. This perspective emphasises the common causes of Eurasia's crises of authority in this period, stressing the importance of adverse climatological changes, reduced crop yields and over-population in catalysing revolts throughout the Eurasian ecumene.[73] Although this last perspective is the most general in its application, it nevertheless serves as a useful reminder that the Thirty Years War constituted but one expression of a larger crisis that was hemispheric in its scope.[74]

Fortunately, it is not necessary here to adjudicate between these frameworks. In reality, the conflict was sufficiently complex that it can only be adequately understood by briefly canvassing all dimensions that are emphasised in these contrasting narratives. Turning first to the conflict's German dimension, the clash between Ferdinand and the princes bears resemblances to the earlier struggle between Charles V and the princes waged almost a century earlier. This parallel is to be expected, given the continuing deterioration of imperial

---

[71] On the German-centred character of traditional accounts of the conflict, see N. M. Sutherland, 'The origins of the Thirty Years War and the structure of European politics', *The English Historical Review*, 107(424) (1992), 587.

[72] *Ibid.*, p. 588.

[73] See for example the collection of essays, both critical and supportive of the 'general crisis' thesis, contained in G. Parker and L. M. Smith (eds.), *The General Crisis of the Seventeenth Century* (London: Routledge and Kegan Paul, 1978). Jack Goldstone's interpretation of the underlying causes of revolution and rebellion in the early modern world is also consistent with this approach. See generally J. Goldstone, *Revolution and Rebellion in the Early Modern World* (Berkeley: University of California Press, 1991).

[74] Parker's discussion of the eco-demographic underpinnings of crises across Eurasia, including a very useful map depicting outbreaks of war and rebellion during this period, offers a useful précis of the broad argument informing the 'general crisis' position. See Parker, *Europe in Crisis*, pp. 1–10.

institutions in the decades following the Augsburg Peace, together with the range of outstanding disputes flowing from that settlement. For while the Augsburg Peace bought Germany over six decades of Peace, it failed to resolve many of the religious and constitutional issues dividing the empire. Although the emperor retained nominal suzerainty over the approximately 1,000 territories constituting the 'Holy Roman Empire of the German Nation', effective territorial jurisdiction resided with the burghers, bishops and princes of Germany's petty states and cities.[75] Admittedly, these petty states existed under a penumbra of shared imperial institutions – the Circles, responsible for regional defence; the Supreme Court, charged with adjudicating disputes between rulers; and the Diet, responsible for approving taxation and legislation for the whole empire.[76] But accumulating religious tensions had further corroded these already fragile institutions in the decades after Augsburg. In recognising the principle *cuius regio, eius religio*, the Augsburg Peace had further strengthened processes of confessionalisation within the empire, with popular loyalties and social practices becoming increasingly governed by the dogma, rites, norms and laws formulated and policed by integrated State–Church complexes.[77] By the seventeenth century, mutually antagonistic Lutheran, Calvinist and post-Tridentine Catholic identities had thus become deeply ingrained within Germany's social fabric, enervating imperial institutions and imperilling the prospects for continued peace.

The interlocking processes of petty-state formation, intensified social disciplining and the confessionalisation facilitated by the Augsburg Peace enhanced political and cultural integration within Germany's petty states, but at the expense of promoting further political and cultural disintegration within the empire as a whole. In this respect, the Augsburg Peace contained the seeds of its own destruction, even without considering the emperor's refusal to extend toleration to Calvinism within the empire. From the 1600s onwards, the Catholic states' dominance of the Supreme Court and Diet triggered further estrangement between the emperor and the Protestant princes.[78] Without adequate constitutional means of venting their grievances, the Protestants established a collective self-defence league – the Evangelical Union – in 1608, a move mirrored one year later with the formation of the Catholic League.[79] From this point onwards, a renewal of religious war in Germany was already likely, an outcome that was further assured by the Jesuit-trained Ferdinand III's

---

[75] *Ibid.*, p. 61.   [76] *Ibid.*, p. 62.
[77] On this process, see generally H. Schilling, 'Confessionalisation in Europe: Causes and effects for church, state, society and culture' in Bussman and Schilling (eds.), *1648: War and peace in Europe*; and also W. Reinhard, 'Pressures towards confessionalization? Prolegomena to a theory of the confessional age' in S. Dixon (ed.), *The German Reformation: The essential readings* (Oxford: Blackwell Publishers Ltd, 1999), pp. 169–92.
[78] Parker, *Europe in Crisis*, p. 62.   [79] *Ibid.*, p. 63.

election to the imperial dignity in August 1619. by Ferdinand's election to the throne, the familiar collision between a centralising emperor and an intransigent coalition of princes played itself out again, only with far greater intensity and for far longer than had been the case in the time of Charles V.

The constitutional struggle between emperor and princes provided the immediate context for the war and its proximate trigger, but the conflict was entwined also within a larger struggle for European supremacy between the Habsburg bloc and its rivals. Geoffrey Parker observes that, by the early 1600s, Europe had become polarised between a Counter-Reformation axis – dominated by Habsburg Spain and encompassing Madrid, Brussels, Munich, Vienna and Rome – and an eclectic coalition united by little more than their opposition to Habsburg power.[80] Once again in an echo of the past, France would ultimately emerge as the Habsburgs' most formidable rival. Nevertheless, this would occur only after a period of equivocation during Louis XIII's minority, and then only after the defeat of renewed Huguenot rebellions and Cardinal Richelieu's assertion of foreign-policy dominance over the ultra-Catholic *devots* faction at Louis's court.[81] Alarmed at Ferdinand's initial triumphs over the German Protestants, first Denmark and then Sweden intervened in the German war both to defend Lutheranism and to advance their own geopolitical interests in the Baltic basin and in Germany.[82] Finally, the Thirty Years War was punctuated by a resumption of the war between Spain and Holland, with the Dutch harrying Spain both in Europe and in the New World.[83]

The Thirty Years War thus constituted a German religious and constitutional conflict embedded within a larger and more enduring struggle for power between the Habsburg family conglomerate and its many rivals. These intertwined conflicts were themselves anchored within a larger hemispheric crisis of political authority, driven by institutional frailties intersecting with the eco-demographic factors alluded to previously. Between 1450 and 1600, it is estimated that Europe's population may have doubled.[84] This demographic expansion reflected generally buoyant economic conditions throughout the Eurasian ecumene, and paralleled processes of political consolidation manifest across the hemisphere during this period.[85] Conversely, from the late 1620s onwards the European economy experienced a severe cyclical downturn. This downturn was disastrously exacerbated by climatological changes that brought

---

[80] Parker, 'The Dutch revolt and the polarization of international politics', p. 66.
[81] Church, *Richelieu and Reason of State*, pp. 87–8.
[82] S. J. Lee, *The Thirty Years War* (London: Routledge, 1991), pp. 14–15.
[83] Parker, 'The Dutch revolt and the polarization of international politics', p. 68. See also Parker, *Europe in Crisis*, p. 111.
[84] Parker, *Europe in Crisis*, p. 5.
[85] On the early modern period as a Eurasia-wide period of commercial growth and political consolidation, see Bayly, *Imperial Meridian*, p. 16.

declining temperatures, reduced harvesting times, lower crop yields and ultimately a reduction in Europe's food supply.[86] Coming at a time of pervasive conflict, when rulers were already lifting taxes and debasing currencies in an effort to mobilise a greater percentage of resources from stagnant or shrinking economies, this exogenous shock precipitated a chain of crises throughout Eurasia. In Europe alone, the 1640s witnessed revolts or revolutions in Scotland, Ireland, England, France, Portugal, Spain, Sicily, Naples, Austria, the Polish Commonwealth and Muscovy.[87] Further afield, the *celali* revolts in the Ottoman Empire, the Ming dynasty's collapse in China, the rebellion against Mughal power in India and even the Kyushu rebellion in Japan betray through their very synchronicity the broader Eurasian dimension of the crisis that roiled Europe at the time of the Thirty Years War.[88]

To summarise: the proximate catalysts for the Thirty Years War lay in constitutional and religious controversies within Germany, the origins of which lay in tensions between the imperial office and princely particularism left unresolved by the Augsburg settlement. This conflict in turn was located within a more protracted struggle between the Habsburgs and their adversaries for regional pre-eminence, a struggle made more bloody and intractable by the absence of a European international order for a century following Christendom's collapse. The chaos generated by this conflict was itself amplified by roughly synchronous eco-demographic changes of global scope, changes that interacted with existing institutional frailties and the pressures of war to trigger large-scale crises of authority across Eurasia. The Thirty Years War can thus be characterised as a series of nested crises encompassing German, European and Eurasian dimensions. A full comprehension of the conflict requires an acknowledgement of the forces operative at these micro, meso and macro levels of analysis. However, as the focus of this inquiry lies at the European level of analysis, the remainder of this discussion will concentrate on the Thirty Years crisis as both an expression of the absence of international order and also a catalyst for its eventual reconstruction.

The Thirty Years War as a symptom of systemic chaos

This discussion is not the place for an extensive narrative of the course of the Thirty Years War, and the main contours of the crisis have already been sketched in their broad form.[89] Generally, however, the conflict can be divided into two halves. In the first half, battlefield victories predominantly accrued to the imperial side. The Bohemian revolt was quickly crushed; Frederick, the Elector Palatine, was evicted from Bohemia and dispossessed of the

---

[86] Parker, *Europe in Crisis*, pp. 5–10.   [87] *Ibid.*, pp. 2–3.   [88] *Ibid.*

[89] Lee's *The Thirty Years War*, which I have relied upon below, provides a very succinct and accessible narrative of the conflict.

Palatinate; and the Danish intervention in support of Germany's Protestants was quickly vanquished.[90] The high tide of imperial power was marked by Ferdinand's 1629 Edict of Restitution, in which he demanded the restitution of all lands illegally taken from the Church since the Augsburg Peace.[91] The indiscriminate enforcement of this edict against all Protestant states – regardless of whether or not they had remained loyal to Ferdinand – firmed the resolve of anti-Habsburg forces, encouraged foreign interventions in support of the Protestants, and thereby contributed to the Habsburgs' eventual containment and defeat.[92]

Under Gustavus Adolphus's leadership, the Swedes carved deep into southern Germany, realising greater gains than their enemies had feared or their allies had desired.[93] The Dutch meanwhile held the Spanish at bay and undercut their position abroad, further squeezing Habsburg finances and thus curtailing their military power.[94] Following a brief Habsburg resurgence at Nordlingen in 1634, the French directly entered into the conflict upon multiple fronts, further hastening the Habsburgs' defeat.[95] As German princes began to negotiate separate peaces with the occupying foreign powers, Ferdinand's position became untenable. When it was finally concluded in 1648, the Peace of Westphalia ended the Eighty Years War between Holland and Spain by officially recognising the former's independence. It additionally ended the Thirty Years War in Germany, further institutionalising religious pluralism within the empire, confirming the princes' liberties, and indefinitely postponing the consolidation of an Absolutist state in Germany. Most importantly, while it failed to settle the struggle between Bourbon France and Habsburg Spain, the Westphalian peace did mark a definitive conclusion to Europe's international Wars of Religion and the beginning of the Absolutist age.[96]

The Peace of Westphalia was of vital importance in creating the climate necessary for the reconstruction of a sovereign international order after a century of turmoil. But to apprehend the true significance of the peace, it is first necessary to revisit the chaotic milieu out of which it emerged. Like the French wars that preceded it, the Thirty Years War reflected in microcosm the broader absence of international order afflicting Europe after Christendom's collapse. The conflict, Europe's bloodiest prior to the two world wars, occurred during a half-century of war and revolution, one in which Europe knew not one

---

[90] *Ibid.*, pp. 1–6. [91] *Ibid.*, p. 6. [92] *Ibid.* [93] *Ibid.*, pp. 6–7.
[94] Parker, 'The Dutch revolt and the polarization of international politics', p. 68.
[95] Lee, *The Thirty Years War*, pp. 7–8.
[96] On this point, see generally H. Schilling. 'War and peace at the emergence of modernity: Europe between state belligerence, religious wars, and the desire for peace' in Bussman and Schilling (eds.), *1648: War and peace in Europe*, pp. 13–22; and also J. Burkhardt, 'The summitless pyramid: War aims and peace compromise among Europe's universalist powers' in Bussman and Schilling (eds.), *1648: War and peace in Europe*, pp. 51–60.

year without international conflict.[97] In the absence of a shared framework
for mediating and containing conflicts, the Thirty Years War demonstrated
the same tendencies towards internationalisation as had the French wars,
only for a longer period and with a greater number of actors involved. In the
absence of norms of mutual recognition and non-intervention, the conflict
within Germany was not able to burn itself out, but was rather continuously
prolonged through foreign powers' continuous injections of troops and subsidies. Domestically, the institutional and social strains produced by war-time
mobilisation and eco-demographic crisis precipitated a chain of revolts and
revolutions across Western Europe in the war's final decade, with Europe's
governments buckling under the burden of sustaining ever larger armies
engaged in continuous warfare. Meanwhile, within the empire itself, the
collapse of effective government is most starkly illuminated through a consideration of the parasitism of the approximately 1,500 private military entrepreneurs who sustained themselves through the systematic plunder of occupied
populations.[98]

Most crucially of all, the war represented a breakdown in moral order, with
ingrained sectarian hatreds interacting with the surge in private military violence to produce a style of warfare dominated by scorched earth tactics and
the calculated use of terror and atrocity to subdue civilians. The 1631 sack
of Magdeburg, in which imperial armies slaughtered approximately three-
quarters of the town's 30,000 inhabitants, constituted only the most notorious
instance of the pervasive and largely indiscriminate violence that defined the
conflict.[99] With chivalric norms long since fallen into desuetude, sectarian
hatreds and the spirit of Holy War still alive, and modern laws of war yet to
be formulated, the violence that convulsed Europe during this period raged
largely in the absence of effectively institutionalised ethical restraints. In the
conflict's later stages in particular, the war in Germany became progressively
unmoored from its original religious and political rationales, with increasingly
autonomous military entrepreneurs devoting themselves exclusively to a form
of institutionalised banditry against occupied civilians committed on a mass
scale.

In the Thirty Years War, one thus finds the symptoms of Europe's
overarching crisis of order – a surge in war and revolutions, governmental

---

[97] On the debate surrounding the demographic and economic impact of the Thirty Years
War on the lands of the Holy Roman Empire, see C. J. Friedrichs, 'The war and German
society' in Parker (ed.), *The Thirty Years' War*, pp. 186–91. The conservative estimate
placed here on German losses is 15–20 per cent of the pre-war population (a loss
proportionately greater than that experienced by Germany in World War II), rising to
over half of the total population in some regions.

[98] On the role of German military entrepreneurs during the Thirty Years War, see G. Parker,
'The universal soldier' in Parker (ed.), *The Thirty Years' War*, pp. 175–6.

[99] On the siege of Magdeburg, see Parker, *Europe in Crisis*, p. 161.

breakdown, confessional schism and the collapse of constraints on the exercise of violence – manifesting themselves on an unprecedentedly large scale. As with the French Wars of Religion, the underlying sources of this turmoil can be found in the intersection of confessional polarisation and increased violence interdependence, occasioned respectively by religious schism and military revolution. Similarly, the absence of an ordering framework to contain conflict between polities played an analogous role in the Thirty Years War as it did in the French wars. Nevertheless, for all their commonalities, it would be misleading to read the Thirty Years War as simply a replication of the French Wars of Religion on a larger scale. For while ideological polarisation and increased violence interdependence were pivotal in framing both conflicts, the roles these pressures played were distinct in both cases. Similarly, while the absence of an ordering framework played a permissive role in enabling the prolongation of both conflicts, the mere fact that the Thirty Years War was a general European conflict ensured that its structural consequences would prove more profound.

Religious controversies obviously remained central to the Thirty Years War's course and conduct. The war's origins in the Bohemian revolt lay in the regency government's encroachments on the Bohemian estates' religious and constitutional liberties, and the estates' rebellion against the emperor was explicitly justified in religious as well as constitutional terms.[100] The combustible environment in Germany at the war's outset and the war's rapid spread can also be attributed to Germany's polarisation into opposing Evangelical and Catholic military alliances in the decade preceding the conflict.[101] International diplomatic alignments in the war's first decade were also heavily influenced by confessional sympathies. In the north, England, Holland and the French Huguenots formed a potentially strong anti-Habsburg bloc, while in the east, the Palatinate, Bethlen Gábor (prince of Transylvania) and Protestant minorities in the Habsburgs' hereditary lands formed an additional counter-weight to Habsburg power bound by confessional sympathies.[102] Similarly, the Counter-Reformation provided a powerful ideological bond reinforcing the kinship ties already linking the Austrian and Spanish Habsburg power-blocs. Finally, the persistence of intense religious antagonisms in Europe severely aggravated already acute security dilemmas between polities, contributing to the war's escalation and expansion. Thus, while Scandinavian fears of Ferdinand's plans to roll back Protestantism in Germany were undoubtedly exaggerated, they were nevertheless instrumental in drawing first Denmark and then Sweden into the war.[103]

---

[100] *Ibid.*, p. 118. [101] *Ibid.*, p. 63.

[102] Parker, 'The Dutch revolt and the polarization of international politics', p. 68.

[103] On this point, see generally E. Ringmar, *Identity, Interest, and Action: A cultural explanation of Sweden's intervention in the Thirty Years War* (Cambridge University Press, 1996).

However, while sectarian rivalries continued to resonate in the seventeenth century as they had in the sixteenth, both their intensity and their influence over early modern diplomacy discernibly waned in the latter period. Thus, for example, one does not find in the Thirty Years War the same synthesis of religious fanaticism, revolutionary terror and proto-modern party organisation that characterised either the Catholic League in France or the Water Beggars in Holland a generation earlier.[104] The dehumanising rhetoric and practices of moral exclusion characteristic of the French Wars of Religion featured also in the Thirty Years War, but religious violence was no longer being linked to the advancement of quasi-revolutionary agendas as it had briefly been under the leadership of the Parisian League.[105] Equally, confessional sympathies continued to influence diplomatic alignments, but sectarian divisions had never deterministically shaped rulers' diplomacy, and their influence continued to wane during the Thirty Years War. France's embrace of *raison d'état* under Richelieu from the 1630s onwards bears superficial similarities to Francis's earlier dalliances with the Schmalkaldic League in the 1540s. But the subordination of religious to political objectives under Richelieu was more consistent, more systematic and undergirded by a much more robust and articulated intellectual framework (the discourse of *raison d'état*) than had previously been the case.[106] Domestically also, the prospect of granting toleration to religious minorities had now been grudgingly accepted in a range of kingdoms, most notably France. The maxim *cuius regio, eius religio* continued to undergird rulers' legitimacy claims and call into question the loyalties of heretical minorities. But the idea of sacrificing religious unity for the sake of political unity was no longer unimaginable for Europe's leaders, and merely gained in traction as the war progressed.

Europe continued to be saturated by religious hatreds in the Thirty Years War. However, the fruits of France's religious wars – the ideological construct of Absolutist sovereignty and the demonstrated link between *politique* domestic and foreign policies and the strengthening of rulers' power – profoundly conditioned the conflict's course. Indeed, by the last decade of the war, religious motives had been almost entirely eclipsed by political motives in driving dynastic diplomacy, anticipating the Absolutist order to come. Conversely, this mild tempering of Europe's religious hatreds was offset by the continuing

[104] The activities of the English Puritans in the period of the Civil War and the Commonwealth provide perhaps the nearest seventeenth-century parallel to the revolutionary religious parties of the preceding period; on this point, see generally M. Walzer, *The Revolution of the Saints: A study in the origins of radical politics* (London: Weidenfeld and Nicolson, 1965).

[105] On the revolutionary character of the Parisian branch of the Catholic League during the French religious wars, see Koenigsberger, 'The organization of revolutionary parties', p. 350.

[106] On this point, see J. D. Tracy, *Europe's Reformations 1450–1650: Doctrine, politics, and community*, 2nd edn (Oxford: Rowman and Littlefield Publishers, 2006), pp. 164–7.

expansion in the scale and destructiveness of European warfare. By the onset of the Thirty Years War, a plethora of transformations inaugurated by the military revolution were increasingly in evidence. Artillery fortresses, broadside-firing warships and massed musket-wielding infantry had by 1618 diffused throughout Europe to become definitive weapons platforms of the age.[107] Equally, the size and costliness of armies had by then also dramatically increased. Thus, while the armies that had fought the Italian wars of the sixteenth century had rarely exceeded 30,000 men, armies of over 150,000 soldiers were common in the Thirty Years War.[108]

Ostensibly, the far larger armies fielded by the opposing sides appear to affirm narratives linking military revolution with the waxing of sovereign power. However, a closer consideration of the conflict reveals that such increases in army size did not necessarily reflect increases in rulers' capacity to finance and bureaucratically administer and control such forces. On the contrary, throughout the Thirty Years War, rulers routinely fielded far larger armies than they could possibly sustain, relying on private military entrepreneurs to recruit, administer, financially maintain and lead these armies in the field. Economies of scale dictated that it was far easier to garrison and plunder occupied populations with larger rather than smaller armies, leading to the development of massive itinerant mercenary hosts led by quasi-autonomous warlords.[109] The recruitment of largely foreign mercenaries on little more than the promise of plunder ensured a rapid breakdown in military discipline as the war progressed, with soldiers routinely subjecting civilians to theft, arson, torture and murder to maintain themselves.[110] Already weakened by famine and epidemics, peasants occasionally stood and fought against mercenaries, but more frequently they fled to neighbouring territories, thereby further enlarging the conflict's radius of disruption.[111]

In the French Wars of Religion, the diffusion of destructive capabilities inaugurated by the military revolution had tended to reinforce the dominance of aristocratic factions at the expense of a weakened crown, momentarily reversing the gains in political centralisation achieved under France's Renaissance monarchs. Paradoxically, the immediate consequence of an incomplete military revolution was thus political regression, a return to an earlier era characterised by weak monarchy, over-mighty subjects and endemic aristocratic violence. Conversely, in Germany, the military revolution redounded primarily to the advantage of the military entrepreneurs fighting the war, yielding a qualitatively more radical fragmentation of political and military power. With a pan-European

---

[107] Parker, *Europe in Crisis*, p. 48.   [108] Parker, *The Military Revolution*, p. 24.
[109] Parrott, 'Strategy and tactics in the Thirty Years' War', p. 18.
[110] On this point, see generally Q. Outram, 'The demographic impact of early modern warfare', *Social Science History*, 26(2) (2002), 253–6.
[111] *Ibid.*, pp. 251–2.

pool of commercial military talent on which to draw and in the absence of norms of non-intervention, Europe's rulers were free to continuously inflame the conflict in Germany through the deployment of armies larger than they could possibly afford to finance or maintain themselves.[112] In an era in which rulers' administrative and mobilisational powers had yet to catch up with advances in the technologies and techniques of European warfare, the burgeoning market for military violence offered them a means of pursuing their ambitions at the expense (both literally and figuratively) of local populations. In reality, this expedient merely nurtured the development of parasitic military entrepreneurs and economies of plunder, further accelerating the moral and institutional breakdown within Germany and compounding international disorder.

Despite their commonalities, the French Wars of Religion and the Thirty Years War therefore stand as distinct expressions of systemic disorder. The absolute enmity born of confessional schism featured in both conflicts, but burned more intensely in the former than the latter. By contrast, the military revolution's centrifugal consequences were more evident in the Thirty Years War than in the French Wars of Religion, although again these tendencies were evident in both conflicts. What united both cases was the absence of an ordering framework to prevent the internationalisation and prolongation of these respective conflicts. In the interregnum between Christendom's demise and the constitution of a sovereign international order, Europe's rulers dwelled in an anarchical system, but not an anarchical society. The combination of confessional polarisation and enhanced destructive capacities characteristic of the era would have strained even a robust order. But in the absence of any agreed rules of co-existence, Europe was condemned to a prolonged era of immature anarchy punctuated by division, war, revolution, atrocity and death. It was only after a peace born of mutual exhaustion that Europe's rulers could formulate the principles upon which a successor order to Christendom could eventually be built.

Re-formation, revulsion and reconstitution: The Westphalian moment and the re-imagining of European international order

International relations scholars have long debated the significance of the Peace of Westphalia for both European and world history. Traditionally, the Peace of Westphalia was lauded as 'the majestic portal' signifying the transition from the medieval universalism of the *Respublica Christiana* to the sovereign anarchy of the modern state system.[113] This orthodox reading of Westphalia's importance has in recent years come under devastating attack from a diverse and growing

---

[112] *Ibid.*, p. 254. See also generally H. Munkler, *The New Wars* (Cambridge: Polity, 2005), Ch. 2.

[113] L. Gross, 'The Peace of Westphalia 1648–1948', *The American Journal of International Law*, 42(1) (1948), 28.

body of revisionist scholarship. Writing from a wide range of theoretical perspectives, scholars have cast serious doubt on the 'myth of 1648', and have sought rather to emphasise fundamental continuities bridging the pre- and post-Westphalian periods.[114] These refutations of the 'myth of 1648' are individually persuasive and cumulatively compelling. Consequently, it is not my intention here to entirely refute these claims of continuity, much less to mount an obdurate defence of the Westphalian thesis in its traditional form. Equally, however, I maintain that the emerging revisionist consensus must be seriously qualified, lest it detract from the genuine and profound transformations in political thought and practice that distinguish the Age of Absolutism from the century of chaos that preceded it, transformations that were in turn made possible by the very stability created by the Peace of Westphalia.

Before considering Westphalia's particular historical significance, let us first revisit the seismic cultural transformations – encompassing re-conceptualisations of religion, politics, community and war – that distinguished the international order that matured in Westphalia's aftermath from the order of Latin Christendom that preceded it. Both Christendom and Absolutist Europe legitimised temporal power in large part by infusing it with sacred authority; European international order in both its late medieval and early modern incarnations took shape in and reflected a devoutly religious world. Critically, however, the traumas of the Reformation and the Wars of Religion together propelled a radical re-conceptualisation of the sacred as an ontological category. Noting the disappearance of confessional disagreement as a catalyst for international war following the Peace of Westphalia, some commentators have mistakenly inferred from this a secularisation of European international order after 1648.[115] In fact, Europeans did not become any less fervid in their religious convictions in the post-Westphalian age. If anything, Protestant 'worldly asceticism' invested everyday life with a religious significance that it had never previously possessed, while divine-right Absolutism similarly accorded hereditary monarchy with unprecedented sacred dignity. Rather than becoming less religious, Europeans simply began to conceive of the sacred differently, and in terms that ultimately proved more compatible with

---

[114] See for example E. Keene, *Beyond the Anarchical Society: Grotius, colonialism and order in world politics* (Cambridge University Press, 2002); S. D. Krasner, 'Westphalia and all that' in J. Goldstein and R. O. Keohane (eds.), *Ideas and Foreign Policy: Beliefs, institutions, and political change* (Ithaca: Cornell University Press, 1993), pp. 235–64; Nexon, *The Struggle for Power in Early Modern Europe*; A. Osiander, 'Sovereignty, international relations, and the Westphalian myth', *International Organization*, 55(2) (2001), 251–87; and Teschke, *Myth of 1648*.

[115] See for example B. Straumann, 'The Peace of Westphalia as a secular constitution', *Constellations*, 15(2) (2008), 173–88. The allegedly secular character of the Westphalian settlement has been strongly contested in P. H. Wilson, *The Thirty Years War: Europe's tragedy* (Cambridge, MA: Belknap Press of Harvard University Press, 2009), pp. 758–60.

the maintenance of a religiously plural international order. Specifically, the sacred began to be regarded less as being synonymous with communal adherence to rituals of integration uniting a corporeal 'body of believers', and instead became more closely identified with the individual believer's reflexively held subscription to a codified 'body of beliefs'. A principled commitment to religious toleration did not flow automatically from this transition.[116] But in shifting the focus of religious experience from embodied ritual to reflexively apprehended belief, this re-formation of the sacred at least permitted religion's subsequent re-imagining as a matter of private conscience, and one that was therefore potentially separable from questions of political obedience.

Post-Reformation re-conceptualisations of the sacred occurred in tandem with parallel innovations in political thought. From Christendom's emergence as a coherent international order in the eleventh century, the clash between the competing universalisms of Church and empire had dominated the medieval political imagination. The Reformation crisis and the failure of the Habsburg imperial enterprise signified the final eclipse of the Church–empire polarity as the Latin West's dominant political antagonism. Instead, with the terminal weakening of these universal institutions, the focus of political discourse shifted towards the centralising monarchies of the Atlantic fringe. Within this context, the French Wars of Religion served as a particularly generative trauma, with the protracted contest between the competing authority claims of the crown and the 'lower magistrates' following Henri II's death providing the catalyst for Bodin's articulation of the model of sovereignty – 'perpetual, absolute, indivisible' – that would dominate the age after Westphalia. Bodin's Absolutist vision did not reflect the institutional reality of Europe's monarchies, either before or after 1648.[117] Neither did the Absolutist model of sovereignty acquire universal purchase in the seventeenth century, with post-revolutionary England, the Holy Roman Empire and the Dutch Republic each securing civil peace through reliance on 'shared' sovereignty regimes that departed substantially from the

---

[116] Indeed, Brad Gregory has argued that a greater emphasis on doctrinal disputes in the confessional era left Europe's protagonists strongly predisposed against the possibility of religious settlements premised on modern ideals of toleration. See B. S. Gregory, *Salvation at Stake: Christian martyrdom in early modern Europe* (Cambridge, MA: Harvard University Press, 1999), p. 346. It was only in the more settled context of the seventeenth century's second half, following the consolidation of the Westphalian peace, that ideas of religious toleration could be fully articulated and properly institutionalised, and even then, systematic discrimination against religious minorities would remain a feature of Western European politics down to the nineteenth century. See generally H. Butterfield, *Toleration in Religion and Politics* (New York: Council on Religion and International Affairs, 1980).

[117] On the disjuncture between Absolutist rhetoric and the persistence of earlier patterns of patronage and indirect rule, see generally Black, *Kings, Nobles and Commoners*; and Henshall, *The Myth of Absolutism*.

Absolutist norm.[118] These observations aside, the Absolutist conception of sovereignty as legislative command represented a genuine intellectual breakthrough, and its adoption by the seventeenth century's most powerful European state guaranteed its durability in the more stable systemic context that prevailed following the end of the Thirty Years War.

Shifting conceptions of political authority implied shifting conceptions of political obedience as their necessary corollary. At the onset of Europe's transformative crisis, medieval constitutionalism and ancient republicanism offered the two dominant frameworks informing discussions concerning the nature and limits of political obligation. This changed with the Wars of Religion. Both the violent passions these conflicts evoked and the non-negotiable character of the demands they generated suggested the inadequacy of older and more negotiated models of political obligation.[119] Equally, the military revolution conferred upon both rulers and rebels greater destructive capabilities than had ever been known in ancient and medieval times. This further underscored the fragility of civil order and the necessity of securing peace via an authoritarian solution. Christendom's religious fragmentation threw the individual back upon the resources of their own conscience, paving the way for potentially endless confessional controversy and civil disunion. Thinkers such as Bodin and later Hobbes opined that the solution was to invent a new morality of politics, one that would subdue and partially delegitimise the impulses of aristocratic pride and popular religious passion, and enjoin in their place universal submission to the sovereign ruler in exchange for the promise of civil peace.[120]

Absolutism thus cast obedience to the sovereign as a practical necessity, a rational imperative and a moral virtue. Additionally, it both reflected and reinforced parallel shifts in collective identities brought about by the Reformation and the Wars of Religion. Latin Christendom had been characterised by a combination of ideological universalism and institutional localism. The teachings of the Church and the vague memory of Roman glory constituted the twin threads holding Christendom together. But for the illiterate peasants that constituted the vast majority of Christendom, the boundaries of both economic activity and collective identification did not extend far beyond the local parish. This too changed in the century following the Reformation. Processes of confessionalisation and state-building saw the imposition of new regimes of bodily and spiritual discipline on the general population of a kind

---

[118] On this point, see for example Black, *Kings, Nobles and Commoners*; and also Wilson, *The Thirty Years War*, pp. 761–2.

[119] On the 'rage for order' that characterised Europe in the later stages of the Wars of Religion, and that reached its apogee during and immediately after the Thirty Years War, see T. K. Rabb, *The Struggle for Stability in Early Modern Europe* (New York: Oxford University Press, 1975), pp. 121–2.

[120] Koselleck, *Critique and Crisis*, pp. 28–32.

not previously witnessed outside of a monastic setting, alongside the continuing growth of rulers' extractive capacities.[121] These two processes bit deeply if unevenly into local communities, encouraging the rise of socially inclusive and territorially exclusive collective identities.[122] Confessional polarisation also provided a fillip to the development of print vernaculars at the expense of Latin, further stimulating the growth of proto-national identities among formerly disparate localities.[123] The partial entwining of Counter-Reformation zeal with Habsburg imperialism provided yet a further stimulus to the growth of proto-national identities. For Dutch Calvinists, atrocities such as the 'Spanish Fury' confirmed Philip II's status as a modern-day pharaoh, while the 'miraculous' failure of the Spanish Armada similarly stoked Elizabethan convictions regarding England's status as an elect nation.[124] The advent of modern nationalism as a feature of European politics would have to wait for the revolutions of the late eighteenth and early nineteenth centuries. But the confessional age did nevertheless yield a 'Mosaic moment' that transcended mere xenophobia, with biblical and medieval narratives of ethnic exceptionalism being hybridised to produce coherent imagined communities that would survive the Wars of Religion, and later come to form the nucleus around which more incontestably national collective identities would eventually cohere.[125]

Finally, Europe's century of crisis eventually catalysed fundamental changes in the character of war as a social institution in Western and Central Europe. Prior to the onset of Europe's transformative crisis, organised violence in Christendom had typically taken the form of either feud or Holy War, the first conceived as a form of aristocratic legal redress, and the second being regarded as a divinely ordained sanction against God's temporal enemies. From the fifteenth century onwards, a growing disconnect separated these coercive institutions from Europe's evolving material and normative context. With the increased destructive potential unleashed by the introduction of gunpowder weaponry into Christendom, earlier notions of the feud as an accepted means of aristocratic self-help came to be seen as increasingly anachronistic. The 'feuds' between rulers such as Francis I and Charles V were clearly of a different order of magnitude to those prevalent among the aristocracy during the High Middle Ages, and with the arrival of the military revolution, the gap between feud and war widened still further. Similarly, the interjection of Holy War sentiments into Europe's internecine struggles during the Wars of Religion had fuelled an almost total breakdown of civil and moral order. The re-conception of war as a

---

[121] See generally Gorski, *The Disciplinary Revolution*; and R. P.-C. Hsia, *Social Discipline in the Reformation: Central Europe, 1550–1750* (London: Routledge, 1989).

[122] *Ibid.*   [123] Elton, *Reformation Europe*, p. 212.

[124] See generally Gorski, 'The Mosaic moment.'

[125] *Ibid.* For a strong argument emphasising the influence of early modern religious struggles on the formation of national subjectivities in Western Europe, see A. W. Marx, *Faith in Nation: Exclusionary origins of nationalism* (Oxford University Press, 2003).

sovereign prerogative, to be rationally harnessed for the exclusive cause of advancing the interests of the dynasty *qua* state, took shape as a direct response to the great disorder that convulsed Europe between Augsburg and Westphalia.[126] Once again, it would take time for new conceptions of war as a rational instrument of statecraft to fully take hold. But an instructive contrast can nevertheless be drawn between the limited wars of the eighteenth century, fought by disciplined, regimented armies in the service of dynastic interest, and the bloody chaos generated by the itinerant plunderers that dominated the Thirty Years War.[127] The practice of war changed fundamentally after Westphalia, and this change in turn reflected a fundamental conceptual shift in the understanding of war's social purpose, and its proper relationship to legitimate political authority.

The preceding re-conceptualisations of religion, politics, community and war in early modern Europe collectively constituted nothing less than a transformation of the Western social imaginary, one brought about by the civilisation-rending traumas of the Reformation, the military revolution and the Wars of Religion. Every international order is sustained by a shared set of assumptions regarding the 'problem of order', conceived as the threats to ontological and physical security that collectively necessitate the construction of fundamental authoritative and coercive institutions. In pre-Reformation Christendom, the problem of order was conceived as one of securing the temporal conditions necessary to prepare for eternal salvation in a post-lapsarian world. Latin Christendom was a universe in which sacred authority was unified but political authority remained fragmented, and one in which capacities for organised violence were additionally dispersed among an existentially bellicose warrior nobility. Within this context, an Augustinian political theology and a social ideology of tri-functionality both ratified existing social inequalities, while also seeking to reconcile them with the egalitarian promise of spiritual salvation through the universal Church. Throughout Christendom, the metaphor of 'harmony in integration' provided the dominant social metaphor through which order was envisaged, with the temporal hierarchy of *laboratores*, *bellatores* and *oratores* supposedly corresponding with a cosmic hierarchy ascending from beasts and men through to angels and God.[128]

By the Peace of Westphalia, this imaginary had been swept away, its place taken by an entirely new problem of order that had intruded with the collapse of Christendom's spiritual unity. Both the systemic 'crisis of pluralism' engendered by the Reformation and the crisis of temporal order produced within Europe's composite monarchies by confessional conflict and military revolution forced a comprehensive re-imagining of the problem of order. With the

---

[126] Koselleck, *Critique and Crisis*, p. 44.

[127] M. E. Howard, *War in European History* (London; New York: Oxford University Press, 1976), p. 73.

[128] Walzer, 'On the role of symbolism in political thought', p. 192.

coming of the Reformation, old certainties crumbled.[129] Established theories of correspondence, which suggested the embeddedness of the temporal world within a larger cosmic order, no longer resonated in the way that they once had. Catholics and Protestants alike continued to yearn for spiritual salvation in the seventeenth century's more settled second half. But the earlier confidence that the City of Man and the City of God were anchored within a common divinely ordained order, the two together constituting 'a *concordia* dynamically oriented towards perfection', had vanished following the Wars of Religion.[130] Instead, a combination of revolutionary ideas – in the form of concepts such as Luther's Doctrine of the Two Kingdoms – and generative traumas, such as the French Wars of Religion and the Thirty Years War – had yielded a heightened appreciation of the contingent, constructed and ultimately precarious character of political order. Increasingly, contemporary thinkers sought to address a new problem of order – that is, how to guarantee temporal order in a world in which religious uniformity could no longer serve as the basis for social unity, and in which revolutionary increases in destructive power had subverted the order-maintaining function of established practices of organised violence. Throughout Europe, this challenge was answered in different ways. In some countries, Protestant voluntarism found its expression in theories of government emphasising notions of covenant and contract, while in others, older Thomistic conceptions of an organic social order were wedded to developing notions of divine right Absolutism. These local variations notwithstanding, throughout Europe 'anarchy in motion' was increasingly supplanting 'harmony in integration' as the dominant social metaphor for thinkers concerned with interrogating the problem of order, and the body politic was steadily eclipsing the *corpus Christi* as their primary object of speculation.[131]

The transformation of social imaginaries outlined above was a tortuous and protracted process, and one that was by no means complete by the signing of the Peace of Westphalia. But the transformed conceptions of religion, politics, community and war that emerged from Europe's century of chaos would prove vital in conditioning the shape of the sovereign international order that matured after 1648. New conceptions of religion that made possible the de-linking of religious belief from political allegiance were critical in facilitating the emergence of an ecumenical peace, not only within Europe's political communities, but also between them. Absolutist conceptions of authority and

---

[129] On the crisis of pluralism engendered by the Reformation, see again Philpott, *Revolutions in Sovereignty*, p. 4.

[130] Wolin, *Politics and Vision*, p. 141.

[131] Walzer, 'On the role of symbolism in political thought', p. 201. On this transformation of social imaginaries and corresponding visions of political order within the specific context of early modern England, see generally S. L. Collins, *From Divine Cosmos to Sovereign State: An intellectual history of consciousness and the idea of order in Renaissance England* (Oxford University Press, 1989).

obedience similarly contributed to the development of a new international order by contriving a new morality of political action, which acknowledged the necessity for kings and subjects alike to subordinate religious passions to the overriding task of working to preserve a perpetually precarious civil order. The development of new imagined communities, yoked around proto-modern sentiments of 'Mosaic' nationalism and stimulated by both the spread of vernacular print cultures and the struggle against Habsburg imperialism, contributed also to the growth of a sovereign international order by further entrenching Europe's cultural fragmentation, foreclosing the return to a European order organised on heteronomous or imperial lines. Finally, the re-conceptualisation of war as a sovereign prerogative distinct from either feud or Holy War was also essential to the consolidation of a new international order after 1648. Henceforth, conventional enmities between sovereigns would be expressed through the medium of 'limited' wars guided by the nascent logic of *raison d'état*, while the absolute enmity that had characterised Europe's Wars of Religion would again be exiled to the Occident's bloody borders as it had largely been during the Middle Ages.

So much, then, for the cultural and conceptual changes that facilitated a reconstitution of international order following the Peace of Westphalia. This still leaves the matter of determining Westphalia's specific importance in contributing to this restoration. In accordance with revisionists, I concur that the Peace of Westphalia did not mark a total break with the past, nor should it be taken as inaugurating the emergence of a states-under-anarchy model of order of the kind familiar to contemporary international relations theorists. But in opposition to those who would 'define Westphalia down' to the point of insignificance, I suggest that the Peace was nevertheless fundamentally important in enabling the reconstruction of international order in seventeenth-century Europe. Specifically, I argue that Westphalia was doubly significant, both in the revolutionary conceptual changes that its terms reflected, and in the processes of state-building that it enabled through the international stability the peace secured.

Turning first to the conceptual changes that Westphalia's terms reflected, it is worth recalling that one of the primary causes underlying Europe's century of chaos was the absence between rulers of agreed principles of co-existence. It was the absence of these rules, together with the structurally distinct vulnerabilities of composite monarchies, that propelled rulers to adopt the strategies of reciprocal destabilisation that had done so much to internationalise Europe's religious wars and inhibit the successful consolidation of monarchical authority. Within this context, clause III of the Treaty of Osnabrück in particular assumed a pivotal significance.[132] In institutionalising a universal commitment

---

[132] The full text of the clause reads as follows: 'And that a reciprocal Amity between the Emperor, and the Most Christian King, the Electors, Princes and States of the Empire, may be maintained so much the more firm and sincere (to say nothing at present of the

among the signatories to refrain from providing any form of support or sanctuary to one another's enemies, the treaty expressly forbade practices of subversion and reciprocal destabilisation that had formerly been central to the practice of early modern statecraft. With the Peace of Westphalia, one can thus discern clear signs of the emergence of the most basic rule of practical association common to sovereign orders, namely the obligation to refrain from attempts to actively subvert the authority of another ruler by providing sponsorship or support to their domestic enemies.

In addition to establishing basic rules of co-existence between the signatories, the Peace of Westphalia also reflected a new acknowledgement of the need to actively commit to preserving Europe's religious pluralism if an enduring international peace was to be secured. For revisionists, the clauses of the peace addressing the question of 'religious liberties' within the empire provide firm evidence of Westphalia's deviation from the states-under-anarchy sovereign model, thus debunking traditionalist claims regarding Westphalia's historical importance.[133] On this point, it is true that Westphalia forced a measure of religious toleration on the empire's constituent *Landesherrs*, amending the Augsburg principle of *cuius regio, eius religio* to bring it into closer conformity with the overriding imperative of preserving peace within the empire.[134] The constitution thus continued to strike an uneasy balance between imperial suzerainty and princely sovereignty, and Westphalia's signatories actively sought to leverage this institutional hybridity in arriving at a workable settlement. What is more significant than the re-articulation of imperial and princely authority claims contained in these clauses, however, is the transformed conception of the relationship between religion and international order that the clauses reflect. Under Christendom, temporal order and religious uniformity were seen for centuries as being mutually dependent. Equally, under the Augsburg Peace, this presumption was affirmed and simply devolved downwards to the empire's constituent territories. It is only with the Westphalian settlement that one sees the emergence of a general peace capable of enduring in a post-Reformation world. And this is because it is only with Westphalia that we see a collective recognition that temporal order was in fact crucially dependent on a collective acceptance of Europe's irreducible confessional pluralism.

The Peace of Westphalia has on occasion been characterised as signalling an important shift towards the secularisation of European order.[135] This characterisation sits uneasily with the text of the two constituent treaties, which remain infused with religious language, and also with the self-understandings

---

Article of Security, which will be mentioned hereafter), the one shall never assist the present or future Enemys of the other under any Title or Pretence whatsoever, either with Arms, Money, Soldiers, or any sort of Ammunition; nor no-one, who is a member of this Pacification, shall suffer any Enemys' Troops to retire thro' or sojourn in his Country.'

[133] See for example Krasner, 'Westphalia and all that', p. 244.   [134] *Ibid.*

[135] See again Straumann, 'The Peace of Westphalia as a secular constitution'.

of its principal signatories, who continued to inhabit a deeply devout world.[136] For this reason, I prefer to characterise Westphalia as an ecumenical peace, albeit one that reflected a transformed post-Reformation conception of religion. The quest for salvation continued to preoccupy believers across the sectarian divide. But the earlier certainty, that the stability and solidity of the political order were ultimately guaranteed by its interconnectedness with a divinely ordained cosmic order, was now gone. Instead, the terms of Westphalia explicitly demonstrate a reflexive appreciation of the contingency of temporal order such as had not previously existed. In making Westphalia's interpretation of the balance between princely prerogatives and religious liberties within the empire binding and perpetual, the signatories explicitly incorporated anti-protest provisions forbidding both clerical and secular actors from either within or beyond the empire from challenging the new dispensation.[137] European international order would henceforth be secured by self-consciously excluding religious convictions forever from the range of reasons that could legitimately be advanced for debating the meaning of the empire's constitution, much less justifying external intervention in the empire's affairs. Moreover, rather than relying on ecclesiastical guarantees, the new order within the empire would depend for its preservation on the guarantees of France and Sweden, two temporal powers elevated not by reasons of divine election, but simply by dint of their status as the war's victors.[138] While Westphalia thus signalled the embryonic emergence of norms of non-intervention and respect for religious liberties, what is truly significant is that ultimately even these norms were amended and abridged where necessary to accommodate the overriding goal of maintaining a stable international order among Europe's sovereigns. By the mid-seventeenth century, Europe's leaders were still in the process of working out both the privileges associated with sovereignty, and the rightful possessors of those sovereign privileges.[139] But by 1648, it was already clear that sovereignty was emerging as the organising principle of European international order, and that the challenge of constructing and maintaining the peace between Europe's sovereigns had become the chief problem of order within the Latin West. With Westphalia, we thus see the emergence of a new reflexivity regarding the constructed nature of international order, as well as a new pragmatism with regards to the practice of maintaining it. In short, we are now passing out of a world in which 'All things that are, are set in order by God' (Romans 13: 1), and into a world in which 'Anarchy is what [sovereigns] make of it.'[140]

---

[136] Wilson, *The Thirty Years War*, p. 758.
[137] Straumann, 'The Peace of Westphalia as a secular constitution', p. 180.   [138] *Ibid.*
[139] On this point, see for example Ruggie, 'Territoriality and beyond', p. 163.
[140] A. Wendt, 'Anarchy is what states make of it: The social construction of power politics', *International Organization*, 46(2) (1992), 391–425.

In addition to reflecting fundamental changes in European political thought and practice, the Peace of Westphalia was significant also for the state-building processes that it henceforth enabled. Following Christendom's collapse, processes of confessionalisation and military revolution had greatly complicated efforts to consolidate political authority in Europe's composite monarchies. Paradoxically, however, these processes significantly abetted the centralisation of political authority once they unfolded within the more settled environment provided by the Peace of Westphalia. Processes of confessionalisation, however protracted and uneven, helped strengthen the institutional and affective relations between rulers and ruled in many instances during Europe's century of chaos.[141] This was particularly the case when the consolidation of confessional identities became conjoined with the struggle against Habsburg imperialism. But in the face of endemic practices of reciprocal destabilisation among Europe's composite monarchies, confessionalisation was equally a source of internal division and a catalyst for internationalised civil war. Conversely, the greater freedom from foreign-sponsored subversion provided by Westphalia enabled rulers to build more systematically on confessional legacies, forging more internally cohesive and enduring patrimonies than had previously existed. The resulting imagined communities of 'elect and covenanted peoples' that developed in Europe after Westphalia were neither as coherent nor as consistently articulated as their post-revolutionary nationalist successors, and Europe's Great Powers retained their composite imperial character well into the nineteenth century.[142] This observation aside, the Wars of Religion undeniably yielded new solidarities upon which rulers could build, while the new rules of co-existence established with Westphalia provided the more stable systemic environment in which revived processes of state-building could occur.

Similarly, while the material and organisational changes inaugurated under the military revolution proved highly destructive in the medium term, they would also be implicated in the reconstruction of order following the Westphalian peace. The development of artillery fortresses, infantry musketry volleys and broadside-firing warships qualitatively increased the destructiveness of European warfare following Christendom's demise, as well

---

[141] On this point, see generally H. Schilling, 'Confessionalisation in Europe: Causes and effects for church, state, society and culture', pp. 219–28.

[142] On the interconnections between religious conflict and the formation of proto-national identities in the pre-revolutionary period, see again Gorski, 'The Mosaic moment'; Marx, *Faith in Nation*; and L. Colley, *Britons: Forging the nation, 1707–1837* (New Haven: Yale University Press, 1992). Conversely, for a discussion of the enduringly composite character of the Great Powers down to the nineteenth century, see J. Goldstone, 'Neither late imperial nor early modern: Efflorescences and the Qing formation in world history' in L. A. Struve (ed.), *The Qing Formation in World-Historical Time* (Cambridge, MA: Harvard University Press, 2004), p. 254.

as imposing fiscal and administrative burdens that were beyond the capabilities of most European polities to manage. The changes wrought by the military revolution brought bankruptcy, bloodshed and rebellion in their immediate wake. Equally, however, these changes also eventually provided the material foundation for the establishment of a new international order founded upon the 'internally pacified and hard-shell rimmed' sovereign polities of Absolutist Europe.[143] The order-producing consequences of the military revolution required for their emergence a raft of institutional innovations, such as the establishment of more robust systems of taxation and public credit and the elaboration of bureaucratic structures of military command, that find isolated and incomplete expressions prior to Westphalia. But it was really only in the decades after Westphalia, when rulers could embark on the project of state-building without fear of foreign intervention, that the institutional changes necessary to subordinate the military revolution to sovereign ends could at last be implemented.[144]

The Peace of Westphalia did not constitute an epochal rupture from all that had gone before – this much the revisionists have convincingly shown. But nor, for that matter, should Westphalia be defined downwards towards the point of insignificance.[145] For the Reformation and the Wars of Religion did not simply mark an interruption in long-standing processes of state and system formation, which were then resumed following a Westphalian peace of exhaustion.[146] Rather, they together constituted a protracted civilisational trauma that forever changed the cultural texture of European international politics. In the wake of the Wars of Religion, European understandings of religion, politics, community and war were forever transformed. These conceptual transformations were reflected both in the problem of order that Westphalia sought to address, and in the solutions to this problem that it sought to institutionalise. Westphalia was so important because it provided for the first time a minimal set of principles for co-existence between polities dwelling in the anarchy left by the collapse of Christendom as a viable international order. In the interim between Christendom's collapse in 1555 and the Peace of Westphalia in 1648, Europe's rulers had dwelled in an international system. After Westphalia, they dwelled in an international society. The modernity of Westphalia should not be overstated, for the provisions of the peace related first to constitutional arrangements within the empire, and were only subsequently expanded to encompass

---

[143] J. Herz, 'Rise and demise of the territorial state', *World Politics*, 9(4) (1957), 483.

[144] On this point, see generally J. Black, *A Military Revolution? Military change and European society 1550–1800* (London: Macmillan, 1991).

[145] On 'defining Westphalia down', see Nexon, *The Struggle for Power in Early Modern Europe*, p. 277.

[146] *Ibid.*, p. 287.

Europe itself.[147] This qualification aside, what the Westphalian peace did accomplish was to make explicit principles of international co-existence that had been presupposed in the theory of Absolutism. The Peace of Westphalia did not expunge war from the European international system, nor did it vanquish dynastic rivalries or sectarian hatreds. But in initiating the process of entrenching norms of mutual recognition internationally, the Westphalian peace provided the foundation for the containment of conflict within tolerable bounds, heralding the development of a new international order.

In comparison to modern peace settlements such as Vienna or Versailles, Westphalia remains a modest settlement. But in comparison to the age of disorder that preceded it, Westphalia's novelty is both profound and immediately apparent. In institutionalising mutual recognition in place of absolute enmity, and in proscribing endemic interference in favour of non-intervention, Westphalia helped reconcile diversity and division with conventional enmity and co-existence. In so doing, it provided the anvil upon which the modern state – and with it the modern sovereign international order – could subsequently be forged.

---

[147] On this point, see H. Steiger, 'Concrete peace and general order: The legal meaning of the treaties of 24 October 1648' in Bussmann and Schilling (eds.), *1648: War and peace in Europe*, p. 437.

6 | *The origins, constitution and decay of the Sinosphere*

You shall not deviate from our instructions, but you shall reverently obey and adhere to our imperial command. Heaven looks down on the earth below and the will and laws of Heaven are strict and severe. Our imperial words and codes are brilliant and effective. Always revere Heaven and the throne ...[1]

On 19 July 1864, the city of Nanjing fell to Qing imperial forces, ending history's bloodiest ever civil war. From 1850, an army of holy warriors, numbering at times over a million strong, had fought to overthrow the imperial household and establish a theocratic Heavenly Kingdom in its place. Inspired by a failed candidate for the imperial bureaucracy who saw himself as Christ's younger brother, the Taiping ('heavenly kingdom') faith fused elements of Chinese folk religion with evangelical Christianity to energise a millenarian movement of exceptional resilience and ferocity. For almost fifteen years, the Taiping rebels paralysed the Qing dynasty, spreading from their base in Guangxi province to seize control of the ancient imperial capital of Nanjing, from where they briefly ruled a territory as large as France and Germany combined. By the time leader Hong Xiuquan died and imperial forces had massacred his remaining followers, the rebellion had claimed at least 20 million lives. Coming at a time when the Qing dynasty was already weakened by fiscal crisis and accelerating Western predation, the Taiping rebellion gravely weakened the imperial core of a suzerain state system that had governed East Asia for the better part of the millennium. In so doing, it constituted the most violent of a series of catastrophes that paved the way for the region's absorption into a European-dominated sovereign state system, and that form the subject of the following four chapters.

In the following pages, I will recount the Sinosphere's origins, constitution, decay and collapse, before then detailing the region's subsequent transition to a sovereign international order. In this chapter, I review the Sinosphere's origins, constitution and operation, focusing particularly on the form that it assumed

---

[1] Imperial edict of the Ming Wanli emperor, investing Toyotomi Hideyoshi with the title King of Japan, 1 March 1595. Cited in K. M. Swope, 'Deceit, disguise and dependence: China, Japan and the future of the tributary system, 1592–1596', *The International History Review*, XXIV(4) (2002), 774–5.

following the Manchu conquest of China in 1644. I then explore the latent vulnerabilities and the processes of decay that were afflicting the Sinosphere's Chinese core immediately prior to the First Opium War and the subsequent onset of full-scale European encroachment into North-east Asia.

Whereas Chapter 6 reviews the Sinosphere's constitution and decay, Chapters 7 and 8 detail its protracted disintegration in the face of domestic rebellion and foreign aggression. I open with an account of the Western ideological and military assault on China that accompanied the Opium Wars, before then discussing the cataclysmic mid-century rebellions that followed in its train. Sandwiched between a mass millenarian rebellion and an external 'barbarian' assault, the Qing dynasty barely survived the mid-century crisis. That it managed to endure for another six decades was due to a contingent convergence of interests between Western merchants and officials, the ortho-dox Han scholar gentry, and the Manchu court. The nature of the ensuing collaboration between these parties and the hybrid synarchic order that it produced are discussed in Chapter 7, while the dynamics of its destruction and the Qing dynasty's subsequent overthrow are examined in Chapter 8.[2]

Following the Sinosphere's destruction and the Qing dynasty's collapse, East Asia plunged into a period of immature anarchy from which it would not emerge until after World War II. This chaotic interregnum is detailed in Chapter 9. Central to my narrative is a focus on the interweaving struggles to reconstitute a coherent territorial state in China and a functioning international order in East Asia. Just as Germany in the Thirty Years War became the focal point at which early modern Europe's ideological antagonisms and its first 'military revolution' converged, so too did northern China become the primary arena in which contesting ideologies and an industrial military revolution collided in East Asia in the three decades from 1915. Increased violence interdependence, the power vacuum left by the Qing Empire's collapse, systemic ideological polarisation and the clash between the Japanese Empire and its nationalist nemeses form Chapter 9's dominant motifs, and the backdrop for the halting reconstitution of order along sovereign lines that I articulate at the chapter's close.

The origins, constitution and operation of the Sinosphere

A prefatory note on constitutional dualism and
the Chinese political tradition

Much like Latin Christendom, any examination of the Sinosphere must begin with an acknowledgement of the different traditions that informed its

---

[2] On the character of synarchy, both as an enduring theme in Chinese history and as a distinctive feature of the Anglo-Qing condominium that crystallised in the decades immediately following the Arrow War, see generally J. K. Fairbank, 'Synarchy under the treaties' in J. K. Fairbank (ed.), *Chinese Thought and Institutions* (The University of Chicago Press, 1957), pp. 204–31.

constitutional values and fundamental institutions. In the preceding chapters I noted the Aristotelian and Augustinian dimensions of political thought in the West, which roughly map onto a long-standing idealist–realist divide within the Western canon. As in Christendom, so too did a parallel idealist–realist dualism obtain within the Chinese political tradition, albeit one in which the official balance between the communicative and coercive dimensions of political action was reversed. Christendom's constitutional values derived from two products of the Axial Age, specifically Hellenic rationalism and Jewish revelation.[3] These two traditions found their synthesis through the teachings of the early Church, and received their political expression in Augustinian ideas developed in the context of the Western Roman Empire's accelerating disintegration. Similarly, the Sinosphere's constitutional values also derived from two traditions – specifically Confucianism and Legalism – that also owed their origins to the Axial Age.[4] In East Asia, the Axial Age overlapped with the Period of Warring States, and both Confucianism and Legalism emerged as responses to the moral and political disorder that dominated the period. The two traditions expressed radically opposed reactions to the turmoil of the times, and an awareness of the tensions between these traditions is essential to understanding the Sinosphere's constitution and subsequent evolution.

The belief in an impersonal and immanent order encompassing the cosmic, natural and social worlds is Confucianism's key point of departure. For Confucius and his followers, the question of government could never be addressed independently of an investigation into the nature of the broader cosmic order of which it was a part. Recalling the earlier unity that had characterised China under the ancient Zhou dynasty, Confucians surveyed the anarchy of the Warring States period and observed a disordered universe in urgent need of repair.[5] Through a Confucian lens, the ruler's cardinal responsibility was to maintain both cosmic and temporal harmony through the performance of ancient rites (*li*).[6] These rites were valued not merely for their religious significance, but also for their educative role in cultivating popular moral virtue. Confucians were first and foremost moralists, who believed in the perfectibility of human nature through the power of the ruler's moral example.[7] Furthermore, their holism led them to believe that China's

---

[3] On the Axial Age 'clash of civilisations' between Hellenic and Jewish culture that presaged and enabled this eventual synthesis, see K. Armstrong, *The Great Transformation: The world in the time of Buddha, Socrates, Confucius and Jeremiah* (London: Atlantic Books, 2006), pp. 351–2.

[4] *Ibid.*, pp. 331–3.   [5] *Ibid.*, p. 204.

[6] On the importance of *li* within the Confucian tradition, see M. Loewe, 'The religious and intellectual background' in D. Twitchett and M. Loewe (eds.), *The Cambridge History of China*, I: *The Ch'in and Han Empires, 221 BC–AD 220* (Cambridge University Press, 1986), pp. 706–8.

[7] *Ibid.*, p. 704.

travails during the Warring States period were but the most tangible manifestation of a cosmic disorder brought about by China's abandonment of the ancient rites that had formerly guaranteed a state of universal harmony.[8] Confucians thus argued that the restoration of peace and unity within China was both desirable and possible, and that this could come about if only China's rulers would return to the practices of correct ritual and righteous conduct that had previously underpinned a harmonious universe.[9]

In contrast to Confucians, the Legalists advanced an uncompromisingly worldly philosophy, abjuring philosophical speculation in favour of a more pragmatic concern with perfecting the methods of acquiring and retaining power in a violent and remorselessly competitive environment.[10] Whereas Confucians sought a condition of universal harmony and saw the violence of the Warring States period as a horrifying aberration, the Legalists conversely regarded violent conflict as an inevitable by-product of humanity's irrepressible greed and ambition, and dedicated themselves instead to the task of universal conquest.[11] Confucians advocated a paternalistic conception of government, whereby a benevolent ruler governed for the benefit of the people, and relied on the power of ritual both to maintain cosmic harmony and also to elevate the moral condition of the populace.[12] Conversely, the Legalists were unapologetically despotic in their outlook, favouring instead a combination of material incentives, harsh laws and exemplary punishments to subordinate the popular will to the interests of the ruler.[13]

In the face of Confucian moralism, Legalists advanced instead a self-consciously amoral philosophy of government, one that exceeded even the most sanguine expressions of modern realism in its endorsement of war and militarism. For the Legalists, a ruler should concentrate only on cultivating activities, such as agriculture and warfare, that would strengthen the state.[14] Additionally, Legalists recommended the cultivation of a vigorous martial ethos among the people. Thus Lord Shang, one of the most notorious early Legalists, proffered the following advice to would-be rulers:

---

[8] X. Yao, *An Introduction to Confucianism* (New York: Cambridge University Press, 2000), p. 69.

[9] *Ibid.* See also Armstrong, *The Great Transformation*, p. 209.

[10] For a useful summary of the Legalist tradition, see Fung Y.-L., *A Short History of Chinese Philosophy: A systematic account of Chinese thought from its origins to the present day* (New York: The Free Press, 1976), pp. 155–65.

[11] On Legalists' sanguine attitude towards the subject of war, see A. Waley, *Three Ways of Ancient Thought in China* (London: George Allen and Unwin Ltd, 1969), pp. 220–1.

[12] Loewe, 'The religious and intellectual background', p. 708. The parallel between Confucian political philosophy and Aristotelian conceptions of the state as a moral association is developed explicitly in Fung, *A Short History of Chinese Philosophy*, p. 73.

[13] Fung, *A Short History of Chinese Philosophy*, p. 162.

[14] Waley, *Three Ways of Ancient Thought in China*, p. 221.

Concentrate the people upon warfare, and they will be brave; let them care about other things, and they will be cowardly ... A people that looks to warfare as a ravening wolf looks to a piece of meat is a people that can be used. In general, fighting is a thing that the people detest. A ruler who can make the people delight in war will become king of kings. In a country that is really strong, the father will send his son, the elder brother his younger brother, the wife her husband, all saying as they speed him: 'Conquer, or let me never see you again.'[15]

Confucianism and Legalism thus emerged as diametrically opposite responses to the violent anarchy that characterised the Warring States period. In the short term, it was Legalism rather than Confucianism that was historically vindicated, the western state of Qin forcibly reunifying China in 221 BCE following the implementation of a host of 'self-strengthening' reforms modelled on Legalist prescriptions.[16] These reforms, including the establishment of a centralised bureaucracy and the mobilisation of mass conscript peasant armies, would exert a profound influence on Chinese practices of government thereafter. Critically, however, Legalism's amoral outlook was not merely jettisoned but rather actively repudiated following the Qin dynasty's collapse. Under the first Qin emperor, Legalism's hegemony had been institutionalised, with Confucian scholars persecuted and all schools of thought other than Legalism proscribed.[17] Memories of the violence of the Qin conquest and the tyranny of Qin rule contributed to Legalism's comprehensive delegitimation after the dynasty's demise. From the Han dynasty onwards, Legalism was identified with the brutality, militarism and hubris of the preceding dynasty.[18] Writing from their newly regained position of privilege, the Confucian literati skilfully interwove history and mythology to construct an enduring allegory of bad government centred on the Legalist-inspired misdeeds of the deposed Qin dynasty.[19] In all succeeding dynasties, government authority would derive its moral legitimacy from its perceived concordance with Confucian prescriptions. When it came to the actual practice of rule, however, successive governments

---

[15] *Ibid.*

[16] These reforms are described in D. Bodde, 'The state and empire of Ch'in' in D. Twitchett and M. Loewe (eds.), *The Cambridge History of China*, I, pp. 34–7. For an outstanding account of the Qin dynasty's success in uniting China's warring states that compares ancient China's experience with the persistence of political disunity in early modern Europe, see generally V. T.-B. Hui, *War and State Formation in Ancient China and Early Modern Europe* (New York: Cambridge University Press, 2005).

[17] Hui, *War and State Formation*, pp. 69–72.

[18] M. Loewe, 'The concept of sovereignty' in D. Twitchett and M. Loewe (eds.), *The Cambridge History of China*, I, p. 734.

[19] On the exaggerated character of Qin atrocities in accounts from the Early Han period onwards, see Bodde, 'The state and empire of Ch'in', p. 72.

would rely equally on Confucian benevolence and Legalist severity.[20] The Sinosphere's fundamental institutions clearly represented a synthesis of authoritative and coercive practices drawn respectively from the Confucian and Legalist traditions. But its constitutional values were much more emphatically Confucian in their complexion, and it is with an exploration of these values that we will begin.

The constitutional structure of the Sinosphere

The Sinosphere's constitutional structure was positively pervaded by Confucian values and ideals. Much like Augustine, Confucius had written at a time of great political volatility.[21] Similarly, just as Augustine sought simultaneously to fortify and bridle the temporal powers of his day by tethering their legitimacy to the Church's teachings, so Confucius also attempted to strengthen temporal rulers by bringing their behaviour into closer conformity with the moral imperatives of the cosmos. These similarities in originating circumstances and political intentions notwithstanding, the philosophies articulated by Augustine and Confucius were radically different. For Augustine, the problem of legitimising political authority was profoundly informed by his pessimistic assessment of human nature, and also by his beliefs concerning the existence of a supreme law-giver in the form of an omnipotent God. Augustinian political theology stressed the fact of man's essentially corrupt nature following the Fall, and the concomitant necessity of restraining human wickedness through the imposition of a remedial and authoritarian political order.[22] In Augustinian lights, temporal authority was an evil made necessary by man's initial defiance of God.[23] The injustices of earthly rulers were moreover construed both as a reflection of man's flawed nature, and as a continuing earthly punishment for Original Sin.[24] This justification for temporal rule simultaneously acknowledged its necessity while stressing both its moral imperfection and its subordinate status to the Church, which remained the agency responsible for interpreting God's will and spreading His Word among the faithful.

In contrast to Augustine's belief in the existence of a transcendent and omnipotent law-giver, Confucianism was conversely informed by a belief in the existence of an immanent and impersonal cosmic order.[25] Equally, whereas Augustine proceeded from a radically pessimistic assessment of a human nature forever tainted by Original Sin, Confucius and his followers instead stressed the perfectibility of human nature. For Confucians, humans were equally endowed with an innate moral sense, which it was the responsibility of rulers to cultivate through a combination of exemplary leadership

---

[20] *Ibid.*, p. 90.   [21] On this point, see Chen, 'The Confucian view of world order', p. 29.
[22] On this point, see Deane, *The Political and Social Ideas of Saint Augustine*, p. 117.
[23] *Ibid.*   [24] *Ibid.*   [25] Chen, 'The Confucian view of world order', p. 27.

and systematic moral indoctrination.[26] Unlike Augustinian political theology, Confucianism placed great importance on the moral qualities of the ruler himself, believing that his righteous conduct and proper adherence to pre-scribed ceremonies (*li*) could exercise a profoundly beneficial educative impact on the populace at large.[27] More broadly, Confucians believed that the ruler's righteous conduct and adherence to the proper ceremonies was necessary for the maintenance of cosmic as well as social order.[28] In Christendom, salvation was possible only through the Church, and the divine could be experienced only through the intercession of a celibate priestly caste. Accordingly, a ruler's moral failings were of little spiritual consequence for the faithful, however negatively they might impinge on believers' earthly existence. Conversely, for Confucians, the ruler's moral qualities were of supreme spiritual as well as earthly signifi-cance, with a failure to live in harmony with the moral imperatives of the cosmos inviting catastrophe for all.[29]

The normative complex underpinning the Sinosphere was thus informed by a world-view that conflated the spiritual and temporal worlds, and worked to sustain a hierarchical order with an omnicompetent universal emperor at its pinnacle. At an identity-constitutive level, the purpose of collective association was to achieve a temporal state of peace, fairness and harmony (*ping*) in accord with the rhythms of a larger cosmic order.[30] For successive Chinese dynasties, the emperor was conceived as the Son of Heaven, and the ambit of his rule was *Tianxia*, literally 'all under Heaven'.[31] From this privileged position, the emperor presided over a social order conceived in organic and rigidly hier-archical terms, with actors embedded in fixed relationships of super- and subordination. Of these relationships, the most important were the Three Bonds linking rulers and ruled, husbands and wives, and parents and chil-dren.[32] These bonds entailed actors' subscription to fixed roles involving specific duties that had to be assiduously fulfilled for social and cosmic order to be realised. The Confucian world-view was thus emphatically paternalistic, and envisaged the ideal society as one in which ruler and ruled, husband and wife, and father and son were to be linked in vertical, mutually reinforcing asymmetric ties of benevolence and obedience.[33] At an international level, this pattern was replicated in the relations between the Chinese empire and its tributary polities, with the latter being expected to show the same level of deference and filial piety to the emperor as one would expect from a dutiful son towards his father.[34]

---

[26] On this point, see J. K. Fairbank and M. Goldman, *China: A new history* (Cambridge, MA: The Belknap Press of Harvard University Press, 2006), p. 56.
[27] *Ibid.*, pp. 52–3.   [28] Fairbank, 'A preliminary framework', p. 6.
[29] Loewe, 'The concept of sovereignty', p. 744.
[30] Chen, 'The Confucian view of world order', p. 28.   [31] *Ibid.*, p. 29.
[32] Fairbank and Goldman, *China: A new history*, p. 19.   [33] *Ibid.*
[34] On this point, see specifically Kim, *The Last Phase of the East Asian World Order*, p. 7.

Where earthly preparation for eternal salvation constituted Christendom's *raison d'être*, the Sinosphere was conversely organised for the purposes of realising a state of peace, fairness and harmony in the social and cosmic spheres, which Confucian scholars deemed to be inextricably enmeshed. Similarly, whereas Christian ethics provided Christendom's primary means of normative pacification, the Confucian ethical code fulfilled this function in the Sinosphere. In their distinctive ways, both Christianity and Confucianism were characterised by a series of tensions between the egalitarian and hierarchical threads running through their respective philosophies. Both ethical frameworks began from a position that stressed the moral worth of each individual, either by dint of their status as children of God or alternatively as creatures cosmically endowed with an intrinsic capacity to think and act as moral beings. In this regard, the ethical-prescriptive norms of Christendom and the Sinosphere were very similar, with variants of the Golden Rule conspicuously featuring in both systems.[35] At the same time, however, both ethical systems functioned within highly inegalitarian social milieus, a fact that necessitated very distinctive cultural accommodations with the prevailing social order.

In Christendom, the Church's ideological hegemony was exercised in a highly fragmented political environment, characterised by high levels of corporate organisation among merchant and aristocratic elites. Consequently, Christianity's egalitarian message was diluted by the accommodations the Church was forced to make, particularly with a bellicose nobility. Both the Augustinian political theology and the social ideology of tri-functionality that sustained Christendom reflected this uneasy compromise, as did the co-existence of Christian ethics with a plethora of legal codes that assigned particularised bundles of privileges to discrete social groups.[36] Conversely, in the Sinosphere, ethical obligations were framed more comprehensively in the language of duties rather than reciprocal rights and responsibilities, reflecting Confucianism's inherent paternalism.[37] Additionally, rather than cohering within a social order marked by autonomously organised and functionally distinct estates and corporate groupings, the Chinese order was fractal in its organisation.[38] Instead of being distinguished by particularistic corporate

---

[35] Interestingly, while the Golden Rule is identified most closely with Christianity for most Westerners, Karen Armstrong reminds us that of all the ethical systems that developed out of the Axial Age, it was the Confucian tradition in which the Golden Rule was first formulated. See Armstrong, *The Great Transformation*, p. 208.

[36] On the heterogeneous character of the legal systems prevalent in feudal Europe, see G. Poggi, *The Development of the Modern State: A sociological introduction* (Stanford University Press, 1978), p. 86.

[37] Fairbank and Goldman, *China: A new history*, p. 51.

[38] On the fractal character of imperial China's social constitution, see R. B. Wong, *China Transformed: Historical change and the limits of European experience* (Ithaca: Cornell University Press, 1997), p. 107.

claims, an empire-wide gentry elite was rather united in its commitments to securing the physical safety and material welfare of the peasantry, as well as supervising their moral instruction.[39] Consequently, the Sinosphere's power-legitimating norms were far simpler than those undergirding Christendom. At the apex of the Sinosphere, a sacerdotal conception of kingship legitimised the emperor's suzerainty as the Son of Heaven over the East Asian ecumene.[40] Meanwhile, social relations were pervaded by a paternalistic Confucian world-view, which stabilised and perpetuated an intensely hierarchical order by emphasising the centrality of asymmetric and familial bonds of benevolence and obedience between superiors and inferiors at all levels of social organisation, from the individual household upwards.

At the institutional level, the Sinosphere was ordered around a suzerain state system centred on the sacred authority of the Son of Heaven. Under the *Pax Sinica*, China was held to be the singular centre of civilisation, and the emperor the supreme temporal and spiritual authority within the East Asian ecumene. In keeping with Confucian ideology, Chinese tributary states – including Korea, Annam (Vietnam) and also for a period Japan – stood in an explicit relationship of subordination to the emperor.[41] In contrast to the Westphalian state system that was to succeed it, relations between polities were conceived in moral rather than legal terms, with the same Confucian rhetoric of paternalism infusing traditional East Asian diplomacy as it did the emperor's relations with his subjects within China itself.[42] As was the case with many traditional composite empires, regional diplomacy was conducted along the lines of a 'rim-less wheel', with all interactions concentrated around the Chinese 'hub'.[43] China managed its relations bilaterally with each of its tributaries on different terms, while its tributaries did not generally engage in routine diplomatic interaction with one

---

[39] *Ibid.*

[40] H. L. Miller, 'The late imperial Chinese state' in D. Shambaugh (ed.), *The Modern Chinese State* (Cambridge University Press, 2000), p. 17.

[41] Although it must be noted that the Ming dynasty expelled Japan from the Sinosphere in 1621, after which it continued to have extensive economic relations with regional actors but no longer identified as a formal tributary of the Chinese emperor. See Kang, 'Hierarchy in Asian international relations', p. 63.

[42] Thus, in discussing Sino-Korean relations under the old order, Kim observes: 'Since relations between China and Korea were considered analogous to those between father and son or between elder and younger brother, they imposed on both parties moral rather than legal obligations'; see Kim, *The Last Phase of the East Asian World Order*, p. 7.

[43] The rim-less hub model of empire, which largely reflects the model of traditional diplomacy in the Sinosphere, is characterised by the following features: (i) vertical interaction between core and periphery; (ii) minimal to no interaction between periphery and periphery; and (iii) an absence of multilateral interaction between the core and its satellite polities. See A. J. Motyl, *Revolutions, Nations, Empires: Conceptual limits and theoretical possibilities* (New York: Columbia University Press, 1999), pp. 121–2.

another.[44] Critically, however, and in contrast to most classical empires, the Chinese emperor did little to interfere with the domestic authority of tributary rulers within their own territories.[45] While obliged to acknowledge the emperor's suzerainty through participation in ritual acts of obeisance, rulers such as the successive kings of the Korean Yi dynasty were generally free to govern their people without Chinese interference.[46] At the same time, however, the high culture of China's chief tributary polities was so heavily Sinicised, and China's material power so preponderant, that direct intervention was largely unnecessary to secure Chinese goals within her tributary polities.

Within the East Asian suzerain state system, order was secured through recourse to the same careful admixture of authoritative and coercive power resources as that manifest in all of the orders considered in this book. However, what is most striking about the Sinosphere is the self-consciousness with which authoritative and coercive power resources were distinguished from one another, as well as the conspicuous priority rhetorically accorded to the former in sustaining regional order. Within Confucianism, a clear distinction was drawn between different forms of social power. At one end of the spectrum resided a form of power centring around *li*, a term referring to the traditional customs and rites performed by the Son of Heaven to communicate social norms to others and thus maintain cosmic order.[47] Traditional East Asian diplomacy was highly ceremonial and explicitly public and performative in its forms, with official interactions between China and its tributaries being saturated with religious and symbolic significance. Thus, for example, the coronation of new rulers in tributary states could be legitimised only by an imperial investiture mission, in which the newly appointed ruler would kowtow to symbols of imperial authority provided by the emperor's representatives.[48] This ritual not only legitimised the local ruler in the eyes of the local gentry, but also symbolically reaffirmed the relations of benevolence and obedience obtaining between the emperor and his vassal rulers. The tribute missions despatched by tributary polities to China provided yet another forum for the ritual affirmation of the emperor's suzerainty, with performance of the kowtow

---

[44] On the lack of regular diplomatic interaction between tributary states (with the possible exception of Korea and Japan), see Y. Zhang, 'System, empire and state in Chinese international relations', *Review of International Studies*, 27(5) (2001), 53.

[45] On this point, see for example Kang, 'Hierarchy in Asian international relations', p. 57.

[46] *Ibid.*

[47] On the Confucian concept of the *li/fa* distinction between authoritative and coercive modes of power, see the interesting discussion in Chen, 'The Confucian view of world order', p. 33. See also Bozeman, *The Future of Law in a Multicultural World*, pp. 144–5.

[48] On the broad significance of investiture as an authoritative institution within the Sinosphere, see T. B. Lam, 'Intervention versus tribute in Sino-Vietnamese relations, 1788–1790' in J. K. Fairbank (ed.), *The Chinese World Order: Traditional China's foreign relations* (Cambridge, MA: Harvard University Press, 1968), p. 179.

and the provision of gifts by the representatives of tribute states investing these trade missions with a profound political and spiritual importance.[49]

From a modern vantage point, the ceremonial forms of traditional East Asian diplomacy may seem both arcane and hopelessly archaic. But the temptation to dismiss them as a baroque and irrelevant artifice must be resisted, for doing so elides the fact that these practices were anchored in deeply held inter-subjective beliefs about the nature of social and cosmic order, and reflected the central importance contemporaries accorded to the maintenance of ideological ortho-doxy in sustaining the Sinosphere. Having made this observation, I must add that the normative power centred around *li* was systematically supplemented by reliance on *fa*. In that strand of Chinese thinking that traces its origins to the Legalist tradition, *fa* (regulations) referred to the recourse to the range of material rewards and penalties available to the Son of Heaven to induce compliance from those impervious to the power of ritually communicated virtue.[50] Moreover, while *li* was suffused with sacred significance and formed a major focus of Confucian scholarship, the 'two handles' of material induce-ments and exemplary coercion that constituted *fa* received at least as great an emphasis in ancient Chinese political philosophy.[51] Internationally, *fa* man-ifested itself most conspicuously in China's intermittent resort to armed force to maintain order within the Sinosphere. In some situations, this entailed the suppression of criminal elements (the most conspicuous of these being Japanese pirates), while in others it involved direct Chinese military interven-tion to protect tributary polities from predators originating from beyond the Sinosphere.[52] In all instances, however, the emperor's resort to force was legitimised not by reference to a shared legal code, but rather by invoking the sacred charisma of the Son of Heaven.

At the material level, the Sinosphere subsisted on a foundation of concen-trated coercion and productive capacity qualitatively greater than anything comparable in late medieval Christendom. In fifteenth-century Europe, the diffusion of firearms and modern artillery had irretrievably corroded Christendom's feudal base, facilitating its eventual transition towards a sover-eign international order.[53] Conversely, the Sinosphere's experience was more consistent with that of most early modern Eurasian societies, with the spread of firearms and artillery working to strengthen and expand pre-existing imperial formations. In China's case, the 'general crisis' of the seventeenth century was resolved with the transition from the Ming to the Qing dynasties, a process that occurred roughly contemporaneously with the birth of the Westphalian order

---

[49] *Ibid.* [50] Fairbank and Goldman, *China: A new history*, p. 55. [51] *Ibid.*
[52] China's attempts to protect Korea from Japanese predation and Vietnam from French conquest in the late nineteenth century attest to the durability of China's commitment to fulfilling its responsibilities as regional suzerain even in the Sinosphere's last phase.
[53] See the discussion in Ch. 3 above.

in Europe. From the early seventeenth century, nomadic Manchu pastoralists from the Asian steppe had augmented their existing superiority in cavalry with the introduction of firearms and light artillery into their armed forces.[54] This adaptation, while not as far-reaching as the European military revolution, was nevertheless sufficient to enable them to rapidly conquer China in 1644.[55] The Manchus then employed a combination of mobile cavalry units, artillery and Han Chinese infantrymen to add vast swathes of territory from the south and south-west to their holdings, expanding China's borders to their furthest extent by the end of the eighteenth century.[56]

The stability provided by the Manchu empire enabled an expansion of trade and the continued accumulation of wealth throughout East Asia over the seventeenth and eighteenth centuries. Just as Christendom's consolidation under the papal–imperial diarchy had permitted a surge in wealth accumulation and demographic expansion in eleventh-century Europe, so too did Qing suzerainty enable a similar process of growth in early modern East Asia. Within China itself, historians estimate that the empire's population more than doubled over the course of the eighteenth century.[57] Moreover, this demographic expansion was accompanied, at least up to 1750, by sustained increases in both land and labour productivity, providing the population with a standard of living generally superior to that of most Western Europeans at mid-century.[58] This economic dynamism spurred the growth of trading networks throughout East Asia and beyond, with the bulk of intra-regional trade directed towards serving the voracious Chinese appetite for both staples and luxury goods. The growth of trade in turn fed into the increasing monetisation of East Asian economies, aiding revenue extraction and stimulating the continuing centralisation of political power throughout the Sinosphere's constituent polities.[59] Without the quantum leap in productive and destructive capacities bequeathed by the industrial revolution, the Qing Empire and its tributaries remained vulnerable to the threat of Western predation that eventually materialised from the Opium Wars onwards. But this observation unfairly diminishes the Qing dynasty's achievements, and overlooks the exceptionalism of the Western experience after 1750. More fundamentally, it threatens to obscure the fact that judging by any material measure of productive and destructive

---

[54] This process is discussed in detail in di Cosimo. 'Did guns matter? Firearms and the Qing formation.'

[55] *Ibid.*, p. 153.

[56] On this point, see E. S. Rawski, 'The Qing formation and the early modern period' in L. A. Struve (ed.), *The Qing Formation in World-Historical Time* (Cambridge MA: Harvard University Press, 2004), p. 218.

[57] Goldstone, 'Neither late imperial nor early modern', p. 259.

[58] *Ibid.*, p. 261. Goldstone notes the one exception to this generalisation at 1750 would potentially have been south-east England, then in the early stages of industrialisation.

[59] On this point, see Kang, 'Hierarchy in Asian international relations', p. 67.

capacities, the Sinosphere was by far the most successful of all regional orders in the early modern world down to the late eighteenth century.

Recalling the theoretical framework informing this inquiry, I maintain that all social orders are composed of various networks yoked respectively around principles of kinship, patronage, contract and bureaucratic command. This observation is borne out by a consideration of the Sinosphere's constitution. Throughout the seventeenth and eighteenth centuries, a major foundation of the Qing dynasty's success was the hybrid nature of their empire, with the conquering Manchu Raj exploiting a broad spectrum of social networks to manage and expand the Chinese imperium. Within the empire's sedentary Han core, the Manchus largely relied upon the operation of the long-established imperial bureaucracy to maintain order.[60] A dedicated corps of administrators enforced the emperor's writ at the provincial level, while at the village level an indoctrinated Confucian gentry-scholar elite assumed responsibility for the day-to-day tasks of governance.[61] Conversely, in the Inner Asian periphery, the Manchus chose not to extend the Confucian bureaucracy into recently conquered territories, and instead governed indirectly through a series of local intermediaries.[62]

Given their status as a conquest dynasty, the Manchus wisely mitigated their dependence on a Han-dominated bureaucracy by maintaining extensive kinship ties between the imperial court and allied clans among the Manchu aristocracy.[63] This strategy provided the emperor with an independent power base bonded together by real and imagined ties of kinship, and enabled successive Qing emperors to concentrate powers in the imperial office that far surpassed those of their Ming predecessors.[64] Finally, the Qing dynasty perpetuated the Ming system of tribute trade. In so doing, it sought to dictate the terms upon which foreigners interacted with the empire, and also to guard against the prospect of alternative power formations cohering within the interstices of developing commercial networks. The dynasty's efforts to funnel commercial activities exclusively through the structures of the tribute system were admittedly only partially effective.[65] But considered in their totality, the Manchus' efforts to marshal diverse power resources through the social networks available to them were remarkably successful, enabling the empire's

---

[60] Rawski, 'The Qing formation and the early modern period', pp. 224–5. Rawski notes that while the Manchus retained the bureaucratic structures inherited from the Ming dynasty, as an alien conquest dynasty they also introduced a series of innovations that increased the power of the imperial throne vis-à-vis the bureaucracy. The phrase 'Manchu Raj' is taken from J. Darwin, *After Tamerlane: The global history of empire since 1405* (London: Allen Lane, 2007), p. 132.

[61] Wong, *China Transformed*, p. 107.

[62] Rawski, 'The Qing formation and the early modern period', pp. 225–6.

[63] *Ibid.*, pp. 224–5.   [64] *Ibid.*

[65] On the extent to which regional trade managed to slip the bonds of the tributary system, see Kang, 'Hierarchy in Asian international relations', p. 65.

wealth, population and territory to grow continuously during the eighteenth century.

The final dimension of the Sinosphere that is salient to this investigation is its level of violence interdependence. Simply stated, Qing China was the most powerful and enduring of the early modern gunpowder empires, and it was largely on the basis of the Qing Empire's military predominance that order in East Asia rested. In the north-west, the ancient threat of invasion from nomadic pastoralists had effectively been neutralised following the Manchu conquest of China in 1644.[66] Manchu military strategy admittedly paid less heed to maritime threats from East Asia.[67] But in the pre-steamship era of the seventeenth and eighteenth centuries, Europeans lacked the capacity to project power along China's riverine arteries, and it was possible for the Manchus to confine them to limited coastal enclaves.[68] At the same time, Japan's self-imposed isolation under the Tokugawa Shogunate removed from contention the one potential regional challenger to Chinese supremacy over the East Asian littoral. With the threat of pastoralist invasion from the steppe eliminated, and the maritime threat from the West and from Japan yet to emerge, China enjoyed regional military supremacy beyond challenge. This military supremacy helped sustain regional order without serious challenge down to 1800.

The Sinosphere's constitutional order is schematically presented in Table 6.1. The same caveats that applied to my discussion of Christendom obtain equally here. International orders are constituted by an elaborate amalgam of normative, institutional and material elements that fit together imperfectly, and are beset by tensions and inconsistencies that are elided in schematic portraits. Equally, schematic outlines convey a sense of stability that belies international orders' provisional and ultimately transient nature. These qualifications aside, the following snapshot of the Sinosphere nevertheless provides a useful point of departure for an examination of the dynamics that led to its destruction.

---

[66] On the Qing dynasty's subjugation of nomadic peoples and rival polities on its Inner Asian frontier in the eighteenth century, an enterprise that Rawski explicitly compares to the colonising activities undertaken by the European powers in other regions, see Rawski, 'The Qing formation and the early modern period', pp. 218–21.

[67] On the long-standing failure of successive Chinese dynasties to defend their maritime frontier from attack and its long-term geopolitical consequences for the East Asian region, see generally J. J. Grygiel, *Great Powers and Geopolitical Change* (Baltimore: Johns Hopkins University Press, 2006), Ch. 6.

[68] On China's relations with Great Britain in the pre-steamship era, Daniel Headrick writes as follows: 'Like an elephant and a whale, China and Britain evolved in two different habitats. At sea, Britain was invincible and could destroy any Chinese fleet or coastal fort. China, on the other hand, was a land empire with few interests beyond her shores and few cities along her coasts. As long as the Europeans were incapable of pushing their way inland, the Celestial Empire was invulnerable.' See D. R. Headrick, *The Tools of Empire: Technology and European imperialism in the nineteenth century* (Oxford University Press, 1981), p. 45.

Table 6.1 *The international order of the Sinosphere, 1644–1850*

Normative complex	Governing institutional framework	Order-enabling material context
Identity-constitutive norms Achievement of a temporal state of harmony (*ping*) in concordance with cosmic order	**Ordering framework** Suzerain state system governed by the Chinese emperor as Son of Heaven	**Aggregate capacities for production and destruction** Proto-capitalist mode of production organised within the framework of centralised gunpowder empire
Ethical-prescriptive norms Confucian ethics	**Authoritative institutions** Ritual enactment of shared identities (*li*) through investiture missions and tribute trade	**Dominant mobilisational networks** Dominance of imperial bureaucracy and centralised imperial patronage networks
Power-legitimating norms Sacerdotal conception of emperor and Confucian norms of asymmetric benevolence and obedience	**Coercive institutions** Imperial resort to judicial sanctions and violence (*fa*) to rectify error and restore cosmic order	**Violence interdependence** High concentration and low accumulation of coercive means (moderate violence interdependence)

The decay of the Sinosphere

Latent vulnerabilities

For all its strengths, the Sinosphere was nevertheless beset with a range of vulnerabilities that became increasingly manifest from the late eighteenth century onwards. The most basic of these was the extremely loose nature of the suzerain order over which China presided, and the dependence of this order upon the continued strength of the Chinese Empire. During periods of dynastic ascendancy, the modest character of China's authority claims over its tributary states assured local rulers a high level of autonomy, thereby minimising resistance to Chinese hegemony. In times of dynastic decline, by contrast, East Asia's Sino-centrism also ensured that domestic instability within China rapidly translated into a deterioration of order internationally as well. This co-variance between dynastic decline and regional instability was evident for example in the Ming dynasty's dying decades in the late sixteenth and early seventeenth centuries. During this period, the Japanese ruler Toyotomi Hideyoshi launched an attack on Korea that was motivated as much by an aspiration to assert equal status with the Ming emperor as it was by a desire for territorial aggrandisement.[69] While imperial forces managed to repel Japan and further strengthen China's bonds with Korea in the process, the conflict nevertheless drained the imperial treasury and thus hastened the dynasty's eventual fall to Manchu conquerors in 1644.[70] More fundamentally, however, the convoluted diplomatic manoeuvrings that accompanied China's early efforts to secure Japan's withdrawal from Korea revealed the fragility of the consensus underpinning the Sinosphere's diplomatic structure. Ambiguity remains as to whether Toyotomi's demand to be recognised as an equal of the Chinese emperor was reflective of an ignorance of the Sinosphere's norms, or whether he was actively seeking to revise these norms through the use of force.[71] What the protracted negotiations between Chinese, Korean and Japanese envoys nonetheless illustrated was the openness of these norms to contestation, particularly at times when China was weak. Consequently, although it was undeniably important as a mechanism for regional order maintenance, China's tributary system was also susceptible to reinterpretations that deviated – sometimes substantially – from the rigid bonds of benevolence and obedience favoured by the imperial court.

While serious in its long-term implications, the existence of a gap between prescription and practice in the Sinosphere's operation is unexceptional from a comparative perspective, being rather illustrative of the imperfections that trouble all international orders. In China's case, however, departures from prescribed norms were particularly dangerous given the disproportionate emphasis accorded to the maintenance of Confucian orthodoxy as a prop for imperial power. The conflation of the sacred and temporal realms in imperial ideology provided ruling dynasties with a great source of strength during times of peace. But in times of dynastic decline, the conjoining of the sacred and temporal realms conversely encouraged actors to interpret the empire's political troubles in spiritual terms. Consequently, failures in governance were often popularly conceived as signifying that the emperor's Heavenly Mandate had been withdrawn, and that the imperial household must consequently be

---

[69] On this point, see Swope, 'Deceit, disguise and dependence', p. 766.

[70] To convey a sense of the scale of the conflict, Toyotomi's invasions from 1592 to 1598 are said by some to have inflicted more destruction, hardship and misery on the Korean people than the Korean War of 1950–3. See *ibid.*, p. 758.

[71] Although Swope characterises Toyotomi's campaigns as 'a revisionist attempt to break the [tributary] system apart', his own meticulously detailed analysis of the diplomacy surrounding the conflict does nevertheless convey a strong sense of the Japanese leader's ignorance of many of the Sinosphere's most fundamental constitutional norms. See *ibid.*, p. 757.

overthrown. For this reason alone, China's insistence that foreigners conform to the rites and practices of the tributary system is understandable, given that a failure of 'barbarians' to observe these rites constituted an explicit challenge to the Confucian order that threatened the emperor's authority domestically as well as internationally. More generally, the religious legitimation of imperial authority ensured that oppositional movements within Chinese society cast their grievances in similarly absolute and eschatological terms. Thus, while barbarian invasion from the Asian steppe constituted the greatest external threat to successive dynasties, the threat of millenarian rebellion constituted the greatest domestic danger to the perpetuation of imperial authority.

The fragility of the tributary system during periods of dynastic decline and the threat of millenarian rebellion together constituted the Sinosphere's two great historical sources of structural vulnerability. Under the Qing dynasty, these vulnerabilities were overlaid by a third and more historically contingent weakness, namely the Han majority's xenophobic hostility towards their Manchu masters. For while the Manchus followed the path trod by previous steppe conquerors of China, becoming progressively sedentarised and Sinicised following their victory over the Ming dynasty, they nevertheless retained a distinctive corporate identity that marked them out as separate from and superior to the Han majority. In southern China in particular, the resulting Han xenophobia assumed a self-consciously political form in the emergence of armed secret societies dedicated to the overthrow of the Manchus and the restoration of the Ming dynasty.[72] In time, this anti-Manchu sentiment would ripen and progressively assume first millenarian and then nationalist incarnations, which would first weaken and then ultimately destroy the Qing imperium.

The onset of internal decay

Like Christendom before it, the Sinosphere eventually became a victim of its own success, with the rapid demographic and commercial expansion of the mid-Qing period seeding the Chinese social landscape with tensions that would eventually imperil the empire's survival. Despite the Qing dynasty's impressive territorial expansion during the eighteenth century, the empire's population grew so rapidly that the land–population ratio diminished over time.[73] The introduction of New World crops such as sweet potatoes and maize enabled the

---

[72] For a historical genealogy of the immediate predecessors of anti-Qing 'secret societies' in southern China, see generally D. Ownby, *Brotherhoods and Secret Societies in Early and Mid-Qing China* (Stanford University Press, 1996), Ch. 1.

[73] S. M. Jones and P. A. Kuhn, 'Dynastic decline and the roots of rebellion' in D. Twitchett and J. K. Fairbank (eds.), *The Cambridge History of China*, X: *Late Ch'ing 1800–1911*, Pt I (Cambridge University Press, 1978), pp. 108–10.

cultivation of marginal lands, thus forestalling the risk of widespread famine.[74] But declining per capita acreage of land, combined with intermittent poor harvests, ensured that increasing numbers of peasants were forced into bankruptcy.[75] Thus compelled to leave the land, many drifted towards work in non-agrarian sectors, others became vagrants, while others still joined a growing pool of itinerant bandits and urban gangs.[76] Given that the Manchus generally imposed few effective barriers to internal migration within their empire, population pressures in densely populated regions could be partially relieved by peasant migration to more sparsely settled territories. But in the absence of revolutionary advances in agricultural productivity, such expedients only temporarily alleviated the empire's accumulating demographic pressures. Worse still, migration towards less settled areas engendered tensions between migrants and established communities, particularly where ethnic differences distinguished migrants from the native population.[77]

In addition to demographically induced social tensions, creeping processes of institutional decay also beset the empire by the late eighteenth century. These processes manifested themselves most keenly in the central state's declining capacity to fulfil the paternalistic promises of Confucian orthodoxy as the century progressed. The Qing state's declining institutional capacity was explicable partially as a result of the Emperor Kangxi's decision in 1713 to permanently fix his subjects' tax quotas in perpetuity.[78] While the emperor's edict was politically astute at the time of issue, his successsors' willingness to maintain this edict contributed to a steady decline in the real value of state revenues, thanks to the continuous inflation induced by robust commercial expansion over the eighteenth century.[79] The decline in real revenues had predictable consequences for state capacity. The government gradually withdrew from governance functions, such as stockpiling food in state granaries to moderate food prices and ensure the masses' food security, which had earlier been central to the dynasty's cultivation of popular legitimacy.[80] Corresponding to the decline in state activism, the state also tolerated – and in some cases tacitly encouraged – local office-holders' efforts to make good the shortfall in central revenues through the arbitrary imposition of additional taxes at the municipal and provincial levels.[81] Both the atrophying of central government and the growth of arbitrary taxation at the local and provincial levels nurtured widespread corruption which, in turn, fed back into a vicious cycle of diminishing governmental capacity and escalating popular disillusionment.

[74] *Ibid.*, p. 109.
[75] H.-F. Hung, 'Early modernities and contentious politics in mid-Qing China, *c.*1740–1839', *International Sociology*, 19(4) (2004), 482.
[76] *Ibid.*   [77] Jones and Kuhn, 'Dynastic decline and the roots of rebellion', pp. 108–9.
[78] Hung, 'Early modernities and contentious politics', p. 483.   [79] *Ibid.*   [80] *Ibid.*
[81] *Ibid.*, pp. 483–4.

Demographic expansion, accumulating social tensions, and diminishing governmental capacity and legitimacy had all featured in prior cycles of dynastic decline. These problems were joined at the eighteenth century's end by the eruption of a series of violent rebellions against Qing rule. The most destructive of these was the White Lotus revolt, which shook parts of northern and central China from 1796 to 1804. Subscribing to a Manichean offshoot of Buddhism, White Lotus adherents venerated the Eternal Mother, the universal progenitor from whom all humans had originated, and from whom they had become estranged upon their entry into the temporal world.[82] Like many millennial sects, White Lotus practitioners construed contemporary social strife as a symptom of humanity's estrangement from the divine. Similarly, they emphasised familiar millennial themes concerning the transient nature of the temporal world and the imminent approach of the apocalypse. The Qing dynasty's looming collapse would be accompanied by devastation on a truly cosmic scale, with the Eternal Mother visiting horrifying punishments on the non-believers. Thus it was prophesied: 'for an entire day and night, a black wind will rise up and blow, killing countless people, leaving mountains of white bones and oceans of blood'.[83] Predictably, a happier fate awaited believers in the Eternal Mother. For them, salvation would be provided through the intercession of the Maitreya, the Buddha of the Future, who would spare them from annihilation and secure their reconciliation with the Eternal Mother.[84]

The foregoing comments imply a potentially misleading homogeneity in the beliefs that drove various sects to participate in the White Lotus rebellion. This qualification aside, the rebellion is relevant to this inquiry for several reasons. First, the rebellion reflected both the depth of popular hostility towards the Qing dynasty and the frailty of governing institutions in the face of armed challenge. Despite the fragmented nature of sectarian resistance, it took imperial forces the better part of a decade to defeat the rebellion. The costs of suppression were also immense, draining the imperial treasury of the equivalent of five years' revenue and thereby eliminating the surplus built up under the Qianlong emperor's long reign.[85] Besides its material costs, the rebellion also inflicted severe reputational damage on the Qing dynasty.[86] In a pattern that would be repeated on a radically larger scale fifty years later, the White Lotus resistance inspired rebellions in other parts of the country, further

---

[82] On the cosmology of the White Lotus movement, see S. Naquin, *Millenarian Rebellion in China: The Eight Trigrams uprising of 1813* (New Haven: Yale University Press, 1976), pp. 9–12.

[83] Quoted in *ibid.*, p. 12.   [84] *Ibid.*, p. 10.

[85] B. A. Elleman, *Modern Chinese Warfare, 1795–1989* (New York: Routledge, 2001), p. 10.

[86] Fairbank and Goldman, *China: A new history*, p. 191.

compounding the empire's woes.[87] More revealingly still, the rebellion was also reflective of the proliferation of clandestine and potentially subversive social networks throughout the empire. Despite the authorities' efforts, White Lotus congregations persisted in northern and central China following the crushing of their eponymous rebellion, their sectarian tradition informing subsequent insurgencies down into the twentieth century.[88] In Taiwan and the south-eastern provinces of Fujian and Guangdong, meanwhile, the late eighteenth century also saw the growth of 'secret societies', including the so-called Triads. While presenting mainly as a criminal rather than a political threat, the Triads nevertheless subscribed to Ming restorationism, and were involved in fomenting rebellion in Taiwan as early as 1787.[89] In the south-western edges of the empire, the province of East Turkestan also presented challenges for the Manchus. Having only recently been conquered, the province remained connected to the neighbouring khanate of Kokand through overlapping ties of faith, kinship and trade. Now exiled in Kokand, Turkestan's former rulers retained influence in East Turkestan due to their leadership of a Sufi brotherhood that straddled the border between the two territories. This brotherhood and the saintly families attached to it would eventually provide the primary vehicles through which successive jihads would be launched against the Qings in Turkestan throughout the nineteenth century.[90]

In an empire as vast as the Qing imperium, it would be unreasonable to have expected the authorities to have detected and suppressed all or indeed even most of the clandestine networks spreading throughout its territory. Nevertheless, in confronting its domestic enemies, the Qing dynasty increasingly adopted short-term expedients that served only to further weaken its grip on power. Thus, in the case of the White Lotus rebellion, the imperial forces'

---

[87] The most notable of these rebellions were the Miao rebellion of 1795–1806, and the Eight Trigram Sect revolt of 1813. The former rebellion was largely driven by the aboriginal population's resentment of the creeping usurpation of their land and power by encroaching Han settlers, and as such lacked the overtly sectarian character of the White Lotus rebellion. Conversely, the Eight Trigram Sect was an offshoot of the White Lotus movement, with the 1813 uprising demonstrating the movement's persistence years after its alleged suppression by imperial forces.

[88] While White Lotus repertoires of rebellion, including the practice of magical rites of invulnerability, informed subsequent rebellions in North China in particular in the twentieth century (specifically the Boxer rebels and the Red Spears), Elizabeth Perry has argued convincingly against earlier suppositions claiming a direct ideological or organisational ancestry between White Lotus practitioners and later rebel movements. See generally E. J. Perry, *Rebels and Revolutionaries in North China, 1845–1945* (Stanford University Press, 1980).

[89] Ownby, *Brotherhoods and Secret Societies in Early and Mid-Qing China*, p. 5.

[90] On this point, see J. Fletcher 'Ch'ing Inner Asia' in Twitchett and Fairbank (eds.), *The Cambridge History of China*, X: *Late Ch'ing, 1800–1911*, Pt I, pp. 89–90.

repeated failures to crush the rebels drove the authorities to rely on popular militias financed and led by the local gentry to contain the insurgency. In hindsight, the establishment of these militias may have been unavoidable, given the weakness of imperial forces and given also the ineffectiveness of the mercenaries who were also hired at ruinous expense to suppress the rebellion.[91] But for all their ostensible commitments to upholding Confucian orthodoxy, the militias also signified a diffusion of military power from the central state to the localities, and also from the conquering Manchus to the conquered Hans. More worryingly still for the Manchus, the militia system could not be rolled up following the defeat of the rebellion. Instead, given the state's fiscal weakness and the unabating accumulation of social pressures accruing from continued population growth, the dynasty was forced to accept the militia system as a vital component of the empire's security apparatus. In this way, the rebellion accelerated the dispersal of armed force within the empire, further corroding the Sinosphere's imperial core.

Finally, in addition to the internal processes of decline buffeting the Qing dynasty, the Sinosphere was weakened from the late eighteenth century by destabilising regional developments intimately connected to the dynasty's decay. Specifically, the enormous surge in Chinese prosperity during the first century of Qing rule had spurred the growth of regional trading networks throughout maritime East Asia.[92] The growth of these networks, and the parallel thickening of commercial linkages between the East Asian ecumene and regional economies centred on the Indian and Atlantic oceans, in turn placed significant strain on the Sinosphere's system of tributary trade.[93] Court officials in the late eighteenth and early nineteenth centuries continued to recognise the political importance of caging China's commercial relations with its neighbours within the insulating framework of the tributary system. But the quasi-monopolistic privileges afforded to the imperial court by the tributary system also lent themselves to abuse. As China's fiscal position deteriorated due to reasons already discussed, the temptation to abuse this privilege proved impossible to resist.

Consequently, from the late eighteenth century, the Qing court increasingly manipulated the tribute trade for short-term commercial advantage, demanding larger volumes of tributary goods from its vassals in exchange for devalued imperial 'gifts', which frequently took the form of a steadily more debased

---

[91] On the great financial cost of employing mercenaries to defeat the White Lotus rebels, and the political dangers involved given the mercenaries' dubious and mercurial loyalties, see P. A. Kuhn, *Rebellion and its Enemies in Late Imperial China: Militarization and social structure, 1796–1864* (Cambridge, MA: Harvard University Press, 1970), p. 50.

[92] T. Hamashita, 'The intra-regional system in East Asia in modern times' in P. Katzenstein and T. Shiraishi (eds.), *Network Power: Japan and Asia* (Ithaca: Cornell University Press, 1997), p. 125.

[93] *Ibid.*, pp. 124–8.

Chinese paper currency.[94] Previously, vassal states had reconciled themselves to Chinese paramountcy because of the disproportionate material benefits they had derived from their participation in the tribute trade. But the Qing dynasty's manipulation of the tribute system for its own fiscal convenience corroded the commercial basis for this political accommodation. A parallel system of unofficial trade correspondingly grew in importance as both Chinese merchants and their overseas counterparts sought to evade the strictures of the old order.[95] Long-standing sub-regional systems of tribute trade such as that linking Vietnam with its neighbouring vassals similarly expanded, further solidifying a multilateral regional trading order that departed substantially from the idealised 'hub and spokes' model of the classical Sinosphere.[96]

The significance of this expansion in regional and extra-regional trading networks was as much political as it was commercial. For as the intra-Asian trade became ever more lucrative, its gravitational pull stimulated the growing involvement of extra-regional powers that neither comprehended nor respected the cultural norms underwriting the Sinosphere's constitution. Europeans had of course been commercially involved in the Pacific from as far back as the fifteenth century. But the expansion of intra-Asian trade significantly strengthened Western traders' incentives to entrench themselves as brokers within the widening webs of intra-Asian commerce after 1800 – similarly, the contemporaneous increase in European production of raw materials in Asia (e.g. rubber), both to fuel their industrialisation and also to sell their industrial products to Asia, created further incentives to link intra-Asian markets with international markets through the creation of Asian entrepôts in which balanced trade between the two markets could be conducted.[97] For the better part of the nineteenth century, Westerners would pursue their commercial goals via contradictory policies of negotiation and confrontation, seeking to insinuate themselves within the pre-existing tributary system, while also overlaying it with an incompatible system of unequal diplomacy reflecting the forms and ideals of an expanding Western global state system.[98] It would be the failure to synthesise these different systems that would eventually condemn the Sinosphere to oblivion.

Conclusion

By 1800 CE, the Qing dynasty was showing unmistakable signs of decline. In a technologically stagnant environment with limited scope for further increases in agricultural productivity, the empire was running out of the arable land

[94] *Ibid.*, p. 125.   [95] *Ibid.*, pp. 125–6.   [96] *Ibid.*, p. 123.   [97] *Ibid.*, pp. 127–8.
[98] On the hybrid nature of the resulting order, see generally T. Hamashita, 'Tribute and treaties: East Asian treaty ports networks in the era of negotiation, 1834–1894', *European Journal of East Asian Studies*, 1(1) (2001), 59–87.

needed to sustain its burgeoning population. While China was fortunate to be spared Malthusian correctives of the magnitude that had swept Christendom in the mid-fourteenth century, the absence of empire-wide famines or plagues ensured steadily declining per capita acreage, increasing peasant indebtedness and bankruptcy, thereby further fuelling social and political instability. Like Christendom before it, China was also experiencing widespread institutional decay, manifest in declining central state revenues and activism, together with a concomitant growth in the powers of arbitrary and corrupt local officials.

Faced with both growing social tensions and declining governmental capacity, sections of the population became increasingly receptive to sectarian calls to overthrow the Qing dynasty. Whereas lay pietist movements within pre-Reformation Christendom had generally shied away from calls to over-throw the temporal authorities, in China sectarian rebels refracted the holistic cosmology of the ruling dynasty in their own conjoined impulses towards political and spiritual renewal.[99] The dynasty's responses to the resulting rebellions in turn accelerated the diffusion of military power towards local Han gentry-officials, cultivating the growth of orthodox private militias to counter heterodox clandestine networks. In this way, late Qing policies partially reversed the centralisation and bureaucratic rationalisation of violence that had accompanied China's absorption of the first 'military revolution' in the mid seventeenth century. Finally, the imperial court's opportunistic efforts to manipulate the tribute trade system – in part to compensate for the costs of suppressing internal rebellions – inadvertently drove a surge in unofficial intra-Asian commerce that further undercut the Sinosphere's 'hub and spokes' format. In so doing, it thereby indirectly helped draw Western actors further into Asian commercial networks that were sufficiently dismissive of the Sinosphere's norms to disrupt it, and sufficiently materially powerful to destroy it once they judged that it could not be adapted to serve their purposes.

The above observations notwithstanding, the Sinosphere's weakness at this time should not be exaggerated. Undeniably, centrifugal forces were at work by century's end, but large-scale public disorder had yet to penetrate the empire's economic heartland around the middle and lower Yangtze regions. Although the demographic and institutional drivers of dynastic decline were universally prevalent, it was largely on the fringes and remote badlands of the Qing imperium rather than within the Han metropole that organised hostility towards the dynasty first manifested itself. Despite the great costs and debilitat-ing institutional legacies spawned by the suppression of these rebellions, the empire's economic heartland remained secure, enabling the imperial household

---

[99] For an interesting discussion of the contrast between the lay pietism of late medieval Christian sects and the activist political posture of Chinese sectarian rebels, see F. Wakeman Jr, *Strangers at the Gate: Social disorder in South China, 1839–1861* (Berkeley: University of California Press, 1966), pp. 123–5.

to retain a misplaced optimism in the dynasty's future. Internationally also, the Sinosphere seemed intact in 1800 CE. The cultural scaffolding of Confucian orthodoxy remained in place throughout East Asia, and while the empire was rotting from the inside, this had yet to be reflected in the growth of concerted international predation. For the moment, China's regional primacy remained beyond challenge, and its diplomatic practices of tribute trade and investiture continued to function. In the absence of systemic ideological challenges, a centuries-old international order continued to prevail, even as the system's custodians began to falter in their management of their own internal challenges.

Two vignettes drawn from the period illustrate both the Sinosphere's resilience and its vulnerability at century's end. The first concerns China's successful management of a succession conflict within her southern tributary of Annam (Vietnam). From 1788 to 1790, the emperor used a combination of military intervention and his powers of investiture to manage and ultimately resolve a conflict between the incumbent king of Vietnam and a pretender to the throne.[100] Initially, China provided refuge to the fleeing incumbent and sent an expeditionary force to help restore him to the throne.[101] Later, this policy was reversed, with the emperor deciding that the incumbent had indeed lost his Heavenly Mandate, and that it was necessary to legitimise the pretender's succession to the throne.[102] What is important about this anecdote is less the outcome of the conflict itself, and more the fact that all parties acknowledged China's powers of investiture and intervention as legitimate.[103] What is more, in the aftermath of the dispute, Vietnam's tributary missions to China dramatically increased, with the ceremonial and diplomatic bonds between suzerain and vassal intensifying rather than diminishing over subsequent decades, even as the Qing dynasty grew weaker rather than stronger over time.[104]

The second vignette concerns the emperor's rejection of a foreign visitor's entreaties to establish trading relations with China in 1816. While the visitor brought goods from his homeland in apparent observance of the requirements of tributary diplomacy, he remained unfamiliar with the rituals expected of a visiting vassal, and refused to perform the kowtow at the imperial court. In light of this failure to observe the Sinosphere's norms, the emperor refused either to meet the visitor or to grant him trading privileges. The emperor's subsequent reprimand to the visitor's distant sovereign, indicative of the supreme confidence worthy of the Son of Heaven, is worth quoting directly:

> You live at such a great distance from the Middle Kingdom that these Embassies must cause you considerable inconvenience. Your envoys, moreover, are wholly ignorant of Chinese ceremonial procedure, and the bickering which follows their arrival is highly displeasing to my ear. My

---

[100] The following vignette is taken from Lam, 'Intervention versus tribute in Sino-Vietnamese relations', pp. 165–79.
[101] *Ibid.*, p. 169.   [102] *Ibid.*, p. 171.   [103] *Ibid.*, p. 178.   [104] *Ibid.*, p. 177.

dynasty attaches no value to products from abroad; your nation's cunningly wrought and strange wares do not appeal to me in the least, nor do they interest me. For the future, O King, if you will keep your subjects in order and strengthen your national defences, I shall hold you in high esteem, notwithstanding your remoteness. Henceforth, pray do not trouble to dispatch missions all this distance; they are merely a waste of time and have their journey for nothing. If you loyally accept our sovereignty and show dutiful submission, there is really no need for these yearly appearances at our Court to prove that you are indeed our vassal. We issue this mandate to the end that you may perpetually comply therewith.[105]

In the face of this intransigence, Lord Amherst and the other representatives of the British East India Company had no choice but to withdraw. The next time the British sought trading privileges from the Celestial Empire, they would prove less easy to rebuff.

---

[105] Chinese imperial edict, quoted in J. M. McCutcheon, '"Tremblingly obey": British and other Western response to China and the Chinese kowtow', *Historian*, 33(4) (1971), 570–1.

7 | Heavenly Kingdom, imperial nemesis: Barbarians, martyrs and the crisis of the Sinosphere

> Both in Heaven and on earth is the Heavenly Kingdom of the Divine Father. Do not imagine that it refers solely to the Heavenly Kingdom in Heaven. Thus the Great Elder Brother formerly issued an edict foretelling the coming of the Heavenly Kingdom soon, meaning that the Heavenly Kingdom would come into being on earth. Today the Heavenly Father and the Heavenly Elder Brother descend into the world to establish the Heavenly Kingdom ...[1]

In the mid-nineteenth century, China experienced a conjunction of internal crisis and external calamity that permanently weakened the Qing dynasty, thus guaranteeing the Sinosphere's eventual destruction. From the First Opium War onwards, the Manchu Raj confronted a barbarian menace on its maritime frontier that directly threatened its economic heartland, and could be subdued neither through the force of arms nor through the munificence of imperial largesse. Confounding historical precedents, whereby pastoral conquerors from the steppe had been progressively Sinicised and thus 'civilised' into conformity with the Sinosphere's norms, the seaborne barbarians of the British East India Company proved incapable of instruction or assimilation. Worse still, the British carried with them heretical beliefs that soon found purchase among south-eastern China's alienated peasantry, fuelling a wave of rebellions that came within an ace of toppling the imperial household. From a population of approximately 410 million in 1850, China's population is estimated to have fallen to approximately 350 million by the time the last of the mid-century rebellions was suppressed in 1873.[2] Beyond the enormous human toll these conflicts wrought, their chief institutional legacy was to accelerate the cascading downwards of military and fiscal power to regional strongmen, gravely compromising the dynasty's subsequent 'self-strengthening' programme of

---

[1] Hong Xiuquan, leader of the Taiping rebellion and self-proclaimed younger brother of Christ, cited in Wakeman Jr, *Strangers at the Gate*, p. 125. The terms 'Heavenly Father' and 'Elder Brother' respectively refer to the Christian God and to Jesus Christ.

[2] Figures cited in Fairbank and Goldman, *China: A new history*, p. 216.

defensive modernisation.[3] More broadly still, the confluence of millenarian rebellion and Western encroachment terminally destabilised the Sinosphere's normative foundations, contributing to its subsequent obliteration and absorption into an international society of sovereign states.

This chapter details the nature of the mid-century crisis and considers its consequences for regional order. The first section sketches both the geopolitical and ideological aspects of the Western challenge to the Qing dynasty. The second section focuses on the domestic ramifications of the Western intrusion, exploring these within the specific context of the Taiping rebellion, the most protracted, damaging and ideologically subversive of the revolts that convulsed China during this time. The Taipings' eventual defeat and its consequences for political order, both within China and throughout the region, are examined. I argue that the post-Taiping era witnessed the emergence of a synarchic order in China founded internationally on an Anglo-Qing condominium and domestically on a restored modus vivendi between the Confucian gentry and the Qing court. The character of the synarchic order that emerged following the mid-century crisis, and the underlying fragility that ensured its eventual destruction, are discussed in the chapter's concluding section.

Opium, gunboats and the Cross in the opening phase of Western encroachment

The First Opium War comprised merely one expression of a hemispheric collision that unfolded during the nineteenth century between an ascendant industrialising West and Eurasia's declining gunpowder empires.[4] In West Asia, Napoleon's Egyptian expedition anticipated accelerating Occidental incursions into the Ottoman Empire following the Bourbon Restoration. These probes were given further impetus from the 1820s by the growing national and religious self-consciousness of minorities within the empire, and Europeans' willingness to exploit these internal ructions to advance their own interests in the eastern Mediterranean. In South Asia, meanwhile, the East India Company was progressively tightening its stranglehold over the subcontinent's commercial heartland, with its domination of Bengal and its relentless extension of British authority up the Gangetic valley, steadily hollowing out the decrepit Mughal imperium.[5] Finally, in East Asia itself, the gravitational pull of the region's surging intra-Asian commercial flows was drawing Westerners

---

[3] On this point, see for example J. E. Sheridan, *China in Disintegration: The republican era in Chinese history, 1912–1949* (New York: The Free Press, 1975), p. 18.

[4] This struggle is described in some detail in McNeill, *The Global Condition*, pp. 124–5.

[5] See generally C. A. Bayly, *Rulers, Townsmen, and Bazaars: North Indian society in the age of British expansion, 1770–1870* (Cambridge University Press, 1983).

inexorably into a regional order maintained by norms that they found incomprehensible and restrictions on trade that they found intolerable.

What eventually tipped the Eurasian military balance decisively in the West's favour was the invention of the shallow-draught ironclad steamship in the early nineteenth century. From the early modern military revolution onwards, the countries of Western Europe had acquired an unrivalled advantage in naval warfare through their development of broadside-firing battleships. However, while this naval supremacy enabled Western Europeans to gradually establish control over strategic sea lanes, up until the nineteenth century their colonial presence in the Old World was largely restricted to networks of fortified coastal enclaves dispersed across the Afro-Eurasian littoral.[6] European naval power was not matched by European land power sufficient to overawe imperial mega-states such as China. Given Europeans' historic inability to project military power into the Eurasian interior, the Chinese could for a long time regard them as a manageable irritant on a par with Japanese pirates, rather than perceiving them as a serious strategic threat. This situation changed fundamentally with the development of shallow-draught gunboats, which could navigate Eurasia's riverine arteries and thus dominate the hydrographic centres around which Asia's economic hubs were concentrated. The gunboat's introduction into Asian waters dramatically increased regional violence interdependence, and enabled the catastrophic inversion of the civilised/barbarian dichotomy that had for centuries helped constitute the Sinosphere. This process was inaugurated by the First Opium War, the origins and consequences of which I will now consider.

The Opium War: Its origins and outcomes

Westerners had maintained a continuous commercial presence in East Asia from the sixteenth century.[7] However, their demands for unfettered access to Chinese markets had previously been moderated by the fact that China had been too economically self-sufficient to be tempted and too militarily strong to be coerced into granting Westerners anything more than highly restrictive trading privileges. In the years leading up to the Opium War, however, neither of these conditions continued to obtain. Within Britain itself, the growing prosperity begotten by the industrial revolution fuelled increasing demand for precious commodities from China, most particularly tea. Given China's lack of

---

[6] On this point, see W. R. Thompson, 'The military superiority thesis and the ascendancy of Western Eurasia in the world system', *Journal of World History*, 10(1) (1999), 147–8.

[7] The Portuguese were the first Westerners to arrive in China in 1514. Apparently being regarded by the Chinese authorities as 'a harmless sort of people', they were granted permission to establish the first Western trading post in China in Macao in 1557. See M. Mancall, *China at the Center: 300 years of foreign policy* (New York: The Free Press, 1984), pp. 72–3.

interest in British manufactures, Chinese tea could initially be paid for only with scarce precious metals. For the British, this unhappy situation improved after 1820, as growing Chinese demand for opium provided them with a tradeable bulk commodity that could be exchanged for Chinese tea, thereby staunching the eastern flow of Britain's bullion reserves.[8] From this point onwards, a triangular trade flourished between India, China and Britain – opium was cultivated on the East India Company's Indian plantations, to then be exchanged for Chinese tea, which was then exported onwards to Britain.[9]

Britain's gains from the opium trade were substantial. Not only did the trade promise to resolve Britain's trade deficit with China, but opium also yielded one-seventh of British India's total revenues in the nineteenth century, thereby facilitating the consolidation of the subcontinental core of Britain's overseas empire.[10] For the Chinese, by contrast, the opium trade exacerbated social disorder and further stimulated the growth of criminal and potentially subversive elements such as the Triads. Chinese officials also correctly blamed the opium trade on China's rising outflows of silver. Thanks to China's bi-metallic currency system, in which peasants' land taxes were paid in copper but assessed and transmitted to the central government in silver, the rising relative value of silver to copper increased peasants' real tax burden without yielding any compensatory increase in the central state's income.[11] In the minds of Chinese officialdom, the opium trade was thus linked via its mediation through the tax system to growing popular distress and anti-government sentiment. This perception contributed along with the trade's more obvious evils to the government's decision to ban the trade and consumption of opium in 1836.[12]

The opium ban further strained an already fraught Sino-British relationship. Given Britain's long-standing ambitions to circumvent China's trade restrictions, and given also China's countervailing determination to minimise foreign contacts by enforcing these very same restrictions, the subsequent slide towards war was perhaps inevitable. The course of the ensuing Opium War has been

---

[8] On the rapid growth in Chinese demand for opium from the 1820s onwards and its massively deleterious impact on China's world balance of payments, see F. Wakeman Jr, 'The Canton trade and the Opium War' in Twitchett and Fairbank (eds.), *The Cambridge History of China*, X: *Late Ch'ing, 1800–1911*, Pt I (Cambridge University Press, 1978) pp. 172–3.

[9] On this point, see Headrick, *The Tools of Empire*, p. 44. [10] *Ibid.*, p. 45.

[11] Wakeman Jr, 'Canton trade and the Opium War', p. 178.

[12] Wakeman notes that there were purely domestic reasons for the changing ratio of exchange between silver and copper, including the declining production of the Yunnanese copper mines and the central government's subsequent decision to circumvent this problem by minting more coins and thus debasing the currency. He nevertheless emphasises that the opium trade's drain on Chinese silver reserves remained the *perceived* cause of the problems, thus contributing to the government's decision to ban the opium trade. *Ibid.*, pp. 178–9.

explored in numerous studies elsewhere, and its precise details need not detain us here.[13] What is relevant to this inquiry is a consideration of the causes of China's defeat, which lay primarily in the West's introduction of compartmentalised iron steamships into Chinese littoral waters after 1840. Whereas Britain's deep-draught sailing ships had been restricted to coastal harassment of Chinese forces, shallow-draught steamships such as the *Nemesis* were capable of navigating China's complex network of estuaries and shallow channels, and could snake up its riverine arteries deep into the Chinese interior.[14] This capability, together with the *Nemesis*'s complement of mobile cannons, enabled her to destroy Canton's defending junks and forts at will in the war's opening stages.[15] More fundamentally, the gunboats' ability to traverse China's internal river systems enabled the British to score the conflict's decisive victory. In June 1842, the British fleet entered the Yangtze River destined for Zhenjiang, a city lying at the intersection of the Yangtze and the Grand Canal.[16] Given that the Grand Canal was the principal trade route along which rice was transported from the southern rice-bowl provinces to the capital of Beijing, the seizure of Zhenjiang effectively cut the Chinese empire in half, thus 'crushing the throat' of the Qing dynasty and compelling it to sue for peace in July.[17]

The gunboat's introduction into East Asia fundamentally altered the Sinosphere's material foundations. Prior to the First Opium War, a gigantic agrarian gunpowder empire had dominated the region, its rulers' focus fixed principally on deterring land-based threats emanating from the northern steppe. After the First Opium War, the Sinosphere's strategic centre of gravity began to shift decisively away from the steppe and towards the Western Pacific. Following China's forced opening to foreign trade in 1842, the gunboat featured conspicuously in subsequent Western campaigns to secure regional dominance. The arrival of Commodore Perry's ships in Japan in 1853, the Second Opium War (1856–60), the Second and Third Anglo-Burmese Wars (1852–3 and 1885), and the French conquests of Tonkin (1873–4) and Annam (1883) each testified to the novel power projection capacities accruing to the Western

---

[13]   Although for an interesting interpretation of the Opium War as merely the first episode of a single protracted inter-systemic conflict (the Twenty-One Years' War) between the Empire and an expanding world-capitalist ecumene led by the United Kingdom, see Mancall, *China at the Center*, pp. 113–18.

[14]   Headrick, *The Tools of Empire*, p. 50.   [15]   *Ibid.*   [16]   *Ibid.*, p. 52.

[17]   *Ibid.*, p. 53. The analogy of 'crushing a man's throat' came initially from a Ming dynasty official who presciently anticipated the dangers of relocating the imperial capital away from Nanjing, where it remained relatively close to its primary taxation base and source of staple food crops, and to Beijing, from where the imperial household would be dependent on the Grand Canal to connect it with its major resource base. On the failure of first the Ming and then the Qing dynasties to lessen their dependence on the Grand Canal by maintaining naval forces sufficient to secure an alternative supply route from the southern provinces to the capital via coastal supply lines, see Grygiel, *Great Powers and Geopolitical Change*, pp. 217–18.

maritime powers as a result of industrialisation.[18] From mid-century onwards, the Western powers' abilities to project power globally would be further enhanced due to technological innovations (e.g. the telegraph), improved knowledge systems (e.g. improved coastal mapping techniques) and organisational adaptations (e.g. the Royal Navy's development of a transcontinental network of coaling stations).[19] These revolutionary changes guaranteed that the strategic initiative slipped irretrievably away from China after the First Opium War. More crucially still, they delivered regional preponderance towards a precocious host of 'barbarian' maritime powers that were both unfamiliar with and contemptuous of the region's diplomatic norms and practices. Beyond the material dislocation induced by the West's maritime ascendancy, it would be this disregard for the Sinosphere's norms that would prove most subversive to the established order.

Civilisations clashing, cosmologies colliding: The ideological impact of China's defeat in the First Opium War

However humiliating it might have been for the empire, court officials did not perceive defeat in the Opium War as heralding an existential crisis for the monarchy. Throughout Chinese history, barbarians had exploited periods of dynastic weakness to extort trading privileges, and the Chinese had correspondingly developed a repertoire of 'barbarian management' techniques to minimise the political threats thereby presented by external predation. From Beijing's perspective, the Treaty of Nanjing, which formally concluded the First Opium War in August 1842, fell squarely within this barbarian-management tradition. The opening of five treaty ports to trade with the British, the cession of Hong Kong in perpetuity, the standardisation of China's tariff regime – these concessions and more were all understood by Beijing as gestures of imperial magnanimity that would sate the foreigners' greed and thus subdue their aggression. Likewise, in granting foreigners the right to exercise extraterritorial jurisdiction within the treaty ports, the Chinese were again merely institutionalising their long-standing preference that foreigners govern and police themselves within clearly demarcated enclaves, replicating a practice that had been applied to resident Arab traders as far back as the thirteenth century.[20] Provided that the British observed the mandatory rituals of obeisance the

---

[18] Headrick, *The Tools of Empire*, p. 54.

[19] J. Black, 'War and international relations: A military historical perspective on force and legitimacy', *Review of International Studies*, 31 (Special Issue) (2005), 131.

[20] Abu-Lughod, *Before European Hegemony*, p. 200. Abu-Lughod notes that regular commercial exchanges were occurring between the Arabs and the Chinese as far back as the eighth century CE, and cites documents indicating China's management of a 'treaty port' system involving the supervision of substantial resident Arab commercial settlements by the thirteenth century.

emperor expected in exchange for his generosity, the imperial dignity would not be unduly tarnished by the latest concessions, and the political threat posed by the West's encroachment could be contained.

That the British and subsequent waves of European predators failed to abide by the Sinosphere's norms can be explained by the profound dissonance in the respective world-views informing Western and Chinese conceptions of international order. Recapitulating briefly, the Sinosphere was hierarchical in its conception, moral in its character, and deliberately flexible and ambiguous with respect to its key mechanisms of operation. It was hierarchical, inasmuch as the emperor presided over the cosmic and social order, and was placed in a position of explicit superiority and authority in relation to other polities. It was moral, in that the emperor was bound to vassal states through asymmetric bonds of benevolence and obedience that were imagined in explicitly moral and familial terms. And it was deliberately flexible and ambiguous, in that the tribute trade system allowed the emperor to buy off barbarians when China was weak, and control or limit their access to Chinese markets when China was strong, at all times overlaying the barbarians' commercial activities with rituals of obeisance that symbolically affirmed a Sino-centric regional order.[21]

Conversely, Western conceptions of international order were superficially egalitarian and legalistic in character.[22] Thus, Western international law from the late eighteenth century increasingly emphasised notions of sovereign equality, contradicting the hierarchical assumptions upon which the East Asian order was based.[23] In place of the paternal moralism characteristic of East Asian diplomacy, Westerners conceived international relationships as being mediated through a depersonalised, formal, rationalised corpus of international law.[24] Finally, rather than abiding by the flexibility and ambiguity that marked the Sinosphere's system of tributary trade, Westerners demanded that contracting parties' rights be explicitly codified in treaty form.[25] To the extent that scope existed for a revision of parties' rights and responsibilities, it could be secured only through a renegotiation of said treaties, which was in turn frequently driven by the stronger party's insistence and the weaker party's acquiescence.

---

[21] Horowitz additionally notes that the tributary character of East Asian diplomacy, in which tributaries frequently received larger gifts than they themselves gave to their nominal suzerains, left tributary diplomacy open to differing interpretations about the meaning of specific transactions by the respective parties. This arguably endowed it with a constructive ambiguity and flexibility lacking in the more rigidly legalistic mode of Western diplomacy that succeeded it. See R. S. Horowitz, 'International law and state transformation in China, Siam and the Ottoman Empire during the nineteenth century', *Journal of World History*, 15(4) (2004), 478.

[22] *Ibid.*, pp. 450–2.   [23] *Ibid.*, p. 452.

[24] On this point, see generally G. W. Gong, *The Standard of 'Civilization' in International Society* (Oxford: Clarendon Press, 1984), pp. 17–18.

[25] *Ibid.*, pp. 139–40.

The contradiction between Chinese familial moralism and Western contractual legalism thus prevented the emergence of a stable modus vivendi between the two parties following the First Opium War. More unsettling still for the Chinese was the fact that Western notions of sovereign equality co-existed uneasily with a parallel 'standard of civilisation' that elevated the West to a position of global pre-eminence, and conferred upon Westerners a duty to civilise 'barbarian' and 'savage' peoples by introducing them to the ameliorative influences of Christianity, free trade and 'responsible government'. As Edward Keene has demonstrated, Western international society had from its very beginning been characterised by the simultaneous co-existence of logics of toleration and civilisation.[26] However, in the nineteenth century, a constellation of forces strengthened Europeans' inclinations and abilities to coercively impose their writ on non-European societies. I have already discussed the technological innovations that enabled Western states to pry East Asia open to European influence, and will not elaborate further save to stress that this growing material supremacy served to reinforce Western notions of cultural superiority.[27] Within the East Asian context, this chauvinism constituted a significant departure from the admiration with which Westerners had previously regarded Chinese civilisation. Whereas the Chinese had once been lauded for their industriousness, their allegedly superior system of Confucian public morality and their stable system of rule, Westerners in the nineteenth century reconceived China as a land plagued by economic stagnation and cursed by an arbitrary and despotic form of government.[28] Within Britain in particular, this re-imagining took place at a time when the country's cultural landscape was itself being transformed by the forces of free trade liberalism and evangelical Christianity.[29] These forces profoundly conditioned Britain's view of the East, which henceforth revolved around a juxtaposition between a liberal trinity composed of Responsible Government, Free Trade and Protestant Piety, opposed to an imagined counter-constellation composed of Oriental Despotism, Protectionism and Idolatry.[30]

---

[26] See generally Keene, *Beyond the Anarchical Society.*

[27] On this point with broader respect to relations between Europeans and non-Europeans more generally during the nineteenth century, see M. Adas, *Machines as the Measure of Men: Science, technology, and ideologies of Western dominance* (Ithaca: Cornell University Press, 1989).

[28] On eighteenth-century Europeans' admiration of China, and particularly their appreciation of a system of government that they perceived as both more rational and more moral than the European despotisms of the time, see D. M. Jones, *The Image of China in Western Social and Political Thought* (New York: Palgrave, 2001), pp. 23–8.

[29] On this point, see generally E. Stokes, *The English Utilitarians and India* (Oxford; London: Clarendon Press, 1959), pp. 40–7.

[30] *Ibid.*

The potent cocktail of mercantile greed and religious fervour that developed in Britain in the years immediately prior to the First Opium War thus infused British imperialism with a decidedly expansive and even revolutionary aspect. Evangelicals interpreted the sheer swiftness with which Britain had acquired its Indian empire as a providential sign that their country was destined to redeem the peoples of the East by introducing them to the civilising influences of law, faith and commerce.[31] Thus, the historian Eric Stokes observes that British imperial expansion in Asia henceforth became increasingly driven by a merchant–missionary alliance, which believed in the power of Western faith and commerce to morally transform subject peoples and thus free them from Oriental Despotism.[32] While this transformative impulse found its most comprehensive expression in British India (at least up until the Indian Mutiny), it also powerfully conditioned Britain's relations with China. Wary of having Britain assume responsibility for governing yet another declining Asian empire alongside Mughal India, British government officials strove doggedly to contain the expansive tendencies of the merchant–missionary alliance.[33] But this attempt to confine the subversive impact of the colonial presence to the treaty ports failed spectacularly in the long run. In part, this was because it was impossible for government officials to completely monitor and control the activities of merchants and missionaries.[34] Consequently, it became impossible to fully sequester their economic and cultural impact within the boundaries of the treaty ports. More generally, however, it was because merchants, missionaries and government officials all affirmed a discriminatory 'standard of civilisation' that radically up-ended the Sinosphere's hierarchical foundations. The very logic underpinning the British presence in China inverted the binary division between civilised and barbarian on which imperial authority had always depended. This inversion of the established order would have disastrous consequences, which would ramify first within the empire, and then throughout East Asia as a whole.

Thy kingdom come: The rise and demise of the Heavenly Kingdom of Great Peace

The Taiping rebellion: Its enabling ideological context

The Manchus' defeat in the Opium War heightened popular perceptions in some quarters that the dynasty had lost its Heavenly Mandate, and was set

---

[31] *Ibid.*, pp. 30–1.   [32] *Ibid.*, pp. 36–7.
[33] G. S. Graham, *The China Station: War and diplomacy, 1830–1860* (Oxford University Press, 1978), p. 420.
[34] This task was further complicated by the persistent divisions and disagreements that marked relations between civilian administrators and the naval leadership of the China squadron in Britain's concessions. On this point, see generally *ibid.*, Ch. 10.

on a course of irreversible decline.[35] Such sentiments were far from novel within the broad sweep of Chinese history. But what marked the post-1842 situation as distinctive was the intrusion of ideas that explicitly contested the monarchy's cosmological foundations. Previous cycles of dynastic decline had played out within a context in which contending parties accepted that the emperor's purpose was to serve as the pivot linking the cosmic and the mundane worlds, and were contesting only the degree to which the incumbent dynasty retained the Heavenly Mandate. Conversely, the Western 'standard of civilisation' repudiated sacerdotal conceptions of political legitimacy, and cast the emperor as merely one of a number of nominally equal sovereigns operating within a formally anarchic state system. More threatening still for the monarchy were the heterodox beliefs that missionaries brought with them, and which they sought with resolute conviction to disseminate among the empire's subjects.

The evangelical Christianity the missionaries introduced into China contained a host of ideas that challenged Confucian orthodoxy. Whereas Confucianism projected an unreservedly hierarchical and familial conception of social order, Christianity emphasised the equality of all humans under God, and provided only qualified and ambiguous justification for political and economic inequalities in the temporal world.[36] Similarly, whereas imperial ideology conflated the temporal and spiritual realms, Christianity expressly emphasised their distinct character.[37] Finally, whereas Confucianism deified the emperor as the Son of Heaven, Christianity reserved divine status for the Holy Trinity, condemning all attempts to deify earthly rulers as idolatry.[38] Christianity's heterodox implications aroused powerful opposition from the scholar gentry, and this opposition helped ensure that the religion found relatively few converts. But the suppression of Christianity was not completely successful, and its hybridisation with folk Chinese millenarian traditions would go on to animate the most devastating of China's mid-century crises in the form of the Taiping rebellion.

Hong Xiuquan, the founder of the Taiping movement, was a failed candidate for the bureaucracy who first encountered Christianity in 1836 via a pamphlet he received entitled *Good Works to Admonish the Age*. Penned by a recent

---

[35] On the growth of popular xenophobia in Canton after the First Opium War and its role as a harbinger of future revolutionary anti-Manchu sentiment, see Wakeman Jr, *Strangers at the Gate*, pp. 77–8.

[36] On this point, see P. A. Kuhn, 'The Taiping rebellion' in D. Twitchett and J. K. Fairbank (eds.), *The Cambridge History of China*, X: *Late Ch'ing, 1800–1911*, Pt I, p. 277.

[37] See for example J. R. Levenson, 'Confucian and Taiping "Heaven": The political implications of clashing religious concepts', *Comparative Studies in Society and History*, 4(4) (1962), 440.

[38] On the contrast between Confucian and Taiping Christian political theologies, see *ibid.*, pp. 445–6.

Chinese convert to Christianity, *Good Works* was a confusing synthesis of Bible extracts interspersed with the author's own commentary on contemporary Chinese society, and was initially filed away and ignored by Hong after a cursory perusal. Following his third failure to be accepted into the bureaucracy the following year, Hong suffered a mental breakdown. During his convalescence, he experienced many visions, including one in which his internal organs were removed by demons and replaced with new ones, another in which he was introduced to a golden-bearded man who was identified as his father, and yet another in which he fought demons alongside a heavenly elder brother.[39] Upon Hong's fourth failure to pass the imperial exams, he revisited the *Good Works* pamphlet, after which he reinterpreted his earlier visions as a divine revelation calling on him to overthrow the Manchus and establish God's Heavenly Kingdom on earth. In 1847, Hong further clarified his vision through a brief period of instruction under an American missionary based in Canton. By this stage, however, the foundations of the Taiping ideology had already been established, and are briefly summarised below.

Protestant Christian texts and motifs formed the original source material for Hong's vision, and both Taiping adherents and their Confucian detractors characterised the Taiping vision as essentially Christian. In keeping with Christianity, Hong preached that there was only one God, who had sent his son Jesus Christ into the world to redeem mankind.[40] Hong's God was also the God of the Ten Commandments, the self-sufficient moral and legal code to which God's followers were to adhere if they wished to enter Paradise.[41] The rite of baptism, strict observation of the Sabbath and an uncompromising repudiation of idolatry further illustrated the Taiping faith's Protestant origins.[42] Importantly, however, the Taiping religion also placed disproportionate emphasis on evangelical Protestantism's more Manichean and apocalyptic aspects. This is unsurprising given that *Good Words* began with the story of Adam and Eve's fall from grace and concluded with graphic descriptions of the Last Judgement, according little if any attention to Christ's Sermon on the Mount.[43] However, it is also reflective of the fact that the Taiping revelation developed in an environment in which expectations of dynastic decline were rife, and in which millenarian visions of apocalypse and redemption already formed an indelible part of China's spiritual landscape.

For all its Christian influences, the Taiping faith nevertheless also constituted an indigenisation of Christianity that both subverted Confucianism and also perverted the Christian faith. By far the most subversive aspect of

---

[39] *Ibid.*, pp. 447–50.

[40] On the traditional Christian components of Taiping religious beliefs and practices, see E. P. Boardman, 'Christian influence upon the ideology of the Taiping rebellion', *The Far Eastern Quarterly*, 10(2) (1951), 123.

[41] *Ibid.*   [42] *Ibid.*   [43] *Ibid.*

Hong's revelation was his condemnation of Confucianism as idolatrous in its elevation of the emperor to divine status.[44] In opposing the emperor's deification, Hong echoed mainstream Christian teachings. But in justifying his revolutionary political programme, Hong departed radically from Christianity. For whereas Christianity stressed the distinctiveness of the City of Man from the City of God, Hong conceived the Heavenly Kingdom as being both temporal and spiritual in nature.[45] In accounting for China's decline, Hong argued that the Chinese had abandoned their ancient worship of a single and all-powerful God, and that emperors from the Qin dynasty onwards had perpetuated China's estrangement from God by claiming the title of Son of Heaven.[46] As the Heavenly Father's second son and Christ's younger brother, it was Hong's mission to overthrow the Manchu dynasty, after which he would then establish God's Heavenly Kingdom on earth.[47] While he abjured claims to personal divinity, Hong thus located himself within the Heavenly family. More fundamentally, he appropriated the most eschatological themes of Christianity and situated them within traditional Chinese narratives of dynastic decline, creating a hybrid faith that enjoined fanatical opposition not merely to the Manchu dynasty, but to the entire Confucian order.[48]

The Taiping rebellion: Its enabling sociological context

As with Protestantism in sixteenth-century Europe, Taiping Christianity found its prophet in a man who had trained to serve the ruling order as part of its bureaucratic elite. Similarly, as with sixteenth-century Protestantism, the Taiping faith diffused rapidly through pre-existing social networks, and leveraged xenophobic sentiments against foreign rule to further its spread. Finally, and again in comparison to Protestantism in its chaotic early phase, Taiping Christianity provided a powerful new idiom through which disaffected peasants could articulate their opposition to an inegalitarian social order. However, whereas Luther recoiled at the egalitarian impulses that early Protestantism unleashed, the levelling impulse remained a permanent feature of the Taiping vision. This difference can be explained by reference to the distinct social conditions in which Taiping Christianity developed. A consideration of the

---

[44] On this point, see T. H. Reilly, *The Taiping Heavenly Kingdom: Rebellion and the blasphemy of empire* (Seattle: University of Washington Press, 2004), pp. 92–4.

[45] On this point, see specifically P. A. Kuhn, 'Origins of the Taiping vision: Cross-cultural dimensions of a Chinese rebellion', *Comparative Studies in Society and History*, 19(3) (1977), 356.

[46] Reilly, *The Taiping Heavenly Kingdom*, p. 93.   [47] *Ibid.*, pp. 110–13.

[48] F. Michael, *The Taiping Rebellion: History and documents*, 3 vols. (Seattle: University of Washington Press, 1966), I, p. 4. Michael goes so far as to characterise the Taiping movement as totalitarian in its aspirations to completely remake Chinese society, a point to which I will return in greater detail below.

rebellion's sociological basis also helps to explain why the Confucian reaction initially proved more successful than its European counterpart in extirpating heterodoxy and preserving the existing order.

Taiping Christianity originated in Canton as an expression of the cultural miscegenation spawned in Guangdong's cosmopolitan entrepôts by interlocking processes of commercial expansion and imperial decay. However, it was in the neighbouring province of Guangxi that the Taiping faith acquired its popular roots. As with much of China following the First Opium War, Guangxi was convulsed by growing unrest stemming from factors such as rising peasant landlessness, an increasingly regressive taxation system, and a corrupt local bureaucracy.[49] The region had also witnessed the growth of local gentry-led militias in response to increasing insecurity, even as the more desperate or opportunistic of the peasantry threw their lot in with the Triads and other secret societies.[50] Britain's piracy-clearing operations around the Pearl River Delta had meanwhile displaced many pirates upriver, funnelling them into Guangxi.[51] Being separated from other parts of China by mountainous borders, the provinces of Guangdong and Guangxi together constituted a single economic unit.[52] But while Guangdong provided the portal through which Western religious doctrines entered China, it was in Guangxi's conflict-laden milieu that Hong was able to construct his holy army.

The Taiping faith first gained popularity among the Hakkas (literally 'guests'), an ethnic minority that the government had earlier encouraged to migrate into Guangxi to relieve population pressures in Guangdong.[53] While they were culturally Sinicised, the Hakkas retained a distinctive ethnic identity, preserving their own dialect and customs.[54] As recent settlers, the Hakka subsisted either as tenants under the yoke of ethnically different landlords, or alternatively eked out an existence as homesteaders on the region's more marginal lands.[55] Moreover, whereas more-established settlers cohered around localised lineage structures and frequently clustered in single-surname villages, the Hakkas' ability to mobilise in defence of their interests was limited by their more fragmented kinship and settlement patterns.[56] As population pressures increased and feuding between the Hakkas and other ethnic groups escalated, the Hakkas became susceptible to the message of salvation Hong's early converts brought to Guangxi from 1844 onwards.

[49] *Ibid.*, p. 16.   [50] *Ibid.*   [51] *Ibid.*, p. 18.   [52] *Ibid.*, p. 18.

[53] Kuhn, 'Origins of the Taiping vision', p. 361. Parenthetically, Franz Michael notes that nomads originating from Central Asia had earlier forced the Hakkas into southern China as a result of their invasion of northern and central China. See Michael, *The Taiping Rebellion*, I, p. 19.

[54] J. D. Spence, *God's Chinese Son: The Taiping Heavenly Kingdom of Hong Xiuquan* (New York: W. W. Norton and Company, 1996), p. 25.

[55] Kuhn, 'Origins of the Taiping vision', pp. 361–2.   [56] *Ibid.*, pp. 363–4.

As a culturally assimilated but socially disorganised ethnic grouping, the Hakkas were particularly vulnerable to victimisation. Lacking the social cohesion of more established communities, the Hakkas struggled to mobilise in defence of their interests.[57] At the same time, being both culturally Sinicised but collectively distinct by virtue of their dialect and customs, the Hakkas lacked the symbolic vocabulary through which ethnic grievances could be conceptualised, let alone openly articulated.[58] The new religion provided the Hakkas with a symbolic vocabulary with which to conceptualise their shared grievances, as well as with an organisational vehicle (in the form of the newly established God Worshipping Society) through which collective action became possible.[59] The Hakkas' special receptivity to the Taiping message was also aided by the fact that Hong himself was a Hakka, and that simmering social tensions had already seen many Hakkas become landless and therefore available for recruitment into Hong's Heavenly Army.

Taiping Christianity's social roots thus lay in the very specific challenges Guangxi's Hakka minority confronted in the years following the First Opium War. Beginning as a localised rebellion in July 1850, the Taiping armies rapidly swept from Guangxi through the middle Yangtze region, felling successive waves of imperial forces and aggressively proselytising among the local population. Capitalising on popular disaffection with a foreign dynasty, the rebels railed against the Qing forces as 'demons' and 'Tartar dogs'. In so doing, the Taipings combined nativist anti-Manchu sentiment with a Manichean outlook that conceived the ruling dynasty as cosmic enemies who had defied God's laws by blasphemously sacralising the imperial office and the imperial person.[60] Exploiting the vast size and speed of their peasant host to overwhelm poorly paid and poorly led imperial forces, the Taipings managed within three years to conquer the ancient imperial capital of Nanjing, renaming it the Heavenly Capital upon its capture on 19 March 1853. For the better part of the following decade, the Taipings would rule the greater part of the middle and lower Yangtze regions, dominating China's major riverine artery, and with it the empire's most urbanised, populous and economically productive regions.[61] A brief consideration of the main features of the Taipings' Heavenly Kingdom provides some insight into the magnitude of the threat Taiping Christianity posed to the Confucian order, as well as suggesting the reasons for its eventual defeat.

The revolutionary character of the Taiping rebellion

Embracing a code that surpassed the Puritans in its moral repressiveness and an egalitarianism that rhetorically matched those of the peasant levellers of early

---

[57] *Ibid.*, p. 364. [58] *Ibid.*, p. 365. [59] *Ibid.*
[60] Reilly, *The Taiping Heavenly Kingdom*, pp. 93–4. [61] *Ibid.*

modern Germany, the Taipings sought a total spiritual and social transformation of Chinese society. Whereas Confucianism anchored imperial legitimacy within the concept of the Heavenly Mandate, the Taipings invoked the authority of a biblical God to legitimise their establishment of God's kingdom on earth. This alternative legitimising ideology reflected a transcendent conception of the divine, which differed in fundamental ways from the impersonal and immanent conception of the divine informing the imperial tradition.[62] Certainly, the Taipings' departure from imperial tradition was not total, for both Hong and his lieutenants claimed to be God's mouthpieces, and thus invested themselves with an aura of sacred legitimacy that unconsciously echoed the Chinese political tradition.[63] But the Taipings' concept of a Heavenly Kingdom had no precedents in Chinese history, and represented a full-frontal assault on the legitimacy of the imperial office.

More important even than the subversive aspects of Taiping ideology was the revolutionary programme the rebels sought to impose on Chinese society. Its precociously sophisticated bureaucracy notwithstanding, the Chinese model of government had generally comported with the pattern of ideological universalism and institutional localism characteristic of pre-industrial empires. Being at once inculcated with Confucian values and yet embedded within village-level social networks, the scholar gentry served as the bulwark of imperial authority, acting in their capacity as local administrators and civic leaders as the lynchpin linking the universal with the local worlds.[64] The Taipings conversely aimed to dispense with this system and replace it with a pyramidal structure vertically integrating the Heavenly Kingdom from top to bottom. Thus, the population was to be organised into base groups ('platoons') of twenty-five families each, with each family obliged to provide one man or woman for service in the Heavenly Army, and the base groups to be collectively supervised by a 'sergeant', who would simultaneously serve as their military, civic and spiritual leader.[65] All land was to be expropriated from landlords and allotted in varying portions to each man, woman and child, while all agrarian surplus was to be accumulated in local 'Heavenly Storehouses'.[66] While the twenty-five families would function as the basic unit of social organisation, they would be hierarchically integrated into units ('armies'), each of 156 families, led by a general, which would each be integrated in turn within the Heavenly Kingdom's broader pyramidal structure.[67]

Within the Heavenly Kingdom, Chinese society was to be re-cast as a mobilised army of believers dedicated to the fight against the Manchu

---

[62] Levenson, 'Confucian and Taiping "Heaven"', p. 440.
[63] Michael, *The Taiping Rebellion*, I, p. 78.   [64] Wong, *China Transformed*, p. 112.
[65] E. Zurcher, 'Purity in the Taiping rebellion' in W. E. A. van Beek (ed.), *The Quest for Purity: Dynamics of puritan movements* (Amsterdam: Mouton de Gruyter, 1988), p. 207.
[66] *Ibid.*   [67] *Ibid.*

'demons'.[68] Additionally, whereas Confucian norms legitimised inequalities between landlords and tenants, the Taipings conversely favoured a form of theocratic proto-communism.[69] The Taipings' ruthless enforcement of religious homogeneity also departed from the status quo. Although Confucianism had sustained the *ancien regime* as its official ideology, the Qing dynasty had nevertheless respected China's religious diversity, and had charged the scholar gentry with responsibility for supporting locals in their worship of the plethora of local deities that populated the Chinese pantheon.[70] The Taipings, by contrast, rejected any possibility of co-existence with other religious traditions, and violently suppressed all non-Taiping religious practices throughout their territories. Even the patriarchal family, the very foundation of the Confucian model of social order, did not escape revision. Although appearing progressive to the contemporary observer, reforms such as the banning of foot-binding and the establishment of places for women in the Taiping bureaucracy were deeply subversive at the time, undermining the gender norms and conceptions of the family then dominant within Chinese society.[71] Similarly, the reorganisation of villages into platoons of twenty-five families each occurred without heed for pre-existing patterns of lineage settlement. Both the segregation of villages by gender and the enforcement of norms of absolute chastity also had predictably catastrophic consequences for the population wherever they were enforced.[72]

Ironically in view of their spiritual debt to the West, diplomacy proved the one area in which the Taipings remained deferential to Chinese tradition. This manifested itself in the Taipings' intransigent insistence on China as the singular centre of civilisation. While faith forced the Taipings to concede that God had sent his first Son to the barbarian state of Judea to redeem humanity, the Taipings nevertheless affirmed their Sino-centrism in positing Hong Xiuquan as God's second Son, and also in conceiving of China as the seat of God's prophesied Heavenly Kingdom. In keeping with this outlook, Hong regarded Western Christians with benevolent condescension. Visiting foreign delegates to the Taiping court were warmly greeted as fellow Christians, but were nevertheless expected to render due deference to Hong in his capacities as

---

[68] On the militarised character of the Taiping vision, see S. P. MacKenzie, *Revolutionary Armies in the Modern Era: A revisionist approach* (London: Routledge, 1997), p. 79.

[69] Kuhn, 'The Taiping rebellion', pp. 278–9.

[70] On the role of the scholar gentry in supervising local religious rites and practices, see J. K. Fairbank, 'Introduction: The old order' in D. Twitchett and J. K. Fairbank (eds.), *The Cambridge History of China*, X: *Late Ch'ing, 1800–1911*, Pt I, p. 13.

[71] Zurcher, 'Purity in the Taiping rebellion', pp. 207–8.

[72] Kuhn, 'The Taiping rebellion', pp. 276–7. While Kuhn notes that sexual relations even between married couples were initially punishable by death, the policy of complete sexual segregation was (perhaps unsurprisingly) abandoned by 1855.

both God's Chinese son, and the ruler of His Heavenly Kingdom.[73] Consequently, disillusionment soon succeeded the initial enthusiasm with which some Westerners had greeted the rebellion. Westerners were alienated both by the heretical elements of the Taiping religion and by Hong's claims to universal spiritual and political dominion.[74] As it became clear that the Taipings were unable to constitute a functioning government in the territories under their control, this Western disenchantment deepened into enduring estrangement. Thus was foreclosed any possibility of an alliance between the foreigners and the Taiping rebels, and thus was foreshadowed also the coalition of foreigners, gentry and court officials that would preserve the Qing dynasty for another six decades.[75]

The Confucian reaction and the end of the Heavenly Kingdom

It is difficult to overstate the devastation the Taiping rebellion wrought on the Qing dynasty. The sheer scale of the crisis – conservative estimates place the number of dead at 20 million – finds no parallels in Western history prior to the total wars of the twentieth century. Similarly, the intensity of the Taipings' challenge to the Confucian order suggests early modern European comparisons only with the conjunction of religious zeal and levelling impulses that characterised the Peasants' War. However, whereas the Peasants' War was both localised and fleeting, the Taiping rebellion raged across China's economic heartland for almost fifteen years. As East Asia's hydrographic centre, the middle and lower Yangtze regions of southern China constituted the East Asian equivalent of the Rhenish basin in Western Europe. Consequently, the depopulation of these regions during the rebellion shook the empire as a whole, disrupting food supplies, displacing large swathes of the population, and denying the imperial treasury access to land taxes from the region that formed a major part of its revenue. Deprived of one of its primary taxation bases, the dynasty was forced to finance its anti-Taiping campaigns through expedients that merely heightened popular disaffection and spurred anti-government violence in other parts of the empire. In debasing the currency and raising land taxes in the territories still under its control, the government inadvertently

---

[73] This attitude of benevolent condescension is conveyed in the tone of the following Taiping missive to visiting British dignitaries to the Taiping court in Nanjing on 28 April 1853: 'Whereas God the Heavenly Father has sent our Sovereign down to earth, as the true Sovereign of all the nations of the world, all people in the world who wish to appear at his Court must yield obedience to the rules of ceremony. They must prepare representations, stating who and what they are and from whence they come, after previous presentation of which only can audience be accorded them. Obey these commands.' Quoted in Spence, *God's Chinese Son*, p. 195. Unsurprisingly, the subsequent meeting between the British and Taiping representatives failed to yield a British commitment to the Taiping cause.

[74] *Ibid.*   [75] *Ibid.*, p. 117.

fuelled further rebellions throughout the realm.[76] The fiscal and reputational costs inflicted by the Taipings' initial successes thus produced a ripple effect throughout China. The government was consequently confronted with a lengthening front of violence composed of peasant jacqueries, secret-society revolts and separatist uprisings from restive tribal and religious minorities, all at the same time that it struggled to crush the Taiping challenge.[77] The empire's resulting weakness in turn invited renewed Western aggression and the imposition of further concessions on the dynasty following its defeat in the Arrow war of 1856–60.

The mid-century conjunction of 'external crisis and internal calamity' strained the Qing dynasty almost to breaking point, exposing both its institutional weakness and its popular illegitimacy. Nevertheless, in contrast to Christendom, which rapidly crumbled following the Reformation's onset, the Sinosphere demonstrated considerable resilience in the face of crisis. Christendom faltered on the basis of irreconcilable rivalries between its most powerful spiritual and military leaders, with Catholicism's post-Tridentine revival flowering only following the defeat of the Habsburg imperial project and the permanent destruction of Christendom's religious unity. Conversely, in the face of Taiping obscurantism, the Manchus and the Han scholar gentry succeeded in shelving their differences to defeat a common challenge to the Confucian social order. Moreover, whereas Protestantism proved attractive to many of Christendom's princes, offering the promises of spiritual solace, material enrichment and emancipation from the bonds of papacy and empire, Taiping Christianity offered no equivalent compensations to the scholar gentry. On the contrary, the heretical and alien nature of Taiping beliefs, coupled with the threat they presented to the scholar gentry's social status and material wealth, foreclosed any possibility of elite defection to the Taiping camp.

Despite its intense destructiveness, the Taiping rebellion thus catalysed extensive institutional renovations in the empire that preserved both the Qing dynasty and the Confucian social order over which it presided. By far the most important of these was the creation of regional new model armies under the command of loyalist strongmen. Developing first in Hunan under the leadership of general Zeng Guofan, the new model armies differed significantly from the forces that had previously defended the empire. Since its establishment, the imperial Green Standard army had been organised so as to discourage the development of personal bonds of loyalty between higher and lower officers, for fear that such bonds might weaken Beijing's control over the military.[78] Faced with the task of forging a viable army out of the diverse ensemble of different

[76] Kuhn, 'The Taiping rebellion', p. 290.
[77] S.-Y. Teng, *The Taiping Rebellion and the Western Powers: A comprehensive survey* (Oxford: Clarendon Press, 1971), pp. 400–1.
[78] Kuhn, 'The Taiping rebellion', p. 287.

mercenaries, militias and other irregular units that he had inherited in Hunan, Zeng abandoned this tradition, and instead built upon pre-existing lineage and native-place relationships to ensure the army's coherence and combat effectiveness.[79] In the financing of the new regional armies, Zeng and his protégés proved equally innovative, introducing an *ad valorem* tax on goods in stock or in transit, and also upon certain goods such as tea in their place of manufacture.[80] This expedient proved particularly effective in financing the defence of Shanghai, where Zeng's lieutenant, Li Hongzhang, forsook a traditional reliance on land taxes in favour of imposing *ad valorem* taxes on the port city's vast commercial flows.[81]

The regional new model armies proved decisive in defeating both the Taiping rebels and a host of the empire's other internal enemies during the mid-century crisis, and foreshadowed a broader pattern of collaboration between the Manchu court and the Han scholar gentry in defence of orthodoxy that would persist throughout the nineteenth century. This collaborative arrangement was further strengthened by the modus vivendi that developed between the Qing court and the Western powers (most particularly Britain) after 1860. While privately sceptical of the empire's ability to defeat its enemies, the Western powers saw even less hope of advancing their interests with a China under Taiping rule. Following the Indian Mutiny of 1857, the British also despaired at the prospect of inheriting the costs of administering yet another empire from a decrepit central Asian dynasty. Out of a desire to ensure that the Manchus would not follow the Mughals into oblivion, the Co-operative Policy was thus born, with Britain agreeing to help stabilise China's external position in order to assist the dynasty to focus more fully on the task of internal reform. The establishment of a modern foreign office (the Zongli Yamen) and a modern Maritime Customs Service – the last being designed, operated and maintained by Westerners – proved merely the most important and enduring reforms to emerge from this arrangement.

By the advent of the Tongzhi Restoration in 1862, a triangular pattern of collaboration had thus emerged between the imperial court, the Han scholar gentry and the Western powers that would define the contours of political order both within China and throughout East Asia for the next three decades. Within China itself, the new model armies enabled Beijing to defeat first the Taipings and then subsequently the dynasty's other internal enemies, which were largely suppressed by 1875. Similarly, the revenues of the Maritime Customs Service helped sponsor a significant strengthening of China's public finances, thereby providing the resources necessary to fund an ambitious if ultimately

---

[79] *Ibid.*   [80] *Ibid.*, p. 289.
[81] S. Spector, *Li Hung-Chang and the Huai Army: A study in nineteenth-century Chinese regionalism* (Seattle: University of Washington Press, 1964), pp. 63–7.

unsuccessful programme of military modernisation.[82] Internationally, meanwhile, the officials of the Zongli Yamen adapted to Western diplomatic practices with remarkable swiftness, successfully eliciting assistance from the Western powers to fend off piecemeal aggression from both tsarist Russia and imperial Japan in the 1870s.[83] This pragmatic conformity with Western international legal principles coincided with China's continued maintenance of her system of tributary diplomacy, with China's tributary ties with Korea in particular providing her with a strategic buffer against foreign encroachments that would persist in some form or another down to the Sino-Japanese war.

A universe out of harmony: The achievements and limits of the Confucian reaction

That the Qing dynasty succeeded in fending off multiple challenges at mid-century is a testament to its durability, but this resilience should not obscure the profound changes to the East Asian order that the mid-century crisis brought in its wake. Within China itself, the dynasty became ever more dependent for its survival on the fragile alliance that had developed between itself, the Han scholar gentry and its fickle foreign benefactors. The Manchu conquerors had of course always relied heavily on the Han bureaucracy to administer their patrimony, but the nature of this dependence changed after the mid-century rebellions, as Beijing's grip on the military and fiscal levers of power gradually slackened. Admittedly, it would be erroneous to suggest a linear progression from Zeng Guofan's new model armies to China's descent into warlordism following the Qing Empire's collapse in 1912.[84] But if the advent of the new model armies did not make China's subsequent disintegration inevitable, it certainly established important preconditions for this development. Thus, the shifting military balance between Manchu rulers and Han subjects inaugurated by the rebellions rendered the monarchy even more hostage to the sentiments of Han elites, while the advent of military provincialism also created new opportunities for social mobility outside the straitjacket of the imperial bureaucracy. Similarly, the development of armies cohering around ties of patronage and kinship rather than centralised bureaucratic command established ominous precedents, which would eventually recur with more momentous import following the empire's humiliation in the Sino-Japanese war.

---

[82] On 'self-strengthening' and its failure, see Fairbank and Goldman, *China: A new history*, pp. 217–21.

[83] Mancall, *China at the Center*, pp. 138–41, 151–3.

[84] This line of argument is convincingly repudiated in E. McCord, 'Militia and local militarization in late Qing and early republican China: The case of Hunan', *Modern China*, 14(2) (1988), 156–87.

The reforms undertaken after 1860 also substantially increased foreigners' involvement in governing the empire. In collecting and administering both the Imperial Maritime Customs Service and the salt gabelle, foreigners assumed a vital role in administering China's public finances, acquiring important leverage over the monarchy in so doing.[85] Similarly, in interjecting themselves into regional circuits of trade and finance with the assistance of local business partners, Western merchants increasingly yoked China's coastal entrepôts into larger trans-regional structures of accumulation, further accentuating the hybrid nature of the evolving regional order.[86] John Fairbank once noted that the joint administration of China by Chinese and 'barbarians' – a phenomenon he dubbed synarchy – was a recurrent phenomenon in Chinese history, and that Westerners' growing involvement in administering China from the Second Opium War onwards bore important parallels with earlier periods of Chinese history.[87] Arguably this synarchic order was already manifest in the alliance between Manchu conquerors and Han bureaucrats that had existed since the Ming–Qing transition. However, this latest expression of synarchy departed from historical precedents in that it was the 'barbarians' who assumed themselves superior to the civilisation they now jointly governed along with Manchu courtiers and Han bureaucrats. Whereas previous barbarian conquerors had allowed themselves to be acculturated into Chinese civilisation, the Western powers instead sought to redeem China by transforming it into a 'civilised' nation. This cultural chauvinism only intensified after 1860, and the inevitable clash of values that resulted significantly impeded the dynasty's efforts to reconcile the practical imperative of reform with the cultural imperative of preserving Confucian orthodoxy.

Internationally, meanwhile, the years following the Tongzhi Restoration witnessed the emergence of a more hybrid and in many ways more incoherent regional order. Resigning itself to the necessity of reform, the Chinese government increasingly interacted with Western powers using the forms and practices of Western diplomacy.[88] At the same time, the Chinese government's diplomatic ambidexterity was evident in its maintenance of the Sinosphere's traditional diplomatic practices in its dealings with tributary states. China's ability to simultaneously inhabit two different worlds diplomatically testified to its ability to grant both its practical and ideal interests their due. Nevertheless, China's capacity to maintain this uneasy compromise remained hostage to foreign powers' willingness to moderate their regional ambitions accordingly. Conversely, any sustained external effort to incorporate China's vassal states into modern diplomatic structures risked exposing the increasingly fictitious character of Chinese regional hegemony, thereby humiliating China and gravely undermining regional stability.

[85] Fairbank, 'Synarchy under the treaties', pp. 222–3.   [86] *Ibid.*, pp. 221–2.
[87] *Ibid.*, pp. 216–17.   [88] Mancall, *China at the Center*, p. 138.

The order that developed in the aftermath of the mid-century crisis was thus inherently fragile, resting on a contingent convergence of interests between court, gentry and foreigners, rather than cohering around a thick constellation of shared values. Within China itself, the imperial court sought to finesse the tensions between a commitment to Confucian orthodoxy and a commitment to reform by adopting an *à la carte* approach to modernisation. While court officials recognised the value of Western practical knowledge and sought to adapt their political and military structures accordingly, such renovations could only be undertaken within the limits prescribed by the abiding moral norms and principles of a cosmically valid Confucian order.[89] Confucian disregard for the merchant classes thus proscribed any sustained effort to nurture an indigenous commercial efflorescence, thereby impeding the development of a revenue base sufficient to adequately fund modernisation efforts.[90] Consequently, as the inadequacy of China's reform efforts gradually became apparent, elite opinion steadily polarised between competing progressive, reformist and reactionary factions, further sapping the monarchy's energies and undermining its legitimacy.

As the early promise of the Tongzhi faded, China's international position also appeared ever more tenuous. Before the First Opium War, China remained East Asia's uncontested hegemon. Western maritime incursions remained at the level of manageable nuisance, the Russian threat to the north had yet to materialise and Japan remained safely somnolent in its isolationist cocoon. By the 1870s, none of these conditions still held. Through force of arms, the Western powers had entrenched themselves in a network of treaty ports on China's coast, compelled China to conform to Western diplomatic practices, and established significant control over the empire's public finances. Additionally, while a common interest in securing the dynasty's survival had restrained British avarice momentarily, Russia's expansionist designs on China's northern frontier were becoming ever more overt. Most significantly of all for China, its one-time vassal state of Japan had responded far more energetically to the Western challenge, and was already showing worrying signs of preparing to challenge Chinese authority within its shrinking penumbra of tributary polities. While the monarchy had endured the mid-century crisis, its survival now rested upon the common interests it shared with foreign 'barbarians' rather than upon the common values that had previously sustained the Sinosphere. As subsequent events would demonstrate, such interests would prove an exceedingly fragile foundation on which to base regional order.

---

[89] Y.-P. I. Hao and E.-M. Wang, 'Changing Chinese views of Western relations, 1840–1895' in J. K. Fairbank and K.-C. Liu (eds.), *The Cambridge History of China*, XI: *Late Ch'ing, 1800–1911*, Pt II, p. 201.

[90] On the formidable ideological barriers retarding China's economic development at this time, see Wright, *The Last Stand of Chinese Conservatism*, p. 195.

8 | *Into the abyss: Civilisation, barbarism and the end of the Sinosphere*

> They ought to have learned, from the beating the Japanese pupils of European civilization gave them, that there were not two systems in the world deserving to be called civilization, but one only, and that whatever opposes or rejects this is a higher or lower form of barbarism, doomed to defeat and disappearance. They might have learned this from observation; they have insisted upon learning it from experience ...
>
> 'An Army of Civilization', *New York Times*, 20 June 1900.[1]

In 1900, 'civilisation' went to war with China. More precisely, in August of that year, an eight-power expeditionary force entered Beijing with the express goals of relieving the diplomatic legations from besieging Boxer rebels and punishing a dynasty that had sided with Eastern 'barbarism' over Western 'civilisation'. For several agonising weeks, foreign observers had been transfixed by stories of heroism and cruelty emanating from the imperial capital, as besieged diplomats and their families fought valiantly to fend off hordes of xenophobic religious fanatics intent on their destruction. That the vast majority of these stories later proved apocryphal was irrelevant, for they resonated powerfully within a ripening global mythoscape opposing Eastern savagery and irrationality to Western enlightenment and civilisation.[2] From the First Opium War onwards, Westerners had cast themselves as the standard-bearers of civilisation, who would shake the Confucian world from its torpor and unleash the creative energies of Asia's millions by introducing them to the beneficent influences of Christianity, free trade and constitutional government. By 1900, this inversion of the Sinosphere's civilised/barbarian dichotomy remained in place, but had assumed a decidedly more pessimistic and immutable cast. Amid a global context characterised by the growth of 'scientific' racism and accelerating geopolitical competition, the Boxer rebellion appeared as yet another expression of

---

[1] 'An army of civilization', *New York Times*, 20 June 1900, p. 6.
[2] On this point, see generally C. A. Bayly, 'The Boxer uprising and India: Globalizing myths' in R. Bickers and R. G. Tiedeman (eds.), *The Boxers, China and the World* (Plymouth, UK: Rowman and Littlefield Publishers, 2007), pp. 151–2.

Eastern fanaticism, to be situated alongside roughly contemporaneous outrages such as the Mahdist rebellion in Sudan, pan-Islamic political mobilisation in Egypt and the *fin de siècle* surge in Indian anti-colonial terrorism in Bengal.[3] In this febrile atmosphere, China was no longer recognised as the Middle Kingdom, admired by Western *philosophes* and venerated by its neighbours as East Asia's political and commercial hub. Nor was it even regarded – as it had been during the era of the Co-operative Policy – as a venerable sovereign monarchy in the process of being civilised and modernised through Western tutelage. Instead, China by the time of the Boxer rebellion was seen as a dying nation ruled by a doomed dynasty, with its pending disintegration portending a renewed era of regional instability. While China would eventually confound its eulogists, the predictions of regional catastrophe that accompanied its humiliation would prove tragically prescient.

This chapter continues the story of East Asia's transition from a suzerain to a sovereign international order, focusing specifically on the Sinosphere's dismemberment and the regional disorder that followed in its wake. In the Taiping rebellion's aftermath, a hybrid synarchic order had developed in East Asia, based on an alliance of convenience between Manchu courtiers, Han scholar bureaucrats and 'barbarian' benefactors. This chapter charts the dissolution of this alliance, and the consequences of the ensuing collapse of East Asian synarchy. My analysis proceeds in six sections. The first two sections focus on China's catastrophic loss of international legitimacy following its defeat in the Sino-Japanese war, and recounts the instability that followed as the Great Powers forsook earlier hopes for reform in Beijing, and instead embarked on a competitive 'scramble for concessions' within the territories of the prostrate empire. The second section considers the domestic consequences of China's defeat in the Sino-Japanese war, concentrating on the crisis in the Confucian social imaginary that followed as growing numbers of Chinese intellectuals abandoned notions of cosmological kingship in favour of more overtly nationalistic conceptions of political order. The third section examines the Qing dynasty's response to its growing domestic and international isolation, focusing in particular on the dynasty's quixotic revolt against international 'civilisation' at the time of the Boxer rebellion. The radicalisation of Chinese opposition to the Qing dynasty, combined with the concurrent processes of provincial military mobilisation that together led to the dynasty's overthrow in 1912, form the subjects of the fourth section. The chapter concludes by anticipating the two master trends, specifically the growth of Chinese warlordism and the blossoming of Japanese pretensions towards regional hegemony, that would define the character and nature of East Asia's chaotic interregnum in the three decades after 1915.

---

[3] *Ibid.*, pp. 151–2.

Railways, imperialists and 'dying nations': The global and regional contexts of the Sinosphere's destruction

The global context

The Sinosphere had historically rested on China's unchallengeable material might, but during periods of dynastic decline it had relied even more heavily on the region's widespread acknowledgement of China as the centre of civilisation. Following the Tongzhi Restoration, however, it was clear that the Taiping challenge had diminished not only the Qing dynasty's prestige, but also China's cultural magnetism. Consequently, the hybrid order that developed after the mid-century rebellions differed fundamentally from the more ideologically integrated order that had preceded it. During its protracted convalescence following the mid-century crisis, China depended for its protection on barbarian benefactors, especially Britain.[4] Critically, the British interest in preserving the dynasty stemmed from calculations of commercial and strategic self-interest rather than from any deference to Chinese cultural supremacy.[5] Equally, while the Han scholar gentry remained wedded to their Manchu masters on account of their commitment to defending Confucian orthodoxy, this same commitment to orthodoxy simultaneously constrained the dynasty's inclination or ability to modernise along Western lines.[6] The resulting tension between adapting to necessity and preserving orthodoxy expressed itself internationally in the emergence of a hybrid regional order, in which China maintained its tributary ties with vassal kingdoms even while accommodating itself to modern diplomatic practices when engaging with Western states. At its base, this hybrid order depended for its survival upon a continuation of the tenuous alliance that had developed between the Manchu court, the orthodox gentry and the foreign 'barbarians' following the Taiping cataclysm. The stability of the Manchu–barbarian leg of this tripod in turn rested exclusively on bonds of common interest rather than common identity, and proved fragile once these interests diverged.

The Sinosphere's destruction was propelled partially by a shift in global strategic circumstances occasioned by a global intensification of Great Power rivalries from the late 1870s onwards. The material advantages of early industrialisation, coupled with the stabilisation of intra-European rivalries via the Congress system, had provided Britain with both the technological capacity and the strategic latitude necessary to consolidate an empire of global reach in

---

[4] Wright, *The Last Stand of Chinese Conservatism*, pp. 21–3.   [5] *Ibid.*, pp. 25–7.

[6] Although the constraints of orthodoxy did not entirely neuter Chinese efforts at reform, and indeed Wright has argued that the Qing dynasty's moves towards reform appear impressive if juxtaposed to those of the Korean Yi dynasty rather than to those of Meiji Japan, to which China is most often unfavourably compared. See generally M. C. Wright, 'The adaptability of Ch'ing diplomacy: The case of Korea', *The Journal of Asian Studies*, 17(3) (1958), 363–81.

the decades after 1815. While encompassing possessions as far afield as sub-Saharan Africa, Canada, the Caribbean and Australasia, the core of the British imperium crystallised around the southern littoral of the Eurasian landmass.[7] More specifically, Britain's naval dominance enabled her to enfold and then further expand a vast web of commercial exchanges spanning from Aden to Hong Kong.[8] As the British tightened their grip over Mughal India, the subcontinent's vast manpower reserves provided a useful land-power supplement to British naval supremacy, with the Raj's 'martial races' supplying much of the muscle needed to police the empire east of the river Indus.[9]

Both Britain's forced opening of China and its subsequent protection of the Qing dynasty during the Era of Co-operation rested on a combination of British military – especially naval – dominance combined with favourable strategic circumstances. From the late 1870s, however, both technological developments and intensifying geopolitical competition steadily corroded British hegemony, weakening both its will and its capacity to preserve the post-Taiping order in East Asia. Technologically, Britain's advantages as the world's first industrial power inevitably waned as industrialisation spread to other countries, providing states such as Germany and America with the material capacity to contest British hegemony.[10] The further diffusion of innovations such as the telegraph and the railroad also knitted the world together into an ever more integrated geopolitical space, with the resulting increase in time-space compression further raising global violence interdependence.[11]

Industrialisation thus increased the number of players capable of competing with Britain, while simultaneously enlarging the stage on which this struggle would play out. Accompanying these material changes, processes of institutional decay both within and beyond Europe further contributed to a more competitive strategic environment. Within Europe itself, the breakdown of the Congress system following the Crimean War portended a growth in intra-European conflicts in the 1860s.[12] These conflicts in turn bequeathed a unified Reich and a revanchist Third Republic, both of whom looked increasingly

---

[7] H. Munkler, *Empires: The logic of world domination from Rome to the United States* (Cambridge: Polity Press, 2007), p. 11.

[8] *Ibid.*

[9] R. Lim, *The Geopolitics of East Asia: The search for equilibrium* (London: Routledge, 2003), p. 17.

[10] Kennedy, *Rise and Fall of the Great Powers*, pp. 291–2.

[11] This increase in global interconnectedness is for example demonstrated in the dramatic expansion of the global railway network from 1870–1914, which grew from a little over 200,000 km to over 1 million km during this time period. See E. J. Hobsbawm, *The Age of Empire, 1875–1914* (London: Abacus, 2003), p. 62.

[12] L. Dehio, *The Precarious Balance: Four centuries of the European power struggle* (London: Chatto and Windus, 1962), p. 205.

to overseas expansion for prestige, profit and security.[13] Beyond Europe, the decay of the Ottoman Empire, Safavid Persia and Qing China steadily corroded the buffer separating British and Russian spheres of influence in Eurasia. Previously, Eurasia had been roughly divided into northern and southern halves along the mountain ranges from the Caucasus to the Himalayas, with tsarist Russia as Europe's land-power giant dominating the north and Britain as Europe's sea-power giant dominating the south.[14] The decay of Eurasia's gunpowder empires from the mid-nineteenth century threatened to destroy this equilibrium, arousing both expansionist appetites in St Petersburg and corresponding fears for the security of Britain's empire in London.

Reflecting and reinforcing the material and institutional trends already outlined, the last third of the nineteenth century also witnessed cultural and intellectual shifts that further inflamed Great Power rivalries. By the 1870s, the beliefs in human malleability and perfectibility that had earlier infused both the European Enlightenment and the Anglo-American 'Great Awakening' were appreciably in decline. In their place, notions of social Darwinism and 'scientific' racism were ascendant.[15] These constructs, which appeared both to explain and condone the vast inequalities developing between different social classes and different nations under conditions of industrialisation and imperialism, injected an added urgency and prospective finality into international rivalries.[16] Misappropriated Darwinian themes of competitive selection and extinction increasingly pervaded the language of international politics, with the fate of 'barbarous' and 'savage' peoples appearing to offer a cautionary example of the dark destiny awaiting nations that failed to respond vigorously and violently to the challenges of the modern world. Spurred on by fears of cultural and racial degeneration, convinced of the moral legitimacy of conquest, and inspired by a belief in war's regenerative capacities, the Great Powers increasingly embraced an ethos enjoining predatory expansion that boded ill for the future of international order.

The regional context

The growing Great Power rivalry of the late nineteenth century inevitably spilled over into East Asia. Western disappointment with the dilatory pace of Beijing's reforms combined with intensifying Great Power rivalries to catalyse a concerted carve up of China's tributary system from the 1870s, as first the

---

[13] Kennedy, *Rise and Fall of the Great Powers*, pp. 247–8.   [14] Munkler, *Empires*, p. 11.
[15] See generally M. Hawkins, *Social Darwinism in European and American Thought, 1860–1945: Nature as model and nature as threat* (Cambridge University Press, 1997), Ch. 8.
[16] *Ibid.*, p. 203.

European powers and then Japan steadily peeled China's tributary polities from Beijing's grasp.[17] By far the most significant of the conflicts that attended the Sinosphere's dismemberment was the protracted Sino-Japanese struggle over Korea. Following Toyotomi's failed invasion of Korea in the late sixteenth century, Japan had progressively withdrawn from diplomatic relations with other states, and had not participated in the Sino-centric order after this time.[18] Awoken from its slumber by Commodore Perry's black ships in 1853, Japan had initially been buffeted by conflicts between pragmatic reformers and reactionaries, but this struggle was decisively resolved in the pragmatists' favour with the Meiji Restoration in 1868.[19] Unlike the roughly contemporaneous Tongzhi Restoration in China, which remained hamstrung by a commitment to modernising only within the parameters permitted by Confucian orthodoxy, the Meiji reformers recognised the need for a fundamental transformation of Japan's social and political order if Japan was to survive.[20] Consequently, the Japanese proved far more capable than the Chinese of emulating the reforms necessary for Japan to be accepted into a Western-dominated international society. Critically, this emulation was not confined to the area of domestic reforms, but extended also towards the 'mimetic imperialism' that characterised Japanese foreign policy from the 1870s onwards.[21]

Japan's motives for seeking to expand its influence in Korea were multiple, and I will restrict myself here only to those drivers most relevant to the present inquiry.[22] Globally, Japan's emergence as a Great Power coincided with the most frenzied surge of imperial expansion in world history since the Mongol *Blitzkrieg* of the thirteenth century. Between 1876 and 1915, six Great Powers divided up territories totalling a quarter of the world's landmass between them.[23] Within such an environment, the weakness of the reclusive Yi dynasty in Korea constituted both a threat and an opportunity for Tokyo. For the

---

[17] See generally I. C. Y. Hsu, 'Late Ch'ing foreign relations, 1866–1905' in Fairbank and Liu (eds.), *The Cambridge History of China*, XI: *Late Ch'ing, 1800–1911*, Pt II, pp. 84–101.

[18] H. Bolitho, 'The inseparable trinity: Japan's relations with China and Korea' in J. W. Hall (ed.), *The Cambridge History of Japan*, IV: *Early Modern Japan* (Cambridge University Press, 1991), p. 300.

[19] M. B. Jansen, 'The Meiji Restoration' in M. B. Jansen (ed.), *The Cambridge History of Japan*, V: *The Nineteenth Century* (Cambridge University Press, 1989), p. 322.

[20] *Ibid.*, p. 359.

[21] On 'mimetic imperialism' as a constitutive feature of Japan's modernisation programme, see generally A. Iriye, 'Japan's drive to Great Power status' in Jansen (ed.), *The Cambridge History of Japan*, V: *The Nineteenth Century*, pp. 721–82.

[22] The most comprehensive account of Japan's varied motives for expanding into Korea remains P. Duus, *The Abacus and the Sword: The Japanese penetration of Korea, 1895–1910* (Berkeley: University of California Press, 1995).

[23] Hobsbawm, *The Age of Empire*, p. 59.

Japanese, a weak Korea could fall easy prey to external powers, after which it might become a platform from which foreigners could then credibly threaten Japan itself.[24] Conversely, a strong Korea, perhaps modernised under Japanese tutelage, would provide Japan with both a buffer against attack and a potential beachhead for further expansion on the Asian mainland. Japan's subsequent assumption of the burden for 'civilising' Korea did not fully develop until after its expulsion of Chinese influence from Korea following the Sino-Japanese war. But the seeds of this civilising imperative were manifest from the outset of Japan's Korean adventure, and reflected the norms of an ever more hierarchical international society, in which possession of one's own empire was a prerequisite for Great Power status, and recognition as a Great Power was in turn seen as providing the only guarantee of being granted the full panoply of rights and privileges associated with membership of the family of nations.[25]

Just as Japan's initial probes into Korea reflected Tokyo's socialisation into the norms of an encroaching international society, so too was this process of socialisation also evident in the Chinese response. Under the norms of the Sinosphere, China had generally refrained from interfering in Korea's internal affairs, and the Yi dynasty had reciprocated by acknowledging Chinese suzerainty through a policy of *sadae* ('serving the great').[26] From the mid-1870s, however, China's sensitivity to developments in Korea sharpened appreciably, and its commitment to observing the non-intrusive norms of tributary diplomacy correspondingly declined. Initially, China's deviations from Sinospheric norms were incremental, and included encouraging Korea to establish equal diplomatic relations with other countries besides Japan while simultaneously maintaining its tributary ties with China.[27] The thinking behind this policy was that Korea's establishment of diplomatic relations with other states would enable the Yi dynasty to 'balance barbarians with barbarians', thus preserving both Korean autonomy and Chinese security.[28] This strategy was nevertheless soon found wanting, both because of Japan's insistent efforts to extend its influence in Korea, and because of the resistance of influential Korean ultra-conservatives to the country's opening to 'barbarians'. Indeed, so significant was the indigenous resistance to Korea's opening that China was forced to intervene in 1882 to quell a revolt by anti-reformist soldiers, drawing China intimately into Korea's domestic politics and thus closer towards confrontation with Japan.

[24] Lim, *The Geopolitics of East Asia*, p. 23.
[25] S. Suzuki, 'Japan's socialization into Janus-faced European international society', *European Journal of International Relations*, 11(1) (2005), 154–5.
[26] Kim, *The Last Phase of the East Asian World Order*, p. 9.
[27] Wright, 'The adaptability of Ch'ing diplomacy', pp. 379–80.
[28] Kim, *The Last Phase of the East Asian World Order*, p. 278.

Japanese assertiveness and Korean intransigence together thwarted Chinese efforts to protect the empire's interests in Korea through the more indirect strategy of 'balancing barbarians with barbarians'. This left only the more interventionist course of action China was compelled to pursue after the orthodox revolt of 1882, a strategy that sucked China into the ever more factionalised and ideologically polarised ferment of Korean politics.[29] China's own modernisation programme had faltered due to the insuperable challenges of balancing the imperative of reform with the necessity of preserving Confucian orthodoxy. Similarly, Japan's modernisation had also necessitated the defeat of an ideologically orthodox xenophobic movement led by a faction of Japan's samurai elite. Consequently, it is unsurprising that a similar polarisation developed in Korea between an orthodox clique dedicated to defending the Confucian order from foreign heresies, and a reformist faction intent on modernising Korea along Japanese lines.[30] What was especially significant about this polarity within Korea, however, was its intimate association with the growing international rivalry between China and Japan.[31] For the Chinese, a triumph of the orthodox faction was unwanted, for it would merely hasten the Yi dynasty's decline into decrepitude, ensuring the Korean peninsula's domination by foreign powers potentially hostile to Chinese interests. Similarly, however, the reformist faction's affinities with Japan precluded Beijing's support, leaving the Chinese with no choice but to shore up the Korean monarchy. Conversely, while Japan's affinities for the Korean reformists made its allegiance more clear-cut, Tokyo's ability to advance its interests remained stymied by China's influence over the Yi dynasty. Given China's and Japan's opposed interests, the Korean monarchy's weakness, and the growing polarisation of Korea's factions, the prospect of conflict grew ever more likely as the 1880s wore on.

Like Valois France in its twilight, late-nineteenth-century Korea was fast becoming the focal point around which court intrigues, systemic ideological struggles and regional contests for power and prestige explosively intersected. While the ineffectual Korean King Kojong embraced a programme of 'Eastern Ethics, Western Technology' after 1882 under close Chinese surveillance, a chastened but unbowed orthodox faction schemed to repel both Japanese and Chinese attempts to impose foreign heresies on Korea.[32] Meanwhile, the reformist Independence Party plotted its own equivalent of the Meiji Restoration with covert Japanese encouragement, and took advantage of China's momentary distraction in the Sino-French war in Annam to stage a

---

[29] Hsu, 'Late Ch'ing foreign relations', p. 104.
[30] B. Oh, 'Sino-Japanese rivalry in Korea, 1876–1885' in A. Iriye (ed.), *The Chinese and the Japanese: Essays in political and cultural interactions* (Princeton University Press, 1980), pp. 48–50.
[31] *Ibid.*, pp. 52–4.   [32] *Ibid.*, p. 52.

palace coup in 1884.[33] Following the ensuing interventions by both China and Japan, an international conflict was only narrowly averted. The Li-Ito Convention of the following year sought to stabilise the situation by mandating the evacuation of all foreign forces from Korea and committing the signatories to notifying one another in advance of any decision to redeploy troops to the peninsula.[34] But the crises of both 1882 and 1884 had nevertheless demonstrated the fact that the practices of tributary diplomacy that had governed the Sinosphere since the fourteenth century were no longer effective in containing East Asia's rivalries. The short and bitter peace that followed also illustrated that while the old order was dying, a new international order in East Asia had yet to take its place.

The Sino-Japanese War and the crumbling of the Manchu–barbarian alliance

The Sino-Japanese war thus developed out of long-standing processes of rising geopolitical competition, which were exacerbated by the Korean government's continuing decay. Japan after the Li-Ito Convention remained dissatisfied with a settlement that preserved China's de facto pre-eminence over Korea, even as expanding trade ties were drawing Korea inexorably into Japan's economic orbit.[35] More ominous still for Japan was Russia's decision in 1891 to commence construction of the Trans-Siberian Railway.[36] Just as the opening of the Suez Canal in 1869 had significantly shortened the maritime powers' lines of supply and communication, thereby enabling their increasing encroachments into south-eastern China and South-east Asia, so too did the Trans-Siberian Railway threaten to establish Russia as North-east Asia's dominant power.[37] To the Japanese, whose strategic interests in Korea resembled Britain's long-standing interests in the Low Countries, the lengthening shadow of Russian imperialism posed a grave threat to the security of the home islands.[38] Similarly, just as ideological affinities and strategic interests had together drawn Elizabethan England into the Netherlands' wars against Philip II, so too did Japan's interest in securing a Korean buffer state ensure its accelerating involvement in the internal struggle between orthodox Confucians and Meiji-style reformers then convulsing Korea.

The rising regional violence interdependence spurred by the spread of Russian railways lent added urgency to the Sino-Japanese struggle for

---

[33] *Ibid.*, p. 51.   [34] Hsu, 'Late Ch'ing foreign relations', p. 104.

[35] Oh, 'Sino-Japanese rivalry in Korea', p. 55.

[36] S. Lone and G. McCormack, *Korea since 1850* (New York: Longman Cheshire, 1993), p. 25.

[37] Lim, *The Geopolitics of East Asia*, p. 25.

[38] I. H. Nish, *The Origins of the Russo-Japanese War* (London: Longman, 1985), p. 18.

influence in Korea after 1891. Nevertheless, it was a millenarian rebellion within Korea itself that provided the spark for war between the two countries. Originating in the south-western province of Chola in 1860, the Tonghak ('Eastern Learning') religion conjoined temporal concerns for social reform with millennial impulses towards individual and societal spiritual transformation.[39] Endorsing the concept 'Man is Heaven', Tonghak believers contested the privileges of the Confucian literati, arguing instead for the abolition of all classes on the basis of all humans' inalienable equality as expressions of the same divine cosmic force.[40] Unlike their Chinese Taiping predecessors, with whom they shared anti-Confucian levelling sentiments, Tonghak worshippers had remained mostly quiescent for much of their existence prior to the uprisings of 1894–5. But in February 1894, the movement burst into action, helping to galvanise a peasant uprising in Chola province against the incumbent governor. While driven strongly by popular economic distress and dissatisfaction with official corruption, the uprising was also fuelled by prophecies anticipating the end of the Yi dynasty and the coming of an earthly Utopia.[41] In the face of this rebellion, the pro-Chinese faction of the Yi court solicited China's intervention to help suppress the uprising.[42] China's accession to this request provoked a Japanese counter-intervention in its turn.[43] Thus was precipitated a war that would end not only with the Sinosphere's destruction, but also with the disintegration of the fragile Manchu–foreigner alliance that had formerly helped guarantee order in post-Taiping East Asia.

China's defeat in the Sino-Japanese war catalysed a profound transformation in the East Asian international order. At the institutional level, the war marked the definitive end of China's system of tributary diplomacy, and with it the end also of the Sinosphere's last institutional remnants. Article 1 of the Treaty of Shimonoseki thus committed China to the dissolution of its remaining tributary ties with Korea, including the abolition of all tribute payments and the end of the ceremonial diplomatic practices that had previously yoked the states to one another in a hierarchical relationship.[44] King Kojong's subsequent

---

[39] S. T. Lee, *Religion and Social Formation in Korea: Minjung and millenarianism* (New York: Mouton de Gruyter, 1996), p. 106.

[40] *Ibid.*   [41] *Ibid.*, p. 120.   [42] Hsu, 'Late Ch'ing foreign relations', p. 105.

[43] *Ibid.*, pp. 105–6. Interestingly, Hsu argues that Japan lured China into the ensuing confrontation between the two countries by falsely signalling that Japan would not intervene in the event of a Chinese deployment to suppress the rebellion. Japan's calculated desire to exploit the Tonghak crisis to decisively resolve the Sino-Japanese struggle for influence in Korea in Tokyo's favour is further explored in Duus, *The Abacus and the Sword*, pp. 67–8.

[44] Thus, Article 1 of the Treaty of Shimonoseki reads as follows: 'China recognises definitively the full and complete independence and autonomy of Korea, and in consequence, the payment of tribute and the performance of ceremonies and formalities by Korea to China, shall wholly cease for the future.' Text of the Treaty of Shimonoseki, available at: http://www.taiwandocuments.org/shimonoseki01.htm.

elevation to the status of emperor of Korea in 1897, placing him at least nominally in a position of equality alongside both the Chinese emperor and the Japanese emperor, further underscored this transformation in North-east Asian diplomatic arrangements.[45] From this point onwards, relations between the three states would increasingly be mediated by the contradictory Western imperatives of toleration and civilisation, with a formalised system of sovereign equality co-existing in uneasy tension with Japan's increasing invocation of norms of paramountcy to assert its hegemony first in Korea and then subsequently within China itself.[46]

At the material level, the war also witnessed a profound shift in the regional balance of power. With its Peiyang fleet destroyed, China's 'self-strengthening' movement was dealt a devastating blow. The destruction of China's hugely expensive modern fleet had enabled Japanese forces to seize control of the Liaodong and Shandong peninsulas, laying open the approaches to Beijing and forcing the Chinese to sue for peace.[47] Of more enduring significance was the massive war indemnity imposed on China, which starved Beijing of the resources necessary to undertake further reforms.[48] China's cession of Taiwan and the Pescadores to Japan further strengthened Japan's material power and international status, with the abolition of the last of the Western Powers' unequal treaties with Japan at this time contrasting starkly with the frenzied 'scramble for concessions' in China that followed in the years after China's defeat.[49]

Beyond both the dismantling of the last vestiges of the tributary state system and the shift in the regional balance of power, it was the radical revision in international perceptions of Chinese power that was most significant for East Asian order after 1895. China's humiliation in the war cemented its status as a 'dying nation' in the eyes of foreign observers, rendering it ripe for dismemberment. Within the context of its hemispheric struggle for supremacy with the British Empire, Russia had been thwarted twice in its push southwards into the decaying Ottoman Empire.[50] Confronted by concerted resistance in the west, the tsar's attentions were deflected eastwards, where the Manchus' weakness invited aggression, and where Russia's steadily expanding rail network increasingly afforded it the logistical and military means necessary to realise its

---

[45] Duus, *The Abacus and the Sword*, p. 128.

[46] The tendency to adapt Western practices of paramountcy in Japan's engagement with nominally sovereign neighbouring states could be seen even prior to the conclusion of the Sino-Japanese war, when Inoue Kaoru, Japan's former foreign minister and representative of the Japanese government in its dealings with the Yi dynasty, modelled his supervision of the Korean government on the conduct of Lord Cromer, Britain's minister to Cairo and de facto regent of Egypt. See Lone and McCormack, *Korea Since 1850*, p. 29.

[47] Lim, *The Geopolitics of East Asia*, p. 25.   [48] *Ibid.*, p. 26.   [49] *Ibid.*

[50] J. P. LeDonne, *The Russian Empire and the World, 1700–1917: The geopolitics of expansion and containment* (New York: Oxford University Press, 1997), pp. 319–26.

expansionist dreams in North-east Asia.[51] While nominally committed to preserving China's territorial integrity, British diplomats after the Sino-Japanese war were both newly alarmed at Russia's designs on Manchuria, and also ever more contemptuous of the 'loose federation of satrapies' that the Manchu Empire now resembled.[52] The combination of Russian aggression and Chinese weakness thus presented the British in southern China with a dilemma similar to that confronted by both the Chinese and the Japanese in Korea a decade earlier. Uninterested for decades in assuming formal responsibility for governing the vast territory in the Yangtze valley that had from the Opium Wars constituted Britain's sphere of influence, the British nevertheless despaired of the Qing dynasty's capacity to serve as a viable buffer between British India and tsarist Russia. Within this context, the British began tentatively negotiating railway spheres of influence with their Russian nemesis to preserve the security of Britain's Asian empire, all the while searching for a diplomatic means of blocking Russia's further advance.[53]

By the end of the nineteenth century, the Qing dynasty had therefore lost the confidence of its erstwhile foreign supporters. While Britain and America both favoured a preservation of China's territorial integrity, this seemed an increasingly forlorn hope following the Sino-Japanese war.[54] The Manchu–barbarian alliance that had underpinned East Asian synarchy was crumbling, portending a further intensification of Great Power rivalry and regional instability. After 1895, the spectre of China's pending disintegration threatened to become a self-fulfilling prophecy, as statesmen weaned on Darwinian tropes of competitive selection and extinction resigned themselves to China's obliteration as a sovereign nation, and sought to position themselves as favourably as possible for the seemingly inevitable post-mortem mutilation. This predatory fatalism found its sharpest expression in the 'scramble for concessions' that followed the murder of two German missionaries in Shandong in November 1897. German demands for territorial compensation in Shandong following the murders were swiftly followed by comparable demands from Russia, Britain, France and Japan, as each sought to balance concessions to Germany by solidifying their own spheres of influence within China.[55] Far from placating the foreign powers, Beijing's capitulation to these demands merely underscored China's status as the 'sick man of Asia', the Qing dynasty's newly exposed frailty serving as an invitation to further foreign aggression.

The 'scramble for concessions' furthered a process that had begun in North-east Asia in the early 1890s, whereby the geographical locus of international

[51] Nish, *The Origins of the Russo-Japanese War*, p. 18.

[52] T. G. Otte, 'The Boxer uprising and British foreign policy: The end of isolation' in R. Bickers and R. G. Tiedeman (eds.), *The Boxers, China, and the World* (Plymouth: Rowman and Littlefield Publishers, 2007), p. 158.

[53] *Ibid.*, pp. 158–9.   [54] Hsu, 'Late Ch'ing foreign relations', p. 113.   [55] *Ibid.*

rivalry shifted decisively from China's hydrographic centre and economic heartland in the south-east and towards the capital of Beijing and its surrounding territories. China's expulsion from Korea, its cession of Taiwan and the Pescadores to Japan, and its de facto cession of large tracts of Manchuria to Russia denied the Qing dynasty control over the Yellow Sea, leaving the imperial capital directly exposed to the threat of foreign intervention.[56] Moreover, while Beijing had briefly experienced the humiliation of foreign occupation before, in 1860, the spread of Russia's Trans-Siberian Railway and its Manchurian Chinese Eastern Railway threatened to make vulnerability to occupation a permanent feature of China's international environment.[57] Within this context, the concessions granted to the imperial powers in 1898 underscored the genuinely existential threat that China now faced. Defeat in war had already precipitated an international crisis of legitimacy for the Qing dynasty. As China's indignities continued to accumulate, the dynasty's crisis of legitimacy would extend inwards as well, as increasing numbers of educated Chinese called into question not merely the authority of the ruling house, but also the very foundations of the Confucian social order.

Crises of social imaginaries, failures of reform and the breakdown of the Manchu–Han Alliance

'Tearing through the nets': Foreign aggression and the crisis of the Confucian social imaginary

China's immediate response to the 'scramble for concessions' exposed an incipient crisis of social imaginaries among sections of the Chinese literati. Prior to the 1890s, foreign ideas such as nationalism and constitutional government had acquired minimal traction in China. The scholar gentry continued to see subscription to the 'three bonds' of Confucianism – the bonds of asymmetric benevolence and obedience linking rulers and ruled, husbands and wives and fathers and sons – as constituting the basis of both cosmic and temporal order.[58] Consequently, they regarded with bewilderment and disdain any suggestions to dilute China's Confucian system of government, especially through the adoption of any reforms encouraging wider political participation at the expense of the emperor's Heavenly Mandate.[59]

---

[56] Hans J. van de Ven, 'The military in the Republic', *The China Quarterly*, 150 (special issue) (1997), 354.

[57] F. Patrikeeff and H. Shukman, *Railways and the Russo-Japanese War: Transporting war* (London: Routledge, 2007), p. 34.

[58] H. Chang, 'Intellectual change and the reform movement, 1890–8' in Fairbank and Liu (eds.), *The Cambridge History of China*, XI: *Late Ch'ing, 1800–1911*, Pt II, p. 276.

[59] *Ibid.*, p. 281.

From the mid-1890s onwards, however, increasing numbers of Chinese intellectuals began to question key tenets of imperial Confucianism. Confucianism had traditionally embraced an ontological dualism that distinguished material force from animating principle, and this dualism had sustained reform efforts that borrowed Western technological innovations while seeking to preserve a sociopolitical order founded on Confucian ideas of cosmological kingship.[60] But the combination of defeat in war, renewed foreign aggression, and an accelerating infiltration of Western ideas through the foreign concessions forced a fundamental reappraisal of the normative complex that held the Chinese world order together. Hao Chang argues that the ensuing 'crisis of orientational order' that Chinese intellectuals experienced was greater than any that China had endured since the Axial Age.[61] This crisis encompassed sweeping criticisms of the identity-constitutive, ethical-prescriptive and power-legitimating norms of the old order.

At the identity-constitutive level, the 1890s saw the first comprehensive questioning of the theory of cosmological kingship that had undergirded the old Sinosphere. Imperial Confucianism maintained that the emperor served as the lynchpin between the cosmos and the temporal world, and that the over-riding purpose of collective association was the achievement of a state of cosmic and temporal harmony via the mediation of the Son of Heaven.[62] But in the face of the continuing Western encroachment, it became untenable either to exclusively equate civilisation with China, or to reserve for the emperor his earlier role as the pivot whose universal authority linked the cosmic, social and natural worlds. Historically, Chinese thought had always distinguished between *Tianxia*, denoting 'empire' or 'all under Heaven', and *guo*, referring to a local political unit within the empire (or 'nation' in modern parlance).[63] Not merely isolated descriptors, these terms were also relational concepts that connoted lower and higher forms of power – whereas *guo* denoted not merely land and people, but was also identified with 'protection by military force', *Tianxia* conversely referred to the truly 'civilised society', elevated by the inculcation of Confucian virtues via the mediation of a righteous ruler.[64] Under the weight of the Western military and cultural onslaught, the parochial reality of Chinese pretensions towards universalism as represented in the concept of *Tianxia* became clear. Conversely, the question of preserving the temporal survival of the Chinese nation (*guo*) now acquired unprecedented urgency. In the face of a static cosmology that enjoined the emperor's preservation of universal harmony via the ritual enactment of timeless virtues, Darwinian notions of

---

[60] Chang, 'Intellectual change and the reform movement', pp. 282–3.
[61] H. Chang, *Chinese Intellectuals in Crisis: The search for order and meaning (1890–1911)* (Berkeley: University of California Press, 1987), p. 7.
[62] See generally Ch. 6.   [63] Levenson, *Confucian China and its Modern Fate*, I, p. 99.
[64] *Ibid.*, p. 101.

evolution conversely suggested a dynamically fluid universe in which change was constant, and the opposing possibilities of extinction and fundamental moral progress were real historical potentialities.[65] Armed with this new awareness, an increasing number of Chinese intellectuals urged a re-envisioning of the role of the imperial office. In place of his earlier function as mediator between the cosmic and temporal realms, the emperor would henceforth be dedicated to cultivating the wealth and material power of the Chinese nation. In the short term, fulfilment of this obligation would preserve China from the threat of foreign subjugation.[66] In the long term, it was suggested, China's national regeneration would itself assist in propelling a global progress towards a utopian world community founded on sentiments of universal sympathy.[67]

Chinese thinkers at the turn of the century remained loath to abandon aspects of Confucian universalism. But they were now compelled to reconcile this universalism with a new evolutionary cosmology that relativised China's place in the world, and therefore mandated a radical reconceptualisation of the function of the imperial office. Similarly, at an ethical-prescriptive level, the desire to preserve Confucianism's philanthropic core conflicted with a new desire to 'tear through the nets' of Confucian morality as it had been institutionalised in the ritual form of *li* and the doctrine of the 'three bonds'.[68] Tan Sitong, one of the major thinkers of his time, thus argued that the core of Confucianism was *ren*, which he interpreted as referring to the universal love that binds the cosmic and social worlds together and invests meaning in human existence.[69] For Tan, this philanthropic essence of Confucianism had been obscured by the orthodox emphasis on *li*, a ritualised code of moral conduct that legitimised social hierarchy and thus denied the equality and moral independence of the individual.[70] What was needed was nothing less than a Confucian reformation, in which the humanitarianism and respect for the individual's moral independence that were originally central to Confucianism would be restored at the expense of the suffocating hierarchy enacted in *li*.[71]

In seeking to reclaim the essence of a spiritual tradition while purging it of centuries of authoritarianism and ritual excess, the activities of the Confucian reformers unavoidably invite parallels with Martin Luther. Tellingly, it was the reformers themselves who were the first to make this association. Tan Sitong declared that he prayed for a Chinese Martin Luther to revive Confucianism, while his mentor Kang Youwei was similarly identified by another student as the

---

[65] C. Furth, 'Intellectual change: From the reform movement to the May fourth movement, 1895–1900' in J. K. Fairbank (ed.), *The Cambridge History of China*, XII: *Republican China 1912–1949*, Pt I (Cambridge University Press, 1983), pp. 325–6.

[66] Chang, 'Intellectual change and the reform movement', p. 289.   [67] *Ibid.*

[68] Furth, 'Intellectual change', pp. 332–3.

[69] L. Yu-Sheng, *The Crisis of Chinese Consciousness: Radical anti-traditionalism in the May fourth era* (Madison: The University of Wisconsin Press, 1979), p. 34.

[70] *Ibid.*   [71] *Ibid.*, p. 35.

'Martin Luther of Confucianism'.[72] Despite their avowedly reformist intentions, the intellectuals' invocation of Luther necessarily gestured towards the revolutionary implications of their reformist message. For the attempts to reform Confucian cosmology and ethics also inescapably implied fundamental revisions to the power-legitimating norms of the Confucian order. Reformists such as Kang Youwei certainly did not advocate a secularisation of the Chinese political order; Kang's characterisation of Chinese renewal as forming one step in the path towards the progressive realisation of a utopian world community puts paid to such a suggestion.[73] But in divesting the emperor of his sacerdotal function as the lynchpin linking the cosmos and the temporal world, Kang and his disciples were clearly arguing for a desacralisation of the imperial office. Within a society in which supreme political authority had been conceived in terms of cosmological kingship for over 2,000 years, this in and of itself was a revolutionary departure.

Similarly, the assault on *li* was also more subversive than many of the reformers made out. Within Confucian tradition, *li* ritually expressed the truth that the fundamental institutions of Chinese social order – kingship and the family – were embedded within a larger cosmic order.[74] Additionally, *li* also affirmed the essential legitimacy of the hierarchical social relations that kingship and the family embodied. In challenging the legitimacy of *li* and the doctrine of the 'three bonds', the reformers claimed only to be ridding Confucianism of ritual accretions that had suffocated the philanthropy and moral egalitarianism that lay at Confucianism's core.[75] But Confucianism's moral content as an ethical system could not be so easily divorced from its mode of ritual expression. For in attacking *li*, the more iconoclastic of the reformers were not merely denigrating a ritual code; rather, they were also seeking to terminally discredit the hierarchical social relations that ritual affirmed. Prior to 1898, the reformers did not seek to abolish either the office of emperor or the traditional Chinese family.[76] But in questioning both *li* and the doctrine of the 'three bonds', reformist thinkers were emphatically making the case for major changes in these institutions. These ranged from calls for popular sovereignty and the establishment of a constitutional monarchy through to the emancipation of women and the eradication of patriarchy as a feature of family life.[77] Such was the magnitude of the crisis convulsing China following the 'scramble for concessions' that such proposals briefly found support among broad quarters, including within sections of the imperial

---

[72] Yu-Sheng, *Crisis of Chinese Consciousness*, p. 35; Levenson, *Confucian China and its Modern Fate*, I, p. 83.

[73] Chang, 'Intellectual change and the reform movement', p. 289; Furth, 'Intellectual change', p. 331.

[74] Chang, *Chinese Intellectuals in Crisis*, p. 186.   [75] *Ibid.*

[76] Yu-Sheng, *Crisis of Chinese Consciousness*, p. 35.

[77] Chang, 'Intellectual change and the reform movement', p. 290; Yu-Sheng, *Crisis of Chinese Consciousness*, p. 34.

court itself. But official openness to reform would prove fleeting, and the return to reaction would witness the final fraying of the Manchu–Han alliance, and with it the further unravelling of East Asian order.

The Hundred Days' Reform and its failure

The Hundred Days' Reform that briefly blossomed in 1898 constituted an ambitious but ultimately abortive programme advanced by the emperor himself that aimed to modernise China's educational, economic and political institutions. Having previously been exposed to Western thought by his tutors, the young Emperor Guangxu proved receptive to reformers who sought to strip the court and bureaucracy of their powers in favour of the emperor and his advisors, while simultaneously establishing a constitutional government and a national assembly.[78] Such initiatives were intended both to strengthen the executive, and also to pave the way for a shift towards greater popular participation in government.[79] The reforms were significant in that they signalled a new-found willingness on the part of the government to contemplate fundamental reforms to China's governance structures, reforms that went well beyond the 'self-strengthening' initiatives undertaken from the Tongzhi Restoration onwards. As such, the Hundred Days' Reform signified a palpable loosening of Confucian orthodoxy over the imperial imagination. Additionally, it also indicated the emperor's preparedness to collaborate intensively with reformist sections of the Han scholarly elite to work together towards the common project of national renewal. Conversely, however, the modernisation of Chinese government also implied a dilution of the powers of both court and bureaucracy.[80] In much the same way as the sixteenth-century papacy continued to oppose conciliarist moves to reform the Church in the face of the Reformation, so too did the Empress Dowager and her courtiers work assiduously to thwart the reforms in order to safeguard their own interests.

In August 1898, the Hundred Days' Reform was brought to an abrupt end by a coup d'état within the imperial court, when the reformist emperor was placed under house arrest and a more reactionary power constellation centred on the Empress Dowager was reinstated.[81] The significance of this coup for order both within China and throughout the region was profound. Within China itself, the disappointment of reformist hopes fed a further intellectual and political radicalisation of Chinese dissidents. Whereas the Hundred Days' Reform had briefly suggested the Qing dynasty's capacity for renewal, the crushing of the reforms instead confirmed for many the regime's irredeemably moribund character. Previously, many educated Han Chinese had sublimated their

---

[78] Chang, 'Intellectual change and the reform movement', pp. 320–1.   [79] *Ibid.*, pp. 326–7.
[80] *Ibid.*, p. 327.
[81] J. D. Spence, *The Search for Modern China* (New York: W.W. Norton, 1999), p. 229.

distaste for the Manchus in the hopes of harnessing the monarchy as an agent of national renewal. In the aftermath of the Empress Dowager's coup d'état, however, such sentiments gave way to a more rancorous and uncompromisingly racialist nationalism.[82] Following the crushing of the Hundred Days' Reform, growing numbers of Chinese would regard the Manchus as a parasitic alien force, as illegitimate and inimical to Chinese interests as the European and Japanese imperialists then also infesting the country.

By itself, the resurgence of anti-dynastic sentiment in China at a time of growing instability was unexceptional. However, what distinguished dissent in late Qing China from historical precedent was the novel matrix of ideas through which it was now being expressed. Throughout their reign, the Manchus had fended off Han challenges to dynastic rule that based their appeals on Ming restorationism.[83] During the Taiping rebellion, the Manchus had also prevailed by collaborating with the Han scholar gentry and 'barbarian' allies of convenience to defend the Confucian sociopolitical order in the face of an existential danger.[84] In both instances, whether confronting threats borne out of xenophobic nostalgia or millenarian hope, the Manchus had survived by identifying their dynasty with the preservation of Confucian orthodoxy and the sociopolitical order within which it inhered. What distinguished the post-1898 period from past periods of turmoil was that Confucianism's hitherto uncontested hegemony was now also being questioned.

Previously, the Qing dynasty's identification with orthodoxy had partially insulated it from Han nativist sentiment. Following the failure of the Hundred Days' Reform, this same identification with orthodoxy merely inflamed the hostility of those now scrutinising Confucianism through newly critical eyes. As we have seen, the intellectual and cultural ferment that immediately preceded the Hundred Days' Reform was marked by a growing cultural reflexivity on the part of China's would-be reformers, as well as a corresponding willingness to critique the Confucian institutions of cosmological kingship and the patriarchal family. Increased exposure to foreign cultural influences had unsettled conceptions of cosmic and social order organised around the master concept of 'China as civilisation' (*Tianxia*), at the same time as the foreign military threat had underscored the urgency of preserving 'China as nation' (*kuo*) from extinction. As a result of these developments, a growing dissonance of threat perceptions separated the imperial court from reformist sections of the Han intellectual and cultural elite. Dynastic preservation remained the Manchus' paramount concern, and this project was legitimised through its presumed concordance with the task of ruthlessly defending the Confucian order. Conversely, reformers sought above all the preservation of a newly imagined Chinese nation, even if

---

[82] *Ibid.*, p. 234.   [83] Wakeman, *Strangers at the Gate*, pp. 129–31.
[84] J. R. Levenson, *Confucian China and its Modern Fate*, 3 vols., II: *The Problem of Monarchical Decay* (London: Routledge and Kegan Paul, 1964), p. 110.

this necessitated radical revisions to the Confucian order. The resulting polarity between civilisational and nationalist conceptions of China fuelled a growing rift between the dynasty and important sections of Han Chinese opinion.[85] As China's humiliations accumulated further following the crushing of the Hundred Days experiment, this rift grew wider still, feeding into an internal legitimacy crisis that would eventually condemn the Qing dynasty to oblivion.

The Boxer rebellion and China's war against 'civilisation'

The rebellion: Its origins and course

Despite its suppression of reformist sentiments after the Hundred Days' Reform, the Qing dynasty nevertheless remained in an exceptionally precarious position. On top of China's defeat in the Sino-Japanese war and the indignities imposed by the 'scramble for concessions', the crushing of the Hundred Days' Reform further disillusioned foreign observers already exasperated by the dynasty's apparent unwillingness to reform. Simultaneously, the reform episode itself had also dramatised Confucianism's weakening as a centripetal force within the empire. Compounding the dynasty's declining legitimacy among foreigners and sections of the Han elite, a combination of official corruption and ecological catastrophe were also stoking growing popular unrest in the country's north. Already the emerging epicentre for international rivalry in North-east Asia, the provinces around Beijing were further destabilised by floods and droughts in the late 1890s.[86] Within Shandong in particular, site of the newly acquired German concession, the resulting peasant unrest had by the summer of 1898 produced a virulently xenophobic heterodox movement known as the Boxers United in Righteousness.[87] Originally informed by hostility to the Manchus, as well as by opposition to foreign imperialism, the Boxers threatened to further destabilise a dynasty already beset by foreign imperialism and internal dissent.[88] Left unchecked, the Boxers would likely open up a plebeian third front of opposition to the ruling house. Conversely, however, if the Manchus could somehow deflect the Boxers' violent energies outwards, the movement could contrarily serve as a potent weapon for use against the dynasty's other enemies. As the Boxer movement grew steadily stronger and

---

[85] Levenson, *Confucian China and its Modern Fate*, I, pp. 98–100.

[86] On the broad social factors driving the emergence of the Boxer rebellion, see for example J. W. Esherick, *The Origins of the Boxer Uprising* (Berkeley: University of California Press, 1987), pp. 173–81.

[87] Spence, *The Search for Modern China*, p. 230.

[88] On the anti-Manchu sentiments that originally animated the Boxers, as well as the Boxers' eventual shift towards a pro-dynastic position, see I. C. Y. Hsu, *The Rise of Modern China* (Oxford University Press, 1995), p. 391. Hsu nevertheless notes elsewhere that a minority of the Boxers retained their anti-Qing convictions throughout the duration of the rebellion; see Hsu, 'Late Ch'ing foreign relations', p. 118.

began to spread beyond Shandong into neighbouring territories, the appeal of co-opting it would eventually prove irresistible for sections of the imperial government. It was out of the resulting collusion between the Manchus and the Boxers that China's brief and disastrous war against international 'civilisation' was born.

The Boxer movement formed part of a mosaic of xenophobic millenarian movements that erupted in East Asia towards the turn of the century in response to governmental decay and encroaching foreign imperialism.[89] Like the Korean Tonghak movement and the Santa Iglesia movement in the Philippines, the Boxers drew upon a heterodox range of beliefs in crafting their anti-imperialist message.[90] Unlike the Tonghaks, however, the Boxers lacked a formally codified body of beliefs, and instead drew their inspiration primarily from a pantheon of spirits and protectors drawn from local folk religions.[91] Taking their name from the distinctive callisthenics and martial arts routines they undertook to acquire invulnerability from their earthly and spiritual enemies, the Boxers lacked a detailed political programme, confining their ambitions to the expulsion of foreigners from China and the extermination of all Christians, be they foreign missionaries or Chinese converts.[92] In their beliefs and their clandestine organisational structure, the Boxers represented a heterodox deviation from Confucianism of the kind that had perennially plagued imperial authorities. But in the face of seemingly relentless foreign intrusions, the Boxers offered a beleaguered dynasty a powerful resource for resisting further pressures for reform. With the protective insulation of the traditional tributary state system now dismantled, China remained brutally exposed to the competitive pressures of an encroaching international society. In leveraging plebeian anti-foreigner violence, the Dowager Empress and her advisors sought to push back the incoming tide of international 'civilisation', thereby preserving both the imperial household and the Confucian social order over which it ruled.

The imperial household's decision to embrace the Boxer cause was the product of an entangled series of events that unfolded in Beijing in June 1900. Having drifted into Beijing and Tianjin early in the month, roaming gangs of Boxers began to harass, intimidate and even kill both foreigners and Chinese

---

[89] Hsu, *The Rise of Modern China*, p. 390.

[90] On the Korean Tonghak rebellion as both a religious and anti-imperialist movement, see generally B. B. Weems, *Reform, Rebellion, and the Heavenly Way* (Tucson: The University of Arizona Press, 1964). On the Santa Iglesia movement in the Philippines, which incorporated millenarian Christian and folk themes with a proto-nationalist hostility towards first Spanish and then American occupiers, see generally I. Setsuho, 'Uprisings of Hesukristos in the Philippines' in I. Yoneo (ed.), *Millenarianism in Asian History* (Tokyo: Institute for the Study of Languages and Cultures of Asia and Africa, 1993), pp. 143–74.

[91] Hsu, *The Rise of Modern China*, p. 391.   [92] *Ibid.*

Christian converts.[93] In the face of an initially vacillating dynasty, Western forces seized the forts at Dagu on 17 June in preparation for a possible intervention to protect foreign residents in the imperial capital.[94] This prompted the Boxers to lay siege to the foreign legation areas in retaliation, at which point the Empress Dowager then sanctified the movement as a loyalist force dedicated to the righteous cause of hastening the 'barbarians' expulsion.[95] With this decision to endorse the Boxers, the Qing dynasty thus began a double-barrelled assault on international society. In siding with the Boxers, the Qing dynasty abandoned earlier efforts to mollify the foreigners through conciliation and incremental reforms. Instead, Beijing now adopted a strategy of full-frontal confrontation, targeting both the official diplomatic representatives of the foreign powers, and the merchant–missionary alliance that had long formed the spearhead of the 'barbarian' presence in China. The Boxers' siege of the diplomatic legations, undertaken with the dynasty's complaisance, thus represented a deliberate repudiation of the most fundamental rules of co-existence defining Western international society. Similarly, attacks on foreigners and local converts were conceived as a form of violent catharsis, the attacks serving to purge China of 'pollutants' that embodied the foreign presence in its most disruptive and malignant form.[96]

For international society's self-appointed guardians, the Boxer rebellion was an intolerable provocation, and retribution was not long in coming. In both their murderous xenophobia and their subscription to seemingly incomprehensible rites of invulnerability, the Boxers seemed to Western observers to exceed even the most extravagant Orientalist stereotypes of Eastern barbarism and irrationality.[97] Boxer attacks on the material manifestations of the Western presence, including attacks on railways and telegraph lines, similarly appeared to connote a pathological aversion to modernity itself, further confirming foreigners in their contempt for Boxer depravity.[98] More egregious still, in the eyes of international society's custodians, was the imperial government's willingness to truck with the rebels, and its moral complicity in the Boxers' atrocities. China's violation of norms enjoining the protection of resident foreigners seemed to signal a moral as much as a political failure, and one that was sufficiently grave as to place China outside the company of 'civilised' nations.[99] Additionally, at a time in which Christianity and civilisation were seen as synonymous by many Westerners, China's connivance in anti-Christian violence against both foreigners and local converts further underscored its

---

[93] Spence, *The Search for Modern China*, p. 231.
[94] *Ibid.*   [95] *Ibid.*, p. 232.   [96] Hsu, 'Late Ch'ing foreign relations', p. 118.
[97] Bayly, 'The Boxer uprising and India', pp. 151–2.   [98] *Ibid.*
[99] J. L. Hevia, 'Looting and its discontents: Moral discourse and the plunder of Beijing, 1900–1901' in Bickers and Tiedeman (eds.), *The Boxers, China and the World*, p. 93.

status as a barbarous and degenerate despotism.[100] Having so ostentatiously rejected the material and moral benefits of 'civilisation', the Chinese had forfeited the privileges of membership within international society, and would accordingly be punished as an outlaw nation.

The rebellion's defeat and its significance

In launching the so-called 'Army for Civilisation' on 4 August 1900, the eight powers party to the Boxer Expedition sought nothing less than to punish Chinese 'barbarism' and enforce a single civilisational order on East Asia. Under the 'era of negotiation' that characterised the preceding synarchic order, the competing standards of Western and Sino-centric civilisation had existed in uneasy equipoise. China partially accommodated Western demands by resorting to 'barbarian management', adopting Western diplomatic practices when dealing with Western states.[101] Equally, Western diplomatic visitors to Beijing rarely insisted on an imperial audience, thus deferring to Chinese sensitivities concerning the sacerdotal character of the imperial office.[102] As security tensions between Japan and China had intensified from the 1870s, Beijing had shifted towards a policy of strategically appropriating Western norms for its own purposes in strengthening its hold over former vassal states. This had in turn culminated in the Sino-Japanese war, the dismantling of the Sinosphere's last elements and the disastrous decline in China's international status that followed.

But with the dynasty's quixotic attempt to expel the 'foreign devils', Western animus towards China shifted to a new phase. What earlier could be dismissed as mere intransigence in the face of reformist pressures was now re-coded as wilful defiance of the standards of international civilisation. Employing a combined force of 20,000 troops operating under a multinational command structure, the Boxer Expedition swiftly defeated the Boxer rebels, before then imposing a peace settlement that was deliberately calculated to chastise and humiliate Beijing.[103] Under the terms of the Boxer Protocol, China submitted to the permanent stationing of foreign troops in Beijing to protect the diplomatic quarter, and was compelled to erect permanent monuments in memory of the Boxers' victims.[104] In addition to a host of other constraints on Chinese sovereignty enacted under the Protocol's terms, the powers also imposed a massive indemnity on China. The sheer size of the Boxer indemnity – the combined debt and accrued interest would not be repaid in their entirety until 31 December 1940 – dramatically curtailed China's ability to finance

---

[100] Hsu, *The Rise of Modern China*, p. 405.   [101] Hsu, 'Late Ch'ing foreign relations', p. 70.
[102] Wright, *The Last Stand of Chinese Conservatism*, p. 261.
[103] Spence, *The Search for Modern China*, p. 232.   [104] *Ibid.*, p. 233.

the modernisation of its industry and armed forces.[105] Similarly, the fiscal arrangements adopted to ensure China's repayment of the indemnity further tightened the foreigners' stranglehold over China's public finances.[106] Having sided with the Boxers in an effort to throw off the shackles of foreign imperialism, China now found itself more systematically subordinated to the foreign powers than ever before.

Internationally, the Boxer debacle and its aftermath heralded dramatic and destabilising shifts within the East Asian international system. In the classical Sinosphere, regional order had rested on a foundation of Chinese hard and soft power. Later, an oligopoly of powers with Britain in the van had managed a hybrid synarchic order in which the Qing dynasty had played a subordinate but essential role. In East Asia after the Boxer rebellion, conversely, China was now so weak as to foreclose the possibility of a regional order predicated in any measure on the strength and authority of Beijing. On the contrary, Chinese weakness and the Great Power competition that it elicited now stood as the region's primary source of instability. By the early 1900s, the former hub of the East Asian ecumene had become a vast semi-sovereign space, honeycombed by concessions to foreign powers and unable to marshal the domestic and international legitimacy necessary to secure full recognition of its sovereignty. The old hierarchy of the Sinosphere was gone, but the new hierarchy assembling in its place was as yet underwritten by neither a singularly powerful hegemon nor a shared set of deeply institutionalised constitutional values.

Beneath the veneer of their commitment to enforcing an international standard of civilisation, the powers after the Boxer rebellion were soon jockeying for regional supremacy with renewed vigour. In the north, construction of Russia's Chinese Eastern Railway in Manchuria proceeded apace. Upon its completion in 1903, the railway would plug the Manchus' ancestral homeland directly into the Trans-Siberian Railway, providing the Russians with a seamless 'bridge of steel' through which to project their influence deep into northern China proper.[107] Fearful of the implications of this development for the Eurasian military balance and mindful of their own declining power, the British sought to check Russian power through the conclusion of the Anglo-Japanese alliance.[108] The alliance, together with America's advocacy of the Open Door policy entreating the powers to respect China's territorial integrity, momentarily forestalled China's further mutilation. But the very terms of the

---

[105] *Ibid.* On the fiscal crisis that engulfed the Chinese state in the decade following the Boxer rebellion, see H. J. van de Ven, 'Public finance and the rise of warlordism', *Modern Asian Studies*, 30(4) (1996), 832–4.

[106] Van de Ven, 'Public finance and the rise of warlordism', pp. 834–5.

[107] Patrikeeff and Shukman, *Railways and the Russo-Japanese War*, p. 34.

[108] Hsu, 'Late Ch'ing foreign relations', p. 130. On the broader geopolitical implications of developments in East Asia for Britain's diplomatic posture after 1900, see generally Otte, 'The Boxer uprising and British foreign policy', pp. 157–77.

Anglo-Japanese alliance also disclosed the extent of China's decline. That the two signatories committed themselves to preserving China's territorial integrity, while nevertheless retaining the right to intervene in the event of domestic 'disturbances' to restore order whenever they saw fit, revealed the extent to which the accumulated crises of the previous half-century had diminished China's international status.[109] Similarly, the fact that China was now listed alongside Korea, a former tributary state, as being equally relegated to semi-sovereign status further indicated the degree to which the old East Asian hierarchy had been inverted.[110]

After the Boxer rebellion, regional order in East Asia thus rested on an inherently unstable balance of power, with China's survival guaranteed only because the powers' mutual jealousies momentarily outweighed their covetous contempt for the senescent monarchy. Within China itself, the rebellion's after-effects on the domestic political order were no less momentous. From having for centuries regarded China as the singular embodiment of civilisation, the shocks of the 1890s had already forced some Chinese to revise their outlooks to accommodate China's co-existence alongside other civilisations.[111] The latest humiliation at the hands of the foreign powers prompted even greater introspection. In both reform and revolt, the Qing dynasty had failed to adapt to external challenges, leaving many Chinese to despair of the possibility of national renewal while the Manchus held the Dragon Throne. By contrast, Japan's triumphs in the Sino-Japanese war, its recognition as an equal alliance partner to Britain and its triumph over tsarist Absolutism in the Russo-Japanese war all appeared to vindicate the Meiji Restoration's comprehensive project of cultural and political modernisation.[112] The comparison between China's and Japan's respective encounters with international society was as unflattering as it was unavoidable for China's leading thinkers, and the implications of this comparison for power structures within the country were profound. Japanese success, Chinese failure and Western predation together indicated the need for revolutionary changes in China's culture and politics if it was to survive. Whereas late-nineteenth-century thinkers had sought cultural reformation and political reform within the context of a modernised constitutional monarchy, those writing after 1900 increasingly counselled cultural and political revolution as the only solution to China's woes.[113] In this way, the

---

[109] Article 1 of the Anglo-Japanese Alliance, available at: http://www.jacar.go.jp/nichiro/uk-japan.htm. See also Hsu, 'Late Ch'ing foreign relations', p. 134.

[110] *Ibid.*

[111] Levenson, *Confucian China and its Modern Fate*, I: *The Problem of Intellectual Continuity*, pp. 103–4.

[112] M. Jansen, 'Japan and the Chinese Revolution of 1911' in Fairbank and Liu (eds.), *The Cambridge History of China*, XI: *Late Ch'ing, 1800–1911*, Pt II, pp. 343–8.

[113] Hsu, *The Rise of Modern* China, p. 406; Spence, *The Search for Modern China*, p. 234.

post-Boxer breakdown of order internationally found its echo within China, as both Confucian cultural cohesion and the Qing political power continued to unravel, and the normative and institutional stability of the Chinese order correspondingly grew ever more brittle.[114]

Rising sun, Manchu requiem: The collapse of the Qing dynasty and the dawn of the great disorder

The last decade of Qing rule was marked by continuing volatility, as China's creeping internal disintegration remained inextricably intertwined with growing regional instability. Following Russia's defeat in 1905 at the hands of Japanese forces, the immediate threat to China's territorial integrity admittedly abated, affording the monarchy yet another opportunity to strengthen itself through domestic reforms.[115] However, while the resulting innovations were far from insubstantial, a combination of international and domestic constraints nevertheless fatally compromised the monarchy's belated moves towards comprehensive modernisation. At the same time, the continuing growth of Han nationalism and increasing provincial militarisation respectively corroded the authoritative and coercive foundations of Qing rule. The convergence of these two forces would eventually catalyse the monarchy's destruction, heralding a protracted era of immature anarchy both within China and throughout East Asia.

The Chinese state undeniably underwent substantial renovation in the years following the Boxer rebellion. In a major concession to its critics, Beijing committed to a gradual move towards constitutional government, establishing a National Assembly in 1910.[116] Acknowledging the inadequacies of China's educational system, provincial military academies were also established in 1901 and China's officers were increasingly sponsored to master the art of modern warfare through study in Japan.[117] In 1905, a new Ministry of Education was also founded to supervise the reform of China's education system, while in 1906 the age-old civil service examination system was also finally abolished.[118] This last initiative in particular was potentially revolutionary, given that it theoretically liquidated the primary mechanism through which untold generations of the literati had hitherto been imprinted with Confucianism and thus socialised into reverence for the imperial office. Equally significant was the abolition of the system of institutionalised discrimination that had previously elevated the

---

[114] The crisis of 'orientational symbolisms' that marked this period is detailed further in Chang, *Chinese Intellectuals in Crisis*, pp. 6–7.

[115] Hsu, 'Late Ch'ing foreign relations', p. 141.

[116] C. Ichiko, 'Political and institutional reform, 1901–1911' in Fairbank and Twitchett (eds.), *The Cambridge History of China*, XI: *Late Ch'ing, 1800–1911*, Pt II, p. 398.

[117] *Ibid.*, p. 384.   [118] *Ibid.*, pp. 378–9.

Manchu martial caste above the Han majority. In allowing intermarriage between Manchus and Han Chinese, subjecting both peoples to the same code of decorum and punishment, and waiving privileges that had previously enabled the Manchus to avoid agriculture and commerce in favour of concentrating on their military duties, the Qing dynasty appeared at least willing to blunt the sharper edges of Manchu domination.[119]

These initiatives notwithstanding, a combination of international and domestic constraints nevertheless stifled the full promise of the post-Boxer reforms. Internationally, China remained straitjacketed in a system of unequal treaties that not only entrenched extensive foreign involvement in China's commercial economy, but also legitimised increasing foreign control over China's public finances.[120] Initiatives such as currency reform, improvements to China's parlous railway infrastructure and the modernisation of China's armed forces were consequently often frustrated for want of revenue. With the majority of the Maritime Customs Revenue dedicated to servicing the Boxer indemnity, the government was forced either to borrow even more money from foreign creditors to finance its reforms, or alternatively extract further 'compulsory contributions' from the provinces.[121] The first option threatened to increase the monarchy's already massive foreign debt, while the second promised to further embitter the peasants on whom the burden of such exactions would ultimately fall.[122] The dynasty's recourse to both of these expedients eventually crystallised both dangers without yielding a compensatory improvement in either the pace or success of reform.

Domestically also, Manchu reformism continued to be constrained by long-standing tensions between the imperative of reform and the dynasty's over-riding interest in self-preservation. Comprising no more than a fortieth of China's population, the Manchus had relied heavily on the integrative power of Confucianism to sustain their rule throughout the dynasty's history, but had been equally committed to preserving their identity as a distinct martial ruling caste.[123] The imperative of reform threatened both Confucian orthodoxy and the preservation of Manchu supremacy. Consequently, the dynasty's implementation of major reforms was often desultory and disingenuous. Ostentatious commitments to modernising the curriculum jarred with a continued classroom emphasis on teaching Confucian values, while the abolition of Manchu–Han *apartheid* coincided with renewed efforts to further concentrate real power in the hands of Manchu loyalists.[124]

[119] *Ibid.*, p. 411.
[120] On foreigners' extensive control over late Qing public finances, see van de Ven, 'Public finance and the rise of warlordism', p. 834.
[121] On the fiscal reforms of the late Qing period and their corrosive impact on central-local relations throughout the empire, see *ibid.*, p. 841.
[122] *Ibid.*   [123] Ichiko, 'Political and institutional reform', p. 411.
[124] Hsu, *The Rise of Modern China*, pp. 414–15.

Founded upon the spiritual authority of Confucian universalism and the coercive power of the Manchu conquerors, the Qing Empire thus remained at its twilight a quintessentially archaic remnant of the early modern age of gunpowder empires. At the same time, China's forced incorporation within a global international system highlighted the costs of this archaism for the Chinese people, stimulating the first systematic expressions of modern Chinese nationalist thought. The failures of Qing reformism and the inspirational counter-example of imperial Japan stirred growing Han nationalist agitation as the decade progressed, with nationalist subversion being concentrated in both the long-established treaty ports of south-eastern China, and also among the Chinese diaspora.[125] That nationalist sentiment would develop most precociously in these cosmopolitan milieus was hardly surprising, given it was these environments that afforded educated Chinese with both greater exposure to foreign ideas, and also greater freedoms to express dissent and foment anti-government conspiracies.[126] It is nevertheless worth highlighting the correspondence between China's continuing *integration* within regional commercial networks, and the accelerating *disintegration* of the Qing dynasty's ideological foundations that this process of regional integration thereby produced.

Whereas the growth of revolutionary nationalism directly threatened the Qing dynasty's legitimacy, the contemporaneous growth of military provincialism posed a parallel threat to the coercive basis of Manchu power. By 1900, China's northern maritime gateway around the Shandong and Liaodong peninsulas was under foreign control, while Russia's 'bridge of steel' was expanding throughout Manchuria to imperil the Chinese capital.[127] Spurred by this existential threat and chastened by the Boxer debacle, the Qing dynasty nurtured the creation of modernised regional new model armies, dedicating particular effort to the creation of the Beiyang (North Seas) army charged with defending the capital and surrounding regions from invasion.[128] Against the backdrop of the creeping military provincialism that had developed from the Taiping period, this expedient was both dangerous and necessary. It was necessary because China could not be truly sovereign while the capital cowered under the shadow of neighbouring foreign armies.[129] But it was also dangerous, in that the creation of modernised provincial forces threatened to further weaken the dynasty's command over organised violence and thus endanger its rule.[130]

---

[125] Spence, *The Search for Modern China*, p. 254.   [126] *Ibid.*

[127] Van de Ven, 'The military in the republic', p. 354; Patrikeeff and Shukman, *Railways and the Russo-Japanese War*, p. 34.

[128] See generally Ichiko, 'Political and institutional reform', pp. 383–7; and also van de Ven, 'Public finance and the rise of warlordism'.

[129] E. S. K. Fung, *The Military Dimension of the Chinese Revolution: The new army and its role in the revolution of 1911* (Canberra: Australian National University Press, 1980), pp. 14–18.

[130] Van de Ven, 'Public finance and the rise of warlordism', p. 841; Ichiko, 'Political and institutional reform', p. 384.

From their conquest of China, the Manchus had ruled through reliance on both a praetorian guard of Manchu cavalry, and a reserve of Han infantry that were carefully supervised to prevent the emergence of any would-be Caesars among Han commanders.[131] Military modernisation necessitated that these forces be dissolved, but the new model armies that replaced them were far from reliable as instruments of imperial power. While formally mimicking the bureaucratic structures of Western and Japanese armies, real power in the new armies clustered around the personal patronage networks of Han officers such as Yuan Shikai.[132] To the extent that men such as Yuan continued to identify their interests with the monarchy's preservation, the growth of the new model armies did not automatically jeopardise the authority of the central government.[133] By the same token, however, the contingent and self-interested nature of commanders' commitments to the monarchy necessarily left the dynasty extremely vulnerable to the threat of armed challenges from within. As greater numbers of Chinese officers studied in Japan, and a portion of them became exposed to the ideas of the revolutionary Chinese diaspora, the prospects of such a challenge emerging correspondingly increased.[134]

Revolutionary nationalism and military provincialism constituted the two greatest internal threats to the monarchy, and it was the convergence of these forces that eventually doomed the dynasty. On 9 October 1911, imperial authorities arrested a cell of revolutionary conspirators within the Hubei New Army following an accidental bomb blast in the revolutionaries' meeting house in the Russian concession area of Hankou.[135] Far from being an isolated band, the arrested conspirators were representative of a larger dissident movement within the Hubei New Army troops then stationed in the Wuhan tri-city area, approximately a third of whom were in some way involved in revolutionary societies by the autumn of 1911.[136] The unexpected arrest of their comrades evoked consternation among large swathes of the army, while the authorities' discovery of the membership records of the revolutionary societies in the course of the arrests threatened a more general crackdown.[137] Fearful of capture and execution, the revolutionary soldiers therefore pre-empted the authorities by initiating a more general uprising, which soon spread rapidly throughout other

---

[131] Ichiko, 'Political and institutional reform', p. 383.

[132] On the significance of patronage networks for Chinese efforts at military modernisation in the late nineteenth and early twentieth centuries, see for example generally S. R. MacKinnon, *Power and Politics in Late Imperial China: Yuan Shi-Kai in Beijing and Tianjin, 1901–1908* (Berkeley: University of California Press, 1980); and Spector, *Li Hung-Chang and the Huai Army*.

[133] MacKinnon, *Power and Politics in Late Imperial China*, p. 10; Spence, *The Search for Modern China*, p. 252.

[134] Spence, *The Search for Modern China*, p. 258.   [135] *Ibid.*   [136] *Ibid.*, p. 259.

[137] *Ibid.*

provinces.[138] Despite a desperate rearguard action from loyalist elements, the Qings' parlous military position was swiftly exposed in the weeks that followed. Facing extinction, the monarchy mounted a last-minute bid to stave off collapse by pressing Yuan Shikai out of retirement to serve as premier in a constitutional monarchy.[139] But by year's end, the revolution was unstoppable. On Christmas Day 1911, the Chinese revolutionary leader Sun Yat-Sen returned to China, where he received a hero's welcome. By 1 January 1912, he was provisional president of the Chinese Republic.[140]

After the fall: Chinese warlordism, Japanese imperialism and East Asia's descent into immature anarchy

With the abdication of the boy emperor Puyi on 12 February 1912, more than two millennia of imperial rule in China came to a close, and the Confucian system that had once provided order for virtually the entire East Asian ecumene passed into history. But the collapse of the old order promised greater disorder both within China and throughout the region, for the new republic lacked the advantages of either a firm ideological or military base. Ideologically, Sun Yat-Sen's revolutionary nationalism was undeniably ascendant, but its social base was as yet insufficiently broad to sustain the new government.[141] Militarily, Yuan Shikai's Beiyang Army represented the most powerful node of Chinese coercive power within the republic, but it co-existed alongside a host of provincial armed forces tied together as much by bonds of patronage as by ideology, not to mention the foreign armed forces ensconced in the territorial concessions.[142] Politically, President Sun quickly recognised his military weakness relative to Yuan Shikai, and conceded the presidential office to the latter the day after the emperor's abdication.[143] But Yuan's decision not to relocate the centre of government from Beijing to Nanjing strained relations with Sun's Revolutionary Alliance, exposing the underlying fissures between Yuan's Caesarist inclinations and the southern revolutionaries' advocacy of parliamentary government.[144] Finally, financially, the new government's modernisation efforts foundered on the same obstacles that had frustrated the Manchus, not the least of which remained China's crippling indebtedness and lack of fiscal sovereignty.[145]

Post-revolutionary China therefore remained a vast semi-sovereign giant at the heart of East Asia, with the combination of its sheer size, centrality and

---

[138] *Ibid.*   [139] *Ibid.*, pp. 260–1.   [140] *Ibid.*, pp. 262–3.

[141] E. P. Young, 'Politics in the aftermath of revolution: The era of Yuan Shi-K'ai, 1912–1916' in J. K. Fairbank (ed.), *The Cambridge History of China*, XII: *Republican China 1912–1949*, Pt I (Cambridge University Press, 1983), p. 211.

[142] *Ibid.*, p. 216.   [143] Spence, *The Search for Modern China*, p. 273.

[144] Elleman, *Modern Chinese Warfare*, p. 144; Spence, *The Search for Modern China*, p. 273.

[145] Spence, *The Search for Modern China*, p. 281.

frailty continuing to exert destabilising effects upon the entire region. Within China itself, the country rapidly descended into warlordism following Yuan Shikai's death in 1916. The resulting power vacuum, coupled with the Western powers' preoccupations with the European war, emboldened Japan to make its first bid for regional hegemony, imposing the notorious Twenty-One Demands on the Chinese republic in January 1915.[146] These demands were first diluted by Chinese resistance and then further diminished following Western diplomatic interventions after 1918. But by then the Japanese had firmly signalled their hegemonic ambitions, setting the stage for the regional struggle that would dominate the ensuing decades.

The implosion of the Qing dynasty and the distraction of the Western powers from 1914 onwards produced a fundamentally unstable imbalance of power in East Asia. The following decade would witness an internal struggle for supremacy in China between a host of warlords newly empowered by the unprecedented firepower and mobility afforded by industrial warfare. Like the great mercenary armies that ravaged Germany during the Thirty Years War, these forces would fight mostly for power and profit rather than principle. Similarly, they would also range in an environment punctuated by both fierce ideological rivalries and endemic foreign intervention. For the 1920s would also witness the maturation and polarisation of the Chinese nationalist movement, followed by the subsumption of this struggle within a global contest between Japanese fascism, Soviet communism, European imperialism and American liberal democracy. Finally, this struggle would end, much like its European counterpart, with the defeat of empire, and with the reconstitution of a sovereign international order fundamentally different from that which had preceded it. It is to a more detailed examination of East Asia's Thirty Years crisis that I now turn.

---

[146] Lim, *The Geopolitics of East Asia*, p. 42.

9 | The great disorder and the birth of the East Asian sovereign state system

The old literature, old politics, and old ethics have always belonged to one family; we cannot abandon one and preserve the others. It is Oriental to compromise and only go half way when reforming, for fear of opposition. This was the most important factor behind the failures of reform movements during the last several decades ... [1]

New Youth magazine, 1918.

Political power grows from the barrel of a gun.

Mao Zedong

In 1922, the Great Powers met in Washington to construct a new East Asian order. While remembered today primarily for its naval arms limitation agreements, the Washington Conference addressed a far broader range of issues, with the powers seeking to construct a new Pacific order within an unprecedentedly volatile international milieu.[2] Globally, the schism between socialist and liberal understandings of popular sovereignty that had roiled European politics since 1848 was now playing out on a world stage, thanks to the Bolshevik revolution and the rise of Wilsonian internationalism.[3] Within East Asia, the balance of power that had formerly provided some semblance of order had also now collapsed. With Germany defeated, Russia prostrate, and the European powers still reeling from the war, Japan and America now warily confronted one another as both pursued their ambitions within a radically changed regional setting.[4] Finally, within the Sinic heartland of the traditional East Asian order, China had descended into chaos. Less than a decade after it

---

[1] Cited in C. Tse-Tsung, The May Fourth Movement: Intellectual revolution in modern China (Cambridge, MA: Harvard University Press, 1960), p. 289.

[2] On the order-building character of the Washington Conference, see generally A. Iriye, After Imperialism: The search for a new order in the Far East, 1921–1931 (Cambridge, MA: Harvard University Press, 1965).

[3] G. Barraclough, An Introduction to Contemporary History (London: C. A. Watts and Co. Ltd, 1964), pp. 113–14.

[4] Iriye, After Imperialism, p. 6.

had consumed Western Europe, industrial mass warfare was now convulsing the north China plain, devastating local populations and confounding Beijing's efforts to restore national unity.[5]

This chapter details the emergence of an East Asian sovereign state system out of this chaotic environment. The first section anatomises the context of the post-war disorder, articulating the intertwined challenges of global ideological conflict, regional security rivalries and the multi-faceted 'China problem' as they confronted delegates to the Washington Conference. The second section discusses the 'Washington system' that emerged from the conference, detailing its contours as well as the reasons for its failure. Japan's bid to reconstitute an imperial order in East Asia is discussed in the third section, while the fourth section examines the failure of the Japanese imperial enterprise and the final consolidation of a sovereign East Asian order after 1945.

The context of the great East Asian disorder after World War I

Europe's eclipse and the breakdown of the East Asian balance of power

The problem of order in East Asia after 1918 cannot be understood in isolation from its global context. In 1914, a dualistic world order had prevailed, comprising, horizontally, egalitarian relationships among an oligarchy of 'civilised' nations, and, vertically, ties of vassalage and paramountcy linking these states in varying degrees of supremacy to the world's 'barbarous' and 'savage' peoples.[6] World War I had gravely undermined both the material and normative underpinnings of this order. At the material level, the war had reduced Britain from the world's largest creditor to its greatest debtor, severely weakening its capacity to sustain a global empire that had rested as much on Britain's financial might as it had on the nation's maritime primacy.[7] Tsarist Russia had meanwhile descended into revolution and civil war.[8] In the war's aftermath, then, both the sea- and land-power giants that had formerly contested supremacy within Eurasia were significantly (and in Britain's case, permanently) weakened.

World War I not only warped the old international order's material underpinnings, but also destabilised its normative foundations. Most fundamentally, European pretensions towards civilisational supremacy did not survive the mechanised slaughter of the Somme. The war triggered a crisis of European cultural self-confidence, as well as working globally to undermine the belief that

---

[5] On the explicit parallels between China's industrial military revolution in the 1920s and the earlier European military revolution of the sixteenth and seventeenth centuries, see Waldron, *From War to Nationalism*, p. 57.

[6] See for example Keene, *Beyond the Anarchical Society*, p. 122.

[7] Kennedy, *Rise and Fall of the Great Powers*, p. 363.

[8] Barraclough, *An Introduction to Contemporary History*, p. 114.

European civilisation marked the acme of material and moral progress.[9] Liberals and progressive intellectuals in Africa and Asia, who had formerly measured their societies' progress towards modernity by European benchmarks, would henceforth become increasingly vocal in their opposition to imperial rule.[10] The old order's normative corrosion had meanwhile been further accelerated by the Bolshevik revolution and the rise of Wilsonian internationalism. Both of these ideologies fundamentally challenged the legitimacy of imperial rule, and their rise to global prominence after 1917 profoundly imperilled a world order based on international hierarchy and civilisational supremacy.[11]

Against this backdrop of global instability, East Asia had also experienced changes that further complicated efforts to reconstitute regional order after 1918. With the European powers distracted by the war, Japan had seized the opportunity to bid for regional dominance, conquering German possessions in both China and the South Pacific. These acquisitions, if acknowledged internationally, would significantly strengthen Japan's continental foothold, as well as enhancing its ability to threaten America's sea lines of communication with the Philippines.[12] From an American perspective in particular, Japan's wartime opportunism was made even more unnerving by the prospective renewal of the Anglo-Japanese alliance in 1922. The alliance's renewal threatened to provide Japan with the diplomatic cover necessary to extend its political and commercial dominance over China at America's expense.[13] More fundamentally, it also risked further entrenching a competitive alliance system of the kind that had existed prior to the war, potentially reproducing all of the attendant insecurities that the pre-war system had sustained.[14]

The situation in China: Political crisis, cultural schism and military revolution

Given the global and regional dislocations the war had produced, the task of re-establishing order in East Asia would always have been difficult. But concurrent political, cultural and military transformations in China made an already challenging project even more daunting. Politically, the Qing dynasty's

---

[9] Keene, *Beyond the Anarchical Society*, pp. 136–7.

[10] On the decline in the prestige of Western civilisation in China as a result of World War I, see Furth, 'Intellectual change', p. 364.

[11] Barraclough, *An Introduction to Contemporary History*, pp. 113–15. On the impact of Bolshevik and Wilsonian internationalism on post-war East Asia, see Iriye, *After Imperialism*, p. 12.

[12] Lim, *The Geopolitics of East Asia*, p. 43.

[13] T. C. Lehmann, 'Keeping friends close and enemies closer: Classical realist statecraft and economic exchange in U.S. interwar strategy', *Security Studies*, 18(1) (2008), 126.

[14] *Ibid.*

demise had done nothing to alleviate the climate of violence and instability that had punctuated the monarchy's last days. Far from reviving under republican rule, China had instead witnessed continuing chaos and disunity. After a brief and fractious democratic interlude, President Yuan Shikai had sought to revive the imperial office in 1916 by installing himself as emperor.[15] While Yuan's power-grab proved short-lived, a subsequent Manchu bid to restore the last Qing emperor had further estranged revolutionaries already discomfited by Yuan's Caesarist turn, aggravating political tensions within an already divided country.[16] The political situation deteriorated further with the onset of warlordism after 1916, the breakdown of central authority heralding the emergence of what was effectively a miniature state system in northern China for much of the ensuing decade.[17] In the provinces centred around Beijing, a tripolar contest for hegemony raged intensely between three main warlord factions, while throughout large swathes of the country, a constellation of lesser warlords and their accompanying hordes of mercenaries preyed upon the local peasantry.[18] Finally, at the international level, Japan's bid to assert regional hegemony meanwhile underscored China's seemingly innate inability to ward off foreign aggression, whether under a monarchical or a republican constitution.[19]

The manifold political crises of the early republican era soon triggered a proportionately momentous cultural reaction. For many Chinese thinkers, the republic's failures were but the latest in a litany of maladaptive Chinese responses to external challenge from the 1860s onwards.[20] The 'self-strengthening' initiatives of the Tongzhi Restoration; the Hundred Day's Reform experiment; the post-Boxer reforms; the revolutionary instatement of a republican government – each of these episodes had begun in hope only to end in bitter disappointment. The cumulative impact of half a century of failure suggested to many that the disappointments of the republic were not reducible to the failings of individual statesmen.[21] Rather, they stemmed from inherent flaws in Chinese culture, which would doom the country to extinction if left unrectified.[22]

---

[15] Hsu, *The Rise of Modern China*, p. 480.   [16] *Ibid.*, p. 483.

[17] On the characterisation of northern China as a miniature state system during the warlord period, see generally H.-S. Chi, *Warlord Politics in China, 1916–1928* (Stanford University Press, 1976).

[18] *Ibid.*

[19] J. K. Fairbank, E. O. Reischauer and A. M. Craig, *East Asia: Tradition and transformation* (Boston: Houghton Mifflin Company, 1989), pp. 755–6.

[20] R. Mitter, *A Bitter Revolution: China's struggle with the modern world* (Oxford University Press, 2004), p. 113. Mitter does nevertheless acknowledge that this radical anti-traditionalism was far from universal, but was rather rigorously contested during the warlord and republican eras.

[21] *Ibid.*, p. 37.

[22] Fairbank, Reischauer and Craig, *East Asia*, p. 769.

In the years after 1915, China's cultural landscape was consequently convulsed by a heated struggle between those who wanted either to preserve or reform Confucianism and those who sought nothing less than to construct an entirely new modern Chinese culture.[23] The turn towards cultural introspection in the wake of political defeat was far from new in Chinese history. But what distinguished China's radical 'new culture' movement from earlier reformers was the totalistic character of its rejection of the Chinese past. Ranging across a broad front, 'new culture' intellectuals condemned the alleged passivity of a nation weaned on the corrupting Confucian emphasis on traditional 'virtues' such as moderation and filial piety.[24] In keeping with an ethos of 'totalistic anti-traditionalism', these intellectuals suggested that China's political liberation could come only following a cultural liberation from the dead hand of Confucian tradition.[25]

Favouring secularism, democracy, scientific rationalism and individualism as the foundations of Chinese renewal, the 'new culture' iconoclasts thus waged a relentless *Kulturkampf* against their traditionalist and reformist opponents during the warlord period. Whereas traditionalists sought to revive China's lost unity by establishing Confucianism as China's state religion, China's cultural revolutionaries conversely saw Confucianism as the taproot of China's twin evils of paternalism and despotism.[26] Consequently, efforts to establish Confucianism as the state religion were automatically repudiated for their presumed association with the cause of monarchical restoration.[27] 'New culture' activists held Confucian reformists in similarly low regard. For the radicals, the failed reforms of the preceding half-century served only to illustrate the futility of efforts to adapt Confucianism to modern circumstances.[28] Much like their Kemalist counterparts in post-Ottoman Turkey, China's cultural avant-garde discerned an indissoluble link between the political structures of a failed empire and the spiritual traditions that had for centuries sustained it.[29] In the face of imperial pretenders, domestic warlordism and foreign predation, neither the conservation nor the reformation of existing traditions was sufficient to assure national renewal.[30] Only a complete scouring of the

---

[23] See generally Mitter, *A Bitter Revolution*; V. Schwarcz, *The Chinese Enlightenment: Intellectuals and the legacy of the May fourth movement of 1919* (Berkeley: University of California Press, 1986); Tse-Tsung, *The May Fourth Movement*; and Yu-Sheng, *Crisis of Chinese Consciousness*.

[24] See for example Mitter, *A Bitter Revolution*, p. 109.

[25] The phrase 'totalistic anti-traditionalism' is drawn from Yu-Sheng, *Crisis of Chinese Consciousness*, p. 10.

[26] Mitter, *A Bitter Revolution*, p. 113.   [27] *Ibid.*, p. 116.   [28] *Ibid.*, p. 104.

[29] *Ibid.*, pp. 129–30.

[30] B. I. Schwartz, 'Themes in intellectual history: May fourth and after' in J. K. Fairbank (ed.), *The Cambridge History of China*, XII: *Republican China 1912–1949*, Pt I (Cambridge University Press, 1983), p. 419.

national consciousness would be sufficient to free the Chinese people from the submissive habits of the past, and thus prepare the way for their future emancipation.[31]

Given their long-term influence on Chinese history, it is easy to forget that the 'new culture' radicals represented a distinctly minority opinion among Chinese elites at the time of their emergence, and that their ideas initially had but scant impact on the outlook of the broader population.[32] This caveat aside, the radicals' turn towards totalistic cultural iconoclasm remains profoundly significant for two reasons. First, the activities of the 'new culture' intellectuals signified profound shifts in China's prevailing social imaginary, comparable in their magnitude and significance to the equivalent transformations in social epistemes that John Ruggie argues were so pivotal to the sovereign state system's emergence in early modern Europe.[33] Indeed, in a distinct echo of developments in Christendom towards the time of its dissolution, China's iconoclasts successfully pushed for the displacement of classical Chinese in favour of vernacular Chinese as the country's medium of literary expression.[34] Much as the displacement of Latin by vernacular languages in Europe had reflected shifts in literature's purpose as well as its medium of expression, so too was this the case in China. Whereas classical literary Chinese, as a sacred 'truth language', had primarily sought to convey and instil Confucian ethical principles (*dao*) in the mind of the reader, the vernacular Chinese literature of the 'new culture' movement was justified either on purely aesthetic grounds, or as a means of propagating the values of new secular ideologies such as liberalism and socialism.[35] In this regard, the displacement of classical literary Chinese by vernacular Chinese both reflected and enabled an ongoing reconceptualisation of China, away from a civilisational entity embedded in an immanent and unchanging cosmic order, and towards a national community evolving in the context of secular, linear time.

Embryonic transformations in the Chinese social imaginary were evident not only in reconceptualisations of collective identity, but also in literary representations of the self. Reflecting its emphasis on affirming the sacred nature of the

---

[31] *Ibid.*

[32] It is also worth noting that it was the nationalists rather than the communists who were the immediate victors of China's internal struggle for power in the 1920s, further indicating that Chinese cultural radicals were far from hegemonic either culturally or politically during this time. See Mitter, *A Bitter Revolution*, p. 105.

[33] On transformations in social epistemes as a key driver of the medieval-to-modern transition in Europe, see Ruggie, 'Territoriality and beyond', pp. 157–60.

[34] Tse-Tsung, *The May Fourth Movement*, p. 271.

[35] *Ibid.* On 'truth languages' such as Church Latin, Koranic Arabic and Examination Chinese as sacred languages that differ fundamentally in form and purpose from the vernacular scripts through which imagined national communities are conceived, see Anderson, *Imagined Communities*, pp. 14–15.

'three bonds', the Confucian literary tradition had traditionally downplayed the individual's significance in favour of a focus on the hierarchical web of relationships within which the individual was situated and given meaning.[36] Writers inspired by the 'new culture' movement contrarily evinced a profound interest in modern projections of the autonomous self.[37] This interest manifested itself stylistically in the growing popularity of first-person narratives in the 'new culture' literature, and thematically in a consistent emphasis on individual struggles for self-realisation against the suffocating strictures of Confucian tradition.[38] In this respect also, post-revolutionary China again reflected the experience of early modern Europe, where the growing dominance of the 'I-form' of speech from the Renaissance onwards reflected transformations in social epistemes that eventually heralded the emergence of a sovereign international order.[39] Both the growth of vernacular literature and the artistic discovery of the autonomous self signified a crisis of traditional hierarchies and their accompanying social imaginaries, portending the breakdown of established universalisms and the corresponding growth of more particularistic forms of political community.

At the highest level of abstraction, then, the 'new culture' movement helped to further displace the Confucian social imaginary, hastening the emergence in its place of a modern social imaginary conducive to China's re-conceptualisation as a sovereign national community. In the more immediate term, however, the cultural iconoclasm of the 'new culture' radicals was equally important through its more tangible association with the militant anti-imperialism that developed in China after the war. While originating as a literary and aesthetic movement, the 'new culture' phenomenon arose within a highly febrile political context, in which demands for a revision of China's international status formed a primary focal point for activism and mobilisation among the students and intellectuals most directly involved in 'new culture' avant-gardism.[40] China's entry into the war on the Allies' side in August 1917 had been motivated largely by a desire to secure the reversion of Germany's territorial concessions to Chinese sovereignty following the Central Powers' defeat, and China's diplomats had both hoped and expected this to be the outcome of their mission to Versailles.[41] The Allies' decision instead to award Germany's concessions to Japan rather than China ignited a wave of fury among students in Beijing, culminating in protests and riots on 4 May

---

[36] Mitter, *A Bitter Revolution*, pp. 108–9.
[37] Fairbank, Reischauer and Craig, *East Asia*, p. 768.
[38] *Ibid.* See also Mitter, *A Bitter Revolution*, p. 112.
[39] Ruggie, 'Territoriality and beyond', p. 158. On the significance of the 'new literature' movement for China's subsequent development in the 1920s, see Tse-Tung, *The May Fourth Movement*, p. 271.
[40] Hsu, *The Rise of Modern China*, p. 505.   [41] Spence, *The Search for Modern China*, p. 285.

1919.[42] Although the rioters in Beijing were swiftly dispersed, the sentiments of outrage that fuelled the riots proved enduring, and 4 May would subsequently assume a totemic significance among Chinese nationalists.[43] From a systemic perspective, the combination of this anti-imperialist animus with totalistic cultural iconoclasm made the task of re-establishing an East Asian order on hierarchical foundations infinitely more complicated. Henceforth, regional statesmen would need to either accommodate or confront the demands of radical Chinese nationalists, now estranged from Confucian tradition and alienated equally by the broken promises of Versailles.

In their different ways, the Sinosphere, the East Asian synarchy and the balance-of-power arrangement that had prevailed prior to 1914 had each assumed the legitimacy of international hierarchy. With the rejection of both Confucian hierarchy and foreign imperialism embodied in the 'new culture' and 4 May movements, the cultural preconditions for the preservation of a hierarchical regional order began to disintegrate. Simultaneously, however, the contemporaneous unfolding of a military revolution in northern China was dramatically transforming the existing order's material as well as its cultural foundations, further frustrating efforts to build a stable post-war order. Drawing explicit parallels with Geoffrey Parker's 'military revolution' in early modern Europe, the historian Arthur Waldron has convincingly argued that northern China experienced a military revolution of comparable significance in the decade after 1916.[44] Aided by factors including the emergence of a Chinese military-industrial complex, the dramatic growth of railway tracks and rolling stock in northern China during the Qing dynasty's last decade, and the failure of an international arms embargo to prevent a flood of surplus weaponry from entering the country after 1918, China's already violent warlord conflicts became dramatically more destructive after 1920.[45] This tendency was most marked in the north-eastern provinces around the capital. There, the combination of relatively dense concentrations of roads and modern railways coupled with the flat, open plains of northern China enabled the emergence of a highly modern form of large-scale mobile warfare, one that effectively leapfrogged the more static mode of fighting that had characterised the Western Front prior to the spring offensives of 1918.[46] From 1920 onwards, warlords exploited the greater mobility afforded by armoured trains and the increased firepower of modern artillery to transcend the limits of traditional siege warfare.[47] Increasingly, war was becoming less focused on besieging walled cities – the fortifications of which could now be easily destroyed by modern artillery – and more focused on seizing lines of communication and supply.[48] As the widening arc of destruction churned up the social landscape and dislocated millions of

---

[42] *Ibid.*, pp. 299–300.   [43] *Ibid.*   [44] Waldron, *From War to Nationalism*, p. 57.
[45] *Ibid.*, p. 68.   [46] Chi, *Warlord Politics in China*, p. 128.   [47] *Ibid.*
[48] *Ibid.*, pp. 127–8.

civilians, a growing reservoir of young men were drawn into the warlord armies in hopes of securing economic advancement and physical protection, swelling those armies' ranks and enabling a further expansion in the conflicts' destructive scale and geographical reach.[49]

Like the European military revolution three centuries earlier, the industrial military revolution in North-east Asia would eventually underwrite the consolidation of a sovereign international order. In the immediate term, however, the industrialisation of warfare on the north China plain benefited warlords more than it did the ineffectual government in Beijing. Just as the European military revolution had once empowered over-mighty subjects as much as centralising monarchs, so too were analogous innovations enabling Chinese warlords to adapt the habits of baronial militarism to the material circumstances of the industrial age. In the lead-up to the Washington Conference, the resulting chaos stimulated ever greater unilateral foreign involvement in Chinese politics to secure the powers' interests, at precisely the moment when burgeoning nationalist sentiments were rendering such involvement ever more provocative and destabilising.[50] China's internal weakness had of course long invited foreign aggression. But whereas, under the Qing dynasty, foreign pressures could be brought to bear on a single sovereign centre, with the advent of warlordism the Great Powers were increasingly drawn to preserve their privileges by unilaterally aligning with favoured warlords.[51] Notwithstanding the Great Powers' notional commitment to maintaining China's territorial integrity, Chinese disunity threatened to draw the Great Powers into a competition for influence that would further weaken China while also sharpening international tensions. China's fratricidal disunity was in this way intimately linked to Great Power competition. Consequently, any attempt to construct a stable post-war order would also need to resolve the 'China problem' – in both its nationalist and warlord manifestations – if it was to endure.

The Washington system: Its constitution and its failure

The purposes and constitution of the Washington system

As they convened in Washington, the Great Powers thus dedicated themselves to two interrelated tasks. First, they sought to establish a regional security framework that avoided the instabilities of the old balance-of-power system.[52]

---

[49] *Ibid.*, p. 78.
[50] W. King, *China at the Washington Conference, 1921–1922* (New York: St John's University Press, 1963), p. 54.
[51] *Ibid.* See also J. E. Sheridan, 'The warlord era: Politics and militarism under the Peking government, 1916–1928' in J. K. Fairbank (ed.), *The Cambridge History of China*, XII: *Republican China, 1912–1949*, Pt I (Cambridge University Press, 1983), pp. 303–5.
[52] Iriye, *After Imperialism*, p. 14.

Secondly, the powers aimed to establish an agreed framework for regulating their relations with China, and facilitating the latter's reconstitution as a responsibly governed sovereign nation.[53] Within ten years of its establishment, the 'Washington system' that emerged from the conference would be in tatters, having faltered as a result of its own normative incoherence and institutional fragility. Before I consider the causes of the system's demise, its core features must first be reviewed.

Despite the protracted and often tense negotiations that accompanied it, the Washington Conference initially appeared to establish the basis for a stable regional order. At the level of Great Power relations, the new 'Washington system' sought first to stabilise existing rivalries by committing the three major maritime powers to a preservation of the existing naval balance in the Pacific. Thus, Britain, America and Japan institutionalised the extant 5:5:3 ratio in the size of their respective battle-fleets, while also extending this ratio to apply to aircraft carriers, cruisers, destroyers and submarines.[54] To prevent the risk of a naval arms race, the powers further committed to a ten-year moratorium on the construction of new capital ships, as well as to an agreement not to further fortify their island possessions in the Pacific.[55] In foreclosing the possibility of the Anglo-American battle-fleets massing for an attack against Japan from bases either east of Singapore or west of Hawaii, these non-fortification agreements provided Japan's home islands with a greater margin of security than might have been won through Japan's participation in an unrestrained arms race.[56] In so doing, the agreements aimed to reconcile Japan towards accepting limitations on the size of the Japanese battle-fleet, while also addressing Japanese security concerns in such a way as to foreclose the possibility of renewed Great Power competition.[57]

While the naval arms limitation agreements laid the material foundations for a new order, the Washington delegates also worked to build a robust institutional framework to support the new system. In the face of insistent pressures from America, Britain and Japan agreed not to renew their alliance following its expiry in 1922.[58] Instead, the two countries joined America and France as signatories to the Four Power Treaty, an instrument that reciprocally acknowledged the signatories' authority over their Pacific island possessions while also committing them to the peaceful resolution of international disputes between the signatories.[59] Although scheduled for expiry or renewal after ten years of operation, the ambitions informing the agreement were considerably more far-reaching. Specifically, the Washington system sought nothing less than to replace the competitive logic of alliance politics with a more co-operative

---

[53] *Ibid.*   [54] Lim, *The Geopolitics of East Asia*, p. 49.   [55] *Ibid.*
[56] Fairbank, Reischauer and Craig, *East Asia*, p. 694.
[57] Iriye, *After Imperialism*, p. 19.   [58] *Ibid.*, p. 17.   [59] *Ibid.*

security framework, to be based on the foundations of multilateral diplomacy and international law.[60]

In comparison to the powers' efforts to establish a new regional equilibrium between one another, the task of constructing a new framework for managing their relations with China proved more challenging. The greater difficulties involved in this task stemmed from the contradiction between the old institutional structures of the unequal treaties system, and the new normative context in which that system was now expected to function. The unequal treaties system had initially emerged to regulate relations between two systems of empire, specifically the Celestial Empire of the Qing dynasty and the maritime commercial empires of the Western powers.[61] In its first incarnation, the system had generally comported with Chinese practices of 'barbarian management', and had only gradually become a lightning rod for popular opposition following the first flickerings of Chinese nationalism around 1900.[62] By 1922, however, the government in Beijing, Sun Yat-Sen's revolutionary opposition in Canton and increasing sections of China's literate classes were united in their opposition to the system's preservation.[63] While mass nationalism had yet to take hold, the 'new culture' and 4 May radicals had already succeeded in stigmatising the unequal treaties as an intolerable affront to China's national dignity.[64]

Chinese desires for recognition as a sovereign nation thus yielded corresponding demands for the unequal treaties' speedy abolition. Contrarily, the Great Powers valued the unequal treaties as a vital mechanism for preserving their interests in a country that remained mired in civil war. For the powers, the privileges enshrined in the unequal treaties provided an insurance against the threat of expropriation, either by rapacious warlords or by China's small but increasingly radicalised urban working classes.[65] Similarly, for the Western powers, the preservation of the unequal treaties system also offered a means of diluting Japanese influence within the country, reassuring them against the spectre of Japanese preponderance in China and thus mitigating the temptation to secure foreign interests through recourse to unilateral action.[66]

---

[60] *Ibid.*   [61] *Ibid.*, p. 5.

[62] On the broad significance of the Shandong concession as a catalyst for the first stirrings of modern Chinese nationalism at the century's turn, see generally J. E. Schrecker, *Imperialism and Chinese Nationalism: Germany in Shantung* (Cambridge, MA: Harvard University Press, 1971).

[63] Hsu, *The Rise of Modern China*, p. 531.   [64] *Ibid.*

[65] Iriye, *After Imperialism*, pp. 28–30. See also E. S. K. Fung, *The Diplomacy of Imperial Retreat: Britain's South China policy, 1924–1931* (New York: Oxford University Press, 1991), p. 241.

[66] On the Washington system's broad conception as an alternative to the powers' resort to both unilateral policies within China and exclusive alliances internationally, see generally A. Iriye, *The Origins of the Second World War in Asia and the Pacific* (London: Longman, 1987), pp. 2–3.

Chinese demands for recognition as a sovereign nation therefore collided with the Great Powers' demands for reassurance from the threats to their interests posed respectively by warlord rapacity, radical Chinese nationalism and Japanese ambition. Consequently, the agreed framework for addressing the 'China problem' reflected an uneasy compromise between the imperatives of recognition and reassurance. Central to this framework was a multilateral endorsement of the 'Open Door' principle that America had long championed. The Nine Powers Treaty committed all powers to respecting China's independence and its administrative and territorial integrity, and to the renunciation of aspirations to establish exclusive spheres of influence within the country.[67] In separate negotiations coinciding with the conference, Japan also agreed to restore Shandong to China, while Britain similarly agreed to restore Weihaiwei to Beijing in short order.[68] Finally, the powers also agreed to negotiate towards the progressive restoration of China's tariff and jurisdictional autonomy, and thus towards the eventual abolition of the unequal treaties system. Critically, however, the powers rendered the full restoration of Chinese sovereignty conditional upon China's re-establishment of a viable central government.[69] The resulting agreements thus whetted Chinese nationalist appetites without fully sating them. Indeed, in a tragic paradox, the persistence of a modified unequal treaty system perversely helped fuel revisionist nationalism in China, thereby sustaining the very conditions of instability that justified the system's retention in the eyes of the Great Powers in the first instance. Thus caught between a receding inter-imperial order built on the hierarchical foundation of the unequal treaties system and an emergent regional sovereign state system that had yet to come fully into being, East Asia's Sinic heartland remained dangerously unsettled. The new regional order inaugurated at Washington in 1922 consequently proved exceedingly fragile, and the reasons for its unravelling will now be reviewed.

The Washington system: Its weakness and subversion

Despite its architects' ambitions, the Washington system failed to secure a durable peace. That the system's eventual failure can be attributed in large part to Japanese aggression is beyond dispute. But to attribute the system's collapse exclusively to Japanese malfeasance is to overlook fundamental weaknesses of the system that arguably doomed it from the outset. Specifically, the Washington system lacked sufficiently coherent constitutional values to assure its legitimacy, while its authoritative and coercive institutions were similarly animated by divergent legitimating principles that further compromised the system's durability. Consequently, the system first faltered in the face of Soviet

---

[67] Iriye, *After Imperialism*, p. 18. [68] *Ibid.*, p. 21. [69] *Ibid.*, pp. 21–2.

subversion and Chinese revisionism in the 1920s, before then collapsing entirely with the rise of Japanese militarism after 1931.

In seeking both to accommodate Chinese nationalism and also to safeguard the privileges of the imperialist powers, the Washington system sought to balance two fundamentally contradictory imperatives.[70] These imperatives in turn reflected the radically unsettled normative context out of which the system had itself emerged. Unlike the Sinosphere, which had rested on the solid foundations of imperial Confucianism, no equivalent normative complex underwrote the Washington system. On the contrary, the Washington system emerged in an environment in which a plethora of ideologies contended for supremacy. Western racism, Japanese pan-Asianism, Chinese nationalism and competing Wilsonian and Bolshevik visions of internationalism each unhappily co-existed after 1917, and the resulting tensions begat a hybrid international order lacking stable normative foundations. Alongside a hortatory commitment to recognising Chinese sovereignty, then, the Conference powers remained practically committed to the preservation of imperialist privileges that derived their legitimacy from the civilisational standards of the preceding century.[71] The resulting tensions between prescription and practice left the system open to charges of hypocrisy from both Chinese nationalists and Bolshevik internationalists, paving the way for the revisionist alliance that would do so much to weaken it in the ensuing decade.

The Washington system's inconsistencies were manifest not only in its contradictory purposes and values, but also in its ordering institutions. On the one hand, the system's authoritative institutions reflected distinctly liberal norms of procedural justice and conceptions of political legitimacy. In place of the balance-of-power politics that had characterised the pre-war era, the system committed its signatories to the peaceful resolution of international disputes through reliance on multilateral diplomacy and contractual international law.[72] Similarly, the Nine Powers Treaty also provided a framework for resolving the 'China problem' that officially acknowledged the legitimacy of Chinese aspirations for national self-determination.[73] Conversely, however, the system also relied on the unequal treaties system as one of its primary coercive institutions. As noted previously, the stationing of foreign troops in the territorial concessions provided the imperialist powers with insurance against the threat of expropriation, while also stabilising the Great Power competition for influence in China.[74] As a hierarchical complement to the regional balance of power, the

---

[70] S. Eto, 'China's international relations, 1911–1931' in J. K. Fairbank and A. Feuerwerker (eds.), *The Cambridge History of China*, XIII: *Republican China 1912–1949*, Pt II (Cambridge University Press, 1986), p. 106.

[71] *Ibid.*   [72] *Ibid.*, p. 105.   [73] *Ibid.*

[74] On the significance of 'gunboat diplomacy' as a primary institution for defending the foreign powers' interests in China as late as the mid-1920s, see generally D. Brunero, *Britain's Imperial Cornerstone in China: The Chinese Maritime Customs Service, 1854–1949* (New York: Routledge, 2006), pp. 64–5.

armed foreign enclaves that pockmarked China's coastline were thus directly tied into the regional security architecture conceived at the Washington Conference. Notwithstanding the powers' commitments towards the restoration of Chinese sovereignty, the unequal treaties system played a vital ordering function in East Asia in the 1920s, providing both a shield for foreign investors and a hedge against the unilateral pursuit of hegemony by any one of the Great Powers. Moreover, while the powers increasingly justified such arrangements through appeals to expediency rather than through overt invocations of civilisational supremacy, such manoeuvrings could not conceal the basic inconsistency of this set-up with the Washington system's professed respect for norms of national self-determination.

That the Washington system relied on a combination of both authoritative and coercive institutions to sustain itself is unsurprising, suggesting only the system's affinities with other international orders considered in this study. Where the system differed from other more enduring orders was in its normative incoherence, and in the discrepant principles that respectively informed its authoritative and coercive institutions. The 'organised hypocrisy' that characterised the Washington system thus left it especially susceptible to a crisis of legitimacy of the kind that eventually overwhelmed it.[75] This crisis when it came was stoked by Soviet subversion and sustained by Chinese radicalism, before finally escalating to a system-destroying conflagration with Tokyo's turn towards empire from 1931. Having outlined the structural factors that made this crisis possible, the exact course of this crisis will now be considered.

Explaining the collapse of the Washington system

From the early 1920s, the Soviets pursued an active anti-imperialist agenda in East Asia that influenced Chinese nationalism in ways that significantly contributed to the Washington system's demise. Adopting a dual strategy of diplomacy and revolutionary subversion targeted at Beijing and Canton respectively, the Soviets aimed to simultaneously weaken the imperialist powers in Asia while also distracting the West from events in Central Europe, where Moscow still hoped to export the revolution.[76] Thus in 1924, Moscow abrogated the unequal treaties that had formerly regulated Sino-Russian relations, renouncing also Russia's interest in its portion of the Boxer indemnity.[77] In Canton, meanwhile, Comintern agents diligently cultivated Sun Yat-Sen's Kuomintang (KMT), while also ordering the newly formed Chinese

---

[75] On 'organised hypocrisy' as an enduring feature of world politics, see generally S. Krasner, *Sovereignty: Organized hypocrisy* (Princeton University Press, 1999).

[76] Fairbank, Reischauer and Craig, *East Asia*, p. 777. See also Eto, 'China's international relations', pp. 107–10; and Lim, *The Geopolitics of East Asia*, p. 52.

[77] Lim, *The Geopolitics of East Asia*, p. 53.

Communist Party (the CCP) to co-operate with the KMT as part of a united front against warlordism and imperialism.[78]

The activities of the 'new culture' and 4 May activists had already yielded a nascent nationalist consciousness among sections of China's urban population.[79] But the crushing of the 4 May protestors had also highlighted the political insignificance of these transformations of social identity while they remained confined to such a tiny fraction of the populace. The revolutionary potential of Chinese nationalism furthermore remained muted while it continued to assume a spontaneous and disorganised form. Consequently, Soviet advisors worked closely with Sun Yat-Sen to clarify the KMT's ideology, reorganise it along Leninist lines, and augment its political power through the establishment of a revolutionary party army.[80] By 1925, as a result of these efforts, Chinese nationalism had acquired both a sharper ideological expression, and more potent organisational vehicles – in the form of a Leninist party and a revolutionary army – through which radical Chinese aspirations might be channelled.[81]

With the assistance of their Soviet advisors, China's revolutionaries were soon able to husband the ideological, organisational and military resources necessary to launch a direct challenge to the unequal treaties system. The occasion for such a challenge presented itself on 30 May 1925, when thirteen Chinese protesting the recent shooting of a Chinese worker were themselves killed in Shanghai by British-officered foreign troops.[82] The 30 May incident immediately assumed totemic significance for Chinese nationalists, and in the weeks that followed, China was rapidly convulsed by nationwide strikes and popular anti-imperialist demonstrations.[83] The chief consequences of 30 May were twofold. First, as popular unrest mounted against the foreign presence in China, the semi-sovereign arrangements of the unequal treaties system became ever more difficult to sustain. Following the 30 May tragedy, popular nationalism was stoked further by the massacre of fifty-two Chinese demonstrators by British troops in Canton on 23 June.[84] The ensuing sixteen-month strike in Hong Kong sufficiently unsettled the British to compel major concessions, including the swift retrocession of their concession in Hankou to Chinese rule.[85] From this point onwards, Britain would beat a steady retreat from its sphere of influence in southern China, further emboldening Chinese revisionism and thereby corroding the political foundation for the unequal treaties system.[86]

---

[78] *Ibid.*   [79] Mitter, *A Bitter Revolution*, p. 119.

[80] Eto, 'China's international relations', pp. 110–11.

[81] Hsu, *The Rise of Modern China*, pp. 522–3.

[82] A. Waldron, 'War and the rise of nationalism in twentieth-century China', *The Journal of Military History*, 57(5) (1993), 92.

[83] *Ibid.*, p. 95.   [84] Spence, *The Search for Modern China*, p. 323.

[85] Hsu, *The Rise of Modern China*, p. 567.

[86] See generally Fung, *The Diplomacy of Imperial Retreat*.

Secondly, the success of the 30 May movement provided strong encouragement to the KMT, which had itself played a crucial role in helping to organise protestors and maintain the movement's momentum. At the same time, a resumption of fighting between China's warlord factions threatened to perpetuate China's division and scotch hopes of national reunification.[87] The emergence of an uneasy coalition between two of the most powerful northern warlord factions posed a potentially lethal military threat to the KMT, while the temporary weakening of these forces following their combined offensives against a third warlord faction conversely provided the KMT with a narrow window of opportunity in which to dethrone the warlords while they remained momentarily exhausted.[88] Consequently, in July 1926, Chiang Kai-Shek mobilised the KMT's newly renamed National Revolutionary Army for a massive military campaign aimed at reunifying China.[89] Equipped with a highly trained and indoctrinated party army and assisted by the timely defection of several key northern warlords, the Northern Expedition culminated in 1928 with the country's nominal reunification under KMT rule.[90]

China's reunification in 1928, while undeniably a highly contingent development, was nevertheless explicable at least in part by the organised hypocrisy at the heart of the Washington system. While professing support for the cause of Chinese national self-determination, the powers had also tolerated the preservation of a system that mandated the occupation of China's major commercial centres by foreign troops as one of its key coercive institutions.[91] This left the system open to precisely the revisionist alliance between Comintern officials and Chinese revolutionaries that materialised shortly after the system's establishment. Admittedly, the expedition's success should not be overstated, for the new government in Nanjing remained only nominally in control of large swathes of the country, while the unequal treaties system would not be entirely abolished until 1943. These caveats aside, the 30 May movement and the Northern Expedition together forced significant revisions to the unequal treaties system. These revisions weakened the system's perceived capacity to curb the twin threats of expropriation and unregulated Great Power competition for influence in China, in turn evoking anxieties most strongly in that country which regarded its security and prosperity as being most intimately tied to developments in China. Ironically, then, China's very success in loosening the strictures of foreign domination thereby heightened Japan's feelings of isolation and insecurity, paving the way for the Japanese bid for an East Asian imperium shortly thereafter.

---

[87] Spence, *The Search for Modern China*, p. 324.
[88] Waldron, 'War and the rise of nationalism in twentieth-century China', p. 100.
[89] *Ibid.*, p. 93.   [90] Elleman, *Modern Chinese Warfare*, pp. 174–5.
[91] Hsu, *The Rise of Modern China*, p. 533.

A suzerain system renewed? The Japanese bid
for an imperial new order in East Asia

The Japanese new order in East Asia: The motive
and mode of imperial expansion

Japan's motives for overturning the Washington system and then reconstituting a fleeting imperial order in East Asia in its place were both geopolitical and ideological in character. The onset of the Great Depression painfully exposed Japan's dependence on Western markets – particularly the American market – for hard currency derived from luxury Japanese exports such as silk, as well as for the commodity imports (principally oil) needed to fuel Japanese industries.[92] Washington had already previously exploited Japan's economic dependence on the American market to extort diplomatic concessions, and with Japan's dependence on American oil continuing to rise, its susceptibility to economic coercion looked set to grow accordingly.[93] The growth of US protectionism also threatened to imperil not only Japan's prosperity but also its social and political stability, with the 1925 introduction of universal male suffrage ensuring that international trade dislocations would translate rapidly into domestic political unrest and anti-government agitation.[94]

In Asia, meanwhile, the KMT was steadily chipping away at the unequal treaties system with the increasingly resigned acceptance of the Great Powers, while an influx of primarily American capital in the 1920s had also enabled China to significantly improve the country's infrastructure, facilitating a growth in China's foreign trade and with it a corresponding increase in its custom receipts.[95] Should China's progress towards full diplomatic equality and sustained economic development continue, Japan's relative influence in China would wane, as would its opportunity to establish itself as the regional hegemon with China as its junior partner.[96] At the same time, the Sino-Soviet war in 1929 had also revealed China's military weakness and the persistent spectre of resurgent Soviet influence in Manchuria. For those who saw Japan's security as necessitating the construction of an autarkic empire centred around Manchuria's abundant agricultural and mineral resources, a failure to confront the Soviet threat on the continent thus represented a potentially mortal threat to the country.[97]

---

[92] Iriye, *After Imperialism*, pp. 278–9.
[93] On America's self-conscious cultivation of Japanese dependence on US oil and its geopolitical consequences, see Lehmann, 'Keeping friends close and enemies closer', pp. 144–5.
[94] Iriye, *The Origins of the Second World War in Asia and the Pacific*, pp. 5–6.   [95] *Ibid.*, p. 4.
[96] L. Young, *Japan's Total Empire: Manchuria and the culture of wartime imperialism* (Berkeley: University of California Press, 1998), p. 41.
[97] Elleman, *Modern Chinese Warfare*, p. 110; Fairbank, Reischauer and Craig, *East Asia*, pp. 705–7.

For an influential section of Japanese opinion, particularly among the junior officers of the Kwantung Army stationed in Manchuria, the establishment of a vast autarkic empire on the continent offered Japan the clearest path to security and prosperity. Hemmed in by a combination of American racism, Chinese nationalism and Soviet Bolshevism, Japan's continued investment in the Washington system would leave Tokyo forever hostage to the whims of hostile powers – integration into the existing order would only mean perpetual economic and diplomatic dependence in the eyes of the empire's advocates.[98] Similarly, continued inaction on the continent would likewise promise Japan's permanent marginalisation in Asia, as the Soviet Union gobbled up the spoils in Manchuria while China reconstituted itself under a radical nationalist government.[99] To those enamoured of the idea of security through expansion, only forceful and immediate action could extricate Japan from the dependency-inducing fetters of the Washington system and thus enable it to carve out the empire that was necessary for its survival.

As important as strategic motives were for those agitating for an expanded Japanese empire, it is also essential to note the powerful ideological attractions of the imperial project in sustaining Japanese militarism. Ideologically, Japan's militarists continued to adapt Western discourses of civilisation and race to legitimise Japan's leadership aspirations in Asia.[100] Pan-Asianist ideas of Japan as East Asia's vanguard nation continued to form a vital component of the imperial tradition.[101] In the 1930s, these themes acquired a new resonance as Japanese militarists unilaterally assumed responsibility for defending their Asian compatriots from the depredations of Western imperialism, as well as from the siren songs of communism and radical nationalism. Simultaneously, however, any feelings of solidarity with Japan's neighbours were diluted by the conviction that the Japanese right to dominion derived as much from their divinely ordained status as the 'master race' (*shujin monzoku*) as it did from Japan's political and economic achievements.[102] Much like their Manchu predecessors, the Japanese would thus retain a distinctive sense of themselves as being separate from and superior to their subject peoples as their empire expanded, even while they sought to stabilise their rule by tapping into more universalistic legitimating frameworks.

The Japanese bid to reconstitute an imperial East Asian order was thus sustained by multiple motives, which reflected the extreme uncertainty pervading the international system from the onset of the Great Depression. The immense volatility of the international environment after 1929 provided Japanese militarists with both the opportunity and the perceived necessity of

---

[98] Iriye, *The Origins of the Second World War in Asia and the Pacific*, p. 5.   [99] *Ibid.*
[100] Young, *Japan's Total Empire*, p. 29.   [101] *Ibid.*
[102] A. Chua, *Day of Empire: How hyperpowers rise to global dominance – and why they fall* (New York: Doubleday, 2007), pp. 276–7.

expanding the empire through armed aggression. Critically, however, the mode of Japanese expansion was decidedly haphazard. Thus, the Japanese move towards establishing a new order in East Asia found its genesis in the actions of Kwantung Army opportunists, whose 1931 conquest of Manchuria proceeded without the prior complicity of the government in Tokyo.[103] Subsequently, the consolidation of the newly formed puppet kingdom of Manchukuo was conditioned as much by the partnership between the Kwantung Army and the South Manchurian Railway Company (SMRC) as it was by Tokyo, the SMRC playing a role in Manchukuo analogous to that of the East India Company under the Victorian Raj.[104] With the handicap of hindsight, Japan's subsequent moves to establish itself as regional hegemon all appear as milestones along a path of inexorable imperial expansion.[105] In reality, however, Japan's abandonment of the Washington system was neither immediate nor uncontested at home, and was propelled by predatory opportunism rather than by the unfolding of a carefully considered grand strategy of regional conquest. The improvised and incremental character of Japan's expansion progressively assured its ever increasing diplomatic isolation, thereby perversely appearing to vindicate Japan's quest for autarky and providing the empire's proponents with a warrant for further aggression. The haphazard manner of the empire's expansion also helps to explain the unstable and ultimately ephemeral constitution of the imperial order over which Japan briefly presided, the main features of which will now be considered.

The constitutional structure of the Japanese new order and its structural vulnerabilities

By mid-1942, Japan's imperial project had reached its zenith. From June 1941, the Soviet Union was fully preoccupied with fending off the Nazi threat. This left Japan's flanks secure, freeing imperial forces to sweep southwards to dislodge the Western powers from South-east Asia and so secure Japan's control over the Dutch East Indies' vital oil reserves. In February 1942, Japan's three-month *Blitzkrieg* culminated in the conquest of Singapore, thereby shattering the military foundation of British power in Asia.[106] The assault on Pearl Harbor had also badly damaged American naval power in the

---

[103] Iriye, *The Origins of the Second World War in Asia and the Pacific*, pp. 7–10.

[104] Calvocoressi, Wint and Pritchard, *Total War*, II, p. 139.

[105] On hindsight bias as an enduring problem in the social sciences, see P. E. Tetlock and G. Parker, 'Counterfactual thought experiments: Why we can't live without them and how we must learn to live with them' in P. E. Tetlock, R. N. Lebow and G. Parker (eds.), *Unmaking the West: 'What if?' scenarios that rewrite world history* (Ann Arbor: The University of Michigan Press, 2006), pp. 25–8.

[106] Fairbank, Reischauer and Craig, *East Asia*, p. 809.

Pacific, winning the Japanese crucial time in which to expand and fortify their defensive perimeters against the inevitable American counter-attack.[107] Most importantly, the attacks on Pearl Harbor and the conquest of Singapore had also struck at the credibility of Western assurances of support to China in its continuing struggle against Japan. With Western attentions divided between wars in Europe and the Pacific and the KMT government incapable of throwing off the Japanese yoke without outside support, Japan's military conquests in the Pacific were aimed squarely at so isolating and demoralising the KMT as to compel China to sue for peace.[108] With China reconciled to Japan's domination of Asia and the resources of East Asia at its disposal, Tokyo's militarists anticipated that they would then be well positioned to wait out the Western powers, who would acquiesce to the new dispensation in Asia rather than bear the formidable costs of the long war that would be necessary to reverse Japan's advances.[109]

History shows that Japan fatally underestimated the resolve of both China and the Western powers in its bid for regional hegemony, and that its embryonic new order consequently proved spectacularly short-lived. Beyond the strategic failures that led to the new order's destruction however, it is also necessary to understand the intrinsic limitations of the new order that contributed to its demise. Like all international orders, the Japanese new order comprised an amalgam of normative, institutional and material components. At a normative level, the new order rested on an unstable amalgam of pan-Asian anti-colonialism, militant anti-communism and 'divine race' national chauvinism. In seeking to legitimise its new-found pre-eminence in Asia, Japan relied on harnessing pre-existing resentments of European imperialism to mobilise support for its alternative East Asian order.[110] Conversely, however, this emphasis on anti-colonialism sat uncomfortably with the reality of a 'Co-prosperity sphere' explicitly founded on Japanese dominion. For the Japanese, the tension between pan-Asianist anti-colonialism and Japanese hegemony was easily reconciled. As Asia's most materially advanced nation, the Japanese regarded themselves as objectively the most qualified state to guide East Asia on its passage to modernity.[111] The cult of emperor-worship that had developed in Japan from the Meiji Restoration onwards, and that also emphasised the special superiority of the Japanese as the divine *Yamato* race, provided for the Japanese an additional justification for their claims towards mastery in Asia.[112] Unsurprisingly, however, Japanese particularism failed to resonate among the empire's subject populations. Similarly, the patent inconsistencies between the anti-colonial promises of Tokyo and the harsh realities of life under Japanese

---

[107] *Ibid.*   [108] Calvocoressi, Wint and Pritchard, *Total War*, II, pp. 329–31.   [109] *Ibid.*
[110] Chua, *Day of Empire*, p. 280.   [111] Young, *Japan's Total Empire*, p. 433.
[112] Chua, *Day of Empire*, p. 276.

occupation further diminished the new order's legitimacy, leaving it susceptible to subversion and armed resistance.[113]

The tension between pan-Asian solidarity and divine race chauvinism undoubtedly weakened the new order, but the uniquely debilitating character of this tension can best be apprehended by contrasting it with comparable tensions in the legitimating frameworks of more durable international orders. Upon first consideration, the tensions between the universalistic and particularistic themes pervading the Japanese new order appear historically unexceptional, having routinely existed in past international orders. In Latin Christendom, for example, Rome's Germanic heirs explicitly identified the empire with the divine mission of the Universal Church, but also independently emphasised the origins of the imperial office in the sacred traditions of the Frankish people.[114] Similarly, within the Sinosphere, the Manchu conquerors successfully mobilised imperial Confucianism to sustain their hegemony, while also preserving their social identity as a conquest elite distinct from the Han majority.[115] In both Europe and East Asia, past rulers had relied on the authoritative power of universalistic religious visions to cement their power, but had also preserved distinct social identities that legitimised conquest on the basis of the assumed superiority of a martial caste bound together by imagined ties of collective kinship.

Universalism and particularism, the logics of faith and blood, had thus long underwritten historic international orders without the tensions between the two necessarily culminating in crises of legitimacy. What distinguished the Japanese order from its historical forebears was the qualitatively different systemic milieu within which it developed. On this point, a contrast with the Manchu-dominated Sinosphere is instructive. In the era of Manchu hegemony, China remained a heteronomous society, in which the social order was regarded as but the tangible expression of the larger cosmic order within which it was embedded.[116] The xenophobic misgivings of Ming restorationists aside, existing notions of cosmological kingship proved sufficiently elastic to accommodate a non-Han dynasty, while the Manchus proved prudent enough to embrace imperial Confucianism as the primary foundation of monarchical authority.[117] By contrast, by the advent of the new order, a modern social imaginary was already taking root among indigenous elites in conquered

---

[113] *Ibid.*, p. 281.   [114] Folz, *The Concept of Empire*, pp. 101–2.
[115] Darwin, *After Tamerlane*, p. 350.
[116] On the distinction between heteronomous social orders, in which the social order is conceived as being connected to a larger cosmic order, and autonomous social orders, where no such assumptions are observed and the social order is held rather to exist autonomously of a cosmic order, see C. Castoriadis, *The Imaginary Institution of Society* (Cambridge: Polity Press, 1987), pp. 107–10.
[117] Darwin, *After Tamerlane*, pp. 92–3.

territories, and the social and political order was now increasingly conceived as existing autonomously from any transcendental source of legitimation. In keeping with emergent ideals of nationalism and popular self-determination, political legitimacy was now seen to derive instead from the immanent will of the sovereign people.[118] Within this new context, the option of legitimising Japanese power through the invocation of transcendental religious visions was foreclosed. Emergent nationalist sentiments instead forced a pan-Asianist attempt at accommodation, which proved impossible to reconcile with the 'divine race' chauvinism of a Japanese nation mobilised for total war.

Unlike the more enduring international orders considered in this study, the Japanese new order therefore failed to cultivate a coherent normative complex. This normative incoherence consequently impeded the development of the authoritative and coercive institutions necessary to consolidate the Japanese imperium. Under the Sinosphere, Confucianism had provided the shared cultural scaffolding necessary to sustain the legitimacy of practices of tributary diplomacy and imperial interventions.[119] These institutions had in turn been crucial in mediating China's relations with its tributary polities. Conversely, under the new order, no equivalent cultural foundation existed to underwrite authoritative and coercive institutions of the kind likely to be regarded as legitimate by both Japan and its subject polities. The resulting legitimacy gap between Japan and its satellites impeded the development of the fundamental institutions necessary to effectively manage inter-polity relations within the empire. Additionally, the new order's resulting illegitimacy and institutional weakness was further aggravated by the qualitatively greater economic demands Japan placed on its neighbours in comparison to imperial China. Japan's ambitions to create an autarkic sphere of influence in East Asia meant that it simply could not replicate an international hierarchy as non-intrusive as that which had characterised the Sinosphere. Whereas the enormous size and wealth of Ming and then later Qing China had obviated the need for these empires to impose significant economic demands on tributary polities, Japan's different structural position in Asia conversely demanded of it a much more intrusive role in the administration of its satellites.[120] At the same time, however, the sheer enormity of even China alone precluded the possibility of the Japanese directly ruling and administering its empire as the British had done in India.[121] Consequently, throughout its penumbra of conquered territories, Japan sought to co-opt local nationalists to provide the new order with a veneer

---

[118] Fairbank, Reischauer and Craig, *East Asia*, p. 714.

[119] See Ch. 6.

[120] The extent of Japan's demands on its conquered territories are examined in detail in P. Liberman, *Does Conquest Pay? The exploitation of occupied industrial societies* (Princeton University Press, 1996), Ch. 6.

[121] Calvocoressi, Wint and Pritchard, *Total War*, II, pp. 224–5.

of popular legitimacy, while simultaneously reserving for the imperial Japanese army the task of ruthlessly looting from these societies the resources necessary to sustain the Japanese war effort.[122]

Both the nascent growth of Asian nationalism and the unquenchable rapacity of the Japanese war machine thus conspired to undermine Japanese efforts to imbue the new order with any semblance of Pan-Asian legitimacy. Japan's imperial project was both more chauvinistic and more intrusive than that of the Sinosphere, while it shared with the short-lived Washington system the debilitating characteristics of normative incoherence and institutional frailty outlined above. Ultimately, what therefore sustained Japan's new order throughout its brief existence was the order's material foundation in Japan's regional military supremacy. Just as earlier steppe conquerors had dominated far more populous sedentary societies across Eurasia through their peerless supremacy in the art of mobile cavalry warfare, so too did Japan's early mastery of industrial warfare enable it to momentarily hold sway over its neighbours.[123] However, while conquerors such as the Manchus managed to absorb enough of their host societies' cultural norms and institutions to establish a stable basis for long-term rule, Japan's imperialists proved far less supple in adapting either their aspirations or their methods of rule to local circumstances. Instead, driven by the necessities of total war mobilisation and lacking the legitimacy necessary to cultivate sustained and effective co-operation from local proxies, the Japanese resorted instead to systematic coercion, both to crush local resistance and to cow occupied populations into submission. Nowhere was this policy of coercion and terror applied more intensely than in northern China, where the Japanese fought unsuccessfully for eight long years to extract a favourable peace settlement from the Chinese government. Ironically, it would ultimately be this resort to terror that would solidify the growth of nationalist sentiment among China's rural majority, completing China's metamorphosis into a nation-state and thereby entrenching the basis for a sovereign international order in East Asia.

Imperial violence, 'people's war' and the failure of the Japanese new order in Asia

State involution on the North China Plain and the structural frailty of the Japanese new order

While the Japanese new order was destroyed largely through the application of Western military power, the political failure of the imperial project was most sharply manifest in northern China. From the first Sino-Japanese war onwards,

---

[122] Chua, *Day of Empire*, p. 280.

[123] On the military foundations of the Manchu conquest, see again generally di Cosimo, 'Did guns matter?'

northern China had served as the focal point around which imperial ambitions and Chinese nationalist agitation had explosively converged. In keeping with this pattern, it would be the failure of Japanese imperialism in northern China, together with the radical Chinese reaction that Japanese brutality helped culti-vate, that would most decisively condition the consolidation of an East Asian sovereign international order.

Japan's failure to consolidate its influence in northern China was in large part governed by shifts in the systemic normative milieu already discussed. Recapitulating briefly, by the beginning of the second Sino-Japanese war in 1937, the Confucian cosmology of the Sinosphere had disintegrated, while natio-nalist sentiments were ripening among growing sections of the Chinese popu-lation. Certainly, the breadth and depth of Chinese nationalist sentiment at the war's outset should not be overstated. While the 'new culture' and 4 May move-ments had done much to cultivate radical nationalism among sections of China's urban elites, illiterate or marginally literate peasants continued to form the bulk of China's population, and their concerns remained predominantly parochial and subsistence-focused.[124] This caveat aside, by the 1930s, nationalism represented the common denominator of Chinese political thought.[125] Nationalism's ascendancy among China's political leadership – confirmed anew with the 1936 formation of a renewed KMT–CCP united front against Japanese imperialism – therefore pre-sented the Japanese with a formidable impediment to imperial expansion of a kind that had not confronted earlier conquerors in Chinese history.

With the collapse of Confucian notions of cosmological kingship and the concomitant growth of ideas locating political legitimacy with the immanent will of the sovereign nation, China was becoming ever more indigestible for would-be conquerors. Compounding Japan's inability to legitimise its rule in conquered territories were the institutional weaknesses of its new empire. In northern China, the Japanese were unable to find indigenous collaborators sufficiently numerous and reliable to effectively administer newly conquered territories.[126] Whereas the Japanese in Formosa had ably exploited the *baojia* system of local governance they had inherited from the Qing dynasty following the first Sino-Japanese war, the social environment in northern China after 1937 proved far less conducive to imperial rule.[127] From the Qing dynasty reforms of the 1900s, successive state-building projects in northern China had

---

[124] Johnson, *Peasant Nationalism and Communist Power*, p. 5.
[125] Fairbank, Reischauer and Craig, *East Asia*, p. 714.
[126] On the unreliability of locally recruited personnel in policing and administering Japan's conquest in northern China, see L. P. van Slyke, 'The Chinese communist movement during the Sino-Japanese War, 1937–1945' in Fairbank and Feuerwerker (eds.), *The Cambridge History of China*, XIII: *Republican China, 1912–1949*, Pt II, p. 671.
[127] On the *baojia* system as a critical component of Japan's imperial infrastructure in Formosa, see Chua, *Day of Empire*, pp. 283–4.

extensively corroded established brokerage networks linking the central state with local elites in northern China.[128] In the face of the growing extractive demands of successive republican and warlord regimes, traditional local power-holders had been displaced by a stratum of violent entrepreneurs who nominally extended state power to the village level by serving as tax farmers, but actually engorged themselves at the expense of both the authority of the central state and the welfare of the peasant majority.[129] This decades-long process of state involution had already fostered accelerating local anarchy and institutional deformation prior to the Japanese invasion. Significantly, it would continue to do so throughout the period of Japanese rule, with the hardships that it generated working in tandem with the brutality of the occupation to hothouse peasant nationalism and thus further enervate the new order.[130]

The legacy of long-term state involution in northern China, aggravated by the more recent traumas of war and mass displacement, presented the Japanese with formidable institutional challenges in addition to the legitimation deficit already discussed. Without a structural analogue to the Confucian gentry upon which the Manchus had relied to administer their empire, the Japanese were forced to directly police and administer conquered territories themselves. Given the dissonance between Japan's limited troop numbers and the enormous size of the conquered territories, the Japanese were compelled to limit their military presence to the railways and major urban centres, delegating to 'local bullies' the task of squeezing the peasantry of the resources necessary to fuel the Japanese war economy.[131] With KMT forces defeated and dispersed, and traditional social elites having long since been displaced by violent entrepreneurs as the chief mediating influence between state and peasantry, Japan's resulting neglect of the countryside thus left a power vacuum in northern China in which anti-imperialist forces could prosper. It was precisely within this power vacuum that the CCP consolidated its grip over popular loyalties, and refined the method of 'people's war' that would herald the eventual emergence of a new China unified under CCP rule.

'People's war', popular nationalism and the defeat of imperial Japan

From the advent of warlordism in 1916, northern China had descended into a state of immature anarchy, analogous in its dynamics to the conflict that had

---

[128] P. Duara, 'State involution: A study of local finances in north China, 1911–1935', *Comparative Studies in Society and History*, 29(1) (1987), pp. 136–7.

[129] *Ibid.*

[130] P. Duara. *Culture, Power, and the State: Rural north China, 1900–1942* (Stanford University Press, 1988), p. 253.

[131] *Ibid.*, p. 253. Duara does nevertheless note that Japan's reliance on 'local bullies' to extract resources from the local peasantry was far from unique, being rather characteristic of all the regimes that dominated northern China throughout the republican period.

engulfed the feuding territories of the empire during the Thirty Years War. As the regional epicentre of ideological and geopolitical rivalry, the provinces of northern China after 1937 remained caught in a tripolar clash between imperial Japanese forces, residual KMT elements and Chinese communist guerrillas, the contest being further complicated by the persistent influence of regional warlords and local militias. Within this disordered context, all three of the main protagonists prosecuted projects of competitive state-building, employing a broad repertoire of techniques in order to fully mobilise the human and material resources of territories under their control. Despite the constant military and political pressures to which they were subjected, it was ultimately the communists who proved most successful in harnessing popular loyalties and laying the institutional foundations for a revived Chinese state. A brief consideration of the CCP's state-building efforts during the Sino-Japanese war is therefore essential in comprehending both the failure of Japanese imperialism and the subsequent consolidation of a sovereign international order in North-east Asia.

In seeking to account for the communists' ultimate triumph in reunifying China, a long-standing debate has raged between those emphasising the communists' ability to harness peasant nationalism as the key to their success, versus those who have conversely stressed the appeal of the communists' revolutionary social programme in accounting for their popularity.[132] I suggest here that both the practice of 'people's war' and the development of techniques of mass mobilisation oriented towards social revolution formed indissoluble parts of a common state-building project. This project in turn served first to instantiate and consolidate nationalist social identities in China's rural hinterland, and secondly to establish a militarised and authoritarian model of state–society relations in the communists' base areas that would eventually prevail throughout the country. In Europe's century of chaos, processes of confessionalisation and armed resistance to Habsburg imperialism had culminated in the formation of new imagined communities and new and more intensive practices of rule, which had in turn laid the foundations for a sovereign international order following the Peace of Westphalia. Similarly, in wartime China, the struggle against foreign imperialism also accelerated ongoing transformations in collective identities and structures of governance, yielding similarly profound consequences both domestically and internationally.

While space limitations preclude an exhaustive treatment of communist practices of state-building during the Sino-Japanese war, the broad contours of this project can be briefly described. Caught between the pincers of Japanese repression and renewed 'friction' with their nominal KMT allies, the communists, after 1941, extensively renovated their practices of government in their

---

[132] The foremost respective advocates of the 'nationalist' and 'peasant radicalism' positions in the literature are Johnson, *Peasant Nationalism and Communist Power;* and M. Selden, *The Yenan Way in Revolutionary China* (Cambridge, MA: Harvard University Press, 1971).

remaining base areas to stave off the threat of annihilation. This programme of renovation extended to all aspects of the party's operations, and encompassed ideological, economic, administrative and military reforms that substantially transformed the party's relationship with its host communities. Ideologically, the party embraced a programme of 'rectification' in order to guarantee party unity and forestall the party's threatened unravelling under the stresses of wartime mobilisation.[133] This process entailed both the comprehensive codification of the CCP programme in accordance with the beliefs of Mao Zedong, as well as the establishment of extensive structures of indoctrination, disciplining and surveillance to ensure cadres' universal conformity with Mao's vision.[134] Economically, the middle years of the war also saw the adoption of the co-operative movement, involving the party's direct involvement in co-ordinating peasant production at the village level.[135] This policy was necessary in order to enhance agricultural productivity and thereby strengthen the party's material capacity to sustain the armed struggle under conditions of wartime hardship and a KMT economic blockade.[136]

Administratively and politically, meanwhile, the imperative of extending the party's influence to the village level occasioned sweeping changes in the CCP's relations with its host communities. Prior to the revival of frictions with the KMT and the upsurge in Japanese repression that marked the war's middle years, the CCP was generally limited in the depth of its penetration of host communities in established base areas.[137] Party functionaries typically replicated the practice of past Chinese dynasties in confining their administrative functions to the provincial and county levels, with responsibility for governance within the villages themselves remaining the prerogative of local elites.[138] With the territorial losses that accrued following the failure of the massive Hundred Regiments Offensive in August 1940, however, the party was compelled to increase its extractive demands on the host communities that remained under its nominal control.[139] Wartime exigencies necessitated that the landlords, gentry and 'local bullies' that had hitherto prevailed at a village level either be co-opted or sidelined in order to assure the party war-machine unmediated access to the productive resources of the Chinese country-side.[140] Henceforth, party activists strove diligently to establish structures of direct rule in base area villages, and deployed a network of cadres to host communities to co-ordinate production and supervise the organisation and indoctrination of the peasantry in conformity with Maoist doctrine.[141]

---

[133] Van Slyke, 'The Chinese communist movement', pp. 687–92.　　[134] *Ibid.*, p. 692.

[135] See for example P. Keating, 'Getting peasants organized: Village organizations and the party-state in the Shaan Gan Ning border region, 1934–1945' in F. Chongyi and D. S. G. Goodman (eds.), *North China at War: The social ecology of revolution, 1937–1945* (Oxford: Rowman and Littlefield Publishers, 2000), pp. 46–9.

[136] *Ibid.*　　[137] Van Slyke, 'The Chinese communist movement', p. 693.　　[138] *Ibid.*

[139] *Ibid.*　　[140] *Ibid.*, p. 694.　　[141] *Ibid.*

Employing a host of mass-mobilisation techniques, the CCP's shift towards a model of direct rule over local communities transformed existing power structures, undermining the influence of established local leaders and tightening the organisational and ideological linkages between the party leadership and the peasantry. These changes, in addition to the ideological and economic innovations already outlined, were each in turn motivated by the overriding imperative of sustaining the CCP in its armed struggle against Japanese imperialism. Following the losses incurred in the Hundred Regiments Offensive, communist forces reverted to their traditional preference for guerrilla warfare, continuously harassing the imperial army for the remainder of the Sino-Japanese conflict.[142] Militarily and politically, this strategy undoubtedly had its merits. In the immediate term, it served to tie down hundreds of thousands of Japanese troops in garrison duty in northern China, diverting Japanese resources from the Pacific War and thereby weakening Tokyo's capacity to defend its imperium from its multiplying Western and Chinese enemies after December 1941.[143] Additionally, the reversion to guerrilla warfare also worked to burnish the CCP's nationalist credentials, while preserving the majority of CCP units as a force in being, ready to resume the civil war against the KMT following Japan's expected defeat.[144]

At a deeper level than its long-term strategic dividends, however, the practice of 'people's war' also consolidated nationalist social identities in China's rural heartland, corroding entrenched habits of parochialism and laying the effective foundations for China's subsequent reunification under communist rule. At the level of collective identity, Mao's refinement of 'people's war' – as both a method of warfare and a way of being – served to complete the transition from elite to mass nationalism in China that had begun two decades earlier with the 'new culture' and 4 May movements. The success of guerrilla warfare as envisioned by the communists always presupposed the existence of a commonality of interests and identity between guerrillas and the people in whose name they fought. In the wake of Japanese mass reprisals against the peasantry in 1941 and 1942, the scope for cultivating these bonds of common interest and identity was dramatically enlarged.[145] Notwithstanding the demoralising effects of the reprisals on sections of the Chinese peasantry, the indiscriminate character of Japanese repression also inevitably aroused popular bitterness that could profitably be harnessed to the nationalist cause.[146] However, just as Chinese nationalists in the 1920s had required external tutelage (in the

[142] L. Li, *The Japanese Army in North China, 1937–1941: Problems of political and economic control* (Oxford University Press, 1975), p. 13.

[143] T. I.-W. Wu, 'The Chinese communist movement' in J. C. Hsiung and S. Levine (eds.), *China's Bitter Victory: The war with Japan, 1937–1945* (London: M. E. Sharpe, 1992), p. 103.

[144] L. P. van Slyke, 'The Battle of the Hundred Regiments: Problems of coordination and control during the Sino-Japanese War', *Modern Asian Studies*, 30(4) (1996), 1000–1.

[145] Johnson, *Peasant Nationalism and Communist Power*, p. 5.

[146] Spence, *The Search for Modern China*, p. 444.

form of Soviet assistance) to develop the ideological and organisational vehicles necessary to translate popular xenophobia into concerted political and military action, so too was this the case in wartime northern China. In those areas abandoned by defeated KMT forces but beyond the effective control of the overstretched Japanese, it was the CCP that came to perform this tutelary role.[147] Through their deployment of cadres to the villages, the communists established direct contact with the peasantry, before then using this proximity to propagate their nationalist message, co-ordinate local self-defence activities, and mobilise the peasants' productive energies towards the cause of national liberation.[148] In so doing, the communists were able to give coherent ideological expression and trans-local organisational shape to anti-Japanese peasant resistance. This in turn forged the basis for the revolutionary mass peasant nationalism that would ultimately underwrite China's successful emergence as a sovereign state after 1949.

Sun Yat-Sen once despairingly compared the Chinese people to a loose sheet of sand, lamenting their parochial commitment to ties of kinship and locality, as well as the absence of a broadly shared national identity binding them together.[149] In the wake of the Qing dynasty's collapse, this lamentation was eminently understandable. Without the cement of modern nationalism, post-Qing China was in danger of disintegrating, just as so many other empires had crumbled following World War I. The decade of warlordism that followed Yuan Shikai's death starkly demonstrated the plausibility of such fears, while the powers' failure to fully restore China's sovereign status at the Washington Conference reaffirmed the long-standing association between Chinese disunity and foreign predation. Chinese disunity and the powers' strategic and commercial interests conspired to keep the country locked within the straitjacket of the unequal treaties system, preserving China's semi-sovereign status in a regional order caught uneasily between the dual logics of imperial hierarchy and sovereign anarchy. Liberating China from these external constraints would be possible only once the country had overcome its internal divisions. This would in turn require revolutionary transformations in popular collective identities, and also in the political and military institutions necessary to harness popular energies to the task of establishing China as a unified sovereign state.

The 'new culture' and 4 May movements initiated these transformative processes, respectively dethroning a Confucian social imaginary and pioneering an elite nationalist sensibility capable of sustaining an assertion of Chinese sovereign rights in the face of foreign imperialism. Sun Yat-Sen's administration in Canton further advanced China's sovereign transformation in the 1920s, establishing the institutional vehicles necessary to promote national liberation

---

[147] See for example Hsu, *The Rise of Modern China*, pp. 591–2.   [148] *Ibid.*

[149] J. Fitzgerald, *Awakening China: Politics, culture, and class in the nationalist revolution* (Stanford University Press, 1996), p. 163.

in the form of the KMT party apparatus and its accompanying 'people's army'. Chiang Kai-Shek advanced this process of transformation further still in leading the Revolutionary Army to victory against the country's warlords in the Northern Expedition, before then nominally restoring a national government in 1928. And the Chinese communists completed this task during the Sino-Japanese war, forging in their base areas the revolutionary synthesis of peasant nationalism and mass mobilisation that concluded China's century-long transition from Celestial Empire to sovereign nation-state.

The imperial recessional and the birth of a sovereign international order in East Asia

By the time of the communists' final victory over nationalist forces in October 1949, East Asia's transition from the suzerain world of the Sinosphere towards a modern sovereign-territorial state system was virtually complete. The classical Sinosphere had been an unambiguously heteronomous order, presided over by an omnicompetent emperor charged with performing the rites and observances necessary to guarantee the preservation of temporal and cosmic harmony. The Sinosphere's fundamental institutions had derived their legitimacy precisely from their perceived concordance with the Mandate of Heaven. This mandate resided with the Son of Heaven, and provided legitimating glue necessary to undergird order both within China and also throughout the suzerain state system over which the emperor presided.

By contrast, the international order that had emerged following Japan's defeat and China's reunification was unambiguously free of any cosmological foundation. Certainly, the post-war order remained rent by the ideological rivalries of the cold war. But these ideological differences reflected competing understandings of an international order framed around the common purpose of promoting popular eudemonism. Additionally, these competing ideologies were articulated also within a framework that regarded self-determining nations as the ultimate repository of political legitimacy. Soviet Bolshevism, Maoist communism and American liberalism all constituted different expressions of the popular sovereignty revolution, and all were the product of a modern social imaginary that elevated the satisfaction of temporal human needs as representing the highest purpose of political association. In this respect, the post-war international order institutionalised the sovereign particularism of the modern nation-state, sloughing off the universalist pretensions of the imperial Confucian outlook that had for centuries defined East Asian international order.

As with the Western European experience after the Reformation, so too in East Asia was the transition towards a sovereign international order thus fundamentally associated with entwined crises of faith and empire. Within the Western European context, religion continued to dominate public life following the collapse of Latin Christian unity and the defeat of Habsburg imperialism. But the Wars of Religion had compelled far-reaching reconceptualisations of religion as an ontological category, with new conceptions of religion as referring primarily to a reflexively held body of beliefs enabling the emergence of an ecumenical – but far from entirely secular – international order following the Peace of Westphalia.[150] In East Asia, similarly, the crisis of the Confucian imaginary that attended the Qing dynasty's decline foreclosed the revival of a regional order founded on the binding power of a common religious vision. Indeed, if anything, the crumbling of Confucian universalism as a basis for international order was more complete and the secularisation of regional order correspondingly more total than in the post-Westphalian West. Within post-revolutionary China, Vietnam and North Korea in particular – the heartland of the classical Sinosphere – the break with Confucian 'superstition' was particularly pronounced, with a militant secularism of truly Jacobin severity characterising the domestic political orders of all three countries as the regional order consolidated itself in the immediate post-war period.

The transformation of international order in post-Reformation Europe had been marked not only by reconceptualisations of religion, but also by transformed understandings of politics, community and war. Once again, comparable shifts in the cultural texture of international politics can also be discerned in post-war East Asia. Under the Sinosphere, political life had been informed by notions of cosmological kingship centred round the office of the Imperial Throne, with the emperor responsible for assuring harmony within the universal cosmic and sociopolitical order of *Tianxia*. Within this order, collective identities were articulated primarily in terms of a 'civilised/barbarian' divide, while war was similarly conceived as an imperial prerogative to be used as necessary by the emperor to chastise all who threatened to disrupt the harmony of *Tianxia*. This order vanished forever with the Qing dynasty's collapse and the disintegration of the Confucian social imaginary. In its place, following the generative trauma of the war against Japanese imperialism, a new regional order arose that enshrined sovereign particularism as its overarching principle. Within this new order, the liberation and advancement of self-determining nations would most strongly inform conceptions of both politics and community, while war would similarly lose its prior identification with imperial prerogative, coming instead to be identified as a necessary means of securing national survival under conditions of international anarchy.

In addition to the transformed cultural texture of East Asian international order after 1945, the region also witnessed a concomitant transformation in its fundamental institutions. The years after 1945 witnessed the dissolution of the last vestiges of imperial hierarchy in the region, and the transition to a modern state system founded on the organising principle of sovereign anarchy. The

---

[150] See Ch. 5.

classical suzerain state system of the Sinosphere; the synarchic order that had succeeded it; the Washington system that had briefly prevailed after 1922; and finally the Japanese new order – each of these different orders was distinguishable from the post-1945 order by its reliance on formal hierarchy to regulate the relationship between at least some of its units. Following World War II, and the dismantling of the Japanese and European empires in Asia, the region was finally fully incorporated into an increasingly global sovereign international order. As with all international orders, this system would rely on the operation of both authoritative and coercive institutions to maintain itself. But these institutions now derived their legitimacy from a common commitment to notions of popular sovereignty, and an associated commitment to maintaining a global order predicated on norms of domestic supremacy and sovereign equality.

Finally, at the material level, the coming of industrial and later atomic warfare to North-east Asia comprehensively reconfigured the geopolitical basis of the East Asian regional order. Under the Sinosphere, international order had depended on China's matchless military power as the world's most powerful gunpowder empire. The industrialisation of warfare – beginning in the south with the advent of British gunboat diplomacy in the 1840s and accelerating in the north with the quickening of Russian railway imperialism in the 1890s – irrevocably destroyed the material foundations of Chinese hegemony. With Chinese military power eclipsed and no one foreign power strong enough to reconstitute an enduring alternative East Asian order along imperial lines, the stage was set for the immature anarchy that characterised northern China and Manchuria in the three decades after 1916, as Japanese imperialists, regional warlords and Chinese nationalists and communists each engaged in practices of competitive state-building with a view towards reasserting national (and in Japan's case, regional) hegemony. Only with the revival of Chinese military power – in both the Maoist 'people's war' that had helped instantiate mass Chinese nationalism and then in the CCP's later mastery of conventional manoeuvre warfare that had enabled its eventual triumph – was China's destabilising weakness at last overcome. The growth of mass nationalism, conscript armies and militarised authoritarian party-states, both in China and also in its most important erstwhile tributaries, Korea and Vietnam, would sustain East Asia's most destructive conflicts in the twentieth century's second half. At the same time, however, this development – alongside the birth of a precarious North-east Asian nuclear balance – would also guarantee the persistence of a regional order founded on the principle of sovereign anarchy, relegating to history the patterns of imperial hierarchy that had for so long characterised regional order.

Historical break points are never absolute, and the great East Asian transformation forms no exception to this rule. In October 1949, as routed Chinese nationalist forces completed their ignominious retreat to Taiwan, sections of the American government briefly floated the idea that the KMT regime might be deposed in Taipei and an American or UN-administered protectorate established in its place.[151] The idea was quickly scotched by elements in the Truman administration who hoped to establish a modus vivendi with Beijing, and became in any case a moot point in June 1950 following the onset of the Korean War and the ensuing rehabilitation of the KMT regime in Taiwan.[152] But while the Truman administration would not resurrect formal empire in East Asia, the new regional order over which it soon presided nevertheless contained undeniably imperial features. One year following the outbreak of the Korean War, the San Francisco Peace Treaty with Japan was signed, while by 1954 the foundations of America's 'hub and spokes' Pacific alliance structure were firmly in place.[153] Within this system, non-communist regimes throughout the Asia–Pacific region – most notably Japan and South Korea – agreed to commit to the United States' strategy of containing the 'barbarous' threat of Soviet and Chinese expansionism in exchange for American protection, as well as for preferential access to the massively lucrative American market.[154] Empire was dead in Asia, and the tributary state system of the Sinosphere was no more. But in its place had been established a less formal hierarchy with an 'imperial republic' at its apex, providing security guarantees and extensive commercial privileges to its regional clients in exchange for recognition of America's regional pre-eminence. The tensions between this informal imperium and the particularist aspirations informing an international order founded on the principle of sovereign anarchy would play out – both in East Asia and beyond – for decades to come. In many respects, they are yet to be resolved.

[151] P. Lowe, *The Origins of the Korean War* (London: Longman, 1997), pp. 134–5.
[152] *Ibid.*, p. 135.
[153] See generally K. Calder, 'Securing security through prosperity: The San Francisco system in comparative perspective', *The Pacific Review*, 17(1) (2004), 135–57.
[154] On the significance of civilisational identities and the cold war, and specifically the relationship between civilisational discourses and enduring Western tropes of racial supremacy in the Asia–Pacific region after 1945 and their influence on the hierarchical constitution of the 'hub and spokes' system, see C. Hemmer and P. J. Katzenstein, 'Why is there no NATO in Asia? Collective identity, regionalism, and the origins of multilateralism', *International Organization*, 56(3) (2002), 598.

PART III

Contemporary challenges and future trajectories of world order

10 | *The jihadist terrorist challenge to the global state system*

The situation cannot be rectified, as the shadow cannot be straightened when its source, the rod, is not straight either, unless the root of the problem is tackled. Hence it is essential to hit the main enemy who divided the *umma* into small and little countries and pushed it for decades into a state of confusion.[1]

> Osama bin Laden, 'A declaration of war against
> the Americans occupying the Land of the Two Holy Places'

In 1979, a new century was dawning on the Islamic calendar. Throughout the *umma*, the century's approach was greeted with excitement and apprehension, with a wave of events seeming to foretell an imminent Islamic resurgence. In February, the Ayatollah Khomeini had triumphantly returned from exile to Iran, while on 1 April, the Islamic Republic of Iran was officially proclaimed. November yielded further signs of political Islam's ascendancy. On 4 November, Iranian radicals stormed the American embassy in Tehran, precipitating a 444-day long stand-off that would cement a decades-long estrangement between the ayatollahs and Washington. On 20 November, in a provocation timed to coincide with the advent of the new Islamic century, approximately 200 militants briefly seized and held Islam's holiest place, the Grand Mosque of Mecca, using the occasion to denounce the Saudi monarchy for its perceived profligacy and Westernising tendencies.[2] Finally, as the year drew to a close, the Soviet Union's invasion of Afghanistan further inflamed Islamist sentiments. In the ensuing decade, Afghanistan's plight would evoke an enormous popular response throughout the Muslim world, with thousands of volunteers electing to fight alongside their Afghan brethren.[3] The Islamic Internationale's military contribution to the Soviet Union's eventual defeat

---

[1] Osama bin Laden, 'A declaration of war against the Americans occupying the Land of the Two Holy Places', 23 August 1996, cited in J. Burke, *Al Qaeda: Casting a shadow of terror* (London: I. B. Tauris, 2003), p. 149.

[2] For an outstanding account of the Mecca siege and its long-term consequences for regional and global order, see Y. Trofimov, *The Siege of Mecca: The 1979 uprising at Islam's holiest shrine* (New York: Anchor Books, 2008).

[3] Burke, *Al Qaeda*, p. 58.

would prove negligible.[4] But the Afghan jihad's broader significance would be inestimable, providing the forum for a convergence of émigré radicals who would go on to form the foundation for an ongoing jihadist challenge to international society.

From the Westphalian settlement onwards, European international society has been constituted by distinctive understandings of the 'religious' and the 'secular' as ontological categories. These understandings laid the basis first for the ecumenical sovereign international order that emerged after 1648, and then secondly for the more avowedly secular international society that grew out of the popular sovereignty revolutions of the nineteenth and twentieth centuries. With the Qing dynasty's demise and the disintegration of the Confucian social imaginary that accompanied it, this secularisation of international order was extended to East Asia. In 1924, with the abolition of the office of the caliphate and the rise of modernising dictatorships in Turkey, Iran and elsewhere, this process of secularisation also seemed destined to envelop the Islamic world. But from the 1970s onwards, the rise of transnational Islamic solidarities has confounded secular triumphalists, and the clash between radical Islam and global liberalism has emerged as a pivotal ideological faultline in world politics. Simultaneously, the past three decades have also witnessed the growth of transnational terrorism and expanding nuclear proliferation pressures, which have both been particularly pronounced in the Greater Middle East and South Asia. The growth of radical Islam and the increases in global violence interdependence embodied in transnational terrorism and nuclear proliferation respectively represent profound challenges to the contemporary world order's normative integrity and material underpinnings. At this stage, neither of these challenges approaches the scale of those that destroyed Christendom and the Sinosphere. But their existence nevertheless draws our attention to systemic vulnerabilities within the present order that must be comprehensively confronted if it is to endure.

This chapter evaluates the global state system's resilience in the face of armed challenges to its integrity, focusing specifically on the jihadist terrorist threat to world order. Constituting a tiny fraction of the world's Muslims, transnational jihadists have failed to acquire a broad popular support base since 9/11, while their dreams of a revived caliphate thus far remain nothing more than a totalitarian fantasy.[5] Al Qaeda's political failures notwithstanding, the jihadist phenomenon is nevertheless symptomatic of deeper legitimacy strains manifest in the contemporary world order that we ignore at our peril, and that are discussed in detail below. This chapter is divided into five sections. The first

---

[4] G. Kepel, *Jihad: The trail of political Islam* (London: I. B. Taurus, 2006), p. 147.

[5] On Al Qaeda's failure to cultivate a broad popular support base in the specific context of Iraq and the broader implications of this failing for jihadism as a political movement, see generally A. Phillips, 'How Al Qaeda lost Iraq', *Australian Journal of International Affairs*, 63(1) (2009), 64–84.

section reviews the contemporary world order's constitutional features, before then delineating the structural vulnerabilities that have latterly left it susceptible to challenge from radical Islamists. The second section situates radical Islamism within its broader historical context, foregrounding the ideological and geo-political forces that have nurtured its emergence and worldwide spread in the past four decades. The concept of radical Islamism encompasses a broad gamut of movements contesting various aspects of the present world order. Consequently, to make the following analysis conceptually and empirically manageable, the third section focuses only on the most extreme anti-systemic expression of radical Islamism, namely the transnational Salafi-jihadist terrorist threat embodied in Al Qaeda and its many offshoots. The context, content and character of the Salafi-jihadist threat are detailed in the third section, before an evaluation of the international community's post-9/11 response to this threat is advanced in the fourth section. I conclude with an interim assessment of Salafi-jihadism's current and prospective significance as a threat to world order, anticipating the broader discussion of the global state system's future that will conclude this inquiry.

The constitutional features and latent vulnerabilities of the global state system

The constitutional features of the global state system

Two aspects of the contemporary world order most emphatically distinguish it from its historical predecessors, and must be noted before we can consider its constitutional features in detail. First, unlike either Christendom or the Sinosphere, the global state system lacks overt cosmological foundations. From the Axial Age onwards, a recognition of the existence of a tension between the transcendent and the immanent realms had historically been central in informing the diverse conceptions of the good underpinning interna-tional orders.[6] Conversely, the global state system powerfully reflects Enlight-enment legacies in its constitutional norms, with the goals of human emancipation and material progress in the temporal world entirely replacing religious imperatives as the basis for international order. Secondly, and relat-edly, whereas imperial hierarchy formed a natural and unproblematic feature of past international orders, the global state system conversely grew out of a repudiation of empire as a legitimate form of political association. In both its avowedly 'this-worldly' orientation and its self-consciously egalitarian aversion to empire, the present world order is historically unusual – even exceptional – and this distinctiveness must be borne in mind both when evaluating its contemporary travails and contemplating its long-term prospects.

---

[6] Eisenstadt, 'The Axial Age', p. 296.

Given the extreme cultural diversity of constituent states, it is undeniably tempting to characterise the contemporary state system as being a practical association only, with shared rules of co-existence substituting for normatively 'thick' purposive values as the foundation for international co-operation.[7] In contrast to this view, I maintain that the global state system coheres around a constellation of constitutional norms and fundamental institutions that are sufficiently coherent as to warrant its designation as a purposive association, thereby enabling meaningful comparison with the historical orders already surveyed. At an identity-constitutive level, the present world order is dedicated to the explicitly profane concerns of enhancing the happiness, autonomy and freedom of individuals and nations as its primary *raison d'être*.[8] Popular eudemonism, or alternatively the cultivation of the conditions for human flourishing, forms the alpha and omega of the contemporary order.[9] Whereas in previous international orders, clerical and bureaucratic elites sought to align the actions of temporal authorities with divine imperatives, the global state system is by contrast exclusively profane in its orientation, reflecting its sponsors' faith in the power of unaided human reason to overcome the earthly challenges of war, poverty and tyranny.

The state system's eudemonistic orientation is reflected also in its ethical-prescriptive norms, which are institutionalised in the form of a universal human rights regime. This regime, which emerged in response to the Axis Powers' atrocities during World War II, explicitly repudiated the racial and civilisational hierarchies that had formerly underpinned European international society. In its place, the post-war architects of international order sought to institutionalise a liberal cosmopolitan moral culture, in which the rights-bearing individual was to become both the primary object of international moral concern and also the ultimate fountainhead of political legitimacy.[10] The ascendant values of egalitarianism and cosmopolitanism in the post-war era also found expression in the system's power-legitimating norms, most notably in the consolidation of a regime of international legal equality between sovereign states. International law retains its obligatory character precisely

---

[7] The classic interpretation of contemporary international society as a practical rather than purposive association remains T. Nardin, *Law, Morality, and the Relations of States* (Princeton University Press, 1983).

[8] On this point, I am again greatly indebted to Christian Reus-Smit's conception of both the moral purpose of the modern state and its impact on the design of the fundamental institutions of international society. See Reus-Smit, *The Moral Purpose of the State*, pp. 127–9.

[9] On the cultivation of the conditions for human flourishing as government's primary moral purpose in the modern era, and the associated conception of the political society as a society of mutual benefit, see Taylor, 'Modern social imaginaries', p. 93.

[10] See generally J. Donnelly, 'Human rights: A new standard of civilization?', *International Affairs*, 74(1) (1998), 1–23.

because states' obligations to obey are held to derive from the presumed grounding of international law in the consent of the contracting states.[11] Similarly, both citizens' obligations to observe domestic laws and governments' prerogatives to rule free from external interference are legitimised through reference to the perceived concordance between the laws of the state and the consent of the governed.[12]

The global state system's egalitarian aspirations and its rights-based moral culture radically distinguish it from the hierarchical international orders that preceded it. The historical distinctiveness of the state system holds equally when considering its fundamental institutions. In contrast to either the papal–imperial diarchy or the Chinese imperial monarchy, power in the contemporary world order is dispersed among almost 200 formally equal sovereign states. Following Christian Reus-Smit, I argue that authoritative power within this system is in turn mobilised and channelled primarily through the fundamental institutions of multilateralism and contractual international law.[13] These institutions reflect a conception of law as reciprocal accord, and thus differ markedly from authoritative institutions in both Christendom and the Sinosphere, which derived their legitimacy from their presumed concordance with cosmic sources of authority. Supplementing these fundamental institutions, the state system relies also on a plethora of rational–bureaucratic agencies incorporated within the UN system to co-ordinate international co-operation within specific issue areas. The products of a rationalised world culture, the authority of these agencies derives from the perception that their policies are guided by the expert knowledge of technocratic elites, and that the rational application of this knowledge will produce desired outcomes for the international community.[14] In both their internal constitution and methods of operation, these international organisations rely on technocratic standards of legitimacy that sit uneasily with the state system's democratic ethos. This inconsistency reflects a broader tension between the respective values of reason and consent informing the state system's constitution, one that in practice complicates but does not decisively stymie collective efforts to maintain international order.[15]

In its commitment to the values of liberty and reason, the global state system differs qualitatively from its predecessors. But in its reliance on coercive as well as authoritative institutions to sustain itself, the post-war order shares inevitable resemblances with the other orders considered in this study. The first and

---

[11] Reus-Smit, *The Moral Purpose of the State*, p. 130.   [12] *Ibid.*   [13] *Ibid.*, pp. 131–2.
[14] On the significance of a rationalised world culture as a feature of the contemporary world order, see generally Meyer, 'The world polity and the authority of the nation-state'.
[15] On this tension between democratic and technocratic bases of legitimacy with specific reference to the World Trade Organization, see generally D. C. Esty, 'The World Trade Organization's legitimacy crisis', *World Trade Review*, 1(1) (2002), 7–22.

most critical of the modern state system's coercive institutions consists of the localised monopolies on legitimate violence claimed by its constituent governments.[16] In a world lacking any supreme locus of recognised authority, the maintenance of order depends upon rulers' capacity to concentrate and cage coercive power within state institutions to a degree that has no parallels in the pre-industrial age.[17] Paradoxically, however, the vast destructiveness of modern conflicts has also testified to rulers' formidable capacities to destabilise international order through the immense coercive powers available to national governments. Consequently, local monopolies on force have been supplemented since 1945 by the maintenance of a collective capacity for marshalling force in defence of international order. In establishing the United Nations Security Council and empowering it to sanction the use of violence for the purposes of maintaining international peace and security, the UN's founding states recognised the necessity of supplementing the authoritative power of international institutions with the coercive power of the strongest sovereign states. Thus, while the institution of war remains a vital instrument for enforcing international order, the scope for its legitimate exercise has been limited to include only acts of self-defence, with responsibility for enforcing norms against aggression residing collectively with the UN Security Council.

Lastly, as with all international orders, the global state system remains profoundly shaped by its material context. Whereas Christendom and the Sinosphere were grounded in relatively static environments dominated by subsistence agriculture, the global state system conversely emerged in a milieu in which technological constraints on self-sustaining economic growth have supposedly been transcended. Similarly, whereas Christendom's poverty and the Sinosphere's pre-industrial character placed a definite ceiling on actors' destructive capacities, the advent of industrial and later nuclear warfare has removed all limits to the physical destruction rulers are collectively capable of unleashing. Reinforcing these technological breakthroughs, productive and destructive capacities have been further enhanced by ongoing processes of organisational rationalisation, with mobilisational networks cohering around the principles of kinship and patronage steadily losing importance to those based on contract or bureaucratic command, at least in the world's major centres of wealth and political power.

---

[16] On the evolution of the state's claim to exercise a Weberian monopoly on legitimate violence within its borders, see generally J. E. Thomson, *Mercenaries, Pirates, and Sovereigns: State-building and extraterritorial violence in early modern Europe* (Princeton University Press, 1994).

[17] On the limited control over organised violence exercised by forms of polity preceding the modern nation-state, see A. Giddens, *The Nation-State and Violence* (Cambridge: Polity Press, 1985), p. 57. On this point with specific reference to the monarchies of early modern Europe, see Kaiser, *Politics and War*, p. 135.

Of all the material contrasts between the contemporary world order and its predecessors, the most salient is its level of violence interdependence. Unlike its predecessors, the contemporary order emerged in an environment marked by an exceptionally high concentration and accumulation of armed force.[18] Violence in Christendom had of course been pervasive, but until the introduction of gunpowder and commercial mercenarism in the fourteenth century it was neither particularly intensive nor extensive in its reach. In the Sinosphere by contrast, coercive capacities were highly concentrated, China being for the most part militarily unassailable prior to the nineteenth century. But China's pre-industrial army and aversion to naval expansion from the fifteenth century onwards nevertheless limited the scale and reach of inter-polity violence within East Asia, at least until the Western encroachment from the 1840s onwards.[19] The global state system by contrast developed in an environment of pervasive and extensive high-level violence. The quantum leap in war's destructiveness initiated by the industrial and nuclear revolutions bears special emphasis precisely because it was the memory of industrial total war and the fear of nuclear Armageddon that spurred the United Nations' establishment in the first place. At the same time, the asymmetries in material power produced by these two developments have also formed an important component of the state system's material ballast. The state's concentration and monopolisation of capacities for large-scale organised violence, however imperfectly realised, constituted a fundamental material prerequisite for the world order that took shape after 1945, as did the restriction of nuclear weapons possession to an oligopoly of Great Powers invested in that order's survival. Like Christendom and the Sinosphere before it, then, the present order took shape in a very specific material as well as normative milieu (see Table 10.1). Equally, as with its historical precursors, the integrity of this order will be determined in part by the relative durability or transience of these material foundations.

The latent vulnerabilities of the global state system

Already I have alluded to several critical vulnerabilities that have left the global state system open to challenge. The first of these derives from the cultural particularity of the state system's normative foundations, and more specifically from its distinctly secular character. Superficially, the state system's promotion of popular eudemonism and self-determination presents as being eminently ecumenical, as does its emphasis on the sufficiency of reason over revelation as a guide for state action. However, on closer inspection, the global state system's

---

[18] As indicated previously, the distinction between the accumulation and concentration of the means of violence within social systems is drawn from Tilly, *Coercion, Capital, and European States*, pp. 19–20.

[19] See above, Ch. 6.

Table 10.1 *The global state system, 1945–present*

Normative complex	Governing institutional framework	Order-enabling material context
Identity-constitutive norms Popular eudemonism, human emancipation and augmentation of collective and individual capacities for self-determination	**Ordering framework** Sovereign state system collectively governed by permanent universal concert of formally equal states	**Aggregate capacities for production and destruction** Global-market capitalist system ordered within framework of states possessing industrial (and in some cases nuclear) capacities for violence
Ethical-prescriptive norms Cosmopolitan ethical framework institutionalised within global human rights regime	**Authoritative institutions** Global legal framework based on multilateralism and contractual international law, supplemented by issue-specific regimes claiming technocratic authority (e.g. WTO)	**Mobilisational networks** Dominance of state and inter-governmental bureaucracies and formally depoliticised global commercial networks
Power-legitimating norms National self-determination and international regime of sovereign equality	**Coercive institutions** State monopolies on violence supplemented by collective maintenance of order through use of force authorised by UN Security Council	**Violence interdependence** High concentration and high accumulation of coercive means (high violence interdependence)

normative complex bears the deep imprint of the West's historical experiences. Specifically, the unmooring of political authority from sacred referents that inaugurated the popular sovereignty revolution built on a series of developments in Western and Central Europe dating back to the Reformation. The revolutionaries' de-coupling of the polis from the cosmos after 1789 was made possible only by a prior ontological shift in the Western conception of religion, from a designation referring to an embodied community of believers towards one referring to an abstract body of doctrines and beliefs.[20] With the post-Reformation separation of beliefs and doctrines from practices and communities, the political unity of the temporal state could then substitute for the shattered religious unity of the Church as the primary mechanism of social integration.[21] Despite the enduring confessional intolerance of many European polities after Westphalia, this 'privatisation' of religion was crucial in enabling the revolutionaries to subsequently articulate an entirely secularised vision of political community, conceived as an institutionalised expression of the General Will and entirely shorn of divine legitimations.

From decolonisation onwards, the sovereign state, cast as the embodiment of the General Will and the chief vehicle for advancing human emancipation, has been the central institution sustaining world order. Despite its universality, however, its constitution has often implicitly reflected Western experiences in negotiating a working relationship between the sacred and mundane worlds. Popular beliefs in post-colonial polities concerning the appropriate relationship between religion and politics have frequently departed from the norms encoded into the Westphalian state system.[22] In the Atlantic state system, the secularisation of public life evolved endogenously and over centuries, with the traumas of Reformation and revolution eventually yielding a resolution in the form of the secular nation-state.[23] Conversely, in post-colonial states, secularisation was more often experienced as a traumatic state-directed assault, with authoritarian elites aggressively suborning religious actors and institutions to the imperatives of modernisation.[24] In domestically reproducing dominant Western understandings of the appropriate relationship between religion and the public sphere, many post-colonial governments have thus aggravated existing estrangements between state and society, leaving incumbent regimes acutely vulnerable to religiously informed oppositional discourses.[25] Internationally, meanwhile, the tendency for most Western governments to regard their own conceptions of secularism as being both normative and universally valid has been equally problematic, inhibiting from the outset accommodations with governments and political movements advocating alternative conceptions of the sacred/secular divide.

Following Elizabeth Shakman Hurd, I therefore maintain that the present world order remains infused with culturally particular authoritative understandings of religion and the secular as ontological categories, and that attempts

---

[20] Thomas, 'Taking religious and cultural pluralism seriously', pp. 821–3.

[21] *Ibid.*, p. 823.   [22] *Ibid.*, pp. 823–4.

[23] Although this generalisation should not obscure the different 'laicist' and 'Judeo-Christian' forms of secularity that have prevailed internally even within the Atlantic region. See Hurd, *The Politics of Secularism in International Relations*, Ch. 2.

[24] On this point with specific reference to the Muslim-majority countries of Turkey and Iran, see for example K. Armstrong, *Islam: A short history* (London: Phoenix, 2001), pp. 135–6.

[25] *Ibid.*

to universalise these understandings perversely prime the state system for religiously informed challenges to its legitimacy.[26] The state system's fragility is not, however, confined to the cultural particularity of its normative foundations, but extends also to the institutional frailty of many of its constituent states. As the arbitrary creations of former colonial powers, many post-colonial 'quasi-states' have lacked the institutional capacities necessary to adequately secure their citizens' material welfare.[27] Given the centrality of popular eudemonism to governments' legitimating frameworks under conditions of high modernity, such failures have crippled many governments' popular legitimacy.[28] The resulting vulnerability of these states to domestic challenge has consequently kept many of them dependent on former metropolitan powers for assistance in deterring both internal and external threats to regime security.[29] By their very existence, these socially disembedded client states expose a glaring discrepancy between an international regime of sovereign legal equality and the underlying reality of enduring relations of informal hierarchy.[30] Comparable instances of 'organised hypocrisy' have of course compromised previous international orders without necessarily contributing to systemic destabilisation.[31] But in an era in which international order has been explicitly organised around the values of popular eudemonism and self-determination, this inconsistency has proved particularly damaging, both to the legitimacy of post-colonial rentier states and to the state system's legitimacy more generally.

Finally, at the material level, the global state system threatens to become a victim of its own success, with the continuous economic expansion facilitated by that system now threatening to undercut its material preconditions. This danger has manifested itself in the accelerating global spread of capacities for mass destruction and disruption to both state and non-state actors. Recollecting briefly, the state system assumes both a high level of state control over capacities for organised violence, and the restriction of nuclear weapons possession to the established oligopoly of nuclear weapons states (NWS) recognised in the

---

[26] Hurd, *The Politics of Secularism in International Relations*, pp. 2–3.

[27] On the phenomenon of 'quasi-states' in world politics, see generally R. H. Jackson, *Quasi-States: Sovereignty, international relations, and the Third World* (Cambridge University Press, 1990).

[28] B. Badie and C. Royal, *The Imported State: The Westernization of the political order* (Stanford University Press, 2000), pp. 31–2; K. J. Holsti, *The State, War, and the State of War* (Cambridge University Press, 1996), p. 100.

[29] On this point with specific reference to pre-revolutionary Iran, see K. Armstrong, *The Battle for God: Fundamentalism in Judaism, Christianity, and Islam* (London: HarperCollins Publishers, 2000), pp. 231–2.

[30] On the dissonance between formal equality and informal hierarchy as an essential characteristic of the present world order, see generally D. A. Lake, 'Escape from the state of nature: Authority and hierarchy in world politics', *International Security*, 32(1) (2007), 47–79.

[31] See generally Krasner, *Sovereignty*.

Nuclear Non-Proliferation Treaty (NPT). Both of these preconditions have been progressively corroded as a result of global commercial expansion and technological innovation. Non-state actors' disruptive capacities have been enhanced by factors as diverse as the growing availability of automatic firearms and conventional high-explosives, together with the emergence of global media platforms offering alienated actors a means of leveraging individual acts of terrorism to secure worldwide publicity for their grievances.[32] Meanwhile, the dual-use nature of the knowledge and technologies associated with nuclear weapons has inevitably confounded diplomatic attempts to completely contain their spread, leading to a slow but inexorable corrosion of the Great Power oligopoly enshrined in the NPT.[33] The resulting growth in global violence interdependence has widened the gap between the state system's ordering institutions and its initial material preconditions, thereby further contributing to systemic instability.

The state system's implicit secularism, the prevalence of weak and unpopular post-colonial client states, and growing global violence interdependence are the three framing factors that inform the ensuing narrative. But before proceeding to a consideration of the jihadist challenge to international society, I must illuminate one final feature of the contemporary order that cuts across the ideational, institutional and material dimensions of my analysis, and that has also been integral in making possible the jihadist challenge. Specifically, throughout the post-war period, governments in the developed world have staked their popular legitimacy on their ability to deliver mass prosperity within the material context of industrial (and later, post-industrial) economies.[34] In the immediate post-war decades, this Fordist strategy of legitimation proved exceptionally effective in moderating social conflict and thus staving off the threat of a return to the political extremism of the inter-war period. Nevertheless, the intensified exploitation of the world's fossil-fuel reserves that this strategy also necessitated yielded a host of unintended consequences that now imperil world order. Fordism's ecological consequences and their prospective implications for world order will be briefly canvassed in my conclusion. For now, it is necessary to foreground Fordism's geopolitical consequences, in the form of the developed world's growing dependence on Middle Eastern oil reserves and the intensified Western military involvement in the region that has flowed from this. Following the 1973 oil shock, and as the true extent of the rich world's dependence on Middle Eastern oil first became

---

[32] J. Robb, *Brave New War: The next stage of terrorism and the end of globalization* (Hoboken, NJ: John Wiley and Sons, 2007), pp. 3–11.

[33] F. C. Iklâe, *Annihilation from Within: The ultimate threat to nations* (New York: Columbia University Press, 2006), pp. 55–7.

[34] E. Gellner, *Plough, Sword, and Book: The structure of human history* (London: Paladin Grafton Books, 1991), pp. 259–60.

apparent, First World governments were drawn ever more deeply into the region. With access to cheap energy deemed vital for sustaining the mass prosperity necessary to maintain social and political stability, the United States in particular was compelled to tie its fortunes closely to the region's major oil-producers.[35] The resulting entanglement of First World interests with those of autocratic local clients left the former dangerously exposed to the animus of dissident elements within these client states, paving the way for the eventual confrontation between global jihadism and international society.[36] The state system's secularism, post-colonial state weakness and increasing violence interdependence each left the present world order vulnerable to challenge. But it was the rich world's addiction to Middle Eastern oil, flowing in turn from its embrace of a Fordist legitimation strategy guaranteeing domestic stability through the promotion of mass prosperity, which largely determined the geographical origins and specific character of that challenge. It is thus towards a more extensive examination of the deep origins of the radical Islamist challenge that I now turn.

The deep origins of the jihadist threat to world order

In order to apprehend the nature of the jihadist challenge to international society, it is necessary to locate its origins within a long-standing clash between secular nationalism and political Islam that has intermittently raged since the caliphate's abolition in 1924. As early as the 1920s, the state system's privileging of the nation-state over the transnational community of believers prompted a countervailing mobilisation of the faithful in the *umma's* defence. In 1919–24, the *Khilafat* movement in British India lobbied unsuccessfully for the preservation of the Ottoman Empire's borders and the retention of the office of the caliphate as a symbol of global Islamic solidarity.[37] Equally, modernising leaders' attempts to confine Islam to the private sphere in countries such as Turkey and Iran generated fierce popular opposition, prefiguring a contest for the soul of the nation that would play out in many Muslim-majority states after decolonisation.[38] The clash between the Muslim Brotherhood and Nasser in post-colonial Egypt; the *Darul Islam* rebellion against Sukarno in Indonesia; the

---

[35] M. T. Klare, *Blood and Oil: The dangers and consequences of America's growing petroleum dependency* (New York: Metropolitan Books/Henry Holt and Co., 2004), p. 4.

[36] *Ibid.*, p. 27.

[37] See generally G. Minault, *The Khilafat Movement: Religious symbolism and political mobilization in India* (Delhi: Oxford University Press, 1999).

[38] Thus for example, in Atatürk's Turkey, the government's aggressive secularising policies (including laws forbidding women to wear the veil and dissolving the country's *madrasahs*) eventually sparked a rebellion led by the head of the Naqshbandi Sufi order. The rebellion was crushed, swiftly and efficiently, by Atatürk's army within two months. See Armstrong, *The Battle for God*, p. 192.

protracted contest between Iran's ayatollahs and the shah – each of these struggles constituted local expressions of a larger battle over the legitimate role of Islam in public life within Muslim-majority societies.

It was in the larger context of this global struggle that the Egyptian Islamist ideologue Sayyid Qutb formulated the philosophical basis for what would eventually mature into the jihadist challenge to world order. Qutb's philosophy began with the intuition that the corruption, poverty and injustice prevalent in Nasser's Egypt were symptomatic of a far broader spiritual malaise infecting the modern world. Following the Pakistani Islamist Mawlana Mawdudi, Qutb characterised the modern world as subsisting in a condition of *jahiliyya*, referring to the time of ignorance in which the tribes of Arabia had lived prior to the coming of the Prophet.[39] Qutb further averred that while the Enlightenment had conferred upon Europeans technological advantages that had facilitated their conquest of the Islamic world, Westerners remained preoccupied with the mundane to the exclusion of the transcendental, their culture crippled by a decadent emphasis upon material well-being and a corollary reliance on purely utilitarian and pragmatic reasoning.[40] Seen through this prism, Nasser's secularism and his socialist agenda appeared to embody a wholesale importation of the spiritual disease that had engulfed the West, and that now threatened to lead also to Islam's destruction if left unchallenged.[41]

While Qutbism originated as a repudiation of Nasserism, it was therefore always embedded within a far broader critique of Western secular modernity, and was for this reason from the beginning profoundly incompatible with the state system's constitutional values. For Qutb, the very notion of popular sovereignty was blasphemous, for true sovereignty could reside only with God.[42] Equally, while the faculty of reason enabled humans to apprehend and apply divine law as embodied in the Sharia, the very existence of this divine legal code rendered it unnecessary to grant legislative sovereignty to any human agency, be it either a single ruler or the broader populace.[43] In place of the

---

[39] On Mawdudi's influence on Qutb and his jihadist descendents, see Kepel, *Jihad: The trail of political Islam*, pp. 31–5.

[40] Wright cites Qutb's writings from his time based in Greeley, Colorado, on the essential banality and materialism of the Western mindset: 'The soul has no value to Americans … There has been a Ph.D. dissertation about the best way to clean dishes, which seems more important to them than the Bible or religion …'. Cited in L. Wright, *The Looming Tower: Al-Qaeda and the road to 9/11* (New York: Knopf, 2006), p. 27. Given the religiously devout character of the United States, particularly in the 1940s, this quote says much about Qutb's degree of estrangement and detachment from his host country at the time of his American sojourn.

[41] *Ibid.*, p. 28.

[42] On the supreme emphasis placed on the notion of divine sovereignty (*hakimiya*) within jihadist thought, which stemmed directly from the inspiration of Qutb and others, see F. A. Gerges. *The Far Enemy: Why the Jihad went global* (Cambridge University Press, 2005), pp. 4–5.

[43] *Ibid.*

modern emphasis on the promotion of collective and individual autonomy, Qutb stressed that true liberation was possible only through unquestioning submission to the will of God.[44] Moreover, where liberals and socialists both prioritised the promotion of popular eudemonism in the temporal world as government's primary purpose, Qutb instead subordinated materialistic considerations to the promotion of the *umma*'s spiritual well-being.[45]

Qutbism's incompatibility with the values underpinning the global state system was further evident in Qutb's hostility towards nationalism. Where Nasser's entire career was devoted to the aggrandisement of the Arab nation, Qutb and his followers regarded nationalism as a form of modern idolatry introduced by the West to divide and weaken the *umma*.[46] Certainly, within the Arab world, the artificiality of the borders imposed by the Mandate powers had been a genuine source of popular resentment. However, whereas even the most ardent Arab nationalists proposed only the unification of the Arab nation, Qutb harkened back to Islam's early history, during which time the entire Islamic community had been united under the caliph's temporal and spiritual leadership.[47] In embracing the vision of a (re)unified *umma*, Qutb rejected the territorial particularism characteristic of all sovereign state systems. This rejection flowed as a corollary of Qutb's denunciation of popular sovereignty and modern nationalism, further distinguishing his world-view from the values underpinning the post-war order.

From its inception, Qutbism thus constituted a holistic negation of the state system's normative complex. In place of the state system's emphasis on popular eudemonism and self-determination, Qutb proposed that humanity's purpose was to submit to God's will and to live in harmony with His divine commands. Where the state system crystallised around a rights-based regime of cosmopolitan ethics, Qutb found the Koran entirely self-sufficient as a guide for moral action. In place of power-legitimating norms authorising acceptance of state power due to its presumed concordance with the popular will, Qutbism insisted upon the supremacy and inviolability of divine sovereignty (*al hakimiya*), arguing that the only legitimate polities were those that implemented God's law as revealed in the Koran. Such a stance carried weighty implications for the global state system's fundamental institutions. If divine command was to replace popular consent as the basis for all authoritative institutions, then both the United Nations and the fundamental institutions of multilateralism and contractual international law would need to be torn down and replaced by a

[44] E. Goldberg, 'Smashing idols and the state: The Protestant ethic and Sunni radicalism', *Comparative Studies in Society and History*, 33(1) (1991), 16–17.

[45] *Ibid.*

[46] On Qutb's evolution away from an earlier support for Arab nationalism and towards a more unequivocally Islamist stance in the 1940s, see J. C. Zimmerman, 'Sayyid Qutb's influence on the 11 September attacks', *Terrorism and Political Violence*, 16(2) (2004), 228.

[47] Armstrong, *The Battle for God*, p. 241.

universal caliphate built upon the foundations of Sharia law.[48] Similarly, through Qutbist lights, the only legitimate violence was that undertaken in God's name; thus the modern state's monopoly on violence could only be legitimate when subordinated to God's law. In the meantime, Qutbism mandated individual believers to employ unlimited violence to overturn the existing order.

Qutb's critique of secular modernity – in both its Western form and also in its indigenised Nasserist incarnation – exerted a powerful influence on Egyptian Islamist dissidents even prior to his execution in 1966. In the years following Qutb's martyrdom, however, a series of developments conspired to further destabilise an already volatile regional environment, creating in their turn a permissive environment for Qutbism to mutate into a global anti-systemic movement. The first of these was Britain's decision to withdraw all British forces stationed east of the Suez Canal by December 1971. Whitehall's decision to liquidate Britain's remaining Asian military commitments was at the time eminently rational, acknowledging as it did the United Kingdom's limited capacity to maintain itself as a global power in the post-colonial era.[49] Nevertheless, its unintended consequences for the Greater Middle East – and particularly the Persian Gulf region – were profound. From 1820 onwards, Britain had served as the Persian Gulf's primary security guarantor, employing its unmatched naval power to establish itself as the regional hegemon and chief arbiter of relations between the region's feuding sheikhdoms.[50] The resulting arrangement had formed the basis of a remarkably durable peace in the region, albeit one that had inevitably favoured British interests. Consequently, Britain's military drawdown after 1971 created a post-imperial power vacuum in the Persian Gulf, inflaming local security rivalries in a region that was then rapidly growing in its global strategic and economic importance.[51]

Britain's imperial retreat coincided with a period of growing ideological ferment and strategic instability in the Middle East and South Asia. In 1967, the Six Day War had seen the humbling of Arab military power at the hands of Israeli forces, in the process widely discrediting Nasserism among large sections of the Arab public. Meanwhile 1971 saw Pakistan's defeat in the Indo-Pakistani war and East Pakistan's subsequent secession to form the new country of Bangladesh. In both the Middle East and South Asia, defeat at the hands of

---

[48] This antipathy towards the United Nations and the institution of international law has in fact subsequently been borne out by subsequent jihadist statements on this theme. On this broader point, see B. Mendelsohn, 'Sovereignty under attack: The international society meets the Al Qaeda network', *Review of International Studies*, 31(1) (2005), 62–3.

[49] P. M. Kennedy, *The Rise and Fall of British Naval Mastery* (London: A. Lane, 1976), p. 326.

[50] The origins of the *Pax Britannica* in the Persian Gulf are described in greater detail in J. Onley, *The Arabian Frontier of the British Raj: Merchants, rulers, and the British in the nineteenth-century Gulf* (New York: Oxford University Press, 2007), pp. 44–7.

[51] Klare, *Blood and Oil*, p. 42.

'infidels' brought with it agonising cultural introspection, as influential actors turned to the works of thinkers such as Qutb to make sense of their situation.[52] For those that subscribed to the Islamist philosophy that Qutb and others had helped forge, the defeats of 1967 and 1971 could only be perceived as divine punishment. Both East Jerusalem's capture and the mutilation of Pakistan were perceived as markers of divine displeasure, provoked by Muslims' embrace of the false idols of nationalism, socialism and secular modernity.[53] From this diagnosis flowed prescriptions for a radical transformation of Muslim-majority societies, entailing the overthrow of incumbent governments and the establishment in their place of authentically Islamic regimes governed by Sharia law.[54]

The late 1960s and early 1970s saw not only the steady growth of Islamist dissent, but also important military innovations that emerged as a direct response to the events of 1967 and 1971. Within the Middle East, the Six Day War indefinitely foreclosed the possibility of Palestine's liberation by conventional Arab forces. In response, Palestinian radicals increasingly turned to transnational terrorism, exploiting the international mobility afforded by the growth of civil aviation and the unprecedented publicity opportunities afforded by a global mass media to perpetrate a series of high-profile atrocities intended to advance their cause.[55] In South Asia, meanwhile, Pakistan's 1971 defeat had likewise exposed Islamabad's conventional military inferiority relative to India, prompting Prime Minister Ali Bhutto's subsequent frenzied effort to secure a Pakistani nuclear deterrent.[56] Neither the growth of Palestinian transnational terrorism nor the birth of the Pakistani nuclear programme were at the time directly linked to the radical Islamist sentiments that were meanwhile gaining momentum in both regions. Nevertheless, these military innovations exacerbated the instability arising from Britain's imperial retreat, as well as increasing systemic violence interdependence in ways that further destabilised international order.

By the early 1970s, a significant section of the Muslim world was being buffeted by the interweaving forces of imperial decline, escalating regional rivalries, military innovation and the growth of religiously inspired ideological dissent. The 1973 oil shock and its aftermath complicated matters still further. OPEC's decision during the Yom Kippur war to withhold oil supplies to Israel's First World allies sparked an overnight quadrupling of world oil prices, dramatising for the first time the extent of the developed world's dependency on

---

[52] On this point, see generally Kepel, *Jihad: The trail of political Islam*, pp. 60–5.

[53] Armstrong, *The Battle for God*, p. 243.   [54] *Ibid.*

[55] On the internationalisation of terrorism from the 1960s onwards, of which Palestinian terrorism formed the most sophisticated expression, see generally B. Hoffman, 'The internationalization of terrorism' in B. Hoffman (ed.), *Inside Terrorism* (New York: Columbia University Press, 1998), pp. 67–86.

[56] S. Ahmed, 'Pakistan's nuclear weapons program: Turning points and nuclear choices', *International Security*, 23(4) (1999), 183.

Middle Eastern oil.[57] The significance of the oil shock for jihadism's subsequent emergence was twofold. First, in highlighting the developed world's dependence on Middle Eastern oil, the oil shock confirmed the Persian Gulf's inestimable strategic importance, stimulating America's gradual emergence as the region's chief security guarantor. Still nursing its wounds from Vietnam, the United States initially abjured direct military involvement in the Gulf, preferring to delegate responsibility for maintaining regional stability primarily to the shah of Iran.[58] Augmenting America's relationship with the shah, Washington also sought after 1973 to renegotiate and strengthen its relationship with Saudi Arabia. This renegotiation would eventually include large-scale recycling of petro-dollars into investments in America, as well as the establishment of both a Joint Commission on Economic Co-operation and a Joint Security Co-operation Commission between the two countries.[59] Following the Iranian revolution and the Soviet invasion of Afghanistan, America's military involvement in the region would become even more intensive. Thus in 1980, the Carter Doctrine rendered explicit America's security guarantees to its Persian Gulf allies, a commitment that was further strengthened with CENTCOM's subsequent establishment in 1983.[60] Incrementally, America thus succeeded Britain as the region's primary security guarantor, eventually presiding over an informal empire of alliances with regional potentates every bit as elaborate as that which had once assured the security of the Raj's Arabian frontier.

In addition to stimulating the growth of an informal American empire in the Persian Gulf, the second consequence of the 1973 oil shock was to cultivate the development of a transnational Islamic imaginary. The overnight quadrupling of oil prices following OPEC's embargo produced a massive financial windfall for the oil-rich Gulf monarchies. Following the first oil shock, the region's strategic and economic centre of gravity thus shifted away from the radical Arab republics and towards monarchies such as Saudi Arabia. The Gulf States had long emphasised the primacy of tribal and religious themes in their legitimating strategies, and had historically regarded Pan-Arabism and socialism with profound unease.[61] With the enormous influx of wealth following the first oil shock, Saudi Arabia in particular sought to seize the initiative by subsidising efforts to proselytise its own creed of Wahhabi Islam throughout the Muslim world.[62]

---

[57] Klare, *Blood and Oil*, p. 11.
[58] R. A. Clarke, *Against All Enemies: Inside America's war on terror* (New York: Free Press, 2004), p. 37.
[59] On this point, see R. Bronson. *Thicker Than Oil: America's uneasy partnership with Saudi Arabia* (Oxford University Press, 2006), pp. 125–8.
[60] Klare, *Blood and Oil*, pp. 45–7.
[61] On the ideological foundations of the conservative Gulf monarchies, see generally F. G. Gause, *Oil Monarchies: Domestic and security challenges in the Arab Gulf States* (New York: Council on Foreign Relations Press, 1994), p. 25.
[62] Kepel, *Jihad: The trail of political Islam*, p. 70.

Saudi efforts from the 1970s to secure conservative Islam's ascendancy over radical populism were not unprecedented, with the monarchy having established the World Muslim League as a foil to Nasserism as far back as 1962.[63] However, following the oil crisis, a range of forces converged to knit together the material foundations of a transnational Islamic imaginary. Within the sparsely populated Gulf States, the oil boom dramatically expanded these states' demand for foreign labour. The resulting increase in short-term migration to the Gulf accelerated processes of regional integration, with states such as Egypt, Jordan and even Syria becoming increasingly dependent on financial remittances from citizens temporarily domiciled in the Gulf States.[64] For Muslim migrant labourers from the Middle East and South Asia, who constituted the majority of the Gulf States' guest workers, temporary residence in the Land of the Two Holy Places and exposure to Wahhabi Islam both served to raise their awareness of the Islamic dimension of their identity.[65] When these labourers returned home they consequently became conduits for the transmission of a heightened sense of Islamic self-awareness back to their home societies.[66] Finally, the exponential growth in migrant remittances within the Islamic world stimulated the expansion of an under-regulated and largely informal *hawala* system of international financial transactions.[67] The growth of this *hawala* system, which complemented the equally prodigious rise of a formal international Islamic banking system, provided a further layer of connective tissue integrating the *umma* within a far denser web of transnational linkages than had previously existed.[68]

During the 1970s, there thus emerged a historical constellation in the Persian Gulf that at least bore superficial resemblances to the pattern that had prevailed in the century up to 1930. On the one hand, order in the region was increasingly the responsibility of America, which had succeeded Britain as the Anglophone hegemon, and which was increasingly relying on forward-deployed naval forces and 'informal' imperial arrangements with local clients to secure its vital interests there. On the other hand, meanwhile, the Gulf States' economic dynamism had worked to partially revive an Islamic ecumene composed of transnational circuits of labour, capital and ideas linking the Middle East to Muslim South Asia. Similarly, just as the Raj had been forced to contend with anti-imperialist sentiments couched in the idiom of Islamic revivalism, so too was American hegemony also attracting the Islamists' ire even prior to the *annus mirabilis* of 1979. What distinguished the two situations from one another was both the magnitude of America's interests in the Gulf and the programmatic character of the Islamists' opposition to the American presence. Whereas Britain maintained its dominance in the Gulf primarily to secure its lines of communication and supply to the subcontinent, by the 1970s access to Middle Eastern oil had become central to the global economy and thus pivotal

---

[63] *Ibid.*, p. 52.   [64] *Ibid.*, p. 73.   [65] *Ibid.*   [66] *Ibid.*   [67] *Ibid.*, p. 70.   [68] *Ibid.*

to America's ability to maintain world order.[69] Similarly, with the fleeting exception of the *Khilafat* movement (1919–24), Britain had rarely confronted concerted Islamic opposition throughout its dominions, but had instead generally encountered localised resistance from traditionalist sects and charismatic reactionaries who could generally be subdued through either co-optation or repression.[70] Conversely, from the late 1970s, there emerged a growing transnational movement of Islamist radicals united in their subscription to a profoundly anti-systemic ideology, and also viscerally opposed to both American hegemony and the larger system of states that it supported. Fittingly, just as Afghanistan had proved a running sore for the British Empire, so too would it also serve as the cradle for a global movement dedicated to the humbling of her American successor.

The jihadist challenge to international society: Its development and character

The legacy of the first Afghan jihad

Throughout the 1960s and 1970s, Qutbism exerted a powerful influence on Islamist dissidents throughout the Muslim world. But it was only with the catalysing influence of the Afghan jihad that Qutb-inspired radicals began to coalesce into a transnational movement. The Afghan jihad's role in facilitating global jihadism's genesis has been exhaustively explored elsewhere, so I will confine myself here to an overview of the key perceptual, organisational and ideological mutations that the conflict stimulated among the émigré Islamists it attracted.[71] At a perceptual level, the war brought militants together from dozens of countries, nurturing a heightened awareness of their common struggles against secular governments. Despite their varied local circumstances, militants found common cause in Qutbism's core propositions. Militants were united both in their hostility towards Westernising tendencies in their home societies, and also in their privileging of divine sovereignty over human sovereignty as the governing principle of a properly constituted polity.[72] In being exposed to like-minded actors suffering similar experiences of

---

[69] On Britain's strategic motivations for establishing hegemony in the Persian Gulf in the nineteenth century, see Onley, *The Arabian Frontier of the British Raj*, p. 217. On the significance of control of the Persian Gulf's oil supplies for America's ability to realise its economic and strategic interests, see Klare, *Blood and Oil*, pp. 17–22.

[70] On the growth of the *Khilafat* movement as a challenge to British authority in the Indian subcontinent after 1918, see J. M. Landau, *The Politics of Pan-Islam: Ideology and organization* (Oxford: Clarendon Press, 1990), pp. 203–15.

[71] See for example Gerges, *The Far Enemy*, Ch. 2; and more generally S. Coll, *Ghost Wars: The secret history of the CIA, Afghanistan, and bin Laden, from the Soviet invasion to September 10, 2001* (New York: Penguin Press, 2004).

[72] Gerges, *The Far Enemy*, p. 85.

persecution at home, the émigré militants experienced a significant perceptual shift whereby the global dimension of their individual struggles became more boldly illuminated. This perceptual shift was reinforced by the intense social bonds and camaraderie forged among the Islamists as a result of their shared experiences in training camps and on the battlefield.[73] By the end of the Soviet intervention, most jihadists remained focused on resuming their separate struggles back home, and the imperative of confronting the entire modern international order had yet to emerge as a shared goal.[74] But the broadening of jihadist horizons and the social connections forged as a result of the Afghan jihad had now made this development possible.

The Afghan conflict also yielded important organisational and ideological innovations within the jihadist community. At the organisational level, activists such as Osama bin Laden and his mentor Abdullah Azzam worked diligently to co-ordinate and manage the emerging transnational cadre of Islamic militants.[75] As early as 1984, Azzam established the Maktab al-Khadamat (MAK, or Services Bureau) in Peshawar, Pakistan, in which thousands of volunteers were received, trained, housed and supervised prior to deployment in Afghanistan.[76] Complementing this effort, bin Laden established the Al-Faruq military college, a specialised training camp designed to equip volunteers with rigorous military training with a view towards turning out senior officers capable of fighting on behalf of Muslims in Afghanistan and a range of other theatres.[77] Although the relationship between these efforts and Al Qaeda's subsequent emergence was far from one of linear evolution, they nevertheless established an important precedent for future efforts to organise and co-ordinate transnational networks of jihadist militants.

Finally, the Afghan jihad also critically accelerated processes of ideological radicalisation and cross-pollination in jihadist circles. Fawaz Gerges notes that one of the most significant by-products of the conflict was the synthesis it effected between the militant Qutbism of Egyptian Islamists and the puritanical Salafi-Wahhabism of the Arabian Peninsula.[78] The Salafi-Wahhabist strain of Islam that had prevailed in the Arabian Peninsula from the eighteenth century was traditionally an introverted faith, whose adherents advocated a return to the more pure form of Islam said to have been practised by the Prophet and his early companions (*salaf*).[79] This strain of Islam, which bin Laden subscribed to and which had sustained the Saudi monarchy from its establishment, was traditionally isolationist in its international orientation and politically quietist in character.[80] However, in the context of the Afghan jihad, the evangelical puritanism and scriptural literalism of the Salafis fused with the Qutbists' revolutionary agenda and programmatic anti-Westernism.[81] Once again, the

---

[73] *Ibid.*   [74] *Ibid.*, p. 86.   [75] Burke, *Al Qaeda: Casting a shadow of terror*, p. 69.   [76] *Ibid.*
[77] Gerges, *The Far Enemy*, p. 134.   [78] *Ibid.*, p. 86.   [79] *Ibid.*, pp. 131–2.   [80] *Ibid.*
[81] *Ibid.*, pp. 132–5.

import of this development was not immediately apparent, but it nevertheless signified an assimilation of bin Laden into the Qutbist mainstream, and also a further radicalisation of the thinking of those who would subsequently form Al Qaeda's nucleus.

The 'end of history' and the onset of the clash between jihadism and international society

By the end of the Afghan conflict an embryonic global jihadist movement had thus emerged, composed of Sunni radicals whose values totally opposed the state system's normative underpinnings. Nevertheless, this movement's subsequent embrace of anti-systemic violence did not flow automatically from their beliefs, but rather arose in response to several momentous developments that accompanied the cold war's end. The first of these was the growth of transformational liberalism following the cold war's peaceful conclusion. With the fall of the Berlin Wall, political leaders on both sides of the Atlantic anticipated the consolidation of a world order marked by both the strengthening of international institutions and the universal spread of democracy and market capitalism. The post-war order had of course been heavily imbued with the liberal values of its Western patrons, but these had unavoidably been circumscribed by the Soviet Union's military power and ideological influence. Similarly, in the immediate post-colonial period, newly independent states in Asia and Africa had successfully sponsored the growth of a 'negative sovereignty regime' that ostensibly curtailed old hierarchies of privilege and deference associated with defunct Western 'standards of civilisation'.[82] However, with the Soviet Union's collapse and the implosion of a number of post-socialist and post-colonial states in the cold war's aftermath, a newly permissive Western attitude towards state sovereignty began to take form. Throughout the 1990s, the 'liberalism of restraint' gave way to a 'liberalism of imposition', with Atlantic policy elites increasingly invoking 'democratic' and 'market' standards of civilisation in their interactions with weaker states.[83] This belief in the universality of liberal ideals and the inevitability of their worldwide extension was in practice qualified by Western states' limited willingness and ability to impose their preferred system of government on weaker countries. But the

---

[82] See generally Philpott, *Revolutions in Sovereignty*, Ch. 8.

[83] On the distinction between the 'liberalism of restraint' and the 'liberalism of imposition' for contemporary global politics in the post-cold war period, see generally G. Sorensen, 'After the security dilemma: The challenges of insecurity in weak states and the dilemma of liberal values', *Security Dialogue*, 38(3) (2007), pp. 367–8. On the ascendancy of democratic and market 'standards of civilisation' as important aspects of the transformational liberalism that emerged following the cold war's end, see respectively C. Hobson, 'Democracy as civilisation', *Global Society*, 22(1) (2008), 75–95; and B. Bowden and L. Seabrooke (eds.), *Global Standards of Market Civilization* (London: Routledge, 2006).

growth of a more uncompromising and transformationalist brand of liberalism nevertheless stood out as one of the decade's dominant features, and formed a critical part of the backdrop against which the jihadist challenge subsequently played out.

Complementing the growth of transformational liberalism, and indeed providing its geopolitical foundation, was the advent of US unipolarity. With the Soviet Union's collapse, America secured a position of predominance unprecedented in the history of modern world politics.[84] Significantly, however, while the post-cold war 'peace dividend' saw the partial drawdown of US forces in Western Europe and East Asia, the 1990s conversely saw a ramping up of America's military presence in the Persian Gulf. Saddam Hussein's 1990 invasion of Kuwait had prompted a massive response from an America anxious to prevent Iraq from acquiring control over more than a quarter of the world's crude-oil reserves, and US forces had led a thirty-member coalition to swift victory in expelling Saddam from Kuwait six months after his invasion.[85] Critically, however, Saddam's survival following the uprisings that accompanied his defeat necessitated a continuing US military presence in the region. Post-war revelations concerning the scope and sophistication of Iraq's weapons of mass destruction (WMD) programmes supplied an additional warrant for the regime's continuing isolation, while Saddam's intransigence in his dealings with UN weapons inspectors provided the rationale for repeated Anglo-American air-strikes against Iraq in the years that followed.[86] Throughout the 1990s, the one-time seat of the Abbasid caliphate was thus rendered a besieged semi-sovereign entity, with vast areas in the north and south subject to internationally enforced 'no fly zones' at the same time that the bureaucracy of the Iraqi petro-state withered for want of revenue.[87] That this quarantine was being enforced by 'infidel' forces operating primarily from Saudi Arabia served to further aggravate many Muslims, most particularly those that would soon form the vanguard of the global jihad.[88]

Finally, the jihadist challenge to international society was powerfully conditioned by Islamist parties' continued failure to seize power in Muslim-majority countries during the 1990s. Flushed with success from victory in Afghanistan, many jihadist émigrés returned home in the early 1990s determined to overthrow 'apostate' regimes and erect genuinely Islamic states in their place.[89] But with the exception of Afghanistan, Sudan and parts of a now stateless Somalia, jihadist efforts yielded few successes, and by the mid-1990s,

---

[84] On the magnitude of America's material preponderance in the post-cold war period, see S. G. Brooks and W. C. Wohlforth, 'American primacy in perspective', *Foreign Affairs*, 81 (4) (2002), 21–3.

[85] Klare, *Blood and Oil*, p. 50.   [86] *Ibid.*, p. 53.   [87] *Ibid.*

[88] G. Kepel, 'The origins and development of the jihadist movement: From anti-communism to terrorism', *Asian Affairs*, XXXIV(2) (2003), 98.

[89] *Ibid.*, pp. 100–3.

the jihadists' inability either to topple incumbent apostate regimes or to export the jihad to foreign theatres was starkly evident.[90] Despite their lack of popular legitimacy, incumbent regimes in Algeria, Egypt and elsewhere proved eminently capable of suppressing the Islamist threat.[91] Faced with a strategic impasse at home, a radicalised transnational fraction of the Islamist movement underwent profound changes that yielded the global jihadist challenge to international society. The first of these entailed a reorientation away from a focus on the 'near' enemy of incumbent regimes in the Muslim world, and towards a concentration on the 'far' enemy that sponsored these local tyrants, and thus was perceived as being ultimately responsible for Muslims' subjugation. For bin Laden and his followers, attacks on the 'near enemy' were futile while 'apostate' governments retained the confidence of their 'infidel' patrons. Only once this alliance between apostate clients and infidel patrons was broken could the former be overthrown, and liberation be achieved through submission to legitimately constituted Islamic governments.[92]

This reorientation towards the 'far' enemy corresponded with important ideological shifts in the jihadist camp. As with more mainstream Islamists, global jihadists decried the existence of incumbent autocratic governments, whom they regarded as tyrannical on account of rulers' refusal to bind themselves adequately to the observance of Sharia law.[93] Similarly, they attributed the evils of earthly tyrants in part to the moral failings of the Muslim masses, who had become alienated from Allah and thus susceptible to the false promises of worldly despots.[94] In contrast to mainstream Islamist opinion, however, the jihadists placed much greater emphasis on foreign malevolence in accounting for the *umma's* travails. For the jihadists, imported notions of self-determination and nationalism served only to estrange Muslims from Allah and from one another.[95] Moreover, these innovations were held to have been deliberately imposed by the West to foment Muslim disunity and thus facilitate their continuing subordination.[96] In recalling the imagined unity of the early caliphate, the global jihadists sought to transcend the parochialism of their more nationally focused counterparts, and mobilise a transnational community of believers in armed struggle against their common infidel enemies.

The increasingly global character of the jihadists' outlook soon found expression in the worldwide breadth of their armed campaign. From 1996 onwards, Al Qaeda pursued a sustained campaign of 'hit and run' operations targeted at American interests overseas. This campaign, including attacks on US military facilities in Saudi Arabia in 1996, the 1998 African embassy bombings and the attack on the USS *Cole* in October 2000, aimed to ratchet up the costs of America's military presence within the Middle East until such time that

---

[90] *Ibid.*   [91] *Ibid.*, pp. 98–103.   [92] *Ibid.*
[93] M. S. Doran, 'Somebody else's civil war', *Foreign Affairs*, 81(1) (2002), 25.   [94] *Ibid.*, p. 26.
[95] Mendelsohn, 'Sovereignty under attack', p. 60.   [96] *Ibid.*, p. 61.

America resolved to leave the region.[97] With their umbilical cord to their infidel sponsors severed, the jihadists anticipated that abandoned 'apostate' regimes would then be vulnerable to popular revolutions led by the jihadist vanguard.[98] Once state power was seized in multiple states, the ground would then be clear for the establishment of a revived caliphate. A spiritually purified and politically unified *umma*, empowered by the Gulf States' financial wealth and also by the Muslim world's control over much of the world's energy reserves, would then restore Muslims to the privileged position they had enjoyed for the first millennium following the Prophet's revelation.[99]

The strategic logic informing the global jihad, while deeply flawed, was thus relatively straightforward. But to reduce jihadist violence exclusively to the product of instrumental reasoning would be to misapprehend its true nature. For the jihad was conceived as a spiritual struggle between the forces of faith and unbelief, as well as a temporal struggle against Western domination. Accordingly, jihadists imbued their violence with existential as well as instrumental significance. Specifically, jihadist violence aimed to manifest the jihadists' religious devotion, as well as ideally inspiring other Muslims to arms in the *umma's* defence.[100] In this respect, jihadist violence aimed to instantiate and consolidate a transnational Islamic identity among the world's Muslims, to be conceived in terms of its total opposition to the US-dominated world order. The post-oil-shock surge in transnational movements of people, capital and ideas throughout the Indian Ocean littoral had already done much to facilitate the emergence of a nascent global Islamic identity. What the jihadists hoped to do was to infuse this identity with an ethos of existential bellicosity, polarising the world between a mobilised *umma*-in-arms and the doomed supporters of the established order.[101]

By the eve of the millennium, globalisation had compressed the strategic distance between North and South, as well as rendering the 'hard-shelled' sovereign state increasingly permeable. Simultaneously, a combination of state failure and accelerating technological innovation was incrementally corroding the state monopolies on organised violence upon which international

---

[97] Kepel, 'The origins and development of the jihadist movement', p. 104.

[98] Gerges, *The Far Enemy*, p. 149.

[99] This grand strategy emerged prior to 9/11, but it has continued to inform jihadist strategy in the wake of the Iraq War. The latest iteration of this strategy involves the following four steps: (1) expulsion of Coalition forces from Iraq; (2) establishment of an Islamic emirate in Iraq or part thereof; (3) extension of the jihad to secular regimes neighbouring Iraq; (4) engagement in an armed confrontation against Israel, and presumably with the West more generally. See English translation of Ayman Al-Zawahiri's letter to Abu Musab Al-Zarqawi (cited 5 November 2007), http://www.weeklystandard.com/Content/Public/Articles/000/000/006/203gpuul.asp?pg=1.

[100] J. J. Yates, 'The resurgence of jihad and the specter of religious populism', *SAIS Review*, XXVII(1) (2007), 134. See also Phillips, 'How Al Qaeda lost Iraq', 68.

[101] Doran, 'Somebody else's civil war', p. 23.

order relied. Within this protean context, jihadist ideology explicitly challenged the state system's secular constitutional norms, while jihadist violence meanwhile dramatised states' increasingly tenuous monopolies over the use of force. In both its ideas and its practice, jihadism thus challenged both the authoritative and the coercive foundations of world order. Moreover, while it had arisen out of a convergence of long-standing ideological, institutional and material trends, by the late 1990s the jihadist threat to world order was immediate. But in the dying days of the twentieth century, most world leaders failed to appreciate the threat's urgency, and their response to jihadism was unco-ordinated, localised, sporadic and desultory. Then came 9/11.

Global jihadism versus the liberal world order, 2001–present

The day after: International society responds to 9/11

For the preceding quarter of a century, Islamist rebellions had roiled large sections of the Muslim world, and had intermittently struck painful blows against Western interests overseas. Nevertheless, it was only with the 9/11 attacks that the proximity and immediacy of the jihadist threat became universally apparent. Even in their death throes, neither Christendom nor the Sinosphere had experienced an event that so vividly dramatised their fragility as did the 9/11 attacks for the liberal world order. Equally, however, neither of these orders demonstrated the same capacity for defensive adaptation as was evident in the state system's immediate response to the attacks. Beyond the broad outpouring of international sympathy for America that followed 9/11, the assault also catalysed a range of more tangible responses to the jihadist threat. Under American leadership, a suite of policies were introduced or expanded under UN auspices to restrict Al Qaeda's access to personnel, money and matériel.[102] With the convening of the 1540 Committee, the UN Security Council additionally founded an institution explicitly charged with the task of preventing non-state actors from acquiring WMD.[103] Similarly, the founding of the UN Counter Terrorism Committee (CTC) and later the Counter Terrorism Committee Executive Directorate (CTED) also signified the UN's new-found willingness to create agencies charged specifically with the task of defending the state system from jihadist terrorism.[104]

---

[102] On this point, see generally E. Rosand, 'The UN-led multilateral institutional response to jihadist terrorism: Is a global counter-terrorism body needed?', *Journal of Conflict and Security Law*, 11(3) (2007), 399–427.

[103] On the nature and functioning of the 1540 Committee, see G. H. Oosthuizen and E. Wilmhurst, *Terrorism and Weapons of Mass Destruction: United Nations Security Council Resolution 1540*, Briefing Paper 04/01 (London: Chatham House, 2004).

[104] On these institutions, see Rosand, 'The UN-led multilateral institutional response to jihadist terrorism', pp. 409–11.

In addition to strengthening the UN's institutional capacities, the international community also renewed its effort to delegitimate terrorism and state sponsorship of terrorism in the wake of the attacks. In place of the permissive negative sovereignty regime of the immediate post-colonial period, by the 1990s a more demanding conception of 'sovereignty as responsibility' had found increasing favour in the developed world.[105] This trend was reinforced after 9/11.[106] In keeping with this emerging emphasis on sovereignty as responsibility, the United States and its allies successfully sponsored UN Security Council Resolution 1373 under the authority of Chapter VII of the UN Charter.[107] This resolution imposed obligations on all member states to prevent or suppress terrorist activities within their borders.[108] In establishing explicit obligations on member states to suppress jihadist terrorism, the Security Council thus reaffirmed norms upholding the state's claim to exert a monopoly on legitimate violence, while simultaneously aligning the prerogatives of state sovereignty more closely with the imperative of defending the state system against jihadist violence.

Finally, the United States acted swiftly and decisively in October 2001 to drive Al Qaeda from its Afghan sanctuaries. Deprived of its sanctuaries and also of the infrastructure that had previously been such a powerful drawcard for other militant groups, Al Qaeda's capacity to plan major attacks was significantly degraded after the US invasion, as was its ability to attract the allegiance of others within the jihadist diaspora through the provision of in-theatre

---

[105] On the prevalence of a negative sovereignty regime in the immediate post-colonial period, see Jackson, *Quasi-States*, pp. 40–7. The concept of sovereignty as responsibility as it developed in the 1990s related primarily to the emerging practice of humanitarian intervention, with the principle of the 'responsibility to protect' receiving broad endorsement by the international community at the World Summit in 2005. See A. J. Bellamy, 'Whither the responsibility to protect? Humanitarian intervention and the 2005 World Summit', *International Affairs*, 20(2) (2006), 143–69.

[106] From 9/11 onwards, the notion of sovereignty as responsibility has been increasingly extended to the areas of counter-terrorism and counter-proliferation. On the application of the principle of sovereignty as responsibility to the area of counter-proliferation in the post-9/11 era, see generally J. Joseph, 'The exercise of national sovereignty: The Bush administration's approach to combating weapons of mass destruction', *The Nonproliferation Review*, 12(2) (2005), 373–87.

[107] United Nations Security Council, SC Res. 1373 (2001), S/RES/1373, New York, 28 September 2001.

[108] These responsibilities included obligations to suppress terrorist financing, obligations to deny safe haven to terrorist organisations, obligations to implement rigorous border controls to constrict the transnational movement of terrorists and obligations to refrain from providing either active or passive support to terrorist organisations. For further details on the obligations imposed on member states by UNSC Resolution 1373, see generally E. Rosand, 'Security Council Resolution 1373, the Counter-Terrorism Committee, and the fight against terrorism', *The American Journal of International Law*, 97(2) (2003), 333–41.

training and financial assistance.[109] Intelligence acquired as a result of Operation Enduring Freedom (OEF) also assisted in both the subsequent assassination or capture of leading Al Qaeda cadres and the thwarting of at least one major follow-up jihadist attack in Singapore in December 2001.[110] The decimation of the Taliban and regional jihadist allies such as the Islamic Movement of Uzbekistan (IMU) further weakened the jihadists, while the inauguration of a new Afghan government and the country's diplomatic rehabilitation at least initially held out the prospect of long-term regional stabilisation.[111]

In contrast to either Christendom or the Sinosphere, the state system after 9/11 therefore initially seemed to respond rapidly and effectively to an armed assault on its integrity. This adaptive capacity was illustrated through both the post-9/11 renovation of the UN's security architecture described above, and the complementary moves to revise standards of legitimate statehood to more effectively proscribe state sponsorship of terrorism.[112] Equally, the broad international support for the United States' overthrow of the Taliban also disclosed a strong collective willingness to condone the use of force to confront the jihadist threat. The magnitude of the destruction wrought by Al Qaeda on 9/11 evoked worldwide concern not least because of the open challenge it presented to the sovereign state's claim to exert a Weberian monopoly on legitimate violence. Consequently, while the struggle against global jihadism was cast as a struggle to preserve the authority of states and the state system from the violence of non-state predators, broad-based diplomatic support for counter-terrorism measures was generally forthcoming. However, to the extent that the jihadist threat was conceived more narrowly as a challenge to US power in the Greater Middle East, states' interests and therefore their actions were likely to be more varied. That the 9/11 attacks were, by their authors' conception, an assault on both the state system and also on America's informal empire in the Persian Gulf complicated matters considerably, ensuring that 9/11's long-term

M. Kenney, 'From Pablo to Osama: Counter-terrorism lessons from the war on drugs', *Survival*, 45(3) (2003), 195. Kenney does nevertheless qualify this observation by suggesting that while Operation Enduring Freedom certainly weakened Al Qaeda's offensive capabilities, its defensive strengths – in terms of covertness, elusiveness and adaptability – may have been strengthened by the dispersal of Al Qaeda operatives away from their Afghan redoubts.

[110] On this point, see R. Suskind, *The One Percent Doctrine: Deep inside America's pursuit of its enemies since 9/11* (New York: Simon & Schuster, 2006), p. 57.

[111] On this point, see S. E. Cornell, 'The narcotics threat in Greater Central Asia: From crime-terror nexus to state infiltration?', *China and Eurasia Forum Quarterly*, 4(1) (2006), 58. See also E. Troitskiy, 'U.S. policy in Central Asia and regional security', *Global Society*, 21 (3) (2007), 425.

[112] On this point with particular regard to American and UN-led efforts to develop a more rigorous international regime against terrorist financing, see generally B. Mendelsohn, 'English school, American style: Testing the preservation-seeking quality of the international society', *European Journal of International Relations*, 15(2) (2009), 291–318.

consequences would be fundamentally conditioned by the character of the American response. As it was, America's decision to extend the 'war on terror' through its 2003 invasion of Iraq dramatically weakened the post-9/11 counter-terrorism consensus, while also forestalling the consolidation of a favourable peace in Afghanistan. The long-term impact of this lateral escalation of the 'war on terror' – for American power, for global jihadism and for the state system's future – will now be considered.

America's imperial moment and its systemic consequences

The jihadist assault on the state system evolved out of a sweeping philosophical critique of secular modernity, and the extent of the jihadists' animus towards the supposed materialism and idolatry of the modern world must not be downplayed, lest one lose sight of the movement's uncompromisingly anti-systemic character. This caveat aside, the jihadists also sought more specifically to destroy the thickening web of patron–client ties linking America to its Middle Eastern allies. To characterise Washington's relationship to its Gulf State clients as imperial without qualification remains problematic, given the absence of formal ties of command and obedience linking America to its local allies.[113] Nevertheless, the dilemma confronting America in the Persian Gulf after 9/11 was in many respects strikingly imperial in its underlying character. Since the 1970s, the developed world's extractive demands on the region's oil resources had necessitated the United States' establishment of protective alliances with local rulers to guarantee consumer countries' security of supply. Simultaneously, however, local clients had traditionally relied heavily on conservative Islam as a mainstay of their domestic legitimation strategies. This reliance grew ever more intense following both the *annus mirabilis* of 1979 and then the indefinite stationing of American troops in Saudi Arabia from 1990 onwards. The resulting tension between metropolitan resource-extraction demands and the legitimation demands of local clients was historically far from unique, having previously been implicated in crises of empire in settings as diverse as Reformation Europe and the late Ottoman Empire.[114] In both of these cases, actors mobilising around social networks, yoked respectively to categorical confessional or proto-national identities, had at times radically disrupted the ties linking core to periphery in imperial agglomerations.[115] In perpetrating the 9/11 atrocities, Al Qaeda similarly sought to destroy the

---

[113] On the importance of formal ties of command and obedience in constituting international hierarchies, see J. M. Hobson and J. C. Sharman, 'The enduring place of hierarchy in world politics', *European Journal of International Relations*, 11(1) (2005), 69.

[114] Nexon, *The Struggle for Power in Early Modern Europe*, Ch. 4; K. Barkey, *Empire of Difference: The Ottomans in comparative perspective* (Cambridge University Press, 2008), Ch. 8.

[115] *Ibid.*

patron–client ties linking America to its regional allies by goading it into a debilitating military confrontation in the Muslim world. Al Qaeda's expectation was that such a confrontation would simultaneously expose the hypocrisy and impiety of America's Quisling allies, while also awakening the Muslim masses and inspiring them to rally to the *umma's* defence just as they had done during the first Afghan jihad.[116]

From the 1970s, America's web of patron–client ties in the Persian Gulf had grown prodigiously at the very same time that its clients were emphasising their Islamic credentials with ever greater insistence. It was precisely this tension that Al Qaeda sought to exploit by mobilising categorical religious identities in such a way as to render America's informal empire in the Gulf unmanageable. In 9/11's immediate wake, the possibility that the jihadists might succeed in terminally destabilising America's Gulf State allies appeared worryingly plausible to decision-makers in Washington.[117] Faced with the jihadist challenge to America's position in the Gulf, the Bush administration was confronted with a choice of three broad alternatives. The first of these, retrenchment, would have entailed a fundamental revision of America's regional posture, including a substantial drawdown of its military presence as well as a sustained effort to disentangle itself from existing security commitments to local allies. However, given the importance of the region's oil reserves for the functioning of the world economy, the option of retrenchment could never have been seriously considered in the short term. The second and most conservative alternative, that of reinforcing existing allies through intensified intelligence-sharing, counter-terrorism assistance and other forms of security co-operation, became in practice a key component of America's post-9/11 regional strategy.[118] Nevertheless, given the heightened atmosphere of mistrust between Washington and the Saudi monarchy immediately after the attacks, a strategy that remained exclusively dependent on the reinforcement of existing alliances carried distinct disadvantages. Specifically, a reinforcement strategy would do nothing to reduce America's exposure to the international repercussions of the Gulf States' legitimation strains, of which the 9/11 attacks stood as but the most conspicuously malevolent expression. Most importantly, it also would do little to mitigate the threat to global energy supplies that would materialise should strengthened alliances prove insufficient to prevent the Saudi monarchy from being overthrown.

---

[116] Gerges, *The Far Enemy*, pp. 144–5.   [117] Klare, *Blood and Oil*, p. 86.

[118] Although it is worth noting that America's provision of counter-terrorism assistance to Saudi Arabia in particular has been kept deliberately low key to avoid further aggravating the monarchy's internal legitimacy strains, and that the monarchy has additionally sought to mitigate its dependence on America by further broadening its counter-terrorism ties with countries such as Egypt, Jordan, Morocco and Pakistan. See B. Riedel and B. Y. Saab, 'Al Qaeda's third front: Saudi Arabia', *The Washington Quarterly*, 31(2) (2008), 43–4.

It was in the light of the limitations of retrenchment and reinforcement as strategic options that the Bush administration settled on a third alternative, namely the renovation of its informal empire in the Gulf through its coercive extension into Iraq. While the administration undoubtedly possessed multiple motives for invading Iraq, the conflict can most usefully be comprehended as part of a larger strategy of imperial renovation aimed at re-establishing American regional primacy on firmer geopolitical foundations. Since the fall of the shah, the developed world's dependence on Saudi Arabian oil had left it hostage to the monarchy's increasingly precarious fortunes. The events of 9/11 illuminated the extraordinary risks inherent in such an arrangement, as well as dramatising its likely unsustainability over the long term. Conversely, the establishment of a pliant democratic Iraqi regime appeared to promise multiple strategic dividends. At the most basic level, the elimination of the Iraqi Ba'athist regime was expected to remove a major external threat to America's regional allies.[119] This in turn would permit a major reconfiguration of the American military footprint in the region, as forces formerly dedicated to containing Saddam could be freed up for redeployment elsewhere. In particular, Hussein's ouster was expected to permit the withdrawal of US forces then stationed in Saudi Arabia, removing one of the key provocations that had inspired the jihadists and thus strained America's relations with its major Gulf State ally.[120] Finally, and most importantly, the establishment of an alternative client state in Iraq promised to reduce the developed world's relative dependence on Saudi oil, as well as mitigating its exposure to future volatility in the Saudi kingdom.[121] This would potentially liberate America from the constraint of reconciling its foreign policy aspirations with the sensitivies of its established autocratic allies, thereby further strengthening its power over these clients and permitting a more unfettered pursuit of America's regional interests.

As with historic crises of international order in both Christendom and twentieth-century East Asia, the volatility of the immediate post-9/11 period thus also called forth an imperial response. Critically, however, the American imperial turn after 9/11 was far more ambiguous, ambivalent and self-limiting than its historical predecessors. In seeking to crush Protestantism and reconstitute Christendom along imperial lines, the Habsburgs had been unselfconscious in their embrace of empire as their preferred model of order. Similarly, imperial Japan's bid to carve out a new order in East Asia had also been unapologetically pursued, Tokyo's rhetorical concessions to Asian nationalism notwithstanding. By contrast, the legitimacy of American 'empire' after 9/11 was squarely dependent on the idea of it being a self-liquidating enterprise.

---

[119] J. Record, *Dark Victory: America's second war against Iraq* (Annapolis: Naval Institute Press, 2004), p. 71.
[120] *Ibid.*, p. 72. See also Riedel and Saab, 'Al Qaeda's third front', p. 44.
[121] Record, *Dark Victory*, pp. 72–3.

The Counter-Reformation Catholicism of the Habsburgs and the 'master race' ideology of imperial Japan had both legitimised imperial hierarchy in part through reference to its supposed concordance with the divine. Conversely, the legitimacy of American occupations in both Iraq and Afghanistan was ultimately to derive from their role in facilitating the consolidation of democratic sovereignty in both countries. The resulting tension – between the end of strengthening the sovereign state system through democracy promotion and the means of advancing this agenda via the short-term imposition of foreign rule – bedevilled America's imperial project in a way that finds no parallel in the historical cases considered in this study.

At its base, the American project of imperial renovation was frustrated by a triple legitimacy deficit, which was simultaneously operative at a systemic level, at a domestic level within America and within both Iraq and Afghanistan as the intended objects of democratic transformation. At a systemic level, the Bush administration was forced to negotiate the inevitable role strain between its responsibilities as a global hegemon charged with leading the anti-jihadist struggle, and its prerogatives as a Great Power seeking to shore up its regional supremacy through the ouster of the Iraqi regime.[122] In making the case for the Iraq War, the administration tried to finesse this tension by emphasising the allegedly indissoluble linkage between the jihadist challenge and Baghdad's long-standing defiance of international demands for its complete, verifiable and irreversible abandonment of its WMD programme. Embedded within an order in which principles of sovereign equality and non-intervention are enshrined as part of the state system's constitutional norms, the Bush administration was compelled to negotiate support for the war through multilateral channels rather than immediately resort to unilateralism. Additionally, given the existence of systemic norms precluding resort to war except for defensive purposes, the administration was also forced to justify the proposed war as a system-preserving measure. Constrained by the norms of the system it was purportedly seeking to defend, the Bush administration thus argued that the proposed invasion was intended both to uphold the UN's authority in the face of Saddam's defiance, and also to foreclose the possibility of Baghdad transferring WMD to jihadist terrorists.[123] Consequently, once the administration failed to secure the UN Security Council's express imprimatur for the invasion, it suffered a loss of legitimacy that was later further compounded with the post-war failure to locate Iraqi WMD stockpiles. This international legitimacy deficit significantly impeded the administration's subsequent efforts to secure large-scale reconstruction assistance from the international community, forcing America to bear the vast majority of the military and financial costs for Iraq's recovery.[124]

---

[122] B. Mendelsohn, *Combating Jihadism*, p. 186.   [123] *Ibid.*, pp. 198–9.

[124] D. Malone, *The International Struggle over Iraq: Politics in the UN Security Council 1980–2005* (Oxford University Press, 2006), pp. 222–51.

Resistance from within America itself further moderated Washington's imperial ambitions. Given America's self-understanding as a polity dedicated to the promotion of liberalism, neither the outright conquest of Iraq nor its indefinite occupation were ever envisaged as either desirable or domestically sustainable war objectives. In seeking to consolidate its position in the Middle East, then, Washington was therefore limited by an aversion to formal empire that distinguished its situation radically from that of historic imperial powers. Both Counter-Reformation Catholicism and Japanese conceptions of the divine *Yamato* race had legitimised international hierarchy through reference to its presumed concordance with divine imperatives. Conversely, the liberal imperialism that briefly defined US foreign policy after 9/11 publicly relied on no such cosmic guarantees. Instead, foreign rule in Iraq was justified as but a temporary expedient deemed necessary to advance the decidedly mundane goal of establishing a friendly democratic regime in the country. The promise of an occupation that would be rapidly self-liquidating inevitably frustrated the American electorate once Iraq's progress towards democracy proved more painful and protracted than first anticipated. This frustration in turn complicated the Bush administration's capacity to sustain domestic political and financial support for the war in the years that followed, further constraining Washington's ability to consolidate its informal imperium in the Persian Gulf.

Finally, within both Iraq and Afghanistan, local resistance to foreign occupation further impeded the achievement of American ambitions. In their efforts to reconstitute international orders along imperial lines, both the Habsburgs and imperial Japan had been frustrated by local actors mobilising respectively around confessional and national identities. Within both Iraq and Afghanistan, America and its allies similarly encountered substantial armed resistance from local rebels. In contrast to either of my historical cases, however, within Iraq at least a deeply held mass nationalism pre-dated the American occupation, fuelling violent resistance to the occupation from its opening days.[125] Equally, in both Iraq and Afghanistan, the presence of 'infidel' forces in Islamic lands provided a critical opening for global jihadists to establish alliances of convenience with both nationalists and local Islamists. Consequently, foreign efforts to consolidate democratic regimes in both countries were initially frustrated by a motley coalition who were able to violently contest the occupations' legitimacy on both nationalist and religious grounds.[126] The cumulative effect of this resistance was to impede rapid transitions to democratic rule in both countries, and also to foreclose American neo-conservative aspirations to generalise coercive regime change as their preferred means of remaking political order

---

[125] On the long-standing character of Iraqi nationalism, see for example E. Davis, 'History matters: Past as prologue in building democracy in Iraq', *Orbis*, 49(2) (2005), 231.

[126] D. Kilcullen, *The Accidental Guerrilla: Fighting small wars in the midst of a big one* (Oxford University Press, 2009), pp. 34–8.

throughout the Middle East. Just as importantly, however, the conflicts in Iraq and Afghanistan also served to partially conflate the international struggle against jihadist terrorism with more local and limited nationalist struggles against foreign rule.[127] In Afghanistan, this was most likely unavoidable, given the necessity of dislodging Al Qaeda from its sanctuaries and given also the tight alliance between Al Qaeda and its Taliban patrons, which required the latter's removal if the jihadist threat was to be successfully confronted. But in extending the 'war on terror' to Iraq, the Bush administration blurred the boundaries between systemic preservation and the advancement of its own Great Power interests, thereby jeopardising the hard-won international counter-terrorism consensus that had emerged in 9/11's immediate after-math.[128] In undermining this consensus, and in reviving jihadist fortunes following the swiftness of their initial defeat and dispersal in Afghanistan in late 2001, the Bush administration's imperial turn inadvertently undermined its overarching goal of preserving a liberal world order. The theoretical and empirical significance of this mis-step for the preservation of international order will now be considered.

The jihadist challenge and the international response: An interim assessment

Having considered both the widespread international counter-terrorism co-operation that followed 9/11 and then reviewed the imperial turn in American foreign policy that succeeded it, one can posit two plausible albeit contradictory assessments of the state system's resilience in the face of armed challenges to its integrity. An optimistic reading of the state system's resilience would begin by underscoring the multitude of institutional and normative innovations that immediately followed the 9/11 attacks. The extensive renovation of the UN's counter-terrorism architecture, the adjustment of standards of legitimate statehood to more explicitly align sovereign obligations with global counter-terrorism imperatives and the broad international support for America's toppling of the Taliban all indicate the state system's robust capacities for self-preservation. In spectacularly exposing states' increasingly tenuous *control* over organised violence internationally, the jihadists struck at one of the most basic – even constitutive – privileges of sovereign statehood.[129] Consequently, it is unsurprising that the 9/11 attacks provoked such a vigorous inter-governmental effort to reassert the state's *authority* over organised violence, as well as calling

---

[127] *Ibid.*   [128] Mendelsohn, *Combating Jihadism*, pp. 197–8.
[129] On the state's claims to monopolise legitimate violence as a constitutive prerogative of modern state sovereignty, see Thomson, *Mercenaries, Pirates and Sovereigns*, p. 152.

forth a raft of initiatives designed to practically reinforce this authority claim.[130] From the nineteenth century onwards, Great Powers have historically leveraged international campaigns against violent non-state predators to successfully enhance their authority as the custodians of international order.[131] Seen against this historical backdrop, it is easy to situate the campaign against jihadist terrorism as just the latest manifestation of this tendency, with jihadism's pending defeat and suppression signifying merely one more milestone in the global state system's universal spread and consolidation.

An optimistic reading of the state system's resilience appears further vindicated by America's engagement with the United Nations both before and after the invasion of Iraq. That Washington felt constrained to solicit the Security Council's imprimatur prior to the invasion indicated the practical importance key decision-makers assigned to the legitimacy the Council could potentially confer on the pending conflict. Far from demonstrating the UN's irrelevance, then, the fact that the Bush administration felt the need to argue the case for the Iraq War before the UN in the first instance testified to the continuing robustness of the contemporary international order. That the fundamental institutions of international society remain sufficiently sturdy as to constrain the actions of the world's most materially powerful actor contrasts starkly with my two historical cases, in which empires waxed in environments where the fundamental institutions of international order had already broken down. Similarly, the fact that America sought to characterise the Iraq War as a system-preserving measure, and that it was forced to argue for the war's *legality* as well as its perceived necessity, also indicated the continuing normative hold of the institutions of multilateralism and international law at the time of the invasion. Communicative action – in the form of public deliberation within the shared normative and institutional parameters of the UN system – remained a core feature of world politics after 9/11. Once again, this contrasts dramatically with my historical cases, in which the breakdown of constitutional norms and fundamental institutions was total, and in which the preconditions for communicative action between political communities had thus irretrievably dissolved.

Jihadism's failure to cultivate a broad popular base in the years following 9/11 provides a further warrant for optimistically assessing the state system's prospects in the face of the jihadist challenge. The wars in Afghanistan and especially Iraq admittedly granted the jihadists a reprieve following the

---

[130] On the critical distinction between authority and control as they pertain to understandings of state sovereignty see J. E. Thomson, 'State sovereignty in international relations: Bridging the gap between theory and empirical research', *International Studies Quarterly*, 39(2) (1995), 223.

[131] On this point, see generally O. Lowenheim, *Predators and Parasites: Persistent agents of transnational harm and Great Power authority* (Ann Arbor: The University of Michigan Press, 2007).

disorientation and division that engulfed the movement immediately after the Taliban's defeat in 2001. For many Muslims, the Coalition's invasion of Iraq appeared to validate the jihadist narrative of a beleaguered *umma* fighting for its survival, and jihadist volunteers were quick to ingratiate themselves with local insurgents in Iraq and Afghanistan in an effort to expand their recruitment base and so carve out stem-lands for a revived caliphate.[132] But with limited exceptions, the jihadists have been generally unsuccessful in co-opting locally oriented insurgents to the jihadist cause. The ideological inflexibility of Al Qaeda franchises, coupled with their brutality towards host communities and their penchant for indiscriminate violence against 'infidels' and Muslims alike, has further weakened their appeal.[133] Thanks to strengthened international counter-proliferation efforts after 9/11, jihadist terrorists have also failed to acquire and deploy WMD, significantly curtailing their material capacity to destabilise international order through acts of catastrophic terrorism. Despite repeated (and intermittently successful) attempts to perpetrate mass-casualty attacks in Western capitals, international counter-terrorism efforts have also prevented the pulsed series of attacks that would have been necessary to cripple public confidence in governments' ability to protect their citizens from jihadist violence.

As a result of the extreme hubris and dogmatism of jihadism's chief exponents and intensified international counter-proliferation and counter-terrorism efforts after 9/11, the jihadist terrorist threat thus appears for the moment to have been contained, further supporting positive appraisals of the present world order's adaptive capacity and long-term durability. Nevertheless, several countervailing considerations invite a less sanguine assessment of the future of world order. The first of these concerns the growing disconnect that the Iraq War controversy exposed between international society's authoritative institutions and the shifting concentration of coercive power within the international system. John Ikenberry has coined the phrase the 'Westphalian flip' to describe the profound shifts in the global geopolitical landscape that followed the cold war's end.[134] Whereas under the classical Westphalian order, world politics was dominated by Great Power competition and states largely claimed a successful monopolisation of violence internationally, the 'Westphalian flip' saw the advent of unipolarity, coupled with a resurgence of private

---

[132] On Al Qaeda's post-9/11 resurgence, see generally B. Riedel, 'Al Qaeda strikes back', *Foreign Affairs*, 86(3) (2007), 24–40.

[133] See generally Phillips, 'How Al Qaeda lost Iraq'. Al Qaeda's tenacious presence in the Af/Pak region partially qualifies this judgement, but is also explicable by reference to factors that are particular to that theatre rather than being generically observable across the Afro-Asian Islamic crescent. See A. Phillips, 'The Anbar awakening: Can it be exported to Afghanistan?', *Security Challenges*, 5(3) (2009), 38–41.

[134] G. J. Ikenberry, 'Power and liberal order: America's postwar world order in transition', *International Relations of the Asia-Pacific*, 5(2) (2005), 141–2.

international violence most dramatically manifest in the rise of transnational terrorism.[135] The Iraq War controversy demonstrated that the 'Westphalian flip' has introduced a potent tension between international society's chief loci of authoritative and coercive power. Whereas the UN Security Council retains formidable capacities to confer or withhold legitimacy with respect to the use of force in world politics, the UN system as a whole remains disproportionately reliant on the United States to coercively enforce its writ internationally. Equally, while America's presently unrivalled military supremacy remains a critical asset for the maintenance of world order, the Iraq War also revealed America's limited capacity to generate the authority necessary to legitimise its use of force in the face of sustained resistance from the Security Council and the General Assembly.

Upon first analysis, the Iraq War controversy may therefore be read as an aberrant episode in America's relationship to the liberal order that it helped create, one in which the Bush administration's unilateral inclinations led it to overlook the necessary complementarity between American power and international legitimacy as embodied in the UN. But however reassuring such an interpretation might initially appear, it must be offset by a recognition that the growing salience of unconventional security threats is likely to further compound the tensions between the UN and the United States in the years to come. This is because despite significant improvements in the UN's counter-proliferation and counter-terrorism architecture since 9/11, existing multilateral structures are still likely to remain too cumbersome to facilitate the kinds of rapid and decisive responses likely to be favoured by America and other developed states in managing unconventional threats such as jihadist terrorism.[136] Similarly, while the articulation of new standards of sovereign responsibility in the areas of counter-terrorism and counter-proliferation can only be commended, many states' compliance with these standards has frequently been unsatisfactory due to deficiencies in both political will and institutional capacity.[137] Efforts to correct for these failings – respectively through the application of diplomatic pressure and the provision of capacity-building

---

[135] *Ibid.*

[136] For a convincing argument that non-traditional security threats may continue to fuel American imperial adventurism even in the wake of the Iraq War, see generally P. MacDonald, 'Is imperial rule obsolete? Assessing the barriers to overseas adventurism', *Security Studies*, 18(1) (2009), 79–114.

[137] On states' patchy compliance with new sovereign obligations in the areas of counter-proliferation and counter-terrorism, and multilateral efforts to at least address capacity shortfalls through the provision of enhanced technical assistance, see M. Heupel, 'Combining hierarchical and soft modes of governance: The UN Security Council's approach to terrorism and weapons of mass destruction proliferation after 9/11', *Cooperation and Conflict*, 43(1) (2008), 17–18.

programmes – have not been entirely without success.[138] But the sheer magnitude of state weakness in many parts of the developing world will continue to prevent many states from discharging their sovereign obligations to a standard sufficient to allay the security concerns of America and its main allies. Consequently, the temptations to embrace conceptions of preventive defence that featured so prominently in the lead-up to the Iraq War are likely to further intensify. This in turn suggests that the accompanying strains between the state system's chief loci of authoritative and coercive power that marked the Iraq War controversy are also likely to grow, portending greater systemic instability as a consequence.

A consideration of America's diminished strategic position in the Greater Middle East following the wars in Iraq and Afghanistan provides additional grounds for pessimism. While the long-term prospects for democratic consolidation in Iraq and Afghanistan remain difficult to foresee, there is no question but that these protracted conflicts have done much to destabilise American hegemony throughout the Afro-Asian Islamic crescent, most particularly in the Persian Gulf. Ironically, whereas the Bush administration sought in invading Iraq to further strengthen its position as the region's chief security patron, the prolonged war in that country has redounded primarily to the benefit of America's adversaries, most particularly the Islamic Republic of Iran.[139] More generally, the wars in Iraq and Afghanistan have further sharpened the vulnerability of key regional allies to Islamist challenges to their legitimacy, undermining the political basis for the alliances that are the foundation of American power in the region. Having substantially overreached in a thwarted project of imperial renovation, the United States may increasingly be forced to substantially retrench in the region, forfeiting hegemony in favour of a more modest strategy of offshore balancing.[140] Such a shift in posture may be neither avoidable nor altogether undesirable, but its historical significance and prospective import for world order should not be overlooked. Notwithstanding the brief interval in the 1970s between Britain's withdrawal from the Gulf and America's assumption of responsibility for the maintenance of regional security, an Anglophone hegemon has played a critical role in stabilising local rivalries and maintaining order since Britain's conclusion of a treaty with the Trucial States in 1853. A partial retrenchment of American influence in the Persian Gulf is consequently fraught with peril, holding the potential to exacerbate local security anxieties and heighten nuclear proliferation pressures at a

---

[138] See generally B. Mendelsohn, 'Bolstering the state: A different perspective on the war on the jihadi movement', *International Studies Review*, 11(4) (2009), 663–86.

[139] On this point, see generally G. Bahgat, 'Iran and the United States: The emerging security paradigm in the Middle East', *Parameters*, 37(2) (2007), 5–18.

[140] On the case for America's adoption of an offshore balancing strategy in the Middle East, see generally C. Layne, 'America's Middle East grand strategy after Iraq: The moment for offshore balancing has arrived', *Review of International Studies*, 35(1) (2009), 5–25.

time when escalating global demand for the Gulf's energy resources is making the stability of international order ever more vulnerable to regional volatility.

Despite the significant adaptive capacity demonstrated by international order's custodians after 9/11, then, a uniformly positive assessment of that order's long-term stability and resilience cannot be entirely convincing. Far from being atypical, the tensions that attended the lead-up to the Iraq War are unlikely to prove unique, given the Western world's acute sensitivity to rapidly evolving and geographically amorphous transnational threats, and given also the inherent difficulties of decisively responding to these threats within the framework of the UN system of collective security in its present form. The disruptive global consequences of America's imperial overreach in the Persian Gulf must also not be underestimated. Finally, notwithstanding the international community's relative success in limiting the jihadists' capacity for systemic disruption, it must be remembered that the years since 9/11 have seen a further growth of the destabilising forces that facilitated jihadism's rise in the first place. While jihadism has failed to acquire broad popular purchase in the Muslim world, the 'war on terror' has undeniably witnessed a further sharpening of tensions between America and its Western allies on the one hand, and political Islamists of various hues on the other. Essentialist claims of an embryonic 'clash of civilisations' remain as analytically fuzzy and politically dangerous as ever. But the ongoing traumas of the 'war on terror' have inflamed cultural antagonisms in both the West and Muslim-majority countries, with profound disagreements concerning the legitimate role of religion in public life providing a primary focal point for these frictions both domestically and internationally.[141]

From the consolidation of a Hamas statelet in Gaza, through the diplomatic assertiveness of a resurgent Iran, to the continuing rise of the Tehrik-e-Taliban across broad swathes of northern Pakistan, Islamism in its varying forms remains a potent force in world politics, the political failures of global jihadism notwithstanding. The increases in global violence interdependence occasioned by both the spread of transnational terrorism and escalating nuclear proliferation pressures further illuminate the present world order's fragility. Despite a flurry of post-9/11 multilateral initiatives to curb both transnational terrorism and nuclear proliferation, the technological enablers driving these forces remain in place, as do the deeper political antagonisms that continue to spur their evolution. State failure meanwhile remains prevalent across much of the Afro-Asian Islamic crescent, condemning millions to insecurity in countries as diverse as Somalia, Yemen and Pakistan, and thereby feeding political extremism and international disorder. The international community's awareness of

---

[141] On these tensions as they have specifically manifested themselves within the context of the French 'headscarves affair', see O. Roy, *Secularism Confronts Islam* (New York: Columbia University Press, 2007), pp. 26–8.

these challenges has been greatly enhanced following 9/11, but the system's capacity to decisively confront them remains worryingly limited.

In both Christendom and the Sinosphere, the destruction of international orders was heralded by the intersection of ideological polarisation, growing violence interdependence and pervasive institutional decay. In the past four decades, this constellation of forces has manifested itself once again. While the global state system is hardly on the cusp of dissolution, its fragility and susceptibility to disruptive change remains greater than is commonly acknowledged. If the custodians of the present world order are to successfully preserve the global state system's liberal constitutional values, they must first acknowledge the full magnitude of the threat being faced, for only then can a collective response be fashioned that adequately deals with the challenge. The likelihood of such a renewal occurring, and the steps that must be taken to avert continuing systemic decay, form part of the subject of the concluding chapter of this investigation, to which I now turn.

Conclusion

In 1500 CE, from Paris to Beijing, the bulk of the world's population was governed by clerics and emperors. In Latin Christendom, the dream of reuniting Europe under the imperial sceptre continued to fire the hearts of men such as Charles V, while the pope remained unchallenged as Christendom's supreme spiritual leader. Throughout the Muslim world, the *umma's* seemingly unstoppable expansion looked set to continue, with the sixteenth century witnessing both the waxing of Ottoman power and the emergence of new Muslim empires in Safavid Iran and Mughal India. Finally, in the Far East, a far-flung suzerain state system flourished under the Ming dynasty, with the Chinese emperor exercising unchallenged regional hegemony by dint of his status as the Son of Heaven. Throughout the Old World, the ethical power of transcendental religious visions intertwined uneasily with the coercive power of dynastic empires. Faith and empire formed the twin foundations of regional international orders in Christendom, the *umma* and the Sinosphere, with the stability afforded by each facilitating the ensuing global demographic and commercial expansion that heralded the advent of modernity.

In the twenty-first century, emancipation has displaced salvation as the animating purpose of collective association, while the nation-state has eclipsed empire as the world's dominant form of political community. In the preceding chapters, I have sought to chronicle this transition, concentrating on two configurative crises that propelled the state system's genesis and expansion, before then considering the contemporary challenges that now threaten its untroubled perpetuation. My purposes in undertaking this inquiry were to investigate the nature of international order, to account for international orders' transformation throughout history, and to make a preliminary assessment concerning the contemporary state system's long-term durability. In this chapter, I will revisit my main findings, considering in turn this study's contributions to our understanding of the nature of international order, the dynamics of international systems change, the developmental trajectory of world order from 1500 to the present, and the global state system's likely future in the coming decades.

The nature of international order

The notion that there exists a clear distinction between the domestic and the international spheres, whereby the former is dominated by the pursuit of the good life while the latter is dominated by the struggle for survival, has long framed prevailing conceptions of international order. In the post-cold war era, however, the distinction between an international realm of necessity and a domestic realm of freedom has grown increasingly untenable. Internationally, the post-cold war period has witnessed the global ascendancy of transformational liberalism, in which both multilateral institutions and hegemonic power have been harnessed to the task of promoting distinctly liberal visions of the good. Concurrently with this development, state failure in countries such as Sudan, Somalia, Iraq and Afghanistan has plunged many populations back into a condition reminiscent of Hobbes's imagined state of nature. These developments alone suggest the limited utility of traditional dichotomies that locate the imperatives of emancipation and survival respectively in the domestic and international spheres.

More generally, however, this inquiry reaffirms constructivist insights regarding the intimate relationship that exists internationally between shared conceptions of the good and the design of fundamental institutions. In Christendom, the Sinosphere and the modern state system, international orders have been thoroughly suffused with historically particular conceptions of the good. Moreover, in each instance, the maintenance of international order has been highly dependent on practices of communicative action, which have themselves been mediated via authoritative institutions anchored in shared conceptions of legitimacy. Nevertheless, while my investigation reaffirms the existence of an Aristotelian dimension to all international orders, I depart from established constructivist accounts in acknowledging their equally significant Augustinian dimension. In opposition to most realists, I concur with constructivists that shared conceptions of legitimacy and practices of communicative action are central to international orders' constitution and operation.[1] But these authoritative norms and practices are by themselves insufficient to maintain international order. On the contrary, I have argued that it is the combined operation of authoritative institutions with legitimate practices of coercion that works to cultivate co-operation and contain enmity between different political communities. This argument derives from the undeniable reality that violent struggles over power and principle have posed a central challenge to the maintenance of international order in every case I have considered. Both the Augustinian and the Aristotelian purposes of political order – the containment of enmity and the pursuit of the good life – have informed international orders'

---

[1] See for example Bukovansky, *Legitimacy and Power Politics*; Philpott, *Revolutions in Sovereignty*; and Reus-Smit, *The Moral Purpose of the State*.

constitutional structure and fundamental institutions throughout history. For this reason, any attempt to understand international orders by focusing exclusively on the operation of authoritative institutions and practices of communicative action is bound to remain incomplete.

That practices of organised violence have been central to international orders' reproduction will come as no surprise to realists, many of whom have long insisted on war's necessity as an unavoidable mechanism for preserving international order.[2] However, this study departs from conventional realism on two important matters. First, my investigation demonstrates the variability of institutionalised practices of legitimate violence across time and space. Secondly, I have also demonstrated that institutionalised practices of legitimate coercion are profoundly conditioned by prevailing conceptions regarding the moral purpose of collective association. In Christendom, the Sinosphere and the modern state system's differing conceptions of the good yielded differing practices of legitimate violence in addition to different forms of authoritative institutions. Far from being diametrically opposed to one another, authoritative and coercive institutions' modes of social action have historically both been recruited to the task of order preservation. Moreover, in their varied expressions, both authoritative and coercive institutions have been intimately related to one another, owing to their common origins in shared beliefs regarding the ultimate ends of social life.

The argument that practices of organised violence are central to international orders' operation will sit uncomfortably with many constructivists, particularly those who are committed to the goal of supplanting the logic of force with the force of logic as the primary feature of international politics. Nevertheless, I maintain that there is significant compatibility between constructivists' emancipatory objectives and the arguments advanced here. In demonstrating the variability of practices of legitimate coercion across different international orders, I hope to have undermined the realist refrain that human agents are condemned to remain stuck in an endless cycle of recurrence and repetition, with brief intervals of peace being punctuated by renewed outbreaks of violent disorder. For while violence has remained a pervasive feature of international politics throughout history, agents' conceptions of what constitutes legitimate violence and who may wield it have varied markedly in different eras. More fundamentally, agents' tolerance of violence has fluctuated significantly in accordance with the differing visions of the good that have sustained different international orders. For example, whereas the Church duly accommodated itself to the bellicosity of the European nobility in the legitimacy it extended to the institution of the feud, Confucianism restricted legitimate recourse to violence to the emperor,

---

[2] See generally H. Morgenthau, *Politics among Nations: The struggle for power and peace*, 5th edn (New York: Alfred A. Knopf, 1978); and Waltz, *Theory of International Politics*.

and consistently emphasised the superiority of moral example over violence as the preferred method of maintaining cosmic and social order. Stated bluntly, some visions of the good – and thus some international orders – have been more accepting of violence as a feature of everyday social life than have others. In illustrating this variability, I hope to have provided a firm empirical basis for refuting realists' pessimism regarding the possibility of achieving fundamental moral progress from more to less violent forms of international order. Equally, in encouraging constructivists to acknowledge the indispensability of legitimate violence in sustaining international orders, I hope to stimulate greater debate regarding the best means of harmonising the ethical imperative of emancipation with the practical imperative of preserving the liberal world order from either external assault or internal corruption.

The dynamics of international systems change

The research traditions of realism, rationalism and constructivism, framed respectively around the motifs of power, efficiency and identity, all suggest different explanations for international orders' transformation.[3] For realists, for whom the ceaseless struggle for power, prestige and survival remains paramount, international systems change is best conceptualised as a residue of Great Power conflict.[4] Conversely, rationalists are more inclined to account for international systems change by reference to actors' search for more efficient institutional solutions to common problems.[5] Constructivists offer yet another explanation for international systems change, emphasising the transformative significance of revolutionary ideas and new forms of social identity in undermining old orders and providing the normative impetus for the construction of new orders.[6]

While I have argued that valuable insights can be drawn from each of these traditions, my argument does not completely vindicate any of them, but instead supports the more analytically eclectic mode of theorising complex social phenomena that Peter Katzenstein and Rudra Sil have recently advocated.[7] Analytical eclecticism, Katzenstein and Sil argue:

---

[3] On power, efficiency and identity as the key motifs of the dominant research traditions in international relations, see Suh, Katzenstein and Carlson, *Rethinking Security in East Asia: Identity, power, and efficiency*, pp. 8–9.

[4] See for example Gilpin, *War and Change in World Politics*.

[5] See for example Spruyt, *The Sovereign State and its Competitors*.

[6] See for example Bukovansky, *Legitimacy and Power Politics*; Hall, *National Collective Identity*; and Philpott, *Revolutions in Sovereignty*.

[7] Sil and Katzenstein, *Beyond Paradigms: Analytic eclecticism in the study of world politics*.

assumes the existence of complex interactions among the distribution of capabilities (typically emphasised in realism), the gains pursued by self-interested individual and collective actors (typically emphasised by liberals), and the role of ideas and norms in framing actors' understanding of the world (typically emphasised by constructivists). Put differently, eclectic analysis seeks to cut across and draw connections between processes that are normally cast at different levels of analysis, and are often confined to either material or ideational dimensions of reality.[8]

This study affirms that historical events as complex and protracted as transformations of international order are best understood through recourse to eclectic approaches that seek to tease out the knotty interconnections and co-constitutive relations between the material, ideational and institutional aspects of social reality. The emergence of new forms of violence; processes of institutional decay; the polarisation of international orders following the irruption of insurgent ideas and forms of collective identity – each of these developments is of equivalent importance in accounting for international systems change. *More fundamentally, these processes work together in an interactive rather than merely an additive fashion.* International orders falter not simply because they are overwhelmed by the simultaneous accumulation of discrete material, institutional and ideational challenges to their integrity. Rather, these macro-processes interweave and overlap in complex ways to collectively produce transformations of international order. International orders are always susceptible to challenges to their legitimacy, owing to the inevitable discrepancies that exist between the values they purport to protect and their limited success in practically realising these values. However, they are most likely to fracture only when their efficiency and legitimacy is compromised by simultaneous increases in violence interdependence and the emergence of ideological challenges to their animating values. Equally, it is not technologically driven increases in violence interdependence per se so much as the qualitatively new forms of violence that they enable that threaten international order. These new forms of violence are certainly facilitated by material changes, but they are also derivative of both the mobilisational opportunities afforded by institutional failure, and the imperatives to violence implied in insurgent ideologies and their corresponding forms of social identity. Lastly, my analysis confirms that revolutionary ideas and identities acquire their full subversive potential only when international orders are already fragile, and only when increases in violence interdependence have provided anti-systemic actors with the coercive wherewithal necessary to challenge the prevailing order.

In addition to demonstrating the multi-causal and conjunctural character of international systems change, my argument also highlights the highly contingent and largely unintended character of this process. Struggles over power and

---

[8] *Ibid.*

prestige, disputes and bargaining over questions of institutional design, and more fundamental contests over meaning and identity feature heavily in the everyday warp and woof of international politics. However, my analysis suggests that a focus on the agency and intentions of particular actors is likely to be of limited value when considering protracted episodes of international systems change. This is because international orders are not transformed by either Herculean acts of statesmanship, the cool calculations of rational actors seeking optimal solutions to shared problems, or even the apocalyptic visions of prophets seeking to inaugurate the new millennium. Certainly, all three of these behaviours may manifest themselves during periods of systemic flux. But transformations of the scale witnessed in Christendom or the Sinosphere are so vast as to preclude their determination by acts of conscious human will. Reformation ideas were undoubtedly central in dissolving Christendom's spiritual unity, while an elective affinity also existed between many Protestant propositions and the constitution of the early modern state. However, the constitution of the Westphalian state system was conditioned even more profoundly by Absolutist conceptions of state sovereignty. These ideas owed their genesis to the Wars of Religion that the Reformation catalysed, but they did not organically arise out of the Reformation challenge itself. Similarly, in nineteenth-century East Asia, the Taiping vision gravely weakened the Sinosphere, but played no role in constituting the East Asian state system that succeeded it. Jihadism looks similarly unpromising as the inspiration for the emergence of a new international order. Nevertheless, given the dominance of a logic of unintended consequences in guiding past transformations of international order, the possibility that the jihadist challenge may yet catalyse far-reaching revisions in the practice of sovereignty cannot be summarily dismissed, a point to which I will return below.

The direction of international systems change

The ends of history and the historical trajectory of international systems change from 1500 to the present

In emphasising the themes of causal complexity and contingency, my account of international orders' transformation would initially appear to confound teleological readings of world history. Nevertheless, a more holistic consideration of my cases does reveal the existence of undeniable common trends and global patterns. These trends must be acknowledged before any informed evaluation of the global state system's future prospects can be undertaken. The first trend that is evident across my cases is the secularisation of international order from 1500 to the present. From the Reformation onwards, the relationship between the polis and the cosmos has grown increasingly attenuated, first in Western Europe and then throughout the world. In Christendom, this process of disenchantment began with Luther's proclamation of his ninety-five theses at Wittenberg, before being momentarily reversed with the outbreak of the Wars of Religion. The Wars of Religion eventually yielded a reinvention of religion (conceived as a body of beliefs rather than a body of believers), a weakening of the transnational authority structures of Church and empire and a re-conceptualisation of political authority around the innovation of Absolutist sovereignty. The modern separation of religion from politics owes its origins to this crisis, but was only really completed in Europe centuries later with the delegitimation of divine right Absolutism and the elevation of emancipation over salvation as the ultimate end of government.

In East Asia, the secularisation of international order was arguably even more traumatic. There, the combination of Western encroachment and domestic millenarian rebellion gravely undermined the emperor's authority as the Son of Heaven. The successive horrors of imperialism, dynastic collapse and warlordism then cumulatively nurtured a totalistic repudiation of Confucianism in China, followed by the consolidation of radically secular nationalist Marxist regimes in the former Sinosphere's heartland polities in China, North Korea and Vietnam. Finally, within the Islamic world, the caliphate's abolition in 1924 best symbolised the global extrusion of religion from international order in the twentieth century. This process had begun as a localised challenge to the Church in 1517. It was refined and fortified in the Age of Revolution with the delegitimation of divine right Absolutism and the onset of the popular sovereignty revolution. And it was coercively imposed on the polities of Africa, Asia and the Middle East in the nineteenth and twentieth centuries through the successive processes of imperialism and decolonisation.

Alongside this global secularisation of international order, the last half millennium has also been marked by crises of empire and the wholesale delegitimation of foreign rule. At the dawn of modernity, the majority of the Old World's sedentary populations were governed by composite monarchies, ranging from Western Europe's Renaissance kingdoms to the sprawling gunpowder empires of Muscovy, China and the Ottoman domain.[9] From the sixteenth century onwards, successive crises of international order have overlapped with, and partially been driven by, the break-up of these imperial formations. Within Christendom, this manifested itself in the interweaving of struggles for religious freedom and political autonomy that punctuated the Wars of Religion. The defeat of Habsburg imperialism in the sixteenth and seventeenth centuries was driven by a multitude of factors, but local resistance to foreign rule in places like Holland and Bohemia was decisive in driving this process.[10] Even if it is anachronistic to

---

[9] On the consolidation of the early modern gunpowder empires, see generally McNeill, *The Age of Gunpowder Empires*. See also McNeill, *The Global Condition*, p. 116. On the growth of gunpowder empires in the Islamic world at this time, see Bayly, *Imperial Meridian*, Ch. 1.

[10] See for example D. Nexon, 'Religion, European identity, and political contention in historical perspective', pp. 266–70.

label these and other anti-Habsburg revolts as being nationalist in the strictly modern sense, the xenophobic rhetoric, anti-imperial sentiments and demands for local religious and political autonomy characteristic of these struggles bore many family resemblances to the more self-consciously nationalist rebellions that followed them, and that themselves further accelerated the global shift from imperial to sovereign state systems.

In East Asia, the transition from the Sinosphere to the sovereign state system was also accompanied by crises of empire. From the mid-nineteenth century onwards, Han xenophobia played a crucial role in first sapping the Qing dynasty of its legitimacy and then eventually ensuring its destruction. A generation later, a more self-consciously modern revolutionary Chinese nationalism would again prove decisive in shaping regional politics, with Maoist 'people's war' playing a pivotal role in thwarting Japanese designs to re-establish an imperial East Asian order. The Qing dynasty's collapse and the Japanese new order's defeat helped ensure the consolidation of an East Asian sovereign international order, and together represented part of a broader turn from empire that dominated twentieth-century world politics. The collapse of the Qing, Ottoman, Habsburg, Romanov and Hohenzollern realms in the century's second decade; the World War II defeat of the Nazi, Fascist Italian and imperial Japanese totalitarian empires; the post-war liquidation of the European maritime empires; and finally, the collapse of the Soviet Union – each of these convulsions brought national self-determination to successively greater swathes of humanity. More generally, the twentieth-century recess of empire capped a much deeper world-historical process, entailing the delegitimation of international hierarchy generally, and of practices of foreign rule in particular.[11] This process had its antecedents centuries earlier, in the failure of the papal–imperial diarchy and the subsequent defeat of the abortive Habsburg imperium. But it was only universalised in the nineteenth and twentieth centuries, first with the collapse of hierarchical non-Western international orders such as the Sinosphere, and secondly with the eradication of European colonialism and the globalisation of a sovereign state system founded on the principle of national self-determination.

Finally, the last five centuries have seen a dramatic increase in both the scale and scope of violence interdependence internationally, as well as a parallel – if admittedly more sporadic and faltering – 'civilising process', whereby violence has been progressively monopolised by states and then imperfectly corralled within a universal framework of international law. This process began with the consolidation of the Renaissance monarchies and Eurasia's gunpowder empires in the sixteenth and seventeenth centuries. Across the Old World, the introduction of gunpowder weaponry generally favoured the consolidation of states and empires, although in Western Europe, the technological balance – both

---

[11] See generally Jackson, *Quasi-States*; and Philpott, *Revolutions in Sovereignty*, Chs. 8–12.

between rulers and between rulers and subjects – was initially more even than elsewhere, yielding a state system that departed from the Eurasian imperial norm.[12] By the mid-seventeenth century, however, the spread of gunpowder weaponry had shifted the balance of power decisively in favour of sedentary agriculturalists over nomadic pastoralists for the first time since the fall of the Roman and Han Empires.[13] With the threat of nomadic *Blitzkrieg* invasions finally contained, empires such as Muscovy and the Qing imperium were then able to expand rapidly into the Eurasian hinterland.[14] Meanwhile, the 'military revolution' facilitated a similarly rapid European expansion into the New World, as well as enabling the construction of a series of littoral factories and forts throughout Asia and Africa that would subsequently form the launch pads for later European imperial expansion into the Old World.[15]

In the nineteenth and twentieth centuries, a raft of technological, organisational and ideological changes emanating from the Atlantic world further increased global violence interdependence, as well as catalysing intensified state efforts to monopolise violence domestically and constrain its use internationally. The combination of the popular sovereignty revolution, European imperialism and the industrialisation of warfare destroyed the multi-ethnic gunpowder empires of the Old World. The global growth of violence interdependence during this time did however also coincide with attempts to contain and control violence, both through the codification of international laws of war, and also through the establishment of a permanent universal congress of sovereign states dedicated to the abolition of war. Following the 'total wars' of the twentieth century, and under the shadow of nuclear annihilation, this commitment to civilising violence internationally and eventually eradicating it entirely has formed one of the UN system's chief *raisons d'être*. In the post-cold war period, one can cite the steady decline in civil and international wars, as well as the UN's increasing activism in responding to new threats such as global terrorism and the spread of WMD, as indicative of the continued maturation and institutionalisation of this civilising process at a global level.[16]

International systems change: The persistence of contrary dynamics

From 1500 onwards, the world has been wracked by a succession of configurative crises, involving outbreaks of religious radicalism, crises of empire and

---

[12] McNeill, *The Global Condition*, p. 118.   [13] *Ibid.*, p. 116.
[14] McNeill, *The Age of Gunpowder Empires*, pp. 27–8.
[15] See generally Parker, *The Military Revolution*.
[16] On the steady decline in both civil and international wars during the post-cold war period, see generally *Human Security Report 2005: War and peace in the 21st century* (Oxford University Press, 2005).

the emergence of new forms of violence that have threatened the integrity of international orders. These crises have historically been resolved through the secularisation of international orders, the delegitimation of universal empires in favour of sovereign state systems and the corralling of violence within the institutional parameters of the sovereign state. These macro-trends superficially suggest an inevitability in the state system's genesis and its subsequent expansion. Nevertheless, upon closer scrutiny, each of these trends can and must be subject to serious qualifications that militate against an unreservedly optimistic reading of the state system's long-term prospects.

The worldwide growth of politicised forms of religious sentiment sits uneasily with the historical trend towards the secularisation of international order. For optimists, this so-called 'revenge of God' is often cast as a lamentable but transient detour from the path of secular modernity.[17] More pessimistic observers have conversely portrayed this development as forming part of a more enduring anti-modern backlash, which is symptomatic of the unfulfilled promises of development and democracy in parts of the post-colonial world.[18] Neither of these readings is sustainable upon closer inspection, however, for both overestimate the secularism of modernity in their initial assumptions. Certainly, the genesis and expansion of the sovereign state system entailed the *institutional* secularisation of international order. However, what is often overlooked is that the global expansion of a Western-dominated sovereign state system coincided with a synchronous consolidation and globalisation of the major faith traditions, most particularly Christianity and Islam. Thus, the historic eclipse of non-Western international orders corresponded with what historian Christopher Bayly has dubbed the coterminous rise of 'empires of religion'.[19] The rise of these 'empires of religion' encompassed a number of trends, including the growing rationalisation, codification and standardisation

---

[17] This optimistic view is not the sole preserve of liberals, as evidenced in Colin Gray's confident prediction regarding the future of Islamic radicalism: 'Al Qaeda and associated organizations will be a perennial menace, but they will be beaten decisively as the Islamic world comes to terms, culturally in its own ways, with the modern, even the postmodern, world. That process will take two or three decades, at least.' C. S. Gray, 'How has war changed since the end of the cold war?', *Parameters*, 35(1) (2005), 23. The protracted character of the Islamic world's anticipated transition aside, what is telling is the implied assumption regarding the inevitability of this transition.

[18] Evocations of this pessimistic theme can be found in different forms in works such as S. P. Huntington, *The Clash of Civilizations and the Remaking of World Order* (New York: Simon and Schuster, 1996); and R. D. Kaplan, *The Coming Anarchy: Shattering the dreams of the post cold war*, 1st edn (New York: Random House, 2000). In its starkest form, this pessimism extends towards a fear that the process of desecularisation will be forcibly imposed on the West in coming decades by a resurgent Islam. See for example Y. O. Bat, *Eurabia: The Euro-Arab axis* (Madison: Fairleigh Dickinson University Press, 2005).

[19] C. A. Bayly, *The Birth of the Modern World 1780–1914: Global connections and comparisons* (Oxford: Blackwell, 2004), p. 325.

of religious beliefs; the increased bureaucratisation of forms of religious hierarchy; the 'downward' expansion of religions to impose devotional uniformity
and moral regulation and surveillance upon a steadily greater proportion of
society; and the geographic expansion of major faith traditions 'outwards' at
the expense of local folk and animist forms of spirituality.[20]

What is so significant about this trend is that it suggests a key paradox in the
state system's evolution. On the one hand, the state system expanded at the
expense of other non-Western international orders built upon religious foundations. In doing so, it imposed an order upon non-European peoples that
assumed the international separation of religious and political spheres of authority. On the other hand, however, this very process of expansion helped stimulate
the rationalisation and extend the geographic reach of the major world religions,
thereby fuelling the development of forms of subjectivity that were both religious
and in some cases also transnational in character.[21] Seen through this lens, the
relationship between secularisation and modernity becomes significantly more
complex, and the emergence of religiously framed challenges to the contemporary order appears as less obviously counterintuitive than is suggested in conventional 'revenge of God' accounts. For while the state system's expansion led to
an institutional separation of political from religious authority internationally,
it also coincided with the growing homogenisation of structures of religious
belief within different faith traditions, as well as a growth in the importance of
these global faith traditions in shaping individual and collective identities.[22]
Global patterns of institutional secularisation have thus mapped uneasily onto
patterns of popular identification from the moment of the state system's initial
expansion, suggesting that contemporary religious challenges to its constitution
are neither as unusual nor as emphatically transient and 'anti-modern' as is often
assumed.

Equally, the eclipse of empire and other forms of international hierarchy
should not be overstated. At first glance, the modern sovereign state system
presents as a relentless steamroller of modernity, flattening international
society first through the humbling of Church and empire in early modern
Europe, before sweeping aside the Old World gunpowder empires to create a
global system of sovereign national states. However, once again, further analysis
calls this teleology into question. This is so first because, at a regional level,
trace elements of past international orders continue to endure. In Europe, for
example, the project of European integration has seen the partial revival of
regional forms of heteronomy, replicating the multilayered pattern of authority relations that has governed Europe for most of its history.[23] The EU's
stalled efforts to integrate Turkey into its ranks also demonstrates the continuing salience of religious faultlines in demarcating the outer boundaries of

---

[20] *Ibid.*, Ch. 9 *passim.*   [21] *Ibid.*, p. 333.   [22] *Ibid.*
[23] Ruggie, 'Territoriality and beyond', pp. 171–2.

a putatively post-Christian Europe.[24] In East Asia and the Persian Gulf, meanwhile, the hierarchical lineaments of past orders find partial parallels in America's contemporary maintenance of 'empires of bases' in both regions.[25] Globally, the revival of practices of international neo-trusteeship also suggests the continuing vitality of hierarchy as a feature of international politics, even in an officially post-imperial age.[26]

Finally, the post-9/11 era has decisively demonstrated that violence interdependence continues to grow off the back of globalisation and technological advances, and has done so in a manner which has temporarily outpaced the international community's capacities to fully contain its disruptive potential. The spectre of non-state actors acquiring WMD remains a disquietingly plausible possibility, and had already been explicitly invoked by the Bush administration for the purposes of relaxing hitherto sacrosanct norms prohibiting states from engaging in preventative war. Equally worrying, however, is the global diffusion of modern techniques of urban warfare of the kind now being refined in countries such as Iraq and Afghanistan. The widespread use of vehicle-borne and roadside improvised explosive devices in both of these countries, alongside traditional insurgent techniques such as assassinations and guerrilla ambushes, has paralysed both local governments and their foreign allies.[27] These techniques are eminently capable of being adopted by autonomous cells operating in Western metropolises, particularly as the continuing information and communications revolution enables anti-systemic actors to spread both the knowledge necessary to undertake such attacks and the propaganda necessary to justify them in the minds of potential perpetrators.[28]

What both the prospective spread of WMD capabilities to non-state actors and the potential introduction of urban warfare techniques into Western cities

---

[24] On this point, see M. H. Yavuz, 'Islam and Europeanization in Turkish-Muslim sociopolitical movements' in T. Byrnes and P. Katzenstein (eds.), *Religion in an Expanding Europe* (Cambridge University Press, 2006), pp. 250–2.

[25] With reference to East Asia, see for example generally C. Johnson, *Blowback: The costs and consequences of American empire* (London: Little, Brown and Co., 2002). See also C. Johnson, *The Sorrows of Empire: Militarism, secrecy and the end of the republic* (London: Verso, 2004), Ch. 6. With reference to the Persian Gulf, see generally M. J. O'Reilly and W. B. Renfro, 'Evolving empire: America's "Emirates" strategy in the Persian Gulf', *International Studies Perspectives*, 8 (2007), 137–51.

[26] See generally W. Bain, *Between Anarchy and Society: Trusteeship and the obligations of power* (Oxford University Press, 2003), Ch. 6; and also R. Caplan, 'From collapsing states to neo-trusteeship: The limits to solving the problem of "precarious statehood" in the 21st century', *Third World Quarterly*, 28(2) (2007), 231–44.

[27] On this point, see for example B. Hoffman, 'The "cult of the insurgent": Its tactical and strategic implications', *Australian Journal of International Affairs*, 61(3) (2007), 325.

[28] The widespread fear and insecurity the Washington sniper was able to evoke in the autumn of 2002 is indicative of the disproportionately disruptive capacities now available to individuals and small groups. See for example *ibid.*, pp. 325–6.

together portend is an unravelling of the modern state's monopoly over the legitimate use of violence, one which contrasts starkly with past historical experience. In both Reformation Europe and nineteenth-century East Asia, international orders were decisively unsettled by increases in violence interdependence, driven respectively by the early modern military revolution and by the nascent industrialisation of warfare. However, what was noteworthy about both of these material ruptures was their long-term centripetal effect. In both instances, material changes eventually favoured central governments' increased assertion of control over violence. This centralisation of control over violence enabled the development of international institutions to contain its exercise, while the increasing technological scale and scope of violence rendered this 'civilising process' a practical necessity. By contrast, the prospective spread of WMD and the contemporary growth of asymmetric violence both constitute a partial reversal of this process.[29] This observation should not be taken to suggest that the international community will be unable to adapt to the challenges posed by this growth in violence interdependence. But it does convey the fact that the growth of non-state capacities for violence is far from trivial, and that it will require significant institutional adaptations if the 'civilising process' is to progress and the present international order is to be sustained.

The future of the global state system

What, then, are the implications of this study for our efforts to anticipate the future of world order? At the outset of this inquiry, I identified four types of international change, specifically configurative, constitutional, institutional and positional forms of change. The bulk of my investigation has been devoted to understanding episodes of configurative change, while in the preceding chapter I also sought to identify points of fragility evident in the contemporary state system. In concluding this inquiry, I wish to briefly sketch out the likely contours of international systems change in the coming decades.

Although the future of world order remains uncertain, at the very least, we can expect that the twenty-first century will see the rise of the Asian giants and the corresponding decline of Western hegemony. While unipolarity may persist for some time yet, the great chasm in power and wealth that opened up between East and West with the onset of the industrial revolution will narrow dramatically in the coming century. Of the four types of international change identified earlier, positional change thus seems inevitable, barring some as yet unforeseeable calamity such as the disintegration of either China or India. The rise of non-Western Great Powers (and their possible resurgence, in the case of Russia and Japan) will entail significant shifts in the international

---

[29] On this theme, see for example generally Iklâe, *Annihilation from Within*; and W. Laqueur, 'The terrorism to come', *Policy Review*, 126 (August/September) (2004), 49–64.

distribution of power and privileges, as well as wrenching shifts in the West's understanding of its place in the world. From the Age of Discovery onwards, the peoples of Western Europe and their colonial offspring have believed themselves to possess a special claim to world leadership. The basis of this belief has been recast on diverse foundations over different epochs, with Christianity, racial supremacy and economic and political modernity successively being invoked as the foundation of Western claims to exercise dominance over the rest of humanity. In the twenty-first century, the material asymmetry of power that has sustained this Western self-understanding will slip away, as modernity becomes unshackled from its dominant associations with the Atlantic world, and the historic pattern of a multi-centric world economy dominated by the Eastern powers is finally restored.[30]

The future stability of world order will therefore depend in part on the Western powers' ability – the European powers perhaps even more so than America – to come to terms with their relative decline, and to manage the ascendancy of the emerging Great Powers in a manner that accommodates non-Western aspirations for recognition without sacrificing either vital material interests, or the equally important principled interest in promoting and extending the global human rights agenda. The history of failed attempts to manage the rise of past Great Powers is a testament to the inherent difficulties involved in peacefully managing power transitions. These challenges will be further complicated by principled disagreements between democratic and authoritarian Great Powers over the proper balance to be struck between human rights concerns and the preservation of states' sovereign prerogatives within the domestic sphere.[31] Whether the international community will be able to peacefully resolve these tensions is at this point difficult to foresee. Nevertheless, it can definitely be stated that this effort will require at a minimum the preservation of a state system that is both sufficiently stable to support the continuing operation of the global economy, and sufficiently robust to resist subversion by the anti-systemic forces presently agitating for its destruction. Significant revisions in the global state system's fundamental institutions will be required if these minimum conditions of order are to be met.

Historically, the threat of nomadic predators operating from ungoverned sanctuaries was most commonly tackled within the framework of empire. From the collapse of the Western Roman and Han Empires through to the early modern consolidation of gunpowder empires, nomadic pastoralists preyed

---

[30] On the historical precedent of a multi-centred world economy, see generally Abu-Lughod, *Before European Hegemony*.

[31] On the ideological and geopolitical significance of the ascendancy or re-emergence of authoritarian Great Powers, see generally A. Gat, 'The return of authoritarian Great Powers', *Foreign Affairs*, 86(4) (2007), 59–69.

upon and occasionally overwhelmed their wealthier sedentary neighbours. In managing this threat, sedentary rulers across Eurasia oscillated between strategies of trade and tribute on the one hand, and reprisal and conquest on the other, their choice of strategy being governed largely by the balance of power then obtaining between city and steppe.[32] Even with the consolidation of the Eurasian gunpowder empires and the parallel growth of the European maritime empires, the problem of frontier instability persisted from the seventeenth down to the twentieth century. From Kabul to Khartoum, regional potentates resorted to a plethora of coercive and co-optive strategies, seeking to stabilise their porous frontiers while securing the wealth-producing core of their patrimonies from external assault. Empire-builders took for granted the principled legitimacy of foreign rule over subject peoples. At the same time, they also accepted the practical limits of imperial rule. In restive frontier regions where the empire's reach exceeded its grasp, the best that could be hoped for was a fitful stability to be maintained by local clients where possible, and enforced through punitive expeditions when necessary.[33]

Today, empire is defunct, but many of the governance problems that bedevilled past empires have re-emerged in new and more dangerous forms. In place of fractious imperial frontiers, the international community is now struggling to contain the instability emanating from weak and failing post-colonial states. Similarly, transnational predators such as Al Qaeda stand as contemporary analogues to the nomadic marauders that threatened sedentary societies in an earlier age, with the 'Manhattan raid' of 9/11 providing a chilling demonstration of the disproportionate damage non-state actors are now capable of inflicting without warning on global cities.[34] Should anti-systemic actors succeed in acquiring WMD, the vital imbalance of power that has prevailed between state and non-state actors since the seventeenth century would be drastically compromised, imperilling the very foundations of world order. For this reason alone, it is vital that states collaborate effectively to adapt international society's fundamental institutions to comprehensively confront these challenges.

The international community's responses to emerging threats will be conditioned by two realities that distinguish the contemporary period from earlier epochs. First, solutions predicated on some form of indefinite foreign rule over weak and failing states are no longer viable. Nationalism was effectively globalised in the twentieth century, and popular tolerance for foreign rule remains

---

[32] McNeill, *The Global Condition*, p. 116.

[33] On the spatial limits of governance constraining the power of traditional states, see Giddens, *The Nation-State and Violence*, pp. 51–2.

[34] For further development of this analogy, see M. Ruthven, 'The eleventh of September and the Sudanese Mahdiya in the context of Ibn Khaldun's theory of Islamic history', *International Affairs*, 78(2) (2002), 347–50.

low even in the most volatile of polities.[35] Secondly, imperial strategies of containment that sought to quarantine instability in the periphery are not likely to be practically effective, having been superseded by the surge in global interconnectedness facilitated by modern advances in transportation and communication.[36] Neither the normative basis of empire nor its underlying spatial premises survived the twentieth century. The globalisation of the nation-state has made a return to formal empire politically impossible, while global-isation itself has diluted traditional distinctions between core and peripheral zones, rendering traditional imperial strategies of order maintenance practi-cally unavailing. The governance capacity of fragile states will need to be strengthened, and the state system's collective capacity to resist anti-systemic violence reinforced, if international order is to be maintained. But both projects will need to be undertaken within the parameters of a state system in which norms of anti-colonialism, non-intervention and sovereign equality have become deeply entrenched.

The international community has already demonstrated significant adaptive capacities in the face of the jihadist challenge. The establishment of both the Counter Terrorism Committee Executive Directorate and the 1540 Committee stand out as definitive examples of the facility with which states have harnessed existing authoritative institutions to the task of upholding states' monopoly over legitimate organised violence. These initiatives, in conjunction with more ad hoc forms of multilateral co-operation such as the Proliferation Security Initiative, are demonstrative of the state system's resilience in the face of anti-systemic threats. More fundamentally, however, they also reflect evolving con-ceptions of sovereignty as responsibility. The Security Council's post-9/11 activism in the areas of counter-terrorism and counter-proliferation has led to the emergence of a raft of new 'duties to prevent', which the UN's member states are now universally bound to observe.[37] These developments signify the Great Powers' sanctioning of the partial return of a positive sovereignty regime, at least to the extent that all sovereign states are increasingly expected to fulfil certain minimum requirements associated with the preservation of international order if they are to be fully recognised as members of international society.

The institutionalisation of duties to prevent activities such as terrorist financ-ing and WMD proliferation to non-state actors is a welcome and necessary development, as are multilateral efforts to enhance the institutional capacities of weak but willing states to fulfil these duties. Nevertheless, the defence of

---

[35] On the discrepancy between the universalisation of the nation-state and the persistence of classically imperial governance problems in the contemporary era, see B. R. Rubin, 'Constructing sovereignty for security', *Survival*, 47(4) (2005), 94–5.

[36] Once again, the 9/11 attacks are instructive here, being directed from Afghanistan, but having been co-ordinated in meetings in Hamburg and Kuala Lumpur before being perpetrated in New York and Washington.

[37] See generally Feinstein and Slaughter, 'A duty to prevent'.

international order in the coming decades will be possible only if two related challenges are addressed. First, the international community will need to formulate an agreed framework for punishing those states that conspicuously refuse to uphold their core duties as members of international society. In the post-9/11 period, the United States has repeatedly resorted to violence against states that have been perceived to have been thwarting its counter-terrorism and counter-proliferation objectives. Given the magnitude of the threat posed by both terrorism and WMD proliferation, one can reasonably expect this trend to continue in a post-unipolar world, as Great Powers invoke these perils to justify the preventative use of force against recalcitrant 'outlaw' states.[38] If international order is to be preserved, both coercive and authoritative power will need to be mobilised to defeat anti-systemic actors and their passive and active state sponsors, but this must be done in a way that minimises the collateral damage inflicted on norms of non-intervention and freedom from external aggression. In a world in which imperial solutions to anti-systemic threats are unavailable and American hegemony is a rapidly wasting asset, it is imperative that the international community develop common rules to enable the *legitimate* use of violence in future to neutralise imminent threats and to punish those states that are willing to provide sanctuary to the would-be subverters of the present state system.

In addition to formulating clearer rules for dealing with states that refuse to abide by the most basic norms of international society, it will also be necessary to develop more reliable means of managing the threats posed by ungoverned spaces where sovereign power is either weak or totally absent. The strength of anti-colonial norms makes an overtly imperialist solution to the problem of state failure and state collapse impossible. Similarly, the international community's post-cold war experience of short-term international neo-trusteeship in territories such as Kosovo and East Timor has demonstrated the limited generalisability of neo-trusteeship as a method of systemic stabilisation.[39] Given these normative and practical constraints, the Great Powers and regional organisations will need to collaborate to develop new regimes, both to prioritise targeting of the ungoverned spaces that pose the greatest threats to global peace and security, and also to marshal the material and institutional resources necessary to undertake the reconstructive interventions needed to revive failing and collapsed states.

In addition to managing the rise of new Great Powers and the decline of Western hegemony, world leaders will thus also need to adapt the state system's

---

[38] On the significance of 'outlaw states' and informal relations of coercive hierarchy between these actors and Great Powers, and the recurrence of informal forms of coercive hierarchy alongside the formal institution of sovereignty, see generally G. J. Simpson, *Great Powers and Outlaw States: Unequal sovereigns in the international legal order* (Cambridge University Press, 2004).

[39] Caplan, 'From collapsing states to neo-trusteeship', pp. 235–6.

fundamental institutions to more effectively combat transnational predators, chastise their active and passive state sponsors and revive state authority in the state system's ungoverned spaces. These tasks are likely to be rendered more complicated by the possibility of purposive shifts in the nature of international order in the coming decades. The ascendancy of authoritarian and semi-authoritarian Great Powers such as China and Russia will increasingly constrict Western democracies' scope for promoting the transformational liberal agenda that held sway in the immediate post-cold war era.[40] Equally, while the growth of politicised forms of religiosity will have regionally uneven effects, it is nevertheless likely to open up a noticeable dissonance in values between a secular, rich, demographically moribund North, and a pious, predominantly poor, demographically dynamic South.[41] One need not subscribe to civilisational essentialism to acknowledge the historical particularity of the Western experience, and to acknowledge the challenges to world order posed by the existence of multiple forms of modernity. Recognition that the West's post-Reformation conception of the sacred/secular divide is but one of many possibilities that are compatible with modernity should imply neither the inevitability of cross-cultural confrontation, nor the necessity of disengaging from efforts to promote liberal values internationally out of respect for cultural diversity. On the contrary, the core values of popular eudemonism and self-determination that underpin the global state system resonate across different traditions, while violent extremism of the type personified by jihadist extremism offends the key tenets of all the major faiths. Nevertheless, in seeking to promote their own hitherto dominant liberal conception of the state system's core values, Western democracies should proceed with a spirit of humility. More specifically, they must proceed with a willingness to accept the possibility that public piety is not incompatible with popular sovereignty and that, in the Islamic world in particular, a degree of rapprochement with peaceful variants of political religiosity will be essential if the threat of jihadist terrorism is to be decisively defeated.

Positional changes in the global state system will be *inevitable* in the coming decades. Revisions of the state system's fundamental institutions are *likely*, given the necessity of such reforms if anti-systemic threats are to be effectively contained. Purposive challenges to the state system's normative values – particularly in their present liberal incarnation – are *possible*, owing to both the rise or revival of authoritarian Great Powers, and the global ascendancy of intensely politicised forms of religiosity, especially but not exclusively within the Islamic world. In light of these trends, is configurative change on the scale

---

[40] Gat, 'The return of authoritarian Great Powers', pp. 67–8.
[41] For a variation on this theme that focuses on an emerging values gap not between the West and Islam but rather between a secular North and an ascendant Southern Christianity, see generally P. Jenkins, *The Next Christendom: The coming of global Christianity* (Oxford University Press, 2002).

of my historic cases likely in the twenty-first century? I would suggest that configurative change remains a remote but nevertheless imaginable possibility, believing it more likely that the custodians of international order will 'muddle through' the challenges of the coming decades than that we will witness the state system's fundamental transformation. As unipolarity wanes, we are likely to enter an era of 'contested constitutions', comparable in many respects to the decades immediately following the Congress of Vienna.[42] Much like the post-Congress period, the world will be multi-polar in its essential form, but informally underwritten by the dual hegemony of two preponderant powers. In the nineteenth century, Britain and Russia underpinned the Concert system as dual hegemons, while in the twenty-first century their places are likely to be taken by America and China, the two serving respectively as the maritime liberal and continental autocratic anchors of an uneasy but nevertheless relatively stable international order.[43] Globally, the Great Powers will compete for influence in major energy-producing regions, with the lands of the former Ottoman Empire and Central Asia serving once again as the chief foci of rivalry, just as they did in the nineteenth century.[44] As in the post-Congress era, the Great Powers are also likely to disagree on the extent to which insurgent ideologies (liberalism in the nineteenth century, Islamism today) threaten international order, and will disagree too on the scope of states' legitimate prerogatives to intervene to resist Islamist influence in states of vital concern.

In yet another parallel with the post-Congress system, states will also collaborate to suppress shared anti-systemic threats. As with the nineteenth-century struggle to suppress piracy, undertaken largely under British leadership, America is likely for some time yet to take the lead in combating transnational terrorism and non-state WMD proliferation, owing both to its acute vulnerability to these threats, and also to its unparalleled military command of the global commons.[45] However, unlike the post-Congress Concert, initiatives against shared threats will need to be undertaken with at least partial regard to the norms of consultation and consensus now institutionalised in the UN system. Equally, Great Power competition will be muted in the coming century both by unprecedented economic interdependence, and by the

---

[42] On periods of 'contested constitutions' within the history of international orders, see Philpott, *Revolutions in Sovereignty*, p. 26. I would like to thank Heather Rae for first drawing my attention to this aspect of Philpott's argument.

[43] On dual hegemony as the basis of the post-1815 international order, and on the distinguishability of dual hegemony from a bipolar balance of power, see Schroeder, 'Did the Vienna settlement rest on a balance of power?', p. 693.

[44] On this point, see generally F. Leverett and J. Bader, 'Managing China–U.S. energy competition in the Middle East', *The Washington Quarterly*, 29(1) (2005), 187–201.

[45] On America's present military command of the global commons and its likely persistence for the foreseeable future, see generally B. Posen, 'Command of the commons: The military foundations of US hegemony', *International Security*, 28(1) (2003), 5–46.

consolidation of anti-imperialist norms that prevent the resolution of 'great games' through the overt territorial conquest or partition of smaller polities. Finally, in the most profound contrast with the nineteenth century, the international order of the twenty-first century will genuinely be a world of regions. With the global imbalance of power between 'the West and the rest' finally wound back, different regional orders are likely to cohere under the broader glacis of a global state system, with these regional orders reflecting the diverse historical experiences of their constituent polities. The traumas of the past five centuries were of such magnitude and permanence that modern-day facsimiles of either Christendom or the Sinosphere will not re-emerge. Nevertheless, echoes of these old orders are likely to resurface, whether in the more formal structure of a heteronomous European Union, or in the more informal structure of an East Asian order economically dominated by Chinese family business networks, and sustained politically and diplomatically by a regionally preponderant China.[46]

The survival of the global state system, albeit one characterised by continuing Great Power rivalry, persistent transnational security threats and intensifying regional diversity, is likely. It is not, however, guaranteed. The present world order is bedevilled by widespread institutional decay, the emergence of anti-systemic ideologies and increases in violence interdependence. Should the custodians of international order fail to respond decisively to these challenges, it is faintly possible to envisage the state system's continuing decay and accelerating disintegration in the coming century. Such a scenario might begin with growing global anxieties over food, water and energy security. These anxieties would be driven by increasing demand for these necessities, combined with diminishing supply caused by over-consumption and local ecological crises fuelled by anthropogenic climate change. Global warming is expected to impact with particular severity on the already water-scarce societies of the Mediterranean littoral, and would feed into increased popular distress and disillusionment towards government among the rapidly growing populations of North Africa and the Middle East. Simultaneously, rising demands for fossil fuels would draw the Great Powers into further involvement in the Greater Middle East. Great Power competition for resources and influence would aggravate the region's already tense strategic situation. In conjunction with states' existing concerns about the continuing Iranian ascendancy, accelerating Great Power competition could amplify existing regional trends towards conventional arms build-ups and 'nuclear hedging' by concerned

---

[46] On the prospect of a partial return to European heteronomy, see again Ruggie, 'Territoriality and beyond', pp. 171–2. On the (re)emergence of a Sinosphere politically dominated by China and economically dominated by interlocking and regionally dispersed Chinese family business networks, see Hamashita, 'The intra-regional system in East Asia', pp. 134–5.

states.[47] At the same time, increased Great Power involvement in the Middle East would also exacerbate the sense of existential anxiety informing jihadist ideology, leading to a likely surge in jihadist terror attacks both within the region and beyond.

Within an ever more volatile environment, and against the backdrop of rising terror attacks against Great Power interests overseas and at home, states would develop ever more permissive defensive justifications for the pre-emptive use of force against terrorists and their presumed state sponsors. Equally, the temptation to seize hydrocarbon reserves, both to ensure states' own energy security and deny it to rivals, could contribute to a further corrosion of norms against aggression. This would in turn worsen the security anxieties of small energy-rich states, further increasing their incentives to acquire nuclear weapons to deter potential aggressors. A regional nuclear proliferation cascade would in turn raise the likelihood of non-state actors acquiring WMD and deploying it against Western targets. Were this to occur, the global state system – at least in its liberal incarnation – would be in danger of unravelling. Domestically, formerly liberal states would confront the now existential threat posed by terrorism by further winding back civil liberties, adopting an even more permissive attitude towards the use of torture upon terror suspects, and potentially even reviving the World War II precedent of indefinitely interning suspect nationalities. Borders would be sealed to insulate the homeland from subsequent attacks, threatening the continued operation of the global economy. With the fragile bonds of global economic interdependence severed, strong states might be compelled to return to imperialist strategies of wealth accumulation to sustain their popular legitimacy at home. This development would further weaken the norms of sovereign equality, non-aggression and non-intervention that have sustained the state system since 1945, threatening a return to a less liberal, less peaceful and less egalitarian age.

While it is possible to envisage the breakdown of the present international order, it is impossible to reliably predict what form of successor order might emerge on the other side of the abyss. Conceivably, the Great Powers might succeed in reconstituting a global order of sovereign states, albeit one equipped with mechanisms of collective defence more properly attuned to the threats of the twenty-first century. Alternatively, some form of global confederacy might emerge, with states voluntarily surrendering a portion of their sovereignty to

---

[47] On recent conventional arms build-ups in the region, see D. Glaister, 'US accused of fuelling arms race with $20bn Arab weapons sale', *The Guardian*, 30 July 2007. On the increased tendency towards 'nuclear hedging' in the Middle East, as evidenced in the fact that no fewer than 13 Sunni states have declared atomic energy plans within the space of a year in response to the Iranian ascendancy, see D. Murphy, 'Middle East racing to nuclear power', *Christian Science Monitor*, 1 November 2007.

a global authority equipped with the authoritative and coercive wherewithal necessary to confront common threats to global peace and security more effectively than its UN predecessor.[48] Yet another possibility is a reversion to a 'durable disorder' characterised by a plethora of different governance forms interacting with one another in the absence of formal organising principles or shared values.[49] Finally, in the event of a genuinely transformative crisis, technological and ideological possibilities that are as yet unimaginable might facilitate the emergence of the world's first genuinely global empire. Regardless of the exact outcome of such a hypothetical crisis, the historic experience of both Christendom and the Sinosphere teaches us that transformations of international order are singularly traumatic experiences. These cases also warn us of the perils of complacency. Both Christendom and the Sinosphere were underpinned by religious visions that appeared to contemporaries to guarantee the indefinite perpetuation of these orders until it was too late to prevent their dissolution. The global state system by contrast lacks the reassuring certainty of any cosmic guarantee, relying rather on the collective reason of its members to ensure its preservation. Writing this book has given me a vivid appreciation of the horrors entailed in transformations of international order. It has also reinforced my conviction that the contemporary world order is more fragile than is commonly acknowledged. Nevertheless, it has also reaffirmed my belief that the challenges facing the global state system, unlike those that faced its historic predecessors, remain in the last instance eminently surmountable.

St Augustine once argued that the Latin word *religio* derived from the earlier *religare*, meaning 'to bind together'.[50] From Augustine's time down to the Reformation, religion served this vital purpose within Christendom, tying otherwise disparate and feuding communities together through the higher bond of a common faith. Since the sixteenth century, however, religion has receded as the basis for international order, first within Christendom and then subsequently throughout the world. Similarly, with nationalism's universal ascendancy in the twentieth century, empire has also been vanquished as the basis of global order. The volatile synthesis of religious ethics and imperial might that underpinned regional orders for the better part of the past two and a half millennia is now defunct, marking a decisive rupture from humanity's dominant experiences of political order from the advent of the Axial Age

---

[48] This seems to be the preferred vision of Daniel Deudney, who anticipates the possibility of continually rising levels of violence interdependence producing a federal republican world nuclear government incorporating 'negarchical structures of mutual restraint' among the world's political communities. See Deudney, *Bounding Power*, pp. 262–4, 276.

[49] On 'durable disorder' as a possible future, see P. Cerny, 'Terrorism and the new security dilemma', *Naval War College Review*, 58(1) (2005), 29–30.

[50] On the etymology of religion, see M. Warner, 'Introduction' in M. Warner (ed.), *Religion and Philosophy* (Cambridge University Press, 1992), p. 1.

onwards. But the ecumenical world order of sovereign nation-states that emerged from empires' ashes after 1945 remains vulnerable to violent contestation, and neither divine mandate nor historical inevitability guarantees its indefinite survival.

The twenty-first century began with the opposing forces of religious fanaticism and imperial temptation together exposing the fragility of the contemporary world order. Both the specific challenges that jihadism and American military adventurism posed to world order after 9/11 will likely diminish in the long term. But these developments nevertheless illuminated two inescapable imperatives that will forever confront international orders' custodians. First, because all international orders embody distinct visions of the good, they will always be susceptible to violent subversion, and thus will always need to rely partially on coercive power to uphold their values in the face of revolutionary opposition. Secondly, and again because of their identification with historically particular visions of the good, international orders can only be successfully defended when violence in defence of order is effectively harmonised with the ethical imperatives and shared standards of legitimacy that help constitute international orders in the first instance. In this respect, then, Reinhold Niebuhr's observations concerning the inherent dualism of political life remain as relevant today as they did when first penned over five decades ago: 'Politics will, to the end of history, be an area where conscience and power meet, where the ethical and coercive factors of human life will interpenetrate and work out their tentative and uneasy compromises.'[51] For all of the momentous historical changes this book has chronicled, it is this fundamental continuity, the perennial imperative of reconciling conscience and coercion and harnessing both in the service of order, that is and shall remain the basic challenge for the world's leaders in the coming century.

---

[51] R. Niebuhr, *Moral Man and Immoral Society: A study in ethics and politics* (New York: Charles Scribner, 1960), p. 4.

Bibliography

Abu-Lughod, J. L., *Before European Hegemony: The world system* AD *1250–1350* (Oxford: Oxford University Press, 1989).

Adas, M., *Machines as the Measure of Men: Science, technology, and ideologies of Western dominance* (Ithaca: Cornell University Press, 1989).

Ahmed, S., 'Pakistan's nuclear weapons program: Turning points and nuclear choices', *International Security*, 23(4) (1999), 178–204.

Anderson, B., *Imagined Communities: Reflections on the origins and spread of nationalism* (London: Verso, 1991).

Anderson, M. S., *The Origins of the Modern European State System, 1494–1618* (London: Longman, 1998).

Aristotle, *The Politics*, trans. T. A. Sinclair (London: Penguin Books, 1962).

Armstrong, K., *The Battle for God: Fundamentalism in Judaism, Christianity, and Islam* (London: HarperCollins Publishers, 2000).

Islam: A short history (London: Phoenix, 2001).

A Short History of Myth (Edinburgh; New York: Canongate, 2006).

The Great Transformation: The world in the time of Buddha, Socrates, Confucius and Jeremiah (London: Atlantic Books, 2006).

Arquilla, J. and Ronfeldt, D. (eds.), *Networks and Netwars: The future of crime, terror, and militancy* (Santa Monica: RAND, 2001).

Augustine, *City of God* (London: Penguin Books, 1984).

Badie, B. and Royal, C., *The Imported State: The Westernization of the political order* (Stanford: Stanford University Press, 2000).

Bahgat, G., 'Iran and the United States: The emerging security paradigm in the Middle East', *Parameters*, 37(2) (2007), 5–18.

Bain, W., *Between Anarchy and Society: Trusteeship and the obligations of power* (Oxford: Oxford University Press, 2003).

Barkey, K., *Empire of Difference: The Ottomans in comparative perspective* (Cambridge: Cambridge University Press, 2008).

Barkin, J. S., 'Realist constructivism', *International Studies Review*, 5(3) (2003), 325–42.

Barraclough, G., *An Introduction to Contemporary History* (London: C. A. Watts and Co. Ltd, 1964).

Bartlett, R., *The Making of Europe: Conquest, colonization, and cultural change, 950–1350* (Princeton: Princeton University Press, 1993).

Bat, Y. O., *Eurabia: The Euro-Arab axis* (Madison: Fairleigh Dickinson University Press, 2005).

Bayly, C. A., *Rulers, Townsmen, and Bazaars: North Indian society in the age of British expansion, 1770–1870* (Cambridge: Cambridge University Press, 1983).

Imperial Meridian: The British Empire and the world, 1780–1830 (London: Longman, 1989).

The Birth of the Modern World 1780–1914: Global connections and comparisons (Oxford: Blackwell, 2004).

'The Boxer uprising and India: Globalizing myths' in R. Bickers and R. G. Tiedeman (eds.), *The Boxers, China and the World* (Plymouth: Rowman and Littlefield Publishers, 2007), pp. 147–55.

Bean, R., 'War and the birth of the nation state', *The Journal of Economic History*, 33 (1) (1973), 203–21.

Bellamy, A. J., 'Whither the responsibility to protect? Humanitarian intervention and the 2005 World Summit', *International Affairs*, 20(2) (2006), 143–69.

Berger, P. L. and Luckmann, T., *The Social Construction of Reality* (Middlesex: Penguin Books, 1966).

Berman, H., *Law and Revolution: The formation of the Western legal tradition* (Cambridge, MA: Harvard University Press, 1983).

'Religious foundations of law in the West: An historical perspective', *Journal of Law and Religion*, 1(1) (1983), 3–43.

Bisson, T. N., 'The organized peace in Southern France and Catalonia, ca.1140–ca.1233', *American Historical Review*, 82(2) (1977), 290–311.

Bizer, E., Betts, R. R. and Spooner, F. C., 'The Reformation in difficulties' in G. R. Elton (ed.), *The New Cambridge Modern History*, II: *The Reformation, 1520–1559* (Cambridge: Cambridge University Press, 1968), pp. 161–225.

Black, J., *A Military Revolution? Military change and European society 1550–1800* (London: Macmillan, 1991).

Kings, Nobles and Commoners: States and societies in early modern Europe, a revisionist history (London: I. B. Tauris, 2004).

'War and international relations: A military-historical perspective on force and legitimacy', *Review of International Studies*, 31(Special Issue) (2005), 127–42.

Bloch, B., *Feudal Society*, 2 vols., I: *The Growth of Ties of Dependence* (Chicago: The University of Chicago Press, 1961).

Blockmans, W., *Emperor Charles V 1500–1558* (London: Arnold, 2002).

Boardman, E. P., 'Christian influence upon the ideology of the Taiping rebellion', *The Far Eastern Quarterly*, 10(2) (1951), 115–24.

Bodde, D., 'The state and empire of Ch'in' in D. Twitchett and M. Loewe (eds.), *The Cambridge History of China*, I: *The Ch'in and Han Empires, 221 BC – AD 220* (Cambridge: Cambridge University Press, 1986), pp. 20–102.

Bodin, J., *The Six Books of the Commonwealth* (Oxford: Basil Blackwell, 1956).

Bolitho, H., 'The inseparable trinity: Japan's relations with China and Korea' in J. W. Hall (ed.), *The Cambridge Modern History of Japan*, IV: *Early Modern Japan* (Cambridge: Cambridge University Press, 1991), pp. 235–300.

Booth, K. and Dunne, T. (eds.), *Worlds in Collision: Terror and the future of global order* (Basingstoke: Palgrave, 2002).

Bossy, J., 'The Mass as a social institution 1200–1700', *Past and Present*, 100 (1983), 29–61.

Christianity in the West, 1400–1700 (Oxford: Oxford University Press, 1985).

Bowden, B. and Seabrooke, L. (eds.), *Global Standards of Market Civilization* (London: Routledge, 2006).

Bozeman, A., *The Future of Law in a Multicultural World* (Princeton: Princeton University Press, 1971).

Brady, T. A. Jr, 'Confessionalization: The career of a concept' in J. M. Headley, H. J. Hillerbrand and A. Papalas (eds.), *Confessionalization in Europe, 1555–1700* (Aldershot: Ashgate, 2004), pp. 1–20.

Bronson, R., *Thicker Than Oil: America's uneasy partnership with Saudi Arabia* (Oxford; New York: Oxford University Press, 2006).

Brooks, S. G. and Wohlforth, W. C., 'American primacy in perspective', *Foreign Affairs*, 81(4) (2002), 20–33.

Brunero, D., *Britain's Imperial Cornerstone in China: The Chinese Maritime Customs Service, 1854–1949* (New York: Routledge, 2006).

Buchanan, A. and Keohane, R. O., 'The preventive use of force: A cosmopolitan institutional proposal', *Ethics and International Affairs*, 18(1) (2004), 1–22.

Bukovansky, M., *Legitimacy and Power Politics: The American and French Revolutions in international political culture* (Princeton: Princeton University Press, 2002).

Bull, H., *The Anarchical Society: A study of order in world politics* (London: Macmillan Press, 1995).

Bunker, R., 'Epochal change: War over social and political organization', *Parameters*, 27(2) (1997), 15–25.

Burke, J., *Al Qaeda: Casting a shadow of terror* (London: I. B. Tauris, 2003).

Burkhardt, J., 'The summitless pyramid: War aims and peace compromise among Europe's universalist powers' in K. Bussman and H. Schilling (eds.), *1648: War and peace in Europe* (Münster/Osnabrück: Westfälisches Landesmuseum, 1998), pp. 51–60.

Burns, J. H., 'The idea of Absolutism' in J. Miller (ed.), *Absolutism in Seventeenth Century Europe* (London: Macmillan, 1990), pp. 21–42.

Butterfield, H., *Toleration in Religion and Politics* (New York: Council on Religion and International Affairs, 1980).

Buzan, B., *People, States and Fear* (London: Harvester Wheatsheaf, 1983).

Buzan, B., Jones, C. and Little, R., *The Logic of Anarchy: Neorealism to structural realism* (New York: Columbia University Press, 1993).

Calder, K., 'Securing security through prosperity: The San Francisco system in comparative perspective', *The Pacific Review*, 17(1) (2004), 135–57.

Calvin, J., *Calvin: Theological treatises* (London: SCM Press Ltd, 1956).

Calvocoressi, P., Wint, G. and Pritchard, J., *Total War: The causes and courses of the Second World War,* 2 vols., II: *The Greater East Asia and Pacific Conflict* (London: Penguin Books, 1989).

Cameron, E., *The European Reformation* (Oxford: Clarendon Press, 1991).

Cantimori, D., 'Italy and the papacy' in G. R. Elton (ed.), *The New Cambridge Modern History,* II: *The Reformation, 1520–1559* (Cambridge: Cambridge University Press, 1990), pp. 288–312.

Caplan, R., 'From collapsing states to neo-trusteeship: The limits to solving the problem of "precarious statehood" in the 21st century', *Third World Quarterly,* 28(2) (2007), 231–44.

Carr, E. H., *The Twenty Years' Crisis, 1919–1939: An introduction to the study of international relations* (New York: Harper and Row, 1946).

Castoriadis, C., *The Imaginary Institution of Society* (Cambridge, UK: Polity Press, 1987).

Cerny, P., 'The new security dilemma: Divisibility, defection, and disorder in the global era', *Review of International Studies,* 26(4) (2000), 623–46.

'Terrorism and the new security dilemma', *Naval War College Review* 58(1) (2005), 11–33.

Chang, H., 'Intellectual change and the reform movement, 1890–8' in J. K. Fairbank and D. Twitchett (eds.), *The Cambridge History of China,* XI: *Late Ch'ing, 1800–1911,* Pt II (Cambridge: Cambridge University Press, 1980), pp. 274–338.

Chinese Intellectuals in Crisis: The search for order and meaning (1890–1911) (Berkeley: University of California Press, 1987).

Chen, F. T.-S., 'The Confucian view of world order' in M. W. Janis and C. Evans (eds.), *Religion and International Law* (Leiden: Martinus Nijhoff Publishers, 2004), pp. 27–49.

Chi, H.-S., *Warlord Politics in China, 1916–1928* (Stanford: Stanford University Press, 1976).

Chua, A., *Day of Empire: How hyperpowers rise to global dominance – and why they fall* (New York: Doubleday, 2007).

Church, W. F., *Richelieu and Reason of State* (Princeton: Princeton University Press, 1972).

Clarke, R. A., *Against All Enemies: Inside America's war on terror* (New York: Free Press, 2004).

Coll, S., *Ghost Wars: The secret history of the CIA, Afghanistan, and Bin Laden, from the Soviet invasion to September 10, 2001* (New York: Penguin Press, 2004).

Colley, L., *Britons: Forging the nation, 1707–1837* (New Haven: Yale University Press, 1992).

Collins, S. L., *From Divine Cosmos to Sovereign State: An intellectual history of consciousness and the idea of order in Renaissance England* (Oxford: Oxford University Press, 1989).

Cornell, S. E., 'The narcotics threat in Greater Central Asia: From crime-terror nexus to state infiltration?', *China and Eurasia Forum Quarterly*, 4(1) (2006), 37–67.

Cosimo, N., di, 'Did guns matter? Firearms and the Qing formation' in L. A. Struve (ed.), *The Qing Formation in World Historical Time* (Cambridge, MA: Harvard University Press, 2004), pp. 121–66.

Cox, R., 'Social forces, states, and world orders: Beyond international relations theory', *Millennium: Journal of International Studies*, 10(2) (1981), 126–55.

Creveld, M., van, *The Transformation of War* (New York: Free Press, 1991).

Darwin, J., *After Tamerlane: The global history of empire since 1405* (London: Allen Lane, 2007).

Davies, N., *Europe: A history* (London: Pimlico, 1997).

Davis, E., 'History matters: Past as prologue in building democracy in Iraq', *Orbis*, 49(2) (2005), 229–44.

Davis, N. Z., 'The rites of violence: Religious violence in sixteenth century France', *Past and Present*, 59 (1973), 51–91.

'The sacred and the body social in sixteenth century Lyon', *Past and Present*, 90 (1981), 40–70.

Deane, H., *The Political and Social Ideas of Saint Augustine* (New York: Columbia University Press, 1963).

Dehio, L., *The Precarious Balance: Four centuries of the European power struggle* (London: Chatto and Windus, 1962).

Deudney, D., *Bounding Power: Republican security theory from the polis to the global village* (Princeton: Princeton University Press, 2007).

'Regrounding realism: Anarchy, security, and changing material contexts', *Security Studies*, 10(1) (2000), 1–42.

Deutsch, K. W., 'Medieval unity and the economic conditions for an international civilization', *The Canadian Journal of Economics and Political Science*, 10(1) (1944), 18–35.

Deventer, J., '"Confessionalisation": A useful theoretical concept for the study of religion, politics, and society in early modern East-Central Europe?', *European Review of History*, 11(3) (2004), 403–25.

Donnelly, J., 'Human rights: A new standard of civilization?', *International Affairs*, 74(1) (1998), 1–23.

Doran, M. S., 'Somebody else's civil war', *Foreign Affairs*, 81(1) (2002), 22–42.

Doran, S., *England and Europe in the Sixteenth Century* (London: Macmillan Press Ltd, 1999).

Duara, P., 'State involution: A study of local finances in north China, 1911–1935', *Comparative Studies in Society and History*, 29(1) (1987), 132–61.

Culture, Power, and the State: Rural north China, 1900–1942 (Stanford: Stanford University Press, 1988).

Duby, G., *The Chivalrous Society* (London: Edward Arnold, 1977).

The Three Orders: Feudal society imagined (Chicago: The University of Chicago Press, 1978).

Duus, P., *The Abacus and the Sword: The Japanese penetration of Korea, 1895–1910* (Berkeley: University of California Press, 1995).

Eisenstadt, S. N., 'The Axial Age: The emergence of transcendental visions and the rise of clerics', *European Journal of Sociology*, XXIII (1982), 294–314.

Elleman, B. A., *Modern Chinese Warfare, 1795–1989* (New York: Routledge, 2001).

Elliott, J. H., 'Revolution and continuity in early modern Europe', *Past and Present*, 42 (1969), 35–56.

'A Europe of composite monarchies', *Past and Present*, 137 (1992), 48–71.

Europe Divided 1559–1598, 2nd edn (Oxford: Blackwell Publishers Ltd, 2000).

Elshtain, J. B., *Sovereignty: God, state, self* (New York: Basic Books, 2008).

Elton, G. R., 'Constitutional development and political thought in Western Europe' in G. R. Elton (ed.), *The New Cambridge Modern History, II: The Reformation 1520–1559* (Cambridge: Cambridge University Press, 1990), pp. 478–504.

Reformation Europe, 1517–1559 (London: Blackwell, 1999).

Esherick, J. W., *The Origins of the Boxer Uprising* (Berkeley: University of California Press, 1987).

Esty, D. C., 'The World Trade Organization's legitimacy crisis', *World Trade Review*, 1(1) (2002), 7–22.

Eto, S., 'China's international relations, 1911–1931' in J. K. Fairbank and A. Feuerwerker (eds.), *The Cambridge History of China, XIII: Republican China 1912–1949*, Pt II (Cambridge: Cambridge University Press, 1986), pp. 74–115.

Fairbank, J. K, 'Synarchy under the treaties' in J. K. Fairbank (ed.), *Chinese Thought and Institutions* (Chicago: The University of Chicago Press, 1957), pp. 204–31.

'A preliminary framework' in J. K. Fairbank (ed.), *The Chinese World Order: Traditional China's foreign relations* (Cambridge, MA: Harvard University Press, 1968), pp. 1–19.

'Introduction: The old order' in D. Twitchett and J. K. Fairbank (eds.), *The Cambridge History of China, X: Late Ch'ing, 1800–1911*, Pt I (Cambridge: Cambridge University Press, 1978), pp. 1–34.

and Goldman, M., *China: A new history* (Cambridge, MA: The Belknap Press of Harvard University Press, 2006).

Reischauer, E. O. and Craig, A. M., *East Asia: Tradition and transformation* (Boston: Houghton Mifflin Company, 1989).

Feinstein, L. and Slaughter, A.-M., 'A duty to prevent', *Foreign Affairs*, 83(1) (2004), 136–50.

Ferguson, N., *Colossus: The rise and fall of the American empire* (London: Penguin Books, 2005).

Fischer-Galati, S. A., *Ottoman Imperialism and German Protestantism, 1521–1555* (New York: Octagon Books, 1972).

Fitzgerald, J., *Awakening China: Politics, culture, and class in the nationalist revolution* (Stanford: Stanford University Press, 1996).

Fletcher, J., 'Ch'ing Inner Asia' in D. Twitchett and J. K. Fairbank (eds.), *The Cambridge History of China, X: Late Ch'ing, 1800–1911*, Pt I (Cambridge: Cambridge University Press, 1976), pp. 35–106.

Flora, P., Kuhnle, S. and Urwin, D. (eds.), *State Formation, Nation-Building, and Mass Politics in Europe: The theory of Stein Rokkan, based on his collected works* (Oxford: Oxford University Press, 1999).

Folz, R. *The Concept of Empire in Western Europe: From the fifth to the fourteenth century* (London: Edward Arnold, 1969).

Fontana, B., 'Logos and kratos: Gramsci and the Ancients on hegemony', *Journal of the History of Ideas*, 61(2) (2000), 305–26.

Fortin, E. L., 'St Thomas Aquinas' in L. Strauss and J. Cropsey (eds.), *History of Political Philosophy* (Chicago: The University of Chicago Press, 1987).

Freedman, L., *The Transformation of Strategic Affairs*, Adelphi Paper 379 (New York: International Institute for Strategic Studies, 2006).

Friedrichs, C. J., 'The war and German society' in G. Parker (ed.), *The Thirty Years' War* (London: Routledge, 1997), pp. 186–91.

Frum, D. and Perle, R., *An End to Evil: How to win the war on terror* (New York: Random House, 2003).

Fukuyama, F., *State-Building: Governance and world order in the 21st century* (Ithaca: Cornell University Press, 2004).

Fung, E. S. K., *The Military Dimension of the Chinese Revolution: The new army and its role in the revolution of 1911* (Canberra: Australian National University Press, 1980).

    The Diplomacy of Imperial Retreat: Britain's South China policy, 1924–1931 (Hong Kong; New York: Oxford University Press, 1991).

Fung, Y.-L., *A Short History of Chinese Philosophy: A systematic account of Chinese thought from its origins to the present day* (New York: The Free Press, 1976).

Furth, C., 'Intellectual change: From the reform movement to the May fourth movement, 1895–1900' in J. K. Fairbank (ed.), *The Cambridge History of China, XII: Republican China 1912–1949*, Pt I (Cambridge: Cambridge University Press, 1983), pp. 322–404.

Gat, A., 'The return of authoritarian Great Powers', *Foreign Affairs*, 86(4) (2007), 59–69.

Gauchet, M., *The Disenchantment of the World: A political history of religion* (Princeton: Princeton University Press, 1997).

Gause, F. G., *Oil Monarchies: Domestic and security challenges in the Arab Gulf States* (New York: Council on Foreign Relations Press, 1994).

Geary, P. J., 'Living with conflicts in stateless France: A typology of conflict management mechanisms, 1050–1200' in P. J. Geary (ed.), *Living with the Dead in the Middle Ages* (Ithaca: Cornell University Press, 1994), pp. 125–60.

Gelabert, J., 'The fiscal burden' in R. Bonney (ed.), *Economic Systems and State Finance* (Oxford: Clarendon Press, 1995), pp. 539–76.

Gellner, E., 'Patrons and clients' in E. Gellner and J. Waterbury (eds.), *Patrons and Clients in Mediterranean Societies* (London: Gerald Duckworth and Co. Ltd, 1977), pp. 1–6.

    Plough, Sword, and Book: The structure of human history (London: Paladin Grafton Books, 1991).

Gerges, F. A., *The Far Enemy: Why the jihad went global* (Cambridge: Cambridge University Press, 2005).

Giddens, A., *The Nation-State and Violence* (Cambridge: Polity Press, 1985).

Gilpin, R., *War and Change in World Politics* (Cambridge; New York: Cambridge University Press, 1981).

Glaister, D., 'US accused of fuelling arms race with $20bn Arab weapons sale', *The Guardian*, 30 July 2007.

Goldberg, E., 'Smashing idols and the state: The Protestant ethic and Sunni radicalism', *Comparative Studies in Society and History*, 33(1) (1991), 3–35.

Goldstone, J., *Revolution and Rebellion in the Early Modern World* (Berkeley: University of California Press, 1991).

    'Neither late imperial nor early modern: Efflorescences and the Qing formation in world history' in L. A. Struve (ed.), *The Qing Formation in World-Historical Time* (Cambridge, MA: Harvard University Press, 2004), pp. 242–302.

Gong, G. W., *The Standard of 'Civilization' in International Society* (Oxford: Clarendon Press, 1984).

Gorski, P. S., 'The Mosaic moment: An early modernist critique of modernist theories of nationalism', *The American Journal of Sociology*, 105(5) (2000), 1428–68.

    'Historicizing the secularization debate: Church, state and society in late medieval and early modern Europe, *ca.*1300 to 1700', *American Sociological Review*, 65(1) (2000), 138–67.

    The Disciplinary Revolution: Calvinism and the rise of the state in early modern Europe (Chicago: The University of Chicago Press, 2003).

Graham, G. S., *The China Station: War and diplomacy 1830–1860* (Oxford: Oxford University Press, 1978).

Gray, C. S., 'How has war changed since the end of the cold war?', *Parameters*, 35(1) (2005), 14–26.

Gregory, B. S., *Salvation at Stake: Christian martyrdom in early modern Europe* (Cambridge, MA: Harvard University Press, 1999).

Grimmelshausen, H. J. C., von, *Simplicius Simplicissimus* (London: John Calder, 1964).

Gross, L., 'The Peace of Westphalia 1648–1948', *The American Journal of International Law*, 42(1) (1948), 20–41.

Grygiel, J. J., *Great Powers and Geopolitical Change* (Baltimore: Johns Hopkins University Press, 2006).

Habermas, J., *Moral Consciousness and Communicative Action* (Cambridge, MA: MIT Press, 1990).

Hall, J. A., *International Orders* (Cambridge: Polity Press, 1996).

Hall, R. B., *National Collective Identity: Social constructs and international systems* (New York: Columbia University Press, 1999).

Hamashita, T., 'The intra-regional system in East Asia in modern times' in P. Katzenstein and T. Shiraishi (eds.), *Network Power: Japan and Asia* (Ithaca, NY: Cornell University Press, 1997), pp. 113–35.

'Tribute and treaties: East Asian treaty ports networks in the era of negotiation, 1834–1894', *European Journal of East Asian Studies*, 1(1) (2001), 59–87.

Hammes, T. X., 'War evolves into the fourth generation', *Contemporary Security Policy*, 26(2) (2005), 189–221.

Hao, Y.-P. I. and Wang, E.-M., 'Changing Chinese views of Western relations, 1840–1895' in J. K. Fairbank and K.-C. Liu (eds.), *The Cambridge History of China*, XI: *Late Ch'ing, 1800–1911*, Pt II (Cambridge: Cambridge University Press, 1980), pp. 142–201.

Harley, J. B. and Woodward, D. (eds.), *Cartography in Prehistoric, Ancient, and Medieval Europe and the Mediterranean* (Chicago: The University of Chicago Press, 1987).

Hawkins, M., *Social Darwinism in European and American Thought, 1860–1945: Nature as model and nature as threat* (Cambridge: Cambridge University Press, 1997).

Head, T. and Landes, R. A., *The Peace of God: Social violence and religious response in France around the year 1000* (Ithaca: Cornell University Press, 1992).

Headrick, D. R., *The Tools of Empire: Technology and European imperialism in the nineteenth century* (Oxford: Oxford University Press, 1981).

Hemmer, C. and Katzenstein, P. J., 'Why is there no NATO in Asia? Collective identity, regionalism, and the origins of multilateralism', *International Organization*, 56(3) (2002), 575–607.

Henshall, N., *The Myth of Absolutism: Change and continuity in early modern European monarchy* (London: Longman, 1992).

Herz, J., 'Rise and demise of the territorial state', *World Politics*, 9(4) (1957), 473–93.

Heupel, M., 'Combining hierarchical and soft modes of governance: The UN Security Council's approach to terrorism and weapons of mass destruction proliferation after 9/11', *Cooperation and Conflict*, 43(1) (2008), 7–29.

Hevia, J. L., 'Looting and its discontents: Moral discourse and the plunder of Beijing, 1900–1901' in R. Bickers and R. G. Tiedeman (eds.), *The Boxers, China and the World* (Plymouth, UK: Rowman and Littlefield Publishers, 2007), pp. 93–113.

Hirst, P. H., *War and Power in the 21st Century: The state, military conflict, and the international system* (Cambridge, UK: Polity Press, 2001).

Hobbes, T., *Leviathan* (London: Penguin Books, 1985).

Hobsbawm, E. J., *The Age of Empire, 1875–1914* (London: Abacus, 2003).

Hobson, C., 'Democracy as civilisation', *Global Society*, 22(1) (2008), 75–95.

Hobson, J. M., *The Eastern Origins of Western Civilization* (Cambridge: Cambridge University Press, 2004).

and Sharman, J. C., 'The enduring place of hierarchy in world politics', *European Journal of International Relations*, 11(1) (2005), 63–98.

Hoffman, B., 'The internationalization of terrorism' in B. Hoffman (ed.), *Inside Terrorism* (New York: Columbia University Press, 1998), pp. 67–86.

'The "cult of the insurgent": Its tactical and strategic implications', *Australian Journal of International Affairs*, 61(3) (2007), 312–29.

Holsti, K. J., *The State, War, and the State of War* (Cambridge: Cambridge University Press, 1996).

Taming the Sovereigns: Institutional change in international politics (Cambridge: Cambridge University Press, 2004).

Holt, M., *The French Wars of Religion, 1562–1629*, 2nd edn (Cambridge: Cambridge University Press, 2005).

Horowitz, R. S., 'International law and state transformation in China, Siam and the Ottoman Empire during the nineteenth century', *Journal of World History*, 15(4) (2004), 445–86.

Housley, N., *Religious Warfare in Europe, 1400–1536* (Oxford: Oxford University Press, 2002).

Howard, M. E., *War in European History* (London; New York: Oxford University Press, 1976).

Hsia, R. P. C., *Social Discipline in the Reformation: Central Europe, 1550–1750* (London: Routledge, 1989).

Hsu, I. C. Y., 'Late Ch'ing foreign relations, 1866–1905' in J. K. Fairbank and K.-C. Liu (eds.), *The Cambridge History of China*, XI: *Late Ch'ing, 1800–1911*, Pt II (Cambridge: Cambridge University Press, 1980), pp. 70–141.

The Rise of Modern China (Oxford: Oxford University Press, 1995).

Hui, V. T.-B., *War and State Formation in Ancient China and Early Modern Europe* (New York: Cambridge University Press, 2005).

Human Security Report 2005: War and peace in the 21st Century (Oxford: Oxford University Press, 2005).

Hung, H.-F., 'Early modernities and contentious politics in mid-Qing China, c.1740–1839', *International Sociology*, 19(4) (2004), 478–503.

Huntington, S. P., *The Clash of Civilizations and the Remaking of World Order* (New York: Simon and Schuster, 1996).

Hurd, E. S., *The Politics of Secularism in International Relations* (Princeton: Princeton University Press, 2008).

Ichiko, C., 'Political and institutional reform, 1901–1911' in J. K. Fairbank and K.-C. Liu (eds.), *The Cambridge History of China*, XI: *Late Ch'ing, 1800–1911*, Pt II (Cambridge: Cambridge University Press, 1980), pp. 375–415.

Ikenberry, G. J., 'Power and liberal order: America's postwar world order in transition', *International Relations of the Asia-Pacific*, 5(2) (2005), 133–52.

Iklâe, F. C., *Annihilation from Within: The ultimate threat to nations* (New York: Columbia University Press, 2006).

Iriye, A., *After Imperialism: The search for a new order in the Far East, 1921–1931* (Cambridge, MA: Harvard University Press, 1965).

The Origins of the Second World War in Asia and the Pacific (London: Longman, 1987).

'Japan's drive to Great Power status' in M. B. Jansen (ed.), *The Cambridge History of Japan,* V: *The Nineteenth Century* (Cambridge: Cambridge University Press, 1989), pp. 721–82.

Jackson, R. H., *Quasi-States: Sovereignty, international relations, and the Third World* (Cambridge: Cambridge University Press, 1990).

Jansen, M. B., 'Japan and the Chinese revolution of 1911' in J. K. Fairbank and K.-C. Liu (eds.), *The Cambridge History of China,* XI: *Late Ch'ing, 1800–1911,* Pt II (Cambridge: Cambridge University Press, 1980), pp. 339–74.

'The Meiji Restoration' in M. B. Jansen (ed.), *The Cambridge History of Japan,* V: *The Nineteenth Century* (Cambridge: Cambridge University Press, 1989), pp. 308–66.

Jenkins, P., *The Next Christendom: The coming of global Christianity* (Oxford: Oxford University Press, 2002).

Jensen, D. L., 'The Ottoman Turks in sixteenth century French diplomacy', *Sixteenth Century Journal,* 16(4) (1985), 451–70.

Johnson, C., *Peasant Nationalism and Communist Power: The emergence of revolutionary China, 1937–1945* (Stanford: Stanford University Press, 1962).

Blowback: The costs and consequences of American empire (London: Little, Brown and Co., 2002).

The Sorrows of Empire: Militarism, secrecy and the end of the republic (London: Verso, 2004).

Jones, D. M., *The Image of China in Western Social and Political Thought* (New York: Palgrave, 2001).

Jones, S. M. and Kuhn, P. A., 'Dynastic decline and the roots of rebellion' in D. Twitchett and J. K. Fairbank (eds.), *The Cambridge History of China,* X: *Late Ch'ing 1800–1911,* Pt I (Cambridge: Cambridge University Press, 1978), pp. 107–62.

Joseph, J., 'The exercise of national sovereignty: The Bush administration's approach to combating weapons of mass destruction', *The Nonproliferation Review,* 12(2) (2005), 373–87.

Juergensmeyer, M., 'The logic of religious violence' in R. Howard and R. Sawyer (eds.), *Terrorism and Counter-Terrorism: Understanding the new security environment, readings and interpretations* (Guildford, CT: McGraw Hill Dushkin, 2002).

Kaiser, D., *Politics and War: European conflict from Philip II to Hitler* (Cambridge, MA: Harvard University Press, 2000).

Kaldor, M., *New and Old Wars: Organized violence in a global era* (Stanford: Stanford University Press, 2001).

Kang, D., 'Hierarchy in Asian international relations: 1300–1900', *Asian Security,* 1(1) (2005), 53–79.

Kaplan, R. D., *The Coming Anarchy: Shattering the dreams of the post cold war* (New York: Random House, 2000).

Kaufman, S. J., 'The fragmentation and consolidation of international systems', *Internaional Organization*, 51(2) (1997), 173–208.

Keating, P., 'Getting peasants organized: Village organizations and the party-state in the Shaan Gan Ning border region, 1934–1945' in F. Chongyi and D. S. G. Goodman (eds.), *North China at War: The social ecology of revolution, 1937–1945* (Oxford: Rowman and Littlefield Publishers, 2000), pp. 25–58.

Keene, E, *Beyond the Anarchical Society: Grotius, colonialism and order in world politics* (Cambridge: Cambridge University Press, 2002).

Kennedy, P. M., *The Rise and Fall of British Naval Mastery* (London: A. Lane, 1976). *The Rise and Fall of the Great Powers: Economic change and military conflict from 1500 to 2000* (London: Fontana Press, 1987).

Kennedy-Pipe, C. and Rengger, N., 'Apocalypse now? Continuities or disjunctions in world politics after 9/11', *International Affairs*, 82(3) (2006), 539–52.

Kenney, M., 'From Pablo to Osama: Counter-terrorism lessons from the war on drugs', *Survival*, 45(3) (2003), 187–206.

Keohane, N. O., *Philosophy and the State in France: The Renaissance to the Enlightenment* (Princeton: Princeton University Press, 1980).

Kepel, G., 'The origins and development of the jihadist movement: From anti-communism to terrorism', *Asian Affairs*, XXXIV(2) (2003), 91–108. *Jihad: The trail of political Islam* (London: I. B. Taurus, 2006).

Kerr, R. F. (ed.), *The History of the Popes from the Close of the Middle Ages,* 40 vols. (London: Routledge and Kegan Paul Ltd, 1952).

Kiernan, V. G., 'Foreign mercenaries and absolute monarchy' in T. Aston (ed.), *Crisis in Europe, 1560–1660* (London: Routledge and Kegan Paul, 1965), pp. 117–40.

Kilcullen, D., *The Accidental Guerrilla: Fighting small wars in the midst of a big one* (Oxford; New York: Oxford University Press, 2009).

Kim, K.-H., *The Last Phase of the East Asian World Order: Korea, Japan, and the Chinese Empire, 1860–1882* (Berkeley: University of California Press, 1980).

King, W., *China at the Washington Conference, 1921–1922* (New York: St John's University Press, 1963).

Kingdon, R. M., *Geneva and the Coming of the Wars of Religion in France, 1555–1563* (Geneva: Droz, 1956).
'The political resistance of the Calvinists in France and the Low Countries', *Church History*, 27(3) (1958), 220–33.
'International Calvinism and the Thirty Years War' in K. Bussman and H. Schilling (eds.), *1648: War and peace in Europe* (Münster/Osnabrück: Westfälisches Landesmuseum, 1998), pp. 229–35.

Klare, M. T., *Blood and Oil: The dangers and consequences of America's growing petroleum dependency* (New York: Metropolitan Books/Henry Holt & Co., 2004).

Knecht, R. J., *The French Wars of Religion, 1559–1598* (London: Longman, 1989).

Knutsen, T. L., *The Rise and Fall of World Orders* (Manchester: Manchester University Press, 1999).

Koenigsberger, H. G., 'The organization of revolutionary parties in France and the Netherlands during the sixteenth century', *The Journal of Modern History*, 27(4) (1955), 335–51.

'The empire of Charles V in Europe' in G. R. Elton (ed.), *The New Cambridge Modern History*, II: *The Reformation 1520-1559* (Cambridge: Cambridge University Press, 1990), pp. 339–76.

Koselleck, R., *Critique and Crisis: Enlightenment and the pathogenesis of modern society* (Oxford: Berg, 1988).

Krasner, S. D., 'Westphalia and all that' in J. Goldstein and R. O. Keohane (eds.), *Ideas and Foreign Policy: Beliefs, institutions, and political change* (Ithaca: Cornell University Press, 1993), pp. 235–64.

'Power politics, institutions, and transnational relations' in T. Risse-Kappen (ed.), *Bringing Transnational Relations Back In* (Cambridge: Cambridge University Press, 1995), pp. 257–79.

Sovereignty: Organized hypocrisy (Princeton: Princeton University Press, 1999).

Krauthammer, C., 'The unipolar moment revisited', *The National Interest*, 70 (2002/03), 5–17.

Kugler, J. and Organski, A. F. K., 'The power transition: A retrospective and prospective evaluation' in M. I. Midlarski (ed.), *Handbook of War Studies* (Ann Arbor: The University of Michigan Press, 1996), pp. 171–94.

Kuhn, P. A., *Rebellion and Its Enemies in Late Imperial China: Militarization and social structure, 1796-1864* (Cambridge, MA: Harvard University Press, 1970).

'Origins of the Taiping vision: Cross-cultural dimensions of a Chinese rebellion', *Comparative Studies in Society and History*, 19(3) (1977), 350–66.

'The Taiping rebellion' in D. Twitchett and J. K. Fairbank (eds.), *The Cambridge History of China*, X: *Late Ch'ing, 1800-1911*, Pt I (Cambridge: Cambridge University Press, 1978), pp. 264–317.

Lake, D. A., 'Escape from the state of nature: Authority and hierarchy in world politics', *International Security*, 32(1) (2007), 47–79.

Lam, T. B., 'Intervention versus tribute in Sino-Vietnamese relations, 1788-1790' in J. K. Fairbank (ed.), *The Chinese World Order: Traditional China's foreign relations* (Cambridge, MA: Harvard University Press, 1968), pp. 165–79.

Landau, J. M., *The Politics of Pan-Islam: Ideology and organization* (Oxford Clarendon Press, 1990).

Laqueur, W., 'The terrorism to come', *Policy Review*, 126 (2004), 49–64.

Latham, A., 'A Braudelian perspective on the Revolution in Military Affairs', *European Journal of International Relations*, 8(2) (2002), 231–66.

Layne, C., 'America's Middle East grand strategy after Iraq: The moment for offshore balancing has arrived', *Review of International Studies*, 35(1) (2009), 5–25.

Lebow, R. N., *A Cultural Theory of International Relations* (Cambridge: Cambridge University Press, 2008).

LeDonne, J. P., *The Russian Empire and the World, 1700-1917: The geopolitics of expansion and containment* (New York: Oxford University Press, 1997).

Lee, S. J., *The Thirty Years War* (London: Routledge, 1991).

Lee, S. T., *Religion and Social Formation in Korea: Minjung and millenarianism* (New York: Mouton de Gruyter, 1996).

Leff, G., 'Heresy and the decline of the medieval church', *Past and Present*, 20 (1961), 36–51.

Lehmann, T. C., 'Keeping friends close and enemies closer: Classical realist statecraft and economic exchange in U.S. interwar strategy', *Security Studies*, 18(1) (2008), 115–47.

Leonardo, D. M., '"Cut off this rotten member": The rhetoric of sin, heresy and disease in the ideology of the French Catholic League', *Catholic Historical Review*, 88(2) (2002), 247–62.

Lesaffer, R., 'Peace treaties from Lodi to Westphalia' in R. Lesaffer (ed.), *Peace Treaties and International Law in European History* (Cambridge: Cambridge University Press, 2004), pp. 9–44.

Levenson, J. R., *Confucian China and Its Modern Fate,* 3 vols., I: *The Problem of Intellectual Continuity* (London: Routledge and Kegan Paul, 1958).

'Confucian and Taiping "Heaven": The political implications of clashing religious concepts', *Comparative Studies in Society and History*, 4(4) (1962), 436–53.

Confucian China and Its Modern Fate, 3 vols., II: *The problem of monarchical decay* (London: Routledge and Kegan Paul, 1964).

Leverett, F. and Bader, J., 'Managing China–U.S. energy competition in the Middle East', *The Washington Quarterly*, 29(1) (2005), 187–201.

Li, L., *The Japanese Army in North China, 1937–1941: Problems of political and economic control* (Oxford: Oxford University Press, 1975).

Liberman, P., *Does Conquest Pay? The exploitation of occupied industrial societies?* (Princeton: Princeton University Press, 1996).

Liebeschuetz, W., 'The end of the ancient city' in J. Rich (ed.), *The City in Late Antiquity* (London: Routledge, 1992), pp. 1–49.

Lim, R., *The Geopolitics of East Asia: The search for equilibrium* (London: Routledge, 2003).

Lone, S. and McCormack, G., *Korea since 1850* (New York: Longman Cheshire, 1993).

Loriaux, M., 'The realists and Saint Augustine: Skepticism, psychology, and moral action in international relations thought', *International Studies Quarterly*, 36(4) (1992), 401–20.

Loewe, M., 'The concept of sovereignty' in D. Twitchett and M. Loewe (eds.), *The Cambridge History of China*, I: *The Ch'in and Han Empires 221*BC *– AD220* (Cambridge: Cambridge University Press, 1986), pp. 726–46.

'The religious and intellectual background' in D. Twitchett and M. Loewe (eds.), *The Cambridge History of China*, I: *The Ch'in and Han Empires, 221*BC *– AD220* (Cambridge: Cambridge University Press, 1986), 649–725.

Lowe, P., *The Origins of the Korean War* (London: Longman, 1997).

Lowenheim, O., *Predators and Parasites: Persistent agents of transnational harm and Great Power authority* (Ann Arbor: The University of Michigan Press, 2007).

Luther, M., 'The freedom of a Christian' (1520) in J. M. Porter (ed.), *Luther: Selected political writings* (Philadelphia: Fortress Press, 1974).

'To the Christian nobility of the German nation concerning the reform of the Christian estate' (1520) in J. M. Porter (ed.), *Luther: Selected political writings* (Philadelphia: Fortress Press, 1974).

'Against the robbing and murdering hordes of peasants' (1525) in J. M. Porter (ed.), *Luther: Selected political writings* (Philadelphia: Fortress Press, 1974).

McCord, E., 'Militia and local militarization in late Qing and early republican China: The case of Hunan', *Modern China*, 14(2) (1988), 156–87.

MacCulloch, D., *Reformation: Europe's house divided, 1490–1700* (London: Penguin Books, 2004).

McCutcheon, J. M., '"Tremblingly obey": British and other Western response to China and the Chinese kowtow', *Historian*, 33(4) (1971), 557–77.

MacDonald, P., 'Is imperial rule obsolete? Assessing the barriers to overseas adventurism', *Security Studies*, 18(1) (2009), 79–114.

Machiavelli, N., *The Prince*, trans. G. Bull (London: Penguin Books, 1999).

MacKenzie, S. P., *Revolutionary Armies in the Modern Era: A revisionist approach* (London: Routledge, 1997).

MacKinnon, S. R., *Power and Politics in Late Imperial China: Yuan Shi-Kai in Beijing and Tianjin, 1901–1908* (Berkeley: University of California Press, 1980).

McNeill, W. H., *The Rise of the West: A history of the human community* (Chicago: The University of Chicago Press, 1963).

The Pursuit of Power: Technology, armed force, and society since AD 1000 (Chicago: The University of Chicago Press, 1982).

The Age of Gunpowder Empires 1450–1800 (Washington DC: American Historical Association, 1989).

The Global Condition: Conquerors, catastrophes, and community (Princeton: Princeton University Press, 1992).

Mallaby, S., 'The reluctant imperialist: Terrorism, failed states, and the case for American empire', *Foreign Affairs*, 81(2) (2002), 2–7.

Malone, D., *The International Struggle over Iraq: Politics in the UN Security Council 1980–2005* (Oxford; New York: Oxford University Press, 2006).

Mancall, M., *China at the Center: 300 years of foreign policy* (New York: The Free Press, 1984).

Mann, M., *The Sources of Social Power*, 2 vols. (Cambridge; New York: Cambridge University Press, 1986).

'The first failed empire of the 21st century', *Review of International Studies*, 30(4) (2004), 631–53.

Marx, A. W., *Faith in Nation: Exclusionary origins of nationalism* (Oxford: Oxford University Press, 2003).

Matthews, D. J. A., 'Reflections on the medieval Roman Empire', *History – Journal of the Historical Association*, 77(251) (1992), 363–90.

Mattingly, G., *Renaissance Diplomacy* (Baltimore: Penguin Books, 1964).

Mearsheimer, J. J., *The Tragedy of Great Power Politics* (New York: W. W. Norton and Company, 2001).

Mellor, P. A. and Shilling, C., *Re-Forming the Body: Religion, community, and modernity* (London: Sage, 1997).

Mendelsohn, B., 'Sovereignty under attack: The international society meets the Al Qaeda network', *Review of International Studies*, 31(1) (2005), 45–68.

  Combating Jihadism: American hegemony and interstate cooperation in the war on terrorism (Chicago; London: The University of Chicago Press, 2009).

  'English school, American style: Testing the preservation-seeking quality of the international society', *European Journal of International Relations*, 15(2) (2009), 291–318.

  'Bolstering the state: A different perspective on the war on the jihadi movement', *International Studies Review*, 11(4) (2009), 663–86.

Meyer, J., 'The world polity and the authority of the nation-state' in A. Bergesen (ed.), *Studies of the Modern World-System* (New York: Academic Press, 1980), pp. 109–37.

Michael, F., *The Taiping Rebellion, History and Documents*, 3 vols., I: *History* (Seattle: University of Washington Press, 1966).

Miller, H. L., 'The late imperial Chinese state' in D. Shambaugh (ed.), *The Modern Chinese State* (Cambridge: Cambridge University Press, 2000), pp. 15–41.

Minault, G., *The Khilafat Movement: Religious symbolism and political mobilization in India* (Delhi: Oxford University Press, 1999).

Mitter, R., *A Bitter Revolution: China's struggle with the modern world* (Oxford; New York: Oxford University Press, 2004).

Moore, R. I., *The Formation of a Persecuting Society: Power and deviance in Western Europe, 950–1250* (Oxford: Blackwell, 1987).

  'The birth of Europe as a Eurasian phenomenon' in V. Lieberman (ed.), *Beyond Binary Histories: Re-imagining Eurasia to c.1830* (Ann Arbor: The University of Michigan Press, 2002), pp. 139–57.

Morgenthau, H., *Scientific Man vs. Power Politics* (Chicago: The University of Chicago Press, 1946).

  Politics among Nations: The struggle for power and peace, 5th edn (New York: Alfred A. Knopf, 1978).

Motyl, A. J., *Revolutions, Nations, Empires: Conceptual limits and theoretical possibilities* (New York: Columbia University Press, 1999).

Munkler, H., *The New Wars* (Cambridge: Polity, 2005).

  Empires: The logic of world domination from Rome to the United States (Cambridge: Polity Press, 2007).

Murdock, G., *Beyond Calvin: The intellectual, political, and cultural world of Europe's Reformed Churches* (London: Palgrave Macmillan, 2004).

Murphy, D., 'Middle East racing to nuclear power', *Christian Science Monitor*, 1 November 2007.

Naquin, S., *Millenarian Rebellion in China: The Eight Trigrams uprising of 1813* (New Haven: Yale University Press, 1976).

Nardin, T., *Law, Morality, and the Relations of States* (Princeton: Princeton University Press, 1983).

Nau, H. R., *At Home Abroad: Identity and power in American foreign policy* (Ithaca: Cornell University Press, 2002).

Nexon, D., 'Religion, European identity, and political contention in historical perspective' in T. Byrnes and P. Katzenstein (eds.), *Religion in an Expanding Europe* (Cambridge: Cambridge University Press, 2006), pp. 256–82.

The Struggle for Power in Early Modern Europe: Religious conflict, dynastic empires and international change (Princeton: Princeton University Press, 2009).

Niebuhr, R., *Moral Man and Immoral Society: A study in ethics and politics* (New York: Charles Scribner, 1960).

Nish, I. H., *The Origins of the Russo-Japanese War* (London: Longman, 1985).

North, D. C., *Structure and Change in Economic History* (New York: Norton, 1981).

and Thomas, R. P., *The Rise of the Western World: A new economic history* (Cambridge: Cambridge University Press, 1973).

Oh, B., 'Sino-Japanese rivalry in Korea, 1876–1885' in A. Iriye (ed.), *The Chinese and the Japanese: Essays in political and cultural interactions* (Princeton: Princeton University Press, 1980), pp. 37–57.

Onley, J., *The Arabian Frontier of the British Raj: Merchants, rulers, and the British in the nineteenth-century Gulf* (New York: Oxford University Press, 2007).

Oosthuizen, G. H. and Wilmhurst, E., *Terrorism and Weapons of Mass Destruction: United Nations Security Council Resolution 1540*, Briefing Paper 04/01 (London: Chatham House, 2004).

O'Reilly, M. J. and Renfro, W. B., 'Evolving empire: America's "Emirates" strategy in the Persian Gulf', *International Studies Perspectives*, 8 (2007), 137–51.

Osiander, A., 'Before sovereignty: Society and politics in *ancien regime* Europe', *Review of International Studies*, 27(5) (2001), 119–45.

'Sovereignty, international relations, and the Westphalian myth', *International Organization*, 55(2) (2001), 251–87.

Otte, T. G., 'The Boxer uprising and British foreign policy: The end of isolation' in R. Bickers and R. G. Tiedeman (eds.), *The Boxers, China, and the World* (Plymouth: Rowman and Littlefield Publishers, 2007), pp. 157–77.

Outram, Q., 'The demographic impact of early modern warfare', *Social Science History*, 26(2) (2002), 245–72.

Ownby, D., *Brotherhoods and Secret Societies in Early and Mid-Qing China: The formation of a tradition* (Stanford: Stanford University Press, 1996).

Parker, G., 'The Dutch revolt and the polarization of international politics' in G. Parker and L. M. Smith (eds.), *The General Crisis of the Seventeenth Century* (London: Routledge and Kegan Paul, 1978), pp. 57–82.

The Military Revolution: Military innovation and the rise of the West 1500–1800 (Cambridge: Cambridge University Press, 1996).

'The universal soldier' in G. Parker (ed.), *The Thirty Years' War* (London: Routledge, 1997), pp. 171–86.

Europe in Crisis 1598–1648, 2nd edn (Oxford: Blackwell Publishers Ltd, 2001).

and Smith, L. M. (eds.), *The General Crisis of the Seventeenth Century* (London: Routledge and Kegan Paul, 1978).

Parrott, D. A., 'Strategy and tactics in the Thirty Years' War: The "military revolution"', *Militärgeschichtliche Mitteilungen*, 38(2) (1985), 7–25.

Patrikeeff, F. and Shukman, H., *Railways and the Russo-Japanese War: Transporting war* (London: Routledge, 2007).

Perry, E. J., *Rebels and Revolutionaries in North China, 1845–1945* (Stanford: Stanford University Press, 1980).

Phillips, A., 'How Al Qaeda lost Iraq', *Australian Journal of International Affairs*, 63(1) (2009), 64–84.

'The Anbar awakening: Can it be exported to Afghanistan?', *Security Challenges*, 5(3) (2009), 27–46.

Philpott, D., *Revolutions in Sovereignty: How ideas shaped modern international relations* (Princeton: Princeton University Press, 2001).

Poggi, G., *The Development of the Modern State: A sociological introduction* (Stanford: Stanford University Press, 1978).

Poly, J.-P. and Bournazel, E., *The Feudal Transformation, 900–1200* (New York: Holmes and Meier, 1991).

Posen, B., 'Command of the commons: The military foundations of US hegemony', *International Security*, 28(1) (2003), 5–46.

Quester, G. H., *Offense and Defense in the International System* (New Brunswick: Transaction Books, 1988).

Rabb, T. K., *The Struggle for Stability in Early Modern Europe* (New York: Oxford University Press, 1975).

Rawski, E. S. 'The Qing formation and the early modern period' in L. A. Struve (ed.), *The Qing Formation in World-Historical Time* (Cambridge, MA: Harvard University Press, 2004), pp. 207–41.

Record, J., *Dark Victory: America's second war against Iraq* (Annapolis: Naval Institute Press, 2004).

Reilly, T. H., *The Taiping Heavenly Kingdom: Rebellion and the blasphemy of empire* (Seattle: University of Washington Press, 2004).

Reinhard, W., 'Pressures towards confessionalization? Prolegomena to a theory of the confessional age' in S. Dixon (ed.), *The German Reformation: The essential readings* (Oxford: Blackwell Publishers Ltd, 1999), pp. 169–92.

Reus-Smit, C., *The Moral Purpose of the State: Culture, social identity, and institutional rationality in international relations* (Princeton: Princeton University Press, 1999).

'Politics and international legal obligation', *European Journal of International Relations*, 9(4) (2003), 591–626.

American Power and World Order (Cambridge: Polity Press, 2004).

'The politics of international law' in C. Reus-Smit (ed.), *The Politics of International Law* (Cambridge: Cambridge University Press, 2004), pp. 14–44.

'International crises of legitimacy', *International Politics*, 44(2/3) (2007), 157–74.

Riedel, B., 'Al Qaeda strikes back', *Foreign Affairs*, 86(3) (2007), 24–40.

and Saab, B. Y., 'Al Qaeda's third front: Saudi Arabia', *The Washington Quarterly*, 31(2) (2008), 33–46.

Ringmar, E., *Identity, Interest, and Action: A cultural explanation of Sweden's intervention in the Thirty Years War* (Cambridge: Cambridge University Press, 1996).

Robb, J., *Brave New War: The next stage of terrorism and the end of globalization* (Hoboken, NJ: John Wiley and Sons, 2007).

Rosand, E., 'Security Council Resolution 1373, the Counter-Terrorism Committee, and the fight against terrorism', *The American Journal of International Law*, 97(2) (2003), 333–41.

'The UN-led multilateral institutional response to jihadist terrorism: Is a global counter-terrorism body needed?', *Journal of Conflict and Security Law*, 11(3) (2007), 399–427.

Rosenau, J. N., 'Illusions of power and empire', *History and Theory*, 44(4) (2005), 73–87.

Rosenberg, J., *The Empire of Civil Society: A critique of the realist theory of international relations* (London: Verso, 1994).

Rowen, H. H., *The King's State: Proprietary dynasticism in early modern France* (New Brunswick: Rutgers University Press, 1980).

Roy, O., *Secularism Confronts Islam* (New York: Columbia University Press, 2007).

Rubin, B. R., 'Constructing sovereignty for security', *Survival*, 47(4) (2005), 93–106.

Ruggie, J. G., 'Territoriality and beyond: Problematizing modernity in international relations', *International Organization*, 47(1) (1993), 139–74.

Constructing the World Polity: Essays on international institutionalization (London: Routledge, 1998).

Ruthven, M., 'The eleventh of September and the Sudanese Mahdiya in the context of Ibn Khaldun's theory of Islamic history', *International Affairs*, 78(2) (2002), 339–51.

Scharpf, F., 'Economic integration, democracy, and the welfare state', *Journal of European Public Policy*, 4(1) (1997), 18–36.

Schilling, H., 'Confessional Europe' in T. A. Brady Jr, H. A. Oberman and J. D. Tracy (eds.), *Handbook of European History 1400–1600 Late Middle Ages, Renaissance, and Reformation*, II: *Visions, Programs, and Outcomes* (Leiden: E. J. Brill, 1995), pp. 641–81.

'War and peace at the emergence of modernity: Europe between state belligerence, religious wars, and the desire for peace' in K. Bussman and H. Schilling (eds.), *1648: War and peace in Europe* (Münster/Osnabrück: Westfälisches Landesmuseum, 1998), pp. 13–22.

'Confessionalisation in Europe: Causes and effects for church, state, society and culture' in K. Bussman and H. Schilling (eds.), *1648: War and peace in Europe* (Münster/Osnabrück: Westfälisches Landesmuseum, 1998), pp. 219–28.

Schmitt, C., *The Theory of the Partisan: A commentary/remark on the concept of the political* (Detroit: Michigan State University Press, 2004).

Schrecker, J. E., *Imperialism and Chinese Nationalism: Germany in Shantung* (Cambridge, MA: Harvard University Press, 1971).

Schroeder, P., 'Did the Vienna settlement rest on a balance of power?', *The American Historical Review*, 97(3) (1992), 683–706.

Schwarcz, V., *The Chinese Enlightenment: Intellectuals and the legacy of the May fourth movement of 1919* (Berkeley: University of California Press, 1986).

Schwartz, B. I., 'Themes in intellectual history: May fourth and after' in J. K. Fairbank (ed.), *The Cambridge History of China*, XII: *Republican China 1912–1949*, Pt I (Cambridge: Cambridge University Press, 1983), pp. 406–50.

Selden, M., *The Yenan Way in Revolutionary China* (Cambridge MA: Harvard University Press, 1971).

Setsuho, I., 'Uprisings of Hesukristos in the Philippines' in I. Yoneo (ed.), *Millenarianism in Asian History* (Tokyo: Institute for the Study of Languages and Cultures of Asia and Africa, 1993), pp. 143–74.

Sheridan, J. E., *China in Disintegration: The republican era in Chinese history, 1912–1949* (New York: The Free Press, 1975).

'The warlord era: Politics and militarism under the Peking government, 1916–28' in J. K. Fairbank (ed.), *The Cambridge History of China*, XII: *Republican China, 1912–1949*, Pt I (Cambridge: Cambridge University Press, 1983), pp. 284–321.

Sil, R. and Katzenstein, P., *Beyond Paradigms: Analytic eclecticism in the study of world politics* (London and New York: Palgrave Macmillan, 2010 forthcoming).

Simpson, G. J., *Great Powers and Outlaw States: Unequal sovereigns in the international legal order* (Cambridge: Cambridge University Press, 2004).

Skinner, Q., *The Foundations of Modern Political Thought*, 2 vols., I: *The Renaissance* (Cambridge: Cambridge University Press, 1978).

The Foundations of Modern Political Thought, 2 vols., II: *The Age of the Reformation* (Cambridge: Cambridge University Press, 1978).

Slyke, L., van 'The Chinese communist movement during the Sino-Japanese War, 1937–1945' in J. K. Fairbank and A. Feuerwerker (eds.), *The Cambridge History of China*, XIII: *Republican China, 1912–1949*, Pt II (Cambridge: Cambridge University Press, 1986), pp. 609–722.

'The Battle of the Hundred Regiments: Problems of coordination and control during the Sino-Japanese War', *Modern Asian Studies*, 30(4) (1996), 979–1005.

Sorensen, G., 'After the security dilemma: The challenges of insecurity in weak states and the dilemma of liberal values', *Security Dialogue*, 38(3) (2007), 357–78.

'The case for combining material forces and ideas in the study of IR', *European Journal of International Relations*, 14(1) (2008), 5–32.

Spector, S., *Li Hung-Chang and the Huai Army: A study in nineteenth-century Chinese regionalism* (Seattle: University of Washington Press, 1964).

Spence, J. D., *God's Chinese Son: The Taiping Heavenly Kingdom of Hong Xiuquan* (New York: W. W. Norton and Company, 1996).

The Search for Modern China (New York: W. W. Norton, 1999).

Spruyt, H., *The Sovereign State and its Competitors* (Princeton: Princeton University Press, 1994).

Steiger, H., 'Concrete peace and general order: The legal meaning of the treaties of 24 October 1648' in K. Bussman and H. Schilling (eds.), *1648: War and peace in Europe* (Münster/Osnabrück: Westfälisches Landesmuseum, 1998), pp. 437–46.

Steinmetz, G., 'Return to empire: The new U.S. imperialism in comparative historical perspective', *Sociological Theory*, 23(4) (2005), 339–67.

Stokes, E., *The English Utilitarians and India* (Oxford: Clarendon Press, 1959).

Straumann, B., 'The Peace of Westphalia as a secular constitution', *Constellations*, 15(2) (2008), 173–88.

Strayer, J., *On the Medieval Origins of the Modern State* (Princeton: Princeton University Press, 1970).

Subrahmanyam, S., 'A tale of three empires: Mughals, Ottomans, and Habsburgs in a comparative context', *Common Knowledge*, 12(1) (2006), 66–92.

Suh, J. J., Katzenstein, P. J. and Carlson, A., *Rethinking Security in East Asia: Identity, power, and efficiency* (Stanford: Stanford University Press, 2004).

Suskind, R., *The One Percent Doctrine: Deep inside America's pursuit of its enemies since 9/11* (New York: Simon and Schuster, 2006).

Sutherland, N. M., 'The origins of the Thirty Years War and the structure of European politics', *The English Historical Review*, 107(424) (1992), 587–625.

Suzuki, S., 'Japan's socialization into Janus-faced European international society', *European Journal of International Relations*, 11(1) (2005), 137–64.

Swope, K. M., 'Deceit, disguise, and dependence: China, Japan, and the future of the tributary system, 1592–1596', *The International History Review*, XXIV(4) (2002), 757–82.

Tallett, F., *War and Society in Early Modern Europe, 1495–1715* (London: Routledge, 1992).

Taylor, C., *Sources of the Self: The making of modern identity* (Cambridge MA: Harvard University Press, 1989).

'Modern social imaginaries', *Public Culture*, 14(1) (2002), 91–124.

Modern Social Imaginaries (Durham NC: Duke University Press, 2004).

A Secular Age (Cambridge, MA: Belknap Press of Harvard University Press, 2007).

Teng, S.-Y., *The Taiping Rebellion and the Western Powers: A comprehensive survey* (Oxford: Clarendon Press, 1971).

Teschke, B., 'Geopolitical relations in the European Middle Ages: History and theory', *International Organization*, 52(2) (1998), 325–58.

The Myth of 1648: Class, geopolitics, and the making of modern international relations (London: Verso, 2003).

Tetlock, P. E. and Parker, G., 'Counterfactual thought experiments: Why we can't live without them and how we must learn to live with them' in P. E. Tetlock, R. N. Lebow and G. Parker (eds.), *Unmaking the West: 'What if?' scenarios that rewrite world history* (Ann Arbor: The University of Michigan Press, 2006), pp. 14–44.

Thomas, S. M., 'Taking religious and cultural pluralism seriously: The global resurgence of religion and the transformation of international society', *Millennium: Journal of International Studies*, 29(3) (2000), 815–41.

Thompson, W. R. 'The military superiority thesis and the ascendancy of Western Eurasia in the world system', *Journal of World History*, 10(1) (1999), 143–78.

Thomson, J. E., *Mercenaries, Pirates, and Sovereigns: State-building and extraterritorial violence in early modern Europe* (Princeton: Princeton University Press, 1994).

'State sovereignty in international relations: Bridging the gap between theory and empirical research', *International Studies Quarterly*, 39(2) (1995), 213–33.

Tilly, C., *Coercion, Capital, and European States, AD 990–1992* (Cambridge, MA: Blackwell, 1992).

Tracy, J. D., *Europe's Reformations 1450–1650: Doctrine, politics, and community*, 2nd edn (Oxford: Rowman and Littlefield Publishers, 2006).

Trofimov, Y., *The Siege of Mecca: The 1979 uprising at Islam's holiest shrine* (New York: Anchor Books, 2008).

Troitskiy, E., 'U.S. policy in Central Asia and regional security', *Global Society*, 21(3) (2007), 415–28.

Tse-Tsung, C., *The May Fourth Movement: Intellectual revolution in modern China* (Cambridge, MA: Harvard University Press, 1960).

Ullman, W., 'The medieval papal court as an international tribunal' in W. Ullman (ed.), *The Papacy and Political Ideas in the Middle Ages* (London: Variorum Reprints, 1976), 355–71.

Ven, H. J., van de, 'Public finance and the rise of warlordism', *Modern Asian Studies*, 30(4) (1996), 829–68.

'The military in the Republic', *The China Quarterly*, 150 (1997), 352–74.

War and Nationalism in China, 1925–1945 (New York: RoutledgeCurzon, 2003).

Wakeman, F. Jr, *Strangers at the Gate: Social disorder in South China, 1839–1861* (Berkeley: University of California Press, 1966).

'The Canton trade and the Opium War' in D. Twitchett and J. K. Fairbank (eds.), *The Cambridge History of China*, X: *Late Ch'ing, 1800–1911*, Pt I (Cambridge: Cambridge University Press, 1978), pp. 163–212.

Waldron, A., 'War and the rise of nationalism in twentieth-century China', *The Journal of Military History*, 57(5) (1993), 87–104.

    From War to Nationalism: China's turning point, 1924–1925 (Cambridge: Cambridge University Press, 1995).

Waley, A., *Three Ways of Ancient Thought in China* (London: George Allen and Unwin Ltd, 1969).

Waltz, K. N., *Man, the State, and War: A theoretical analysis* (New York: Columbia University Press, 1959).

    Theory of International Politics (New York: Random House, 1979).

Walzer, M., *The Revolution of the Saints: A study in the origins of radical politics* (London: Weidenfeld and Nicolson, 1965).

    'On the role of symbolism in political thought', *Political Science Quarterly*, 82(2) (1967), 191–204.

Warner, M., 'Introduction' in M. Warner (ed.), *Religion and Philosophy* (Cambridge: Cambridge University Press, 1992), pp. 1–22.

Watt, J. A., *The Theory of Papal Monarchy in the Thirteenth Century* (New York: Fordham University Press, 1965).

    'The Papacy' in D. Abulafia (ed.), *The New Cambridge Medieval History*, V: *c.1198–1300* (Cambridge: Cambridge University Press, 1999).

Weems, B. B., *Reform, Rebellion, and the Heavenly Way* (Tucson: The University of Arizona Press, 1964).

Wendt, A., 'Anarchy is what states make of it: The social construction of power politics', *International Organization*, 46(2) (1992), 391–425.

Wheatcroft, A., *The Enemy at the Gate: Habsburgs, Ottomans, and the battle for Europe* (New York: Basic Books, 2009).

Wight, M., *Systems of States* (London: Leicester University Press, 1977).

Williams, C., '"As if a new sun had risen": England's fourteenth century RMA' in M. Knox and M. Williamson (eds.), *The Dynamics of Military Revolution, 1300–2050* (Cambridge: Cambridge University Press, 2001), pp. 15–34.

Wilson, P. H., *The Thirty Years War: Europe's tragedy* (Cambridge, MA: Belknap Press of Harvard University Press, 2009).

Wolin, S. S., *Politics and Vision: Continuity and innovation in Western political thought* (Princeton: Princeton University Press, 2004).

Wong, R. B., *China Transformed: Historical change and the limits of European experience* (Ithaca: Cornell University Press, 1997).

Wright, L., *The Looming Tower: Al-Qaeda and the road to 9/11* (New York: Knopf, 2006).

Wright, M. C., *The Last Stand of Chinese Conservatism: The T'ung-Chih restoration, 1862–1874* (Stanford, CA: Stanford University Press, 1957).

'The adaptability of Ch'ing diplomacy: The case of Korea', *The Journal of Asian Studies*, 17(3) (1958), 363–81.

Wu, T. I.-W., 'The Chinese communist movement' in J. C. Hsiung and S. Levine (eds.), *China's Bitter Victory: The war with Japan, 1937–1945* (London: M. E. Sharpe, 1992), pp. 79–106.

Yao, X., *An Introduction to Confucianism* (New York: Cambridge University Press, 2000).

Yates, J. J., 'The resurgence of jihad and the specter of religious populism', *SAIS Review*, XXVII(1) (2007), 127–44.

Yavuz, M. H., 'Islam and Europeanization in Turkish-Muslim socio-political movements' in T. Byrnes and P. Katzenstein (eds.), *Religion in an Expanding Europe* (Cambridge: Cambridge University Press, 2006), pp. 225–55.

Young, E. P., 'Politics in the aftermath of revolution: The era of Yuan Shi-K'ai, 1912–1916' in J. K. Fairbank and D. Twitchett (eds.), *The Cambridge History of China, XII: Republican China, 1912–1949*, Pt I (Cambridge: Cambridge University Press, 1983), pp. 209–55.

Young, L., *Japan's Total Empire: Manchuria and the culture of wartime imperialism* (Berkeley: University of California Press, 1998).

Yu-Sheng, L., *The Crisis of Chinese Consciousness: Radical anti-traditionalism in the May fourth era* (Madison: The University of Wisconsin Press, 1979).

Zhang, Y., 'System, empire and state in Chinese international relations', *Review of International Studies*, 27(5) (2001), 43–63.

Zimmerman, J. C., 'Sayyid Qutb's influence on the 11 September attacks', *Terrorism and Political Violence*, 16(2) (2004), 222–52.

Zurcher, E., 'Purity in the Taiping rebellion' in W. E. A. van Beek (ed.), *The Quest for Purity: Dynamics of puritan movements* (Amsterdam: Mouton de Gruyter, 1988), pp. 201–15.

Index

Bodin, Jean 125–7, 138, 139
Bohemia, rebellion against empire 130–1, 133
Bologna, University of 63
Boniface VIII, Pope 88
Bourbon house, role in Wars of Religion 118
Boxer rebellion (1900) 196–7, 214–20
  aftermath 218–20, 221
  beliefs 215–16
  international response 216–18
  military suppression 217
  origins 214–15
  peace settlement 217–18
  seizure of foreign legations 216
Buddhism 167–8
Bukovansky, Mlada 41–2
Bull, Hedley 21, 22
Bush, George W./Bush administration 289–90, 291, 293, 294, 296, 311
Buzan, Barry 49

Caliphate, Islamic
  abolition 262, 272, 306
  evocation by jihad movement 274, 282, 283
Calvin, Jean/Calvinism 111–12
  spread in France 118, 120–1
  see also Huguenots
canon law 28, 63, 67–8, 80
  Reformation challenges to 87, 90, 91, 93
Canton, massacre of civilians (1925) 240
Carolingian dynasty 61, 100
Carr, E. H. 21–2
Carter, Jimmy 277
Cateau-Cambrésis, Treaty of (1559) 99, 107, 117
Catherine de Medici, queen of France 117–18, 120
Catholic Church
  anti-Huguenot propaganda 122–4
  assimilation of Classical inheritance 74; problems of 74–7
  challenges to legitimacy 77
  common principles with Protestantism 94, 142
  intercessionary position 155; Lutheran rejection 87

legitimation of violence/inequality 65
  perceived worldliness 76
  persecution of unorthodoxy 76–7
  proposed reconciliation with Protestantism 93–4, 102
  Tridentine reforms 111
  see also Christendom; confessional conflicts; papacy
Catholic League 119, 122–4, 128, 134
centralisation (of political power) 115
  theoretical development 125–6
'century of chaos' 116–17, 142–3, 251
  see also Thirty Years War; Wars of Religion
Cerny, Philip G. 40
Charlemagne *see* Carolingian dynasty
Charles 'the Bold' of Burgundy 85
Charles V, (Holy Roman) Emperor 11, 94–5, 96–7, 98–9, 127, 129, 140, 300
  abdication 104–5
  failure of reunification project 99–104
  relations with papacy 98, 102–3
  religious/political concessions 101
Chiang Kai-Shek 241, 255
China
  (alleged) lack of national identity 254
  anti-imperialist feeling 232–3
  as centre of civilisation 157–8, 189–90, 198; rethinking 210
  defensive flaws 162
  demands for sovereign recognition 236–7
  descent into anarchy 226–7
  formation of modern state 150, 248
  improvements in infrastructure 242
  languages 231
  literature 231–2
  Manchu conquest (1644) 149–50, 160, 161, 162
  military technology 78–9
  nationalist movement 51, 54–5, 56, 220, 222–5, 231, 233, 236, 248, 249, 254–5, 256, 257, 307; influences 239–40 (*see also* Kuomintang)
  Period of Warring States 1, 151–3
  problems facing invaders 249–50

Cambridge Studies in International Relations

DATE DUE

FFR 1 0 2014	